THE DIPLOMAT
A Memoir of Life in the
US Foreign Service
1943-1970

KENNEDY M. CROCKETT
US Ambassador, Retired

EDITED BY   Judith C. Faerron
FRONT COVER PHOTO   Seal of the US Department of State (US Government, public domain)
INTERIOR PHOTOS   © KM Crockett / © Mary C. Crockett / Public Domain (unless noted).
BACK COVER PHOTOS   Top: US Department of State; Bottom: © Mary C. Crockett

AUTHOR'S NOTE   *This collection of stories about life in the US Foreign Service is based on personal experience. Some names have been changed and some incidents dramatized.*

LCCN   2020914718

ISBN   978-0-578-73762-1

Dedication

The children of Mary and Kennedy Crockett,
LAURA, JACK, JUDY, LINDA, and TERRY,
dedicate the publication of this memoir to our parents,
who gave us an appreciation for the great outdoors, a passion
for travel and adventure, and extraordinary childhood memories.
We miss them every day.

Acknowledgments

Many thanks to Rita Lagace and Inson Kim for your meticulous proofreading and constructive comments.

Deepest appreciation to Terry Crockett Esquivel for your invaluable support and skillful assistance in the preparation of our Dad's manuscript. Your drive to honor his intent to publish his memoirs was fundamental to the completion of this massive project he and I undertook so very many years ago. From scanning and massaging the original 634-page typewritten manuscript, to critiquing my edits, checking and rechecking page proofs, contributing two sections, and always being available to help me make dozens of decisions, you have been indispensable every step of the way. I have no doubt Dad is extremely proud and pleased.

Judith Crockett Faerron
Editor

Contents

United States Ambassador Kennedy M. Crockett, with loyal companion Pancho, doing what he loved best, near Pochomil, Nicaragua, 1970.

Foreword

By Teresa Crockett Esquivel

"It may not matter much to you now, but one day you will wish you knew more about your parents." I can still hear my dad's words as though they were spoken yesterday—yet it's been over 25 years since we drove the back roads of the Texas Hill Country that day in his white Ford F-150.

"This will become far more important to you the older you get," he added. "I know, because I have lived it." Over time, the truth in those words has been proven to all his children.

From his first position in 1943 as auxiliary clerk in Nuevo Laredo, Mexico, to his final day as US ambassador to Nicaragua in 1970, Kennedy Crockett took meticulous notes and collected letters, documents, photos and newspaper clippings. He relied on these documents, and others acquired post retirement, as he compiled this memoir.

The pages of this book not only chronicle his 27-year career as a public servant, they also capture the adventures he and our mother, Mary Campbell, experienced as they raised five children during assignments in Honduras, Mexico, Guatemala, Costa Rica, Nicaragua and Washington, DC. Although early feedback from potential publishers suggested otherwise, Kennedy insisted on preserving the family anecdotes. For him, the complete story was the most valuable gift he could leave behind—his written legacy.

Today, as we take in media reports covering the ongoing US immigration crisis, we become increasingly aware of the serious challenges faced by Central Americans in their home countries. What might be much less evident, however, is the significant role the United States played in Central America and the Caribbean over the past century. Through Kennedy's accounts we gain insight on circumstances that led the United States to protect economic interests, help maintain stability, and defend against threats to the potential for democracy in the region.

For example, by the time our father arrived in Honduras in 1946, both the US-based United Fruit Company (now Chiquita) and Standard Fruit Company (now Dole) owned extensive banana plantations there, were the largest employers in the country, and made sizable investments in ports and railroads to support their businesses.[1] Both Puerto Cortés and La Ceiba were primary harbors for banana exports when Kennedy was stationed in those locations as American vice consul, principal officer.[2][3] US investments in Honduras were substantial enough that decades before Kennedy's arrival, troops were deployed there on various occasions, dating back as early as 1903.[4]

Three and a half years before Kennedy's arrival in Guatemala as first secretary and chief of the political section in early 1958, the United States played a key role in ousting then-President Jacobo Arbenz. While the US government denounced his administration as communist influenced, an equally pressing motivation for intervening was his agrarian reforms that risked US bank loans and allowed for confiscation of lands belonging to United Fruit Company, the largest landowner in Guatemala at the time.[5] US troops were also deployed by sea near Guatemala during the 1920 elections.[6]

In the Caribbean, numerous events in the Dominican Republic triggered US involvement as early as 1903.[7] In 1965, while Kennedy was director of Caribbean Affairs at the Department of State, he was responsible for positioning the USS *Boxer* in preparation for deployment of Marines during the Dominican Crisis. Eventually, 20,000 troops would safeguard the evacuation of US citizens from Santo Domingo, protect the US embassy, and help bring stability to the region. Meanwhile, Kennedy played a key role in behind-the-scenes efforts to identify and secure a much needed interim chief of state to coalesce a government capable of running the country peacefully.

Over 50 years before Kennedy arrived in Nicaragua to lead the US delegation, the Bryan-Chamorro Treaty granted the United States exclusive rights in perpetuity to construct a transoceanic canal across Nicaragua. Due to the country's interest in the canal, US Marines intervened in local affairs on several occasions decades before Kennedy's arrival.

As one of his last tasks before leaving Nicaragua, and after the Canal Study Commission decided that building a canal across Nicaragua would not be feasible, Kennedy began negotiations with President Anastasio Somoza and put the revocation of the old treaty in motion.[8]

The current Central American migration crisis is a complex and multifaceted issue many decades in the making. It is not only difficult to imagine that anyone could have foreseen these developments, but important to appreciate that between 1946 and 2016 the United States contributed nearly $86 billion ($176 billion in constant 2016 dollars) in aid to Latin America and the Caribbean.[9]

As you read Kennedy's memoir of life in the US Foreign Service, we hope you will come away with an increased awareness of real events and enjoy the off the beaten path adventures our family was so fortunate to experience during this bygone era.

September 2019

[1] "Agriculture, forestry, and fishing," Encyclopaedia Britannica, accessed September 2, 2019, https://www.britannica.com/place/Honduras/Agriculture-forestry-and-fishing

[2] "Puerto Cortés," Encyclopaedia Britannica, accessed September 2, 2019, https://www.britannica.com/place/Puerto-Cortes

[3] "La Ceiba," Encyclopaedia Britannica, accessed September 2, 2019, https://www.britannica.com/place/La-Ceiba

[4] "Honduras (1902-present)," University of Central Arkansas, accessed September 2, 2019, https://uca.edu/politicalscience/dadm-project/western-hemisphere-region/honduras-1902-present/

[5] "Jacobo Arbenz," Encyclopaedia Britannica, accessed September 2, 2019, https://www.britannica.com/biography/Jacobo-Arbenz

[6] "Guatemala (1903-present)," University of Central Arkansas, accessed September 2, 2019, https://uca.edu/politicalscience/dadm-project/western-hemisphere-region/guatemala-1903-present/

[7] "Dominican Republic (1902-present)," University of Central Arkansas, accessed September 2, 2019, https://uca.edu/politicalscience/dadm-project/western-hemisphere-region/dominican-republic-1902-present/

[8] "Nicaragua Foreign Intervention," Encyclopaedia Britannica, accessed September 2, 2019, https://www.britannica.com/place/Nicaragua/Foreign-intervention

[9] "US Foreign Assistance to Latin America and the Caribbean: FY2018 Appropriations," Congressional Research Service, Federation of American Scientists, accessed September 2, 2019, https://fas.org/sgp/crs/row/R45089.pdf

**Kennedy McCampbell Crockett and Mary Corinne Campbell
on their wedding day, September 8, 1943; Laredo, Texas.**

Prologue
1970

January 18, 1970 fell on a Sunday. With the dry season well under way, the morning sky was clear. The view from the balcony of the embassy's master suite was always breathtaking, and this morning it was spectacular. Managua spread below and to the east, still half asleep on the day of rest. To the north, the perfect symmetry of Momotombo's cone rose against a deep blue sky accentuated by fleecy cirrus clouds. A puff of steam drifted above the blue rim of the volcano's great crater. The surface of Lake Xolotlán shimmered in the early light. A calm, beautiful day. A favorable omen for a special day I had thought about often for many years—with mixed feelings of anticipation and dread.

For better or worse, today would be a defining juncture in my life.

My thoughts turned back almost 30 years. World War II came on the eve of my final year at the University of Texas. My attempts to volunteer for military service were frustrated by poor eyesight. A return to campus was short lived—it seemed a futile exercise with the world in flames. I went home to Laredo to work with a group exporting beef from Mexico to our allies in Europe. The job involved a good bit of contact with the US consulate in Nuevo Laredo, and Consul George H. Winters, my first and most admired chief in the Foreign Service, offered me a six-month appointment in the wartime Foreign Service Auxiliary to help with the consulate's shipping problems. The salary was $1,800.00[1] a year. I took it. It was 1943, and I was 23 years old.

For the first several months, the job was an adequate challenge. We moved truckloads, then freight car loads and finally trainloads of supplies and equipment across the border destined to interior posts or war related projects in Mexico and Central America. We moved more and bigger things as German subs sank increasing numbers of our ships in the Gulf of Mexico and the Caribbean. But regardless of the cargo, being a shipping clerk is not a terribly rewarding occupation, and I wanted to get involved with the more traditional work of the Foreign Service.

As often as I could, I helped the full-fledged consular officers with visa, citizenship, protection and other statutory duties, and took seriously the best piece of advice I ever had from a chief. George Winters urged me to learn the laws and regulations "forward and backward," not so I could enforce them, but to be sure I knew where there was leeway to find a solution to a problem rather than fall back on the easy and traditional (read: *bureaucratic*) way out through adamant negativism.

In those days, the regulations were an uncodified collection of thousands of individual instructions circulated to field posts by the many offices of the Department of State. I studied and indexed all I could find in the consulate's files, and there were reams of them dating back decades.

One day my opportunity came. A vice consul doing visa work got an urgent transfer and there was no replacement in sight. I got his work and his desk, but not his title or his salary. The vice consul sitting at the next desk was to administer the oath and sign the visa of each applicant I approved. I could refuse to issue a visa on my own—after all, the right to say "no" is inherent in being a bureaucrat and requires no title. But each application I approved had to be endorsed by the Old Hand next door, and his criterion was so strict that we spent much of our time in discussion, neither one of us getting much work done. Luckily for me, my arguments usually prevailed when we took an exceptionally sticky case to Consul Winters for resolution.

This arrangement was so clumsy that something had to be done, and it wasn't long until the diplomatic pouch brought the most beautiful parchment scroll I have ever seen. It read:

> To all to whom these Presents shall come, Greetings: I certify that Kennedy M. Crockett has been appointed Vice Consul of the United States of America . . . with all the privileges and authorities of right appertaining to that office . . . done at the City of Washington this eleventh day of April in the year of our Lord one thousand nine hundred and forty four.
> [Signed] Secretary of State Cordell Hull

I was damned pleased and proud.

And now 27 years had passed. How fast they had gone, to have been so many places and done and seen so many things in between! I could not deny that I had enjoyed the Foreign Service. There had been many more good years than bad ones. But was the security I had, and could hold on to, important enough for me to stay on at all costs, or did I want to prove to myself that I could do something else? Today was the day I had long since set to reach a final decision on this question.

What the hell! It was a special day no matter which way it went, and I was a different man today than I had ever been before or would ever be again. Today was my Emancipation Day and I would damned well enjoy it!

The boots, jeans and jacket didn't impress my driver, Octavio. He knew Sunday was "anything goes," and he kept right on polishing the big, black sedan. But his eyebrows shot up when I asked for the Honda trail bike. I had ridden it only a few times, and only on remote country roads or isolated beaches. Since Ambassador Gordon Mein had been gunned down on the street in Guatemala City some months before, the security people hadn't allowed me to drive anything or go anywhere unaccompanied. These restrictions were acutely irksome to me. Octavio knew the rules, but he brought the bike up from the garage and handed me the helmet. I pulled the visor down, made a trial run around the drive and was off for the chancery, managing a wave to the startled guards stationed at the embassy residence gate, machine guns at the ready.

As all bikers know, nothing lifts the spirit like being out on the road. It beats a sports car or a speedboat hands down. After months of not having driven anything or having been alone in the outside world, I experienced a tremendous sense of exhilaration. By the time I turned in the chancery drive, I was in high good humor. The gate was open, so I wheeled up to the main entrance, kicked the stand and shut her down.

In a heartbeat, the Marine guard was out from behind his desk and closing in on me with fire in his eyes. He was fresh from Vietnam and clearly meant business. It dawned on me that I had better flip up my visor or find myself thrown out on the seat of my pants. By then we were eyeball to eyeball. The Marine was already shouting, "What the hell do you think you're doing?" when recognition dawned. He didn't close his mouth, but opened his eyes to match, snapped to attention and saluted smartly. I bade him good morning, walked into the lobby and up the stairs to my office. As I rounded the corner at the landing, I could see he was still at attention, holding his salute, mouth wide open.

The two messages on the desk before me had been prepared days earlier. They were both quite brief. One addressed to President Richard M. Nixon informed him of my decision to resign my appointment. The other asked the director general of the Foreign Service for guidance in effecting my retirement.

This was it, and I had no doubts—the half hour alone riding into town had dispelled them. There were many, many reasons why I had reached this decision. But always near the top of the list was the urgent need I so often felt to be just an average Joe; to be able to do it myself, for myself and by myself.

Beth Beers knocked. Somehow she always knew when I would be in over a weekend, and never failed to show within minutes of my arrival at the chancery. Executive secretaries are like that. She smiled and said, "Good morning, Mr. Ambassador. And Happy Birthday. How does it feel to be 50?"

"Great, Beth!" I smiled. "Would you please see that these two telegrams get off this morning?"

[1]Adjusted for inflation, $1,800 in 1943 was equal to $26,759 in 2019.

Nuevo Laredo
1943

Skinning A Cat

When you don't know much about what you're doing, ingenuity can be your only salvation. During my early years in the Foreign Service, the times when I knew little to nothing about what I was assigned to do were all too frequent.

At the outbreak of World War II, consular establishments around the world used two code books for encrypted messages: The Grey Code and the Brown Code, so named because one book was bound in grey hardback and the other in brown. One of my few remaining memories about them is that the code group for the word monthly was "Kotex." I don't know which came first, the code book or the product. In any event, advancing Nazi armies in Europe captured copies of both books, and a new system was called for.

In due course, we received new equipment for the consulate at Nuevo Laredo, Mexico, by registered US parcel post. As far as I know, the little flashlight battery operated sets were the first electronic encryption devices generally issued to consulates. The old timers had never seen anything like them and had no idea how to set them up.

I didn't either, but being low man on the totem pole, I got the job. That would have been fine, but accompanying instruction dictated that acknowledgment of receipt of the devices must be transmitted to Washington within 48 hours, using the new system of encryption. Even worse, we got the damned things on a Friday during deer hunting season.

There were two devices: one for coding and one for decoding, and their respective designations were "Sigfoy" and "Signoal." Their use involved hand wiring a series of transposers altered regularly according to key instructions, which would also be altered regularly. Thus, if the devices or the keys fell into unfriendly hands, new keys could be circulated by courier and the encryption system would not be compromised for future use.

I set to work on Friday afternoon, studying the machines and accompanying guidance until late in the evening before attempting to encipher and decipher a trial message. It didn't work. I went over the instructions again, checked each of the hand wired circuits carefully and made another try. It still didn't work. I decided to go home and rest during the few remaining hours of darkness to be fresh for a new try on Saturday. Saturday passed the same way, as did Saturday night and the early morning hours of Sunday. Time was growing short and my desperation was growing in geometric proportion.

Sunday was a frantic nightmare, going over and over the same ground as fast as I could. Finally, the deadline came, and I had to get something out acknowledging receipt of the devices and reporting them to be in faulty condition. I locked the machines in the vault, went to the telegraph office and sent the message. In a few hours, I had a reply: "Destroy the instructions and key. Return the devices to Washington by registered United States parcel post." I had them in the mail Monday morning.

It was only then that a horrible thought crossed my mind: what if the machines were OK and I was too stupid to figure out how to work them? I made a U-turn and raced back to the parcel post window to retrieve Sigfoy and Signoal. When I told my high school classmate behind the grill that I needed my parcel back, he said "Sorry, but postal regulations don't permit that." I tried to reason with him. No luck. Heroic measures were called for. Could he talk to me away from the window? I had to come clean.

After he pulled down his grill and came into the post office foyer, I explained that the parcel contained equipment I had been unable to operate and which I had reported to be defective. Now I was worried that maybe I was the defective one and wanted to have one more try. Could I use a private room inside the post office if he couldn't let me have my package back?

"No way!"

I felt desperate, and it must have showed. My schoolmate was sympathetic.

He said, "So you're just worried this equipment might not really be inoperative?"

"Yes!" I replied.

"Well, rest your mind old buddy—you can count on the United States Postal Service. I'll process the package myself, and you can be damned sure that if the gear wasn't defective when it came into this building, it will be when it goes out!"

I turned wearily back to the parking lot, my mind at ease. I never again heard of Sigfoy or Signoal. The system was soon replaced by a simpler and more reliable method of coding and decoding. And who knows—maybe the machines really were defective.

Helga

Business at the visa counter of the United States Consulate in Nuevo Laredo was always brisk. The waiting room bulged with applicants and the air hummed with dozens of whispered conversations from morning to night. The noise was so continuous that none of us noticed it until it unexpectedly stopped one afternoon. Startled, I got up and walked to the door of my office to see what had happened.

There at the counter stood a conversation stopper in anyone's league, and every pair of eyes in the room was turned her way. It was only with considerable effort that I quit gawking and returned to my desk. I knew I would get a closer look when it came time to issue her visa.

Helga's application and her passport came in together, but without Helga. Instead, the clerk laid a bright yellow 3"x 5" index card on the desk, a "lookout notice" from the consulate general in Monterrey. Helga was a resident of that district, said the card, and no visa should be issued to her. Confidential information establishing her ineligibility would be provided on request.

I told the clerk to give Helga the bad news, but he said he already had, and she still insisted on seeing me. I instructed him to try again. We both knew there was nothing to be done but send Helga back to Monterrey to work out her problems there. He tried, but Helga announced she wasn't going anywhere until she had personally explained her problem to the vice consul. Well, that was me, so I told him to show her in.

At close range, she was striking. A classic Nordic, she was tall, slender, very blond and impeccably dressed. Her perfume was light and bright, her smile was radiant. Helga closed the door behind her and took the chair in front of my desk, crossing her long legs gracefully. All she wanted was a "small visa" so she could shop a few days in San Antonio. Then she would go back to Monterrey, and no one would be harmed by so simple a matter. Did I not agree?

Well, I sure did, but I explained with sympathy that since she lived in Monterrey, she would have to return there to get her visa.

"Oh," she pouted, "but I know many from Monterrey who come to the border for their visas to go shop in the United States. Please, can't you help me?"

I truly wished I could, but she would need to mark time in Nuevo Laredo until I could send to Monterrey for authorization to consider her application. "You know, get a waiver of jurisdiction and all that."

Helga knew, all right. She knew what her problem was in Monterrey, although I didn't. But she had a plan, and she unfolded it.

"I can tell you are busy here. So many, many people to see. The afternoon is late. You must be tired. I will not bother you more—now. But I want to tell you about my problem with that old consul general in Monterrey. I am staying at the hotel across the plaza. When you have finished your work here, please come to my room, so we can have a drink and be at ease."

With that, she got up from her chair, picked up her passport, laid a hotel key on my desk and swayed out.

I was dumfounded! I was young and newly married. I buzzed for the messenger to send Helga's key over to the hotel. But Ed stuck his head in the door first. "Boy, oh boy, who was *that*?"

Ed was my supervisor, single and recently arrived at the post. He fancied himself an authority on everything. I described my interview with Helga. His only question was, "What are you going to do with the key?" I told him, "Why, send it over to the hotel with José, what else?" With that, he picked up the key and walked out, mumbling that he would take care of it himself.

There was still lots of work to do, so I tried to forget Helga, scribbling, "Get clearance from Monterrey" across her application and tossing it into the out-box. I knew she would be back in the morning, and I could at least say I had set the machinery in motion to process her out-of-district visa application.

Around midmorning the next day it occurred to me that Helga hadn't showed up. It was a fleeting thought—there was always a throng of applicants to interview. She had probably gone back to Monterrey, and what the hell, there wasn't anything I could do to help her anyhow.

Several days later, the morning mail brought Monterrey's reply to my request for authorization of Helga's out-of-district visa application. It turned out she had been the paramour of a Swedish steel magnate who dealt with Nazi Germany. As a Nazi sympathizer, she was ineligible for a visa. Boy, was I glad

I had stood my ground and Helga hadn't pressed harder for her "small" visa. I took the message into Ed's office for him to read. He didn't say much, but he didn't look too well.

That week was busy and the weekend more so. By early Sunday evening I was fast asleep when my work phone rang. I recognized the deep, heavily accented female voice at the other end as Helga's.

"I call to tell you I have finished my shopping and I fly back to Monterrey within the hour. I have hurt no one and I have caused no problems. I wanted the visa to spend money in your country. I hate the consul general in Monterrey, who makes so much trouble for me—for no reason. But I came anyway, and now I go home." The line clicked dead. I felt uneasy. Where . . . when . . .? I was afraid to wonder how . . . or who.

Gradually the uneasiness abated, and I drifted back to sleep. Deep in my subconscious, I was aware of the telephone, again demanding my attention. The voice at the other end sputtered like a short fuse burning toward a giant firecracker. There was no question my caller was irate—and eventually he managed to get out why. It was the consul general at Monterrey, and he, too, had heard from Helga. It seems she had been less than courteous—I recall he used the term "taunting." He wanted to know *immediately* how Helga got to San Antonio.

I didn't mention the key but told him the rest of the story exactly as it had happened. He made it clear he would take it up with Ed, vowing to get to the bottom of the whole thing, cost what it might.

When I arrived at the office the next morning Ed was already there. He looked pale, but it was a Monday after all. I was eager to tell him about my telephone calls of the previous evening, but he was uninterested. My suspicion that the consul general in Monterrey had already called him was confirmed when he asked me to excuse him—he was getting ready to drive down to Monterrey for the day—a little "area familiarization trip," he said, adding that he might pay a call on the consul general there. I thought it best not to pursue the matter. After all, Ed was my boss.

I never heard of Helga again. The old consul general at Monterrey soon retired. Ed moved on to other work. More than 30 years have passed, and Germany has long since become our staunchest ally. You never hear the term paramour anymore, and the relationship it connotes is hardly noticed now, much less frowned upon.

It's been a long time, and much has changed—but I still remember Helga.

The Bribe

Attempts at bribery in visa work along the Mexican border were common. Some, like Helga's, amounted to no more than a quick wink or a suggestive smile. Others were crude, and in those cases, it was a simple matter to refuse the visa and order the culprit out of the office. My reactions ranged from outrage to pity for a poor devil who only wanted to get into the promised land and didn't know any better.

Some of the attempts were so pathetically bungling that I chose to look the other way and forget it. There were others, however, staged by shrewd operators, whose skill and innovation had to be admired.

For months, I had carried on a lengthy correspondence with an attorney in New York representing an Eastern European refugee. Because of quota restrictions on immigration from this applicant's country of birth, he had no hope of immigrating to the United States for many years to come.

The law was clear, and the facts were simple, but I couldn't convince the lawyer. He must have been more interested in collecting periodic fees than telling his client it was a lost cause, and there was no alternative except to wait his turn. Or maybe it was the client who would not take no for an answer.

One day the attorney telephoned from New York and asked for an appointment to call on me in person to discuss his client's case. He said he understood my position and he had checked the law, but his client insisted. I couldn't believe he would come all this way for nothing but told him I would see him if he did. Maybe he simply wanted a vacation at his client's expense.

Within two weeks the receptionist announced that the attorney was in the outer office waiting to see me. He had made the trip from New York by train, for lack of a priority to come by air. I was incredulous, but there he was. We went over the ground already fully explored in my letters. I amplified by pointing out that quota numbers were controlled by Washington, and consular officers had no discretion when it came to an applicant's place on the quota waiting list. His client would have to wait his turn, and that was that.

He said he understood but his client didn't, adding there was always the outside chance of some quirk in the laws or peculiarity of his client's case that might provide an exception. Would I please grant him one interview to go over the details again before he returned to New York? He had come a long way and wanted to tell his client he had done everything possible. It was a waste of time and I told him so, but agreed to see him again later in the week.

As the attorney rose to go, he reached for a book in his briefcase. It was a novel currently on the bestseller list. He said he had read it on the train, and if I had not read it yet, he would like to give it to me. I thanked him but explained I was already far behind in my leisure reading. He insisted I would find it engrossing and pressed me to at least thumb through it when I had a minute. I was eager to get rid of him and didn't object when he put the book down on the corner of my desk and walked out.

Several days later my datebook reminded me the attorney would soon be in to see me. I hadn't even looked at his client's file because there was no way for me to speed up his case. The attorney's book was still on the corner of my desk—at least I could tell him I had looked at it and wasn't interested. When I picked up the book to thumb through it, it opened readily near the middle. There was a crisp, new $100 bill tucked between the pages. On closer examination, I found four more $100 bills between the pages. I was outraged. The attorney was trying to bribe me!

Book in hand, I rushed into my boss's office and told him what had happened. I was ready to call the FBI or the United States Attorney or someone—anyone—to see that this crook was prosecuted. But the boss had a lot more experience and a much cooler head than I. He pointed out the obvious: I had not been offered a bribe—I had merely found $500 between the pages of a book. I couldn't prove who put them there. The attorney could say he had put the money there for safekeeping on his trip and forgotten about it. If push came to shove, how would I prove there had not been ten $100 bills in the book, instead of five? The attempted bribery had been skillfully planned.

By the time the attorney arrived, I had cooled down and carefully replaced the book exactly where he had left it. At least I would have a little fun out of this awkward situation.

The man was all smiles as the receptionist showed him in. I apologized for keeping him waiting, and said I wished I had been able to find some way to help him, but I knew he understood the law was the law. His smile faded. I shuffled papers on my desk. He made no move to leave. I asked if there was something else he needed. Slowly he rose from his chair, his eyes on the book.

"Did you have time to look at the book?" he asked. "No," I told him, "I haven't gotten around to it." I didn't suggest he take it back—after all, he had offered to give it to me. Let him sweat a little. I shuffled more papers. He shuffled his feet. He clearly wasn't sure what to do next—better yet, he wasn't sure what I was going to do next.

Slowly he turned toward the door. It took an age for him to grasp and turn the knob. He looked back at me as he opened the door, his face a study in sheer agony. He opened his mouth, but no sound came out. Finally, he turned and went through the door.

I called to him right before it closed, "You might as well take the book," I said. "I don't care for that kind of story." He rushed back in, snatched up his book, and was gone. I wondered how long he would be able to wait before he checked to see if the $500 was there.

Bullfrogs

There's a first time for tears in all new marriages. I know that now, but when Mary and I got married I didn't think that time would ever come for us, and certainly not the way it did.

We were both 23 and working—Mary at the Army post in Laredo, and I at the US consulate in Nuevo Laredo. We had known each other for about as far back as either of us could remember and had dated steadily for nearly a decade. Marriage was a logical sequel to an extended courtship, and we knew each other well enough to expect that things would go as smoothly in the future as they always had in the past. Against such a perfect backdrop, it was a real shock to me when the first sign of trouble came.

Our apartment was near the Army post, and it was a rare occasion when Mary didn't get home from work before I did. It was her custom to fix a snack to go along with the cocktails she would have ready and waiting upon my arrival from across the Rio Grande. My homecoming was a joyful occasion for us both. We were very much in love and, after all, hadn't seen each other all day long. Thus, I couldn't have been more surprised to arrive home that fateful afternoon and find Mary sitting on the front porch, her eyes red and face tear streaked. It certainly didn't occur to me that I could have been the cause of her distress.

My instinctive reaction was to take her in my arms, comfort her with my affection and assure her that I would fix whatever or whomever had caused her unhappiness.

"Don't you *dare* touch me!" she wailed, moving out of my reach. "How could you have *done* such a thing?" The tears flowed anew, punctuated by great sobs.

In due course I learned the nature of my transgression. It had actually started many years before our marriage, and Herman O'Keefe was to blame. Herman had a ranch about 10 miles south of Laredo where he built a large earthen dam which impounded an artificial lake covering about 500 acres. It was by far the largest body of water within 100 miles of Laredo, and a favorite spot for fishing when I was a boy. Herman stocked the lake with everything he could think of, including bass, crappie, perch and channel catfish, plus a few alligators to eat the turtles that propagated there on their own. Once he imported several hundred Louisiana bullfrogs to see how they would do. They didn't like Herman's lake well enough to reproduce, but while they lasted, I developed a real taste for frog legs.

I never forgot how good Herman O'Keefe's bullfrogs were and was always on the lookout for a new source. Sadly, there didn't seem to be any within reasonable reach of the South Texas brush country. The nearest natural habitat of these delectable amphibians seemed to be a marshy lake in the state of Michoacán, Mexico, some 600 miles to the south. I never missed a chance to inquire about it of anyone I met from the area, and finally found someone who was familiar with it and willing to ship me a crate of live bullfrogs.

The long awaited shipment had been delivered to my office that morning. There was a baker's dozen in all, and they were truly giant creatures, some 15-inches long. I was thrilled, although considerably distressed to see how dehydrated they had become during the long trip north. Their normally shiny skin was dull, and their eyes were closed to mere slits. They could be induced to move, but only by prodding. But they were alive, and I knew their condition would improve after they soaked up a little moisture. For lack of a better idea, I hurried home during my lunch hour, partially filled the bathtub, dumped them in, and rushed back to work, delighted in the knowledge that I would have a wonderful surprise for Mary when she got home that evening. As it turned out, she was a bit more than surprised.

Mary had arrived at the apartment half an hour before me. Cheered that we would soon be reunited after a whole day's separation, she let herself in, put her purse on the dining room table, and headed for the bathroom to freshen up. It must have been quite a shock when she opened the bathroom door and 13 fully revived bullfrogs sprang from the tub. For a moment, she was too stunned to move. Reassured, the frogs remained calm, maintaining their perches on wash basin, toilet, window ledge and tub rim, gently croaking and keeping a wary eye on what was to them the intruder. Recovering use of her limbs, Mary turned and fled the apartment, slamming the front door behind her and locking herself out in the process.

When she could finally bring herself to speak to me, she announced that she would stay right there on the porch until I rounded up every last one of my "friends" and got them out of her house.

It is hard to corner and catch 13 active bullfrogs, even in a relatively small apartment. The evening was far advanced before the task was complete. But at least Mary had regained her composure by then. And it was not more than a day or two before she spoke to me again. In fact, within the same week I was allowed to return to my place in the bedroom. By then I had gotten tired of keeping company with the frogs out on the back porch. Frogs weren't nearly as good company as Mary.

The Commitment

Although I had thought about a career in the Foreign Service during my youth and had majored in Latin American studies during my university days, I had no desire to live anywhere other than south Texas where I was born and raised. My first love was the outdoors. My main goal was to live comfortably enough to have the time and money needed to enjoy the excellent hunting and fishing found within easy reach of Laredo.

In the beginning, when I thought about the Foreign Service, I thought of Mexico. There were more than 20 posts in Mexico then, most of them small—many located on the Gulf or Pacific coasts where the fishing was good and the hunting nearby. The principal officers at these smaller posts were often old-time, non-career consuls who had spent the better part of a lifetime moving from one post in Mexico to another. To me they were the men to be envied in the Foreign Service, and I coveted an assignment to one of their consulates.

My ambition was to become a vice consul at one of these posts. If I could manage that, I might some day in the distant future be found qualified for appointment as consul and principal officer. But I didn't think about it much because I didn't have any intention of staying in the Foreign Service—and besides, it seemed presumptuous to entertain such grandiose aspirations.

Before I realized it, three years had passed. I had gotten a good taste of command responsibility when I was chosen to take temporary charge of the consulate for several months. I found I liked being in charge—very much. I still didn't think of the Foreign Service as a career, but I didn't look for anything else to do. I liked what I was doing and let things ride—until the day the telegram came transferring me to Puerto Cortés. What a shock! I had no idea where Puerto Cortés was.

There was great excitement at our house that evening. Mary and I read the brief telegram from Washington over and over. We found Puerto Cortés in the world atlas and tried to imagine what it might be like. It was a small dot on the Caribbean coast of Honduras in Central America. At least there would be fishing if we went there. The thought was intriguing, exciting, and the longer we thought about it, inviting! But we couldn't possibly go so far away from home— what health hazards would we face? What about our small daughter? And what about our aging parents? We were both close to our own and each other's parents. Still, we could hardly wait for the post report to come up from Mexico City.

In those days, Foreign Service people got 18 months credit toward retirement for every year served at a "hardship" post. Hardship posts like Puerto Cortés had bad reputations within the Service to begin with, and people assigned to these posts were careful to see that reputation persisted, lest the extra retirement benefit be prejudiced. Thus, we expected the post report to play up the bad aspects of life there. But when it finally came, we were aghast to find there was absolutely nothing good to be said about the place.

Our parents were horrified at the thought of their children and grandchild being exposed to amoebic dysentery, four varieties of typhoid fever, malaria, hurricanes, sand flies, sharks, scorpions, boa constrictors, vampire bats, centipedes, revolutions, and more. But Mary and I found ourselves arguing that the place couldn't be that bad. We didn't know it, but we already had Foreign Service Fever— that rare disease that makes the stricken look longingly at each new horizon.

Mary was always game for anything, and she enjoyed fishing as much as I did. Puerto Cortés had that to offer. And I was excited by the prospect of having my own post. I would be in charge because I would be the only one there. We decided we would go.

The next few weeks were full of excitement and frantic preparations. We needed clothing for the tropics. The hand-me-down furniture we had started housekeeping with would never do for a principal officer. I borrowed $1,500— over eight months' pay—and we shopped in San Antonio for seersucker suits and tropical style furnishings. Then we stocked up on the many things that couldn't be had in Puerto Cortés. It was a busy but happy time.

Finally, the day came when we were ready. Our belongings had been packed and were en route. We had vacated our house and moved in with Mary's parents for the last few days. We were on the eve of leaving for the tropics. Then came the second telegram. Transfer orders were changed—we would not go to Puerto Cortés on the Caribbean but to Tegucigalpa the in the mountains! At 4,000 feet elevation, the climate there was temperate. I would not be the principal officer, but the most junior officer in the embassy. Mary would be the handmaiden to every other officer's wife. There would certainly be no fishing.

As often happens in the Foreign Service, our well-laid plans ended us up where we had no intention of being—and it was too damned late to do a thing about it! Worst of all, we boarded the plane for Tegucigalpa knowing almost nothing about the place.

Turkey hunt: Chief of Consular Section, US Embassy, Tegucigalpa, Honduras, 1947.

Honduras
1946

Tegucigalpa

Our dismay over the last minute change of assignment was great, but not great enough to dampen our enthusiasm for the upcoming adventure. Both of us had traveled extensively within the US by train, and into Mexico by car. But neither of us had ever made a trip by air—nor had we faced the prospect of living abroad. Our excitement knew no bounds as we said goodbye to family and friends in the little terminal building at Nuevo Laredo's fledgling airport and boarded the 21-passenger C-47 that would take us away from the world we knew.

Our flight to Monterrey, Mexico City, Tapachula, Guatemala City, San Salvador and finally, Tegucigalpa, Honduras, took the better part of two days—such was the state of air travel in Central America in 1946. But what a wonderful experience it was! We flew a few thousand feet above the earth's surface, and the rivers, mountains, villages, isolated ranches, impenetrable jungles and ocean were clearly visible as we soared above. It's been a long time since flying was like that, but then it had been less than 20 years since Charles Lindbergh made the first solo flight across the Atlantic. He could not have enjoyed his adventure any more than we enjoyed ours.

What with landing and taking off at the various intermediate stops on our way south, we had become seasoned air travelers before we approached the end of our journey. We had landed in the desert at Monterrey, high among snow covered mountains at Mexico City, in the jungle at Tapachula, and right in town at Guatemala City, where our approach took us just a few feet above the old Spanish colonial aqueduct at one end of the strip. The ultimate test of our nerves had come at San Salvador. The approach there was low over the surface of Lake Ilopango, straight toward the face of a towering cliff that rose

23

from the water's edge. When it seemed we would be dashed to smithereens, we lifted lightly over the edge and set down smoothly on the runway. What a thrill! We were all but jaded veterans by the time we circled over Tegucigalpa in preparation for landing.

Tegucigalpa nestles in a rather narrow valley in the arid Honduran upland. At the end of April—which is also the end of Central America's dry season—three colors predominated on the terrain below. Most prominent were the great expanses of black where the grass and undergrowth had been intentionally burned off. The eye was next drawn to the dull brown of parched grass, shrubs and weeds that had not yet been burned. And finally, there were random expanses of white limestone outcroppings where nothing would grow. Nature had not offered an inviting panorama. What was attractive was the sea of red tile roofs covering just about every building in town. If nothing else, Tegucigalpa was picturesque.

There was no escaping the conclusion that the small, white patch of limestone our pilot maneuvered toward was Toncontín, Tegucigalpa's airport. It appeared much too small to accommodate an aircraft as large as our C-47. On top of that, a rather prominent hill dominated one end of the short strip which terminated abruptly where it intersected with a deep chasm at the other end. In a rather amazing maneuver, our pilot made what must have been close to a three-point landing. We raced to the end of the little strip before we slowed enough to swing around and taxi back through the dense cloud of powdery, white dust we had raised as we came in, finally rolling to a stop beside the small terminal building.

As had been the custom at stops along the way, all the other passengers left their seats and crowded into the aisle near the door at the back of the little plane long before the landing had been completed. They lurched back and forth as we taxied over the rough, unpaved runway toward the terminal building. It was all the flight attendant (they were called stewardesses back then) could do to elbow her way through the crowd to open the door so they could spew forth when we came to a stop.

As Mary, little Laura and I waited for the aisle to clear, we could see there was a crowd gathered in the shade of the terminal porch. Undoubtedly some of those pale faces belonged to people from the embassy who had come out to receive us. But who were the others? We already knew the three of us were the only passengers destined for Tegucigalpa. Finally, we were inside, being introduced, shaking hands, trying to remember names and hoping it would be possible later to connect the right name with the right face. There were so many! These people couldn't all be connected with the US embassy. But if not, who were they? And no matter who they were, why were they out here to meet such a junior addition to the embassy's staff? Everyone was pleasant and cordial. We were welcomed with great warmth and unrestrained enthusiasm by one and all. How very nice it made us feel.

Our luggage had long since been unloaded from the plane and brought into the terminal. The last call for passengers to re-board had come over the loudspeaker for at least the fourth time but nobody made a move to go. At last, all the stragglers were routed out of the bar, herded onto the tarmac and helped up the steps to the plane. No one made a move to leave the terminal until the plane had made its takeoff run and disappeared beyond the horizon. Then everyone said goodbye to everyone else and, as one, headed back to town in a cloud of white dust.

Something about the whole exercise didn't seem quite right until it occurred to me that an arrival or departure by air was an event in isolated Tegucigalpa. People came out to the airport much as people in the old west used to come down to the depot when a train came in. It was a special occasion in a dull existence to be savored to the last drop. And sure enough, I was to learn, while nearly everyone connected with the US government in Tegucigalpa had come out, more than half the crowd had no connection whatsoever with the embassy. They were simply curious and looking over the new arrivals was something to do, to say nothing of watching the plane land and take off.

There was no hotel in Tegucigalpa in 1946, so we were housed across the river in Comayagüela. Our corner room in the small hotel facing the square boasted a balcony that looked out on the main church. We were rather pleased with the spaciousness of our room and thought we would be comfortable here until we could find more permanent quarters.

It was late before we could even think of going to bed. It took a long time to settle down after all the excitement of the trip, the arrival and reception at the airport and, and the number of new friends we had met and entertained at the bar that evening.

It seemed we had hardly settled into sound sleep when all hell broke loose. Without warning there was a series of loud explosions outside our window, accompanied by a frantic clanging of bells. I rushed to the window in the dark as a rocket whooshed past and exploded in the sky. I was sure a revolution had broken out and we were in the center of it. I snatched Laura from her borrowed crib and herded Mary into the relative safety of the bathroom. There we huddled for what seemed like an age before the din came to an end.

Cautiously, I ventured to the window, and although there was hardly any light in the eastern sky, it was enough to silhouette the faithful filing into church across the street. We had witnessed the call to early mass as it was done in Honduras. It had been customary from colonial times—and without the fireworks, the natives wouldn't come to church. They may still do it the same way today, for all I know.

***

The bar in the little hotel in Comayagüela was a favorite gathering place for many lonely souls, some passing through, and some regular fixtures. Two of the latter caught my eye from the beginning. One, named Stevens, was a WWI flying ace. The other was a hard rock gold miner named Corcoran, as Irish as the name implies, and as tough as his profession demanded. The way they happened to catch my eye says something about the Honduras I came to know and love in the mid-1940s.

The entrance to the lobby of the hotel was through a broad, double doorway opening from the sidewalk and facing a cast iron statue of one of Honduras' many military figures of the past, who kept a dignified posture on his pedestal in the center of the little park across the street. The doorway gave direct access to the lobby. Across the lobby from the main entrance was a slightly narrower double doorway opening into the bar. Thus, a patron sitting at the bar could look down its length, across the lobby and through the hotel's main entrance, which framed the statue in the center of the park across the street.

There is a certain rhythm at small hotels in the tropics. At the hotel in Comayagüela things began to liven up around 4:30 each afternoon as the regulars took their places at the bar, ordered their favorite brand of poison and shouted over the ensuing game of *chingona* (played with poker dice) to see who paid for each round. Things were somewhat lively by the time dinner was ready and the doors of the dining room were opened wide. But since you either ate when dinner was served or went hungry, things quickly quieted down as the customers filed into the dining room to partake of the communal fare, seated as always at their customary table in their customary chairs. You quickly learned not to sit at someone else's place.

On this evening, Stevens was moody. He did not file into the dining room with everyone else but stayed at the bar and directed his attention to discovering how many drinks it would take to convert the bottle of scotch before him into another dead soldier. His dedication to this task was undeniable.

The sun had dropped below the rim of the western mountains and twilight had fallen by the time dinner was finished. The hotel's customers relaxed around the lobby or filed back into the bar. It was the quiet period before the usual rowdiness that developed as the evening wore on, and the effects of food were overcome by each customer's libation of choice.

Suddenly, there was a loud explosion from the direction of the bar, followed by a resounding clang from the direction of the statue in the park across the street. In short order, the sequence was repeated. By then, everyone realized the explosions were pistol shots. As is customary under such circumstances, the loungers in the lobby hit the floor and squirmed under whatever cover they could find. All except Corcoran.

Corcoran flattened himself against the wall to one side of the door to the bar. As the third shot rang out, he edged closer to the opening. By the time the fourth shot was fired, Corcoran could see what was going on inside the bar. He sprang through the door with a lunge that would have done justice to a man half his age.

"Gimme that bloody thing. If you've gotta target practice, for God's sake, go somewhere else!"

"Aw hell," came the slurred reply. "I haven't missed one yet, have I? What's all the excitement about?"

But there were no more shots. And when the others dared get to their feet for a look, the .45 caliber automatic lay on the bar between Stevens and Corcoran—who had joined forces in the effort to vanquish the bottle of scotch before them.

***

In time, we were able to lease a house belonging to Virginia and Chuck Abadie, who were on extended vacation in the States. Fully furnished, including a cook and a maid, it was a wonderful deal for us. But like so many things, it didn't last. We were hardly settled in when orders came for us to relieve the man at Puerto Cortés, Honduras, who had been medically evacuated and whose return was uncertain. Thus, within a few weeks of our arrival in Tegucigalpa, we were off for a detail of indefinite length in Puerto Cortés, where we had been headed in the first place. We may not have known much about life in the Foreign Service when we decided to give a try at it, but we sure were learning a lot in a hell of a hurry.

Joe

I never met Joe, although I saw him a couple of times and came to know him well. Joe was killed during World War II before I came to Puerto Cortés, or for that matter, ever heard of that tiny banana port on the Caribbean Sea.

The Puerto Cortés of 1946 was not exactly the kind of tropical paradise you tend to associate with the Caribbean. Built on a sand spit between the bay and a shallow swamp, the maximum elevation above high tide was less than two feet at the town's most prominent feature: the railroad track, which was the only connection between the port and the banana growing regions inland, and also served as the town's main street.

One good thing about Puerto Cortés in those days was that since there was no road, there were very few vehicles to contend with—except for the trains that brought the green gold from the plantations to the United Fruit Company's ships. In this respect, it was a healthy post. Walking was obligatory if you wanted to get anywhere, unless you had time to call the dispatcher and await a clear track for the railroad motor car to come pick you up. This sometimes took less than two days, but not often.

I first heard about Joe from a major US insurance company. The company understood Joe had been run over by a train some time back and was buried at Puerto Cortés. They wanted conclusive evidence that it was really Joe who had been run over by the train. The letter stated that "positive identification" would be an indispensable requirement.

I started checking the files as soon as the sun got low enough on the horizon to make the expenditure of so much energy bearable. And I should make clear that Puerto Cortés was not always hot, humid and sticky. More often it was hellishly hot, suffocatingly humid, and the effort required to lift a highball brought on a drenching sweat.

I found a file on Joe. He was a seaman who had frequented many of the bars along Puerto Cortés' waterfront while his ship was also getting loaded.

As he was crawling, or sleeping, on Puerto Cortés' "main street," the conductor had switched the train, and that was the end of Joe. Next of kin was notified, and he was buried in the local cemetery, Row Seven A, Plot 9.

I carefully tapped out a letter outlining these facts to the insurance company. I then pecked out a copy for the consulate's files, having overlooked inserting a carbon between the pages on my first effort. The copy was a better job than the original, so I sent the copy to the insurance company and filed the original. This struck me as the best way to have gone about it in the first place, so after that I did all my official correspondence that way.

I guess I should mention that the only other employee of the US Department of State (DOS) in Puerto Cortés at that time was the consulate's messenger/janitor, and he didn't know how to type. Thus, I had to do all the typing, which sometimes came to two or three letters a month. This extra burden on the principal officer resulted in considerable efficiency. Correspondence from the United States consulate at Puerto Cortés was uniformly brief and to the point. No big words, either—the dictionary provided by the US government some decades earlier had long since been consumed by termites.

I always felt guilty that I never found time to seek authority to drop the dictionary from inventory. I had, after all, signed for it when I took over, as had every one of my predecessors back through the ages. I could prove it hadn't been misappropriated—part of the cover was carefully safeguarded in the storeroom, along with the remnants of other items consumed by termites over the years. The storeroom was large and quite full—of both remnants and termites.

The consulate was not located in downtown Puerto Cortés but on the beach, a mile or so outside of town. Except for the constant hum from great clouds of mosquitoes and black sandflies, the area was quiet and relatively unpopulated.

It was always an occasion when the consulate entertained a visitor. Today's visitor was quite notable, dressed in a three-piece Brooks Brothers seersucker suit, topped off with a Panama hat and carrying a shiny briefcase. Nobody around Puerto Cortés did that! He seemed surprised when I responded to his request for an audience with the consul by saying "That is I."

I got out of my hammock, buttoned my shirt, slipped on my shoes and invited my visitor into the office. As usual it was sweltering, so I promptly unbuttoned my shirt, having observed the formalities.

My visitor had come to Puerto Cortés on important business for his insurance company. The letter I had written the company about Joe had been most useful. However, the company required conclusive evidence that the seaman buried in the local cemetery was the same man whose life had been insured by his company. The company's representative had come all the way from New York to this end. Both he and the company counted on my assistance.

I noticed there were large, damp spots around the armpits of the Brooks Brothers jacket. It occurred to me that the man would have been more comfortable if he at least unbuttoned it. Then came the shocker. The company wanted to exhume Joe's body! Worse yet, I would be expected to verify the identification. I got an uneasy feeling in my stomach, and immediately started to muster arguments supporting my hope that it could not be done.

Gradually the story unfolded: At the time of Pearl Harbor, Joe had lived a rather lavish life in New York, without visible means of support. There were rumors he had connections with the underworld. It was also thought that Joe was not interested in receiving greetings from his draft board. To avoid this, he had managed to become a union member and had gone to sea for the duration of the war as an able-bodied merchant seaman.

The insurance company was now being petitioned to make good on a double indemnity policy that had been taken out on Joe's life. Given the accidental nature of his demise, the sum in question came to six figures. The company wanted to be damned sure Joe was really dead. There were dental charts to be reconciled—Oh. My. God!

I could see why the company's representative was not impressed by my arguments that the whole thing was out of the question. There was a lot of money involved, and he hadn't been sent all the way to Puerto Cortés to be persuaded he might as well not have come. We walked back into town together to see what could be done about getting the permit required for the exhumation while the uneasy feeling in my stomach gradually increased.

I immediately felt better when the public health official in town pointed out that under Honduran law, a body could not be exhumed until seven years following burial. That would be some years yet in Joe's case, and I would be elsewhere.

I unenthusiastically translated the company representative's arguments for an exception. The public health official stood firm. As we walked back to the consulate, I commiserated with him. My stomach felt pretty good!

The afternoon sun was setting, and the sway of the hammock created a slight stir of air. The sprig of fresh mint in my glass gave the illusion of coolness. Through my half-closed eyes, I spotted the company representative striding down the walkway, waving a legal-size sheet of paper bearing an assortment of fiscal stamps and elaborate signatures. My stomach sank. No need to ask what prompted his eagerness—I knew these things could be arranged. I had even been foolhardy enough to suggest he discuss his problem with a lawyer in town who was a well-known "fixer."

The insurance company representative had the permit. We would get to work first thing in the morning. The uneasy feeling in my stomach returned.

Even in Puerto Cortés there was a marked lack of enthusiasm among the labor force when it came to digging up a body. We eventually found a man willing to take on the job, at a figure roughly equivalent to one week's wages. By that time, it was midmorning and steaming hot. I found a spot of shade under a coconut palm and stretched out on the grass. The company representative covered his three-piece suit with a heavy white smock and hovered over Cayetano—our digger—who, having already been assured a week's wages, paced himself accordingly.

We took a break at lunchtime, some four feet down. It looked like rain. It wouldn't make any difference to the company representative, or to Cayetano, whether it rained or not. Both were soaking wet with perspiration. The company representative did take off his smock for lunch. He did not unbutton his jacket.

As I knew it must, the moment came sometime in midafternoon when Cayetano's shovel made a hollow sound against Joe's coffin. Simultaneously, the rain came down in sheets. The hole quickly filled with water. The sides of the open grave began to cave in. We were through for the day! Someone up there was looking out for me. I was drenched, but my stomach felt better, and I headed for the Fruit Company Bar. In the early part of the evening I toasted the rain, during the latter part of the evening I tried to forget what tomorrow would bring.

I had a hangover the next morning, and felt thoroughly rotten, although thankful that it was still too wet for digging. The company representative complained about the delay, while I silently prayed for more rain. In due course word came that digging could resume, so we trudged over to the cemetery. I took a supply of hangover remedy with me.

Cayetano worked at his normal pace. Time passed. My supply of hangover remedy was fully adequate. I was surprised to discover before long that I didn't care who dug up whom, or why. I remembered a little ditty from my childhood that started out: *Did you ever think when the hearse goes by, that you will be the* next to die? . . . and whose chorus went: *The worms crawl in, the worms crawl out. . .*

By the time the coffin was opened, and the company representative had buttoned his smock and pulled on his rubber gloves, I was humming the tune. I was singing it as he steered me over to the grave, so I could observe the comparison of dental work with his charts. He seemed to miss the humor of it all. He looked a little green and the sweat was pouring off his face. Joe didn't look so good either, but I really couldn't see him that well. I could hear Cayetano vomiting over by the coconut palm. I felt fine.

A week later I had fully recovered and managed to force myself to forget about Joe. That morning I sifted through the bag of mail brought up from the ship that had docked during the night. It was always nice to get mail—so many surprises.

Then I saw it. Somehow, I knew before I opened the letter bearing the return address of another major insurance company that it would involve Joe. And it did: "This company understands that Mr. Joseph Smith was killed by a train at Puerto Cortés and is buried there. . . your assistance is requested in obtaining positive identification . . . a company representative will call on you."

Life in the Tropics

The detail to Puerto Cortés only seemed long. In reality, we were there just a few months. But that was long enough for us to fully appreciate how fortunate we had been to have our assignment switched to Tegucigalpa. Someone up there was looking out for us.

Our assignment may have felt longer because so much happened while we were there—mostly things we wished had never happened at all. There was the trauma of the boa constrictor that squeezed through the cyclone fence around our back yard, ate one of the chickens the cook kept there, and then couldn't get out because he couldn't fit through the mesh for the return trip.

Then there was the time some insect laid a tiny egg under my big toenail. The tiny egg grew into a rather large larvae and things got quite crowded down there until an ancient, toothless granny skilled in such things dug it out with a sharp bamboo splinter. But the old crone met her match when a different variety of local vermin took up residence behind my shinbone. That one braced himself firmly in place whenever any attempt was made to get him to come out through his porthole, and granny finally had to admit he was too much for her.

The fruit company doctor at the nearby town of La Lima told us I was fortunate granny had given up. Had she pierced the larvae's thick hide, a serious infection would have been inevitable, quite likely involving blood poisoning and possibly the loss of the leg. My, but that made me feel better!

The doctor took a different tactic to dislodge my guest: using a long hypodermic needle, he injected ether into the larvae's cavity, prompting its immediate voluntary evacuation. I was glad to be rid of it but am convinced that it would have been considerably less painful to amputate the leg in the first place.

Hurricanes were another new tropical delight, and local architects had provided for them. Like every other building in the beachside fruit company compound, the combined office-residence occupied by the consulate stood on stilts nine feet off the ground. This offered protection from the storm surge accompanying tropical cyclones, which frequently occurred there on the front line of Hurricane Alley, as our location was known. I got up the morning after a particularly wet storm to find water deep enough at the consulate's front stoop to accommodate a boat with enough draft to safely make the trip from there to Cuba.

The pillars also made it more difficult for creepy-crawly things to get inside, although they weren't much of a barrier for the more determined—not to mention winged ones. In addition, they allowed better air circulation, which helped a lot, given the climate, and that air conditioners were unknown in those latitudes in that day and time.

The pillars were ideal, except when it came to seismic activity. Earthquakes are old hat now, but when Mary and I hit Puerto Cortés we had never been through one. One evening, after a pleasant game of bridge, we sat together rocking on the screened porch that ran the length of the building, enjoying a nightcap before going to bed. I had a strange sensation that someone was pushing my rocker. I couldn't stop rocking. At first, there was no unusual sound, but soon the entire building began to creak and groan, much like a wooden-hulled ship sailing before a stiff breeze. Mary gasped and pointed toward the chandelier in the living room: it lurched back and forth in an alarming arch.

By then, the china in the kitchen cabinets began to clatter. Our consternation had grown beyond alarm, but neither of us guessed what the problem was until the cook burst through the door—dressed in her nightgown, her hair up in cotton curlers, her eyes wide with fear—and screamed, "Temblor!" How long it lasted, I don't know, but it seemed that the house swayed forever atop its nine-foot legs. Even after the quake stopped, the chandelier wobbled as the house settled back to normal.

Puerto Cortés was not all bad. There were many opportunities for fishing. Our busiest time of day at the consulate came when a ship sailed, and that was usually in the early morning before daylight. After that, Price Dodson, the port captain, and I often boarded one of the several small boats available to him and set forth for a couple of hours of trolling. Out on the ocean the breeze was cool and there were no sandflies or mosquitoes. The fishing was always good, and sometimes excellent. On most trips we could count on catching mackerel, barracuda, tarpon or kingfish. Sometimes there was high excitement as we hooked a sailfish or wahoo.

But it wasn't all catch and enjoy. Sharks were plentiful and regularly stole our catch—often along with line and lure—before we could get one into the boat. They were especially challenging with schooling fish like albacore. The sharks followed the schools and when they discovered where we were fishing, they stuck close and ended up with more of our fish than we did. Once this started, it was time to close shop and go home. It was annoying, and Price and I decided one day—or more likely one evening in the bar at the company hotel—that we would do something about it.

We made our plans carefully. We would use the small tug *Sula*, which had flush decks and no railing. We would invite four or five friends to go with us to help pull in our catch—sharks in that part of the Caribbean were often upwards of 12 feet long and weighed several hundred pounds.

We would also need a rifle, so we could kill the sharks before hauling them into the boat with us. We needed shark hooks with chain leaders, and heavy line—we thought of everything. Finally, we were ready and sailed out early one morning to take revenge on the sharks.

The albacore were schooling far offshore, but we found them. We put out feather jigs and landed several before the sharks found us. After that all we got into the boat was a head or half a fish at best. We were now ready to go after shark. We baited our hook with half an albacore and played out the heavy line, lashing the end to the towing bit. Right away we had a strike. The line drew taut and there was great excitement as we let the shark work off his fury. At first, he pulled us backwards against the light drag of the idling propeller. As he tired, we tested the line to see if he could be hauled in. When he came to the surface, we were startled by his enormous size, and alarmed to see how many of his buddies followed him up.

After struggling to get him alongside, we watched helplessly as he easily thrashed away, and the process had to be repeated all over again. But at length the fight was out of him and we were ready to haul him aboard. It was then that the rifle was employed to insure he didn't snap off someone's leg once we had him on deck. As the blood spread in the water, the number of sharks circling the boat swiftly doubled. Triangular fins cut the surface on all sides, and we expected them to go after our catch any minute. Heave and pull as we might, he was too heavy to lift over the *Sula*'s gunnel, so several of us scrambled atop the deckhouse to gain the advantage of pulling from up there.

At this point several things happened in rapid succession: the shark we had presumed dead began to thrash and jerk at the line. Someone decided to shoot him again. The shot missed the shark, but cut the line, and the three of us pulling from atop the deckhouse went over backward and landed in the water. I can vividly remember the feeling of terror as I realized I would soon be in the water with those aroused sharks. But I don't remember hitting the water, nor getting back on the boat. The next thing I knew, all three of us were back aboard the *Sula*, breathing heavily, but hardly wet at all. As they say in personnel work, we were motivated.

It was a good thing my zest for fishing was temporarily dampened because our detail to Puerto Cortés was at an end. Our initial disappointment at the change in our assignment had changed to gratitude for that lucky turn of the Foreign Service wheel of fortune. It had been an interesting experience, but the thought that we might easily have had two years of it was chilling. Our attitude about working at the embassy had undergone a most refreshing change, and we were ready to return to the relative civilization of Tegucigalpa.

Termites

There were always problems for the general services officer at Tegucigalpa. One requiring urgent attention when I took over was the physical inventory. Many new furnishings and supplies had been acquired during World War II, but the need to record these items and place inventory numbers on them had been overlooked. It is an easy matter to overlook, until you see an inspection in the offing. The process is tedious and thankless, but you get the hell kicked out of you if the inspectors find you haven't done it. Our post hadn't been inspected in years and was long overdue, so I reluctantly decided I had better try to straighten out our inventory.

The job was more complicated than I anticipated. Many items had been disposed of without anyone bothering to remove them from the inventory. My first task would be to identify what items we still had and were accountable for, and what might have happened to the ones we were accountable for but no longer had. It got worse and worse. There were many objects that had been on hand for decades and I felt sure were covered by inventory cards, but which couldn't be reconciled. Some of them had never been tagged with inventory numbers, while others had been refinished and, in the process, lost any inventory numbers they had carried.

After months of sweating over the problem in my spare time, I got things sorted out. Some lost items were located and reconciled. Authority was obtained to drop many furnishings that had been damaged by termites. We were in pretty good shape except for the bookcase sections. These came in standard sizes and could be stacked to make anything up to a ten-shelf bookcase—and we seemed to have a million of them. Reconciliation of unnumbered items was impossible, and it was obvious that there was only one solution: I submitted the required forms asking for authorization to drop numerous bookcase sections, explaining that they had been eaten by termites. For all I knew, it was true.

There was a long delay before my request was acknowledged by Washington. I got nervous. I didn't know for a fact that the bookcase sections had been consumed by termites, although it was as good a guess as any. Finally, the form arrived. I was authorized to drop my missing bookcase sections from the embassy's inventory.

But at the bottom of the form was a brief note: "The Museum of Natural History requests samples of the termites that consumed the bookcase sections referred to in the embassy's dispatch of November 6, 1946, as the department's records indicate they were made of steel."

Who says bureaucrats don't have a sense of humor?

Choluteca Duck Hunt

A mirror-calm lake spread before the solitude of the blind. An eager golden retriever quivered in anticipation beside me. The decoys were spaced spot on to lure the flock of mallards circling in the distance into good range. I tried a tentative call and the ducks turned toward me. My gun was up, and I got off two shots as they wheeled. The retriever swam out for my kill.

Thus, my imagination brought into focus the scene I anticipated as I thought about the invitation to go on my first duck hunt in Honduras. I was to join the members of the Tegucigalpa Duck Hunt Club at Toncontín Airport before first light on Sunday morning.

The drive through town to the airport was always an adventure. There were no paved streets, although a few blocks in the center of town were surfaced with hand-hewn granite slabs. Otherwise it was cobblestones, and large ones at that. Sewers were scarce, but those that existed were constantly in need of maintenance, and an open sewage ditch across any given street might or might not be marked. Saturday night's revelers were not gathered up until after daylight on Sunday and lay wherever they had fallen, which was usually in the street. There were no streetlights, but there were two safety factors: the streets were too rough for any speed, and there was no other traffic.

My hosts and hunting companions huddled near the Lockheed 10 that would take us to the Choluteca lakes. The number of guns, game bags and other gear being carted aboard was alarming. Every seat would be filled, and the plane looked small for all that load.

It was pitch dark when we boarded and buckled up. Joe Silverthorne, TACA Airlines' operations manager, would be our pilot. My seatmate was Chuck Abadie who owned Casa Uhler, a large general store. Jack Linton, who ran Tegucigalpa's only grocery store, sat across the aisle, next to Norman Scholes, owner of Empresa Dean, Honduras' largest trucking company. Fernando Sempe, Manager of the Banco Atlántida was up front by Ocie Sager, who oversaw operations at the Halliburton gold and silver mine at Agua Fría, and the lumbering operation and ranch at Jamastrán. Clark Anderson, the FBI special agent attached to the embassy, was in the bunch, too. All were to become close friends, although I didn't know any of them well yet.

They seemed unconcerned that we were preparing to take off before dawn, although Toncontín's airstrip was not lighted. If we managed to get up in the dark, we sure as hell would have trouble coming back down if there was an emergency. I tried not to dwell on that possibility as Joe taxied off the rough, unpaved apron onto the equally rough, unpaved strip. I wasn't afraid of flying, but I wasn't used to it, either.

It wasn't bad once we were airborne. There was a distinct band of light along the eastern horizon, although the ground below us remained cloaked in darkness. Chuck said we would be over the lakes at Choluteca in about 20 minutes. I hoped it would be light by then. So far, this had not been exactly the kind of outing I had envisioned. But it still seemed an easy way to get from one isolated location to another yet more isolated location. There was not a mile of paved highway in all of Honduras then, and the overland trip from Tegucigalpa to Choluteca took a full day.

I had managed to relax somewhat until Joe came walking down the aisle toward the back of the plane. This would not have been unusual, except that he was the only one aboard who knew how to fly. I struggled to stay calm, but it was a long 20 minutes before the Choluteca lakes spread below us.

Back at the controls, Joe banked sharply and made a low pass over the largest of the three lakes now visible in the spreading daylight. Clouds of ducks rose from the surface. The lake was hardly as I had imagined it. In fact, it was not a lake at all, but a shallow, overgrown swamp studded with dead trees. Thick shrubs crowded down to the water's edge. I couldn't make out anything that looked like a landing strip. There was simply a small clearing where a variety of livestock grazed.

Joe swung toward it and made a low pass, scattering the animals into the encroaching bushes. We dropped for an approach, and I realized this was the airstrip. My hands cramped from the force of my grip on the armrests. Surely, we weren't going to land on this tiny cow pasture!

The tips of the trees were level with the cabin window. I closed my eyes. We hit the ground, bounced once and raced toward the shrubs at the end of the clearing. I was certain we would crash into them, but Joe wheeled the plane around at the last minute and we came to a stop with a yard or two to spare.

Although there had not been a habitation of any description visible as we circled the lake, a crowd of ragged, barefoot campesinos gathered beside the plane as we disembarked. Greatly excited, they shouted and tugged at our clothing to attract attention. These, Chuck told me, were our "golden retrievers." We selected two and headed for the water.

The lake and surrounding thickets had looked formidable from the air. On the ground, it was considerably less inviting. There were two options for our shooting. We could fashion a blind in the thorn thickets at the swamp's edge, or we could wade into the swamp and seek concealment by one of the dead snags. The bristly bushes looked impenetrable, as did the thorny cactus intermingled with it. And then, this country was home to rattlesnakes, bushmasters, and who knew what else. We opted for the swamp.

Open water was visible some hundred yards from the edge of the bushes. The distance in between was covered with a solid matting of swamp grass and water hyacinth thick enough to bear our weight as we edged out from shore. After a dozen yards, we broke through the quivering mass to stand thigh deep and immobilized.

Here the campesinos took over, hacking a passage with their machetes. I could see they had advantages over golden retrievers, at least in Honduras. My appreciation grew as one expertly sliced in half a six foot, brown and yellow striped snake that slithered out of the heavy growth. I tried not to think too much about that as we worked our way deeper into the swamp and the path closed behind us. Retreat from this morass at more than a snail's pace would be impossible. It was not a comforting thought.

In what seemed like an age, we reached open water. By now we stood armpit deep. I looked for a place to hang my game bag, heavy with 250 rounds of shotgun shells. A greenish-brown log some 10 feet long floated nearby and I edged toward it. It edged away. I made out two small eyes and a snout barely above the water at one end of the log, and a ridged tail at the other. Chuck hadn't said anything about caimans, but I had been to the zoo. I'm sure I left a wake going the other way, muddy bottom and swamp grass notwithstanding.

There were plenty of ducks to shoot at that morning, but I was handicapped, what with one eye looking out for the caiman, and the other looking out for ducks. My Honduran golden retriever and I were loaded down when the time came for us to head back to the plane. Many of our birds were Muscovy ducks weighing six to eight pounds each. Conditions might not have been what I had anticipated, but the bag was beyond my wildest expectation.

There was much excitement and good humor as the hunters drifted back to the plane and gathered in the shade of the wings. Spirits of various vintages and proofs appeared from innermost pockets of hunting jackets and game bags. The morning's shoot had been exceptionally good, and while the golden retrievers plucked, the shooters relaxed and recounted the morning's exploits, which tended to grow in magnitude and reflect ever-increasing skill, in direct proportion to the amount and proof of libation consumed.

Soon no one minded being bone weary and dripping wet from hours of wading around neck deep in the muddy swamp. In fact, we were about as wet inside as out. All of us, that is, except for Fernando Sempe. He had not returned at the appointed hour and we could hear him down at the swamp blasting away. Occasionally someone called, but there was no response.

Joe Silverthorne had his notebook and slide rule out making calculations as he estimated the weight of our kill and subtracted the weight of the ammunition we had used up. At regular intervals, he shook his head and figured some more. At length he announced the load was too heavy for the short stretch of pasture available for our takeoff. Something would have to be left behind.

There was a chorus of anguished protest. What could possibly be left behind? Certainly not our guns—or our ducks. Our ammunition was already gone, and the booze was going fast. What else was there? Joe took off his cap and scratched his head. Maybe we could make it if we stowed our ducks and gear in the nose cargo compartment and crowded together at the front end of the passenger cabin for the takeoff. With the tail thus lightened, we might get off the ground.

Joe sent a crew of those wonderful Honduran golden retrievers to the far end of the cow pasture to top the higher trees we would have to clear as we became airborne. The rest of us pitched in to load the cargo compartment. Then we pushed the tail around and backed the plane to the very edge of the bushes in order to take advantage of every available inch for the takeoff run.

We paid our campesino helpers and somehow managed to crowd, one on top of the other, into the first four rows of seats. With the brakes locked, Joe advanced the throttles until the Lockheed shuddered and the tail bounced. The plane shot forward as he suddenly released the brakes, and we started our takeoff run. My spine tingled, and I held my breath so we would be that much lighter, but thanks to the generous quota of spirits, I wasn't half as concerned as I had been on the flight down. Gradually we became airborne. Joe retracted the wheels. The propellers shredded the uppermost branches of the trees as we cleared the pasture. A cheer went up. We had made it!

At 500 feet Joe banked for a final pass over our landing field. Our campesinos stood with faces upturned, marveling at the miracle of flight. One jumped up and down excitedly, waving his arms as if to catch the plane and come with us. It seemed strange, but no one gave it much thought—until halfway home, when we noticed that Fernando Sempe was not among us.

Zopilotes

Housing was at a premium in Tegucigalpa, and we felt fortunate to locate a lovely new house in Colonia Buena Vista that Henry Guilbert had built. Henry was a US dentist who had moved to Honduras many years before. His house came up for rent about the time we returned from our detail to Puerto Cortés, and we grabbed it, although our furniture had not yet arrived from the US.

Various members of Tegucigalpa's US colony were kind enough to lend us odds and ends of furnishings so we could set up housekeeping, after a fashion, until our own effects arrived. The most memorable of these was a double bed provided by Dr. Flinter of the Rockefeller Foundation. It had been manufactured before the advent of coil springs and the mattress was quite thin and flexible. Thus, there was a definite tendency for everything to gravitate to the exact center of the bed. By the time Mary and I managed to settle in for a night's rest, we, the pillows, the bedding and often our young daughter were lumped together in a mass at the center of a thrashing vortex.

We had camped out at the house in Colonia Buena Vista for many months when word came that our effects had cleared customs in Puerto Cortés and would be arriving in Tegucigalpa any day. It is about 185 miles from Puerto Cortés to Tegucigalpa, but in 1946 it was a long, hard trip. From Puerto Cortés to Potrerillos, cargo was hauled by the Tela Railroad. There was a narrow, winding dirt road from Potrerillos to Tegucigalpa. It was so steep and the turns so sharp that few trucks could navigate it. During the worst part of the rainy season all traffic stopped.

Our effects were off-loaded from the Tela Railroad at the Potrerillos freight yard during the season's heaviest downpour, and there they stayed until the rains let up enough to allow trucks to navigate the Potrerillos-Tegucigalpa highway. Our containers arrived in two dump trucks. As each tilted its bed so the container could slide to the ground, a cascade of water poured forth and streamed down the road toward town.

We knew what to expect when we opened them, but hope springs eternal, and our shock was great when we saw what the tropical rains had done to our new furnishings, bought with such care and shipped from Texas with so much anticipation. The furniture was ruined. Bedding and linens were moldy, pillows were saturated, and everything that could come unglued, had. Mary held back the tears until we were alone. When they came, it was all I could do to keep from joining in. We had learned another lesson about the Foreign Service—and it was one of the hardest to date. But the destruction of our furniture was not the only problem we faced in connection with our occupancy of Henry Guilbert's new house.

The first real inconvenience we found with the house itself was caused by two factors: the linen closet was in the bathroom, and there was no lock on the inside of the bathroom door. It could be locked from the outside, however. This was not an uncommon situation in Honduras where modern carpentry was in its infancy. The resulting problem became evident the first time Mary decided to have the linens on our bed changed. Immediately on being given her instructions, the maid proceeded to the linen closet for fresh sheets, greeting me where I sat in the bathroom with a cheery, "Buenos días, señor," as she came in, and excusing herself as she passed me on the way out with a polite, "Con su permiso."

Then there was the confusion with the plumbing, which we were to find throughout Latin America. The faucet in the shower marked with an H provided cold water, H being the first letter of helado, or icy. The faucet marked with a C provided hot water, C being the first letter of caliente, or hot. The hot water tap in the shower was on the right, while the hot water tap in the bathroom sink was on the left. I never could remember which was which. This wasn't as great a problem as it might have been because we often didn't have any hot water—in fact, most of the time, we had no water at all.

Houses in Tegucigalpa weren't identified by street name or number—most streets didn't have names, and none had numbers. Houses were known by the name of the first occupant, and addresses were given in relation to the nearest place of importance, usually the neighborhood pulpería, the corner store. Thus, our house was to be known as "Casa Crockett" (a designation that continued to identify it years after we were gone) and its location was given as three blocks to the east and above the Empresa Dean—Norman Scholes' place of business. The "above" part was quite appropriate, as Colonia Buena Vista was built on the steep slope of Mount Picacho, of which there was much more up and down than east and west.

Our road passed between Empresa Dean and Joe Silverthorne's house, up past Norman Scholes' home where it turned sharply, and then climbed in front of Clark Anderson's house. There it made another sharp turn to climb by Jack Linton's place, and came to a dead end in front of our house. To the rear, the ground sloped in terraces toward the Olancho road and the ravine far below.

The balcony that opened at the rear of our living room overlooked this vista, as well as Jack Linton's house to one side. That balcony created another serious problem for me.

Jack Linton was from Athens, Georgia. Large, dark haired and rather handsome, he had a Clark Gable mustache and a *Gone with the Wind* drawl. He was a likeable fellow. He happened to be in Honduras because he met and married Marietta Lardizábal while she was going to college in the United States. Marietta was friendly and pleasant, though known to be fussy about her house.

Jack owned the only grocery store in Tegucigalpa worth the name—and it took some stretching to go that far. But he did eventually stock lettuce and loaf bread, which was not to be had when we first arrived. He also started carrying fresh lamb in the meat section, until then an unheard-of luxury.

The lamb was part of the problem. For lack of a better place, Jack slaughtered the lambs in his back yard. No one minded, and there were no sanitation regulations against it. The country's sanitation department consisted of large flocks of *zopilotes* that were everywhere. Those fellows did a great job. They were tough, too. More than once I watched one fight off a good-sized dog for a tasty morsel. I often wondered why they had never been declared the official Honduran bird. They certainly deserved the title. There were always a good number of zopilotes to be found in Colonia Buena Vista, many of them slowly circling above Jack Linton's house waiting for him to slaughter another batch of lambs.

Given the proximity of our houses, there was no way for zopilotes to circle Jack Linton's house without circling ours as well. This didn't create a problem if you were careful to shade your eyes when you looked up and, above all, kept your mouth shut.

I used to watch those birds circle lazily, high above, for hours. It was at one of these times when I was abruptly seized with the idea that they were excellent moving targets for my new .22 rifle. I got the rifle, stretched out flat on my back on the balcony, and began squeezing off shots at the zopilotes high above. It soon became clear that they were in no danger at all. The range was too great and the moving targets too difficult for the state of my art as a trick zopilote shot.

I had about decided that the sharp-eyed birds were dodging my bullets when a big one I hadn't aimed at suddenly folded his wings and plummeted earthward like a falling stone. I was shocked at this evidence that my shots were that wide off the mark. But that shock was nothing compared to my panic when I realized that the zopilote was going to impact near the center of Jack Linton's roof.

Red clay tiles covered flimsy wooden framework on just about every roof in Tegucigalpa. This kept the rain out—most of the time—and allowed hot air from inside the house to escape through the spaces between the tiles. It was a satisfactory, though fragile arrangement. I could imagine what would happen when the zopilote, whose dive was gaining speed by the split second, hit the roof. All I could do was shudder in anticipation

There was a clatter of shattered tile and a loud, sickening thud from deep within Jack Linton's house, followed by piercing screams of alarm in several different keys. I was to learn later that the bird came to rest on the dining room table. Jack told me the shot that brought it down had been clean through the head.

Marietta was distinctly cool toward me after that, although Jack, bless his heart, was kind enough to laugh about it later—after the damage had been repaired and I had sought forgiveness in the humblest manner I could affect.

The Last Prospect

Jim Cokay was old. His hair was grizzled, and his shoulders stooped. He was black. He claimed to be a US citizen, but he preferred to speak Spanish. A prospector, he had lived in Honduras since before the turn of the century. He had discovered a gold mine out near Catacamas many years ago, and now one of the local officials was trying to take it from him. He had walked six days from Olancho to ask for the embassy's help. I wished I could do something for him.

Jim produced a leather folder where he safeguarded time-yellowed papers of importance. He explained that he could not read or write, but assured me I would find the title to his mine in the folder. There was a document on Honduran legal paper with fiscal stamps and flourishing signatures. It might have been a claim registration, but the rural authority who prepared it had been barely literate himself. I couldn't make heads or tails of it. And besides, I didn't know anything about the Honduran Mining Code. I told Jim I couldn't be of any help—he would have to find a lawyer. I don't think he expected much help in the first place. He left without complaint. I felt bad.

Jim sat on the curb with a bundle beside him as I drove home for lunch. He was the picture of dejection. I had to stop. Yes, he was hungry. No, he didn't have any place to eat. We loaded his things in my jeep, and he went home with me. I didn't plan it that way, but he stayed with us for six months.

I didn't have a job for Jim. Honduras was primitive in those days and it took a large staff to keep a house going, but we already had a cook, a maid, a laundry woman and a houseboy-gardener. Besides, Jim was too old to be able to do much. I couldn't find it in me to send him away, and he didn't go on his own.

Our small daughter, Laura, took to Jim immediately, and he entertained her for hours. He could swing an ax, and assumed responsibility for splitting the cook's firewood and keeping a supply dry for her kitchen stove. He slept in the woodshed. He wanted a place by himself, and there wasn't anywhere else.

In time, Jim again became accustomed to speaking English. His soft drawl was from the Deep South. He had come to Honduras from Louisiana and thought he had been born in Tennessee, but he wasn't sure where or when. One day he said, "Ol' Jim Crockett, he jus' forget." I was taken aback and asked since when had he become Jim Crockett instead of Jim Cokay. "Why, ever since I come here. Hondurans can't say Crockett, so they call me Cokay. I don' have nothin' with my name writ on it."

I never knew for sure whether it was the truth or if I had been adopted by a foster son old enough to be my grandfather. I did know that Hondurans often pronounced my name Cokay, with an accent on both the "o" and the "a," and that one branch of the Crockett family had gone to Tennessee from Virginia— Davy Crockett's branch. All Jim had with his name on it had been prepared by a semiliterate Honduran country bumpkin.

Soon after Jim took up residence at our house, he produced from his bundle a china plate, cup and saucer. These had once been white, with bright blue design overlaid. The plate had ridges creating several small divisions to hold assorted foods—and must have once been used to serve a lunch in a cheap restaurant. Jim insisted on having his meals served on his china. We learned that he also insisted on sitting at the table alone, with the servants standing until he had finished his meal. This didn't go over too big, but Jim managed to get his way. Mary and I stayed out of it.

As we became better acquainted, Jim told me about his life in Honduras as a prospector for gold, and about his mine. It turned out not to be a mine at all, but a location where he had found good placer gold deposits and which he had attempted to file a claim on. Jim said that in his younger days he had earned a livelihood panning for gold. Sometimes very good, sometimes not so good. What paid the most had involved the hardest work.

Jim explained that diggings along the streams in the gold country had been worked and reworked, first by the natives, then by the Spanish conquistadores and modern-day prospectors. But high in the mountains, there was still good pay dirt. The problem was that up in the mountains there was no water. He had solved this by taking mule pack trains to the high country, loading them with pay dirt and bringing them back down to the valley where there was water to wash his ore. There had been days, Jim said, when he panned as much as $500 worth of gold this way.

The day came when Jim reached inside his shirt and untied a strap around his waist on which hung a pouch. From this he produced a vial of gold dust and small nuggets—about two or three ounces in all. He didn't offer to hand me the vial, but the contents looked genuine enough. I was impressed. Jim said he longed to go back to prospecting but needed a backer. Would I be interested in buying a share in his mine? I thanked him but said I would not.

As Jim became more accustomed to us, he sought ways of making himself useful. He loved any excuse to walk into town and go to the market, a trip that usually had to be made once or twice a day. He would not go with the cook, but he would take her basket if asked to go by himself. Our drinking water came to the house in five-gallon bottles, and if the delivery truck failed to show, as it often did, Jim would walk into town for water, carrying the heavy load back up the steep road on his shoulder.

When we had guests, Jim guarded their cars in the parking area. Our friends liked him, and I suspected he accepted tips from them, as he always had pocket money, and I couldn't imagine where else he might come by it. We fed and housed him, and even clothed him with my castoffs, but he got no salary, and courteously declined when I offered him spending money.

There was friction between Jim and the servants. To them, he was an unsalaried servant. To him, they were Honduran peons. Mary and I frequently found ourselves forced to arbitrate their squabbles. We tried not to show bias, but our sympathies were with Jim. He was practically a member of the family, and Laura could not have loved him more had he been her own grandfather.

Finally, the showdown came. One Sunday morning I was awakened at daylight by what sounded like a pitched battle in the servants' area. I had a headache and a bad taste in my mouth. Jim and the four servants were all screaming and shoving one another. I tried to establish some order to find out what the trouble was. I caught enough of the response to gather that someone had accused someone else of putting a poisonous toad in the soup, a favorite trick among unfriendly Hondurans. It was much more complicated than that, and each of the five insisted on shouting their version at the same time. I fired them all and went back to bed. Mary reminded me we had company coming for lunch, got up and put everybody back on the payroll.

Some days later, Mary told me she had noticed Jim bringing home packages that were not ours when he went to the market for her. The houseboy told me Jim was accumulating bundles in his woodshed bedroom. I asked Jim about it. At first, he was reluctant, but it finally came out that he was gathering the tools and supplies he would need to go back to prospecting.

Then came the day I discovered Jim had two mules staked out in the bushes near our house. Twice a day he took water and a little grain out to them. I knew the time was near when he would leave us. I was saddened, and worried about how Laura would react. Our daughter had become Jim's constant companion.

I couldn't keep from wondering where Jim was getting his finances but didn't want to ask for fear he would take my questioning as an accusation. I knew he wouldn't part with the little vial of dust and nuggets he treasured so greatly. And that wouldn't have covered his expenses anyway. Mules were costly, and gold was only $35 an ounce.

The early morning air was chilly, but I stood on the balcony watching for Jim and his mules. He had loaded his packs before daylight and started down Mt. Picacho, on the road to Catacamas, which followed the ravine's watercourse north. I caught sight of his stooped figure leading the mules far below. He looked up toward the house but made no sign. I wondered if his old eyes could make out the house, much less my small figure, at that distance. I waved and the lump in my throat grew larger.

Laura wasn't alone in missing Jim. Mary and I did too. I never looked at the winding road down by the ravine without thinking of Jim and wondering if we would ever hear of him again. Our friends who had come to know Jim asked about him too. Like ourselves, each of them had a soft spot in their heart for old Jim. They knew his story, and they also knew about his little vial of gold dust and nuggets—almost every one of them had bought a share in Jim's mine to help fund his last prospect.

Jamastrán Deer Hunt

Some of the best times of my life were spent in the Jamastrán Valley of southeastern Honduras. When I knew the valley in the mid-1940s, getting there was a major undertaking. From Tegucigalpa you took the narrow dirt road leading over the mountains to the Zamorano Valley, and from there a narrower and more difficult track across the Choluteca River and through Jacaleapa to Danlí, near the Nicaraguan border. From Danlí on, there was no road worthy of the name. But there were overgrown logging trails and occasional savannas you could carefully follow in a jeep for the last six miles or so to Jamastrán. The trip was about 60 miles overall, but under the best of conditions it took six to seven long, rough and dusty hours. When it rained, you didn't get through.

For the most part, Jamastrán was virgin jungle. In many respects, it was an outdoorsman's paradise. Rich in natural beauty, the valley abounded in many varieties of game, including deer, peccary, tapir, jaguar, ocelot, peacock, blue rock pigeon, chachalaca, agouti, coati, and several types of monkeys. The rivers draining the valley were well populated with game fish. All of this helped make it an extremely enjoyable place for me, but I came to love Jamastrán because of the men with whom I shared my outings there.

There were five of us: Norman Scholes, Chuck Abadie, Clark Anderson, Ocie Sager, and myself, all duck hunting companions. Ocie was our host when we went to Jamastrán. I've had a good number of close friends over the years, but none better or truer than these four men.

More time was dedicated to deer hunting than to any other sport at Jamastrán, and most of the deer hunting was done at night. Having been raised where hunting with a headlight is viewed with the same distaste as stealing the pennies off a dead man's eyes, I was never able to develop a great deal of interest in it. But I soon learned that it was a hard and dangerous way to go after game in the Central American jungles.

You had to worry about the occasional jaguar, or a constrictor scooping you up as you walked under a low-hanging limb. You also had to watch out for a bushmaster or fer-de-lance on the path before you. This was complicated because night hunting is done in the dark of the moon, and jungle deer greatly prefer areas of heavy cover.

In honesty, I must confess that there was another, more subtle reason why night hunting never held much attraction for me. That incident took place on my first night hunt in Honduras.

We were working a series of small fields that had been hacked out of the jungle and planted in black beans. Deer will come to tender young beans in preference to anything else, and country folk are hard put to save their crops in wild areas where the deer population is heavy. Our hunts were always welcomed by the local farmers.

I had separated from the others and started to hunt when my light picked up a nice buck grazing in the center of a field. He was a little out of range, but when I crawled through the pole fence to get nearer, he spooked and jumped into the next field. I followed, but he managed to stay out of range, catching a mouthful of bean plants whenever he could as we progressed from one field to the next. With each successive but unproductive stalk, I became more determined.

Finally, the opportunity came. The buck cleared a fence into a field bordered by jungle and trotted within good range of the forest before looking back in my direction and then lowering his head to pull up a mouthful of bean plants. I had him where I wanted him, and carefully executed a flanking maneuver I hoped would put him into range of my freezer.

With casual nonchalance, I quartered away from my quarry and then doused my light to feel a little less conspicuous. A couple of hundred yards more and I was over the last fence and into the jungle. The undergrowth was heavy and laced together with hook-thorned vines. In what seemed like an age, I managed to drag, tear and squirm to a point that I estimated was opposite my buck's location. I cautiously crept forward and came out of the jungle at the edge of the field. My sense of direction had been perfect! I could see nothing in the pitch dark, but I could hear my buck moving about as he continued to graze.

I exercised a great deal of willpower to overcome the urge to spring up immediately and blast away. But I waited until I had caught my breath and checked all essential equipment to insure against any last-minute failure. My headlight was aimed in the right direction, and ready to switch on. My 12-gauge automatic shotgun was loaded with five rounds of 00 buckshot. I was breathing heavily, but this was mostly from excitement and anticipation. I was ready to move in for the kill.

I stood up slowly and carefully raised the shotgun. I knew the buck had heard, smelled or sensed me, because the sound of his peaceful grazing was replaced with what sounded like nervous pawing. I had to shoot and shoot fast before he turned and ran. I switched on my headlamp.

Instead of reflecting one pair of eyes, the light glared back red from two pair! My buck had found a friend. Before they could turn to run, I pulled the trigger twice in quick succession. Both animals fell in their tracks. My chest expanded a couple of inches as I casually blew the smoke from my gun barrel.

What a wonderful feeling! For days, as we had prepared for the trip, I had been told how difficult it was to bag a deer at night, how spooky they were, how quick and sure one had to be in his shooting, how I should not expect success until I had more experience. Well, I had showed them. My first nighttime hunt had barely begun, and I already had not one but two deer! What would they say to that?

I crawled through the fence and walked along the bean rows, lighting my way with the headlight. When I saw my kill stretched out on the ground, I realized at once something was wrong. Each animal had a rope around its neck. I distinctly recall the crushing sense of dread accompanying the series of thoughts that flashed through my mind as I fully realized that I had bagged a pair of jackasses!

There were several mitigating circumstances that made it possible to rationalize shooting two donkeys tied in a fenced bean patch. I used to try to explain but have long since given up. After you sift, boil, strain and sort all the facts, the remaining essence is still two dead burros.

Donkeys are valuable critters in the mountains of Honduras, but they are far more valuable when killed by a gringo city slicker. I couldn't blame the owner as we dickered over the transaction. I knew that had I been in his position, those two donkeys would have been as fine a pair of animals as he alleged. I didn't mind paying an exorbitant price to bring the matter to an honorable close. But I did get sick and tired of being repeatedly asked during the next six months if donkey meat really was good enough eating to be worth the price I paid for it.

Dolores

Four steep-sided hills rise from the floor of Jamastrán Valley. Ocie's headquarters camp was built on top of one, and a traditional part of each day spent there was the late afternoon bull session held on the back porch that ran the length of the bunkhouse. It was a beautiful location to watch evening come to the valley. There the day's exploits were recounted, with embellishments in geometric proportion to the number of rapadura Old Fashioneds we had consumed.

Rapadura Old Fashioneds were a traditional part of our trips to Jamastrán. They were like most other Old Fashioneds, except they were made with rapadura instead of regular sugar. Rapadura is a crudely refined brown sugar commonly used in rural areas where sugar is boiled out of home-grown cane in a backyard kettle. It has a distinctive flavor. We all agreed that there was no drink to compare with a rapadura Old Fashioned, drunk on the back porch of Ocie's bunkhouse at Jamastrán. We never had them anywhere else because we were all convinced they could never be mixed to taste the same unless made with rapadura boiled down by Ocie's camp cook, Dolores.

Dolores was a native of the Intibucá region of Honduras. Her rapadura was excellent, even if her cooking was not. With Dolores, there was one way and one speed of doing things: slowly. She seemed unaffected by anything. No matter what happened, she never changed her expression or her pace—well, almost never. I do remember once when she did.

We were having our customary rapadura Old Fashioned bull session on the back porch, and a heated discussion was taking place. I was defending myself as best I could, but conditions didn't favor my position and I was having a hard time of it. The more Norman thought about the whole thing, the madder he got and the harder he pressed. It is true that he had every right to be provoked, but I had no intention of admitting it.

The whole thing had started earlier that afternoon. It was near the end of the dry season and the dust was deep in Jamastrán's rutted logging trails. We had hunted hard, and each drop of perspiration had quickly turned to mud. We were all eager to clean up before settling down to rapadura Old Fashioneds and had agreed that the most pleasant way to accomplish this would be to have a swim in the Guayambre River.

It was a pretty tight squeeze for all five of us to get aboard the jeep. Fortunately, none but Norman was willing to risk damaging his rifle by bringing it along the rough trail to Guayambre.

Norman insisted his rifle went wherever he went and warned that we need not expect to use it if we spotted any game along the way. He added a variety of offensive remarks about hunters who were foolish enough to leave their guns behind. We didn't pay much attention. Norman enjoyed scolding us, and it was a short drive from the camp to the river. There was little likelihood of seeing game.

The water was wonderful, and while we swam Ocie managed to pick up enough fish for supper, using a small spinner on a fly rod. It was a relaxed and jolly bunch that bounced along the trail back to camp. Norman was annoyed because our conversation was loud enough to scare off whatever game might be around. In his efficient British way, he described exactly what type of jack-ass he thought each of us to be. This was a sure sign Norman was enjoying himself enormously, despite having a hard time hanging on to the bouncing jeep and holding his gun safely at the same time. It was at about this point that I spotted the buck standing broadside not 50 yards away.

Maybe because it was the last place you would expect to see a deer at that time of day, none of the others saw him. Ocie stopped immediately on my request, swinging around in his seat to ask what the trouble was. Norman continued his commentary about our worthless frivolity but didn't hesitate when I said, "Hand me your gun, Norman." It wasn't until I had the rifle to my cheek and was steadying the bead behind the deer's shoulder, that the others saw him.

The thought of Norman's righteous ire after I shot the buck with his rifle was so sweet that I chuckled to myself as I squeezed the trigger. Then the impossible happened! The slug that should have been precisely on the mark at that short range kicked up a spurt of dust under the buck's belly, and he kicked up his heels. I knew there was going to be hell to pay!

Norman was so shocked at the beginning that he was speechless. But by the time we neared the bottom of our second round of rapadura Old Fashioneds, he was in full voice, and with such righteousness, his sarcastic commentaries were forceful. He did have a point. Had I killed the buck it would have been a great joke on Norman. Having missed, I was the goat.

Then it dawned on me. Although Norman claimed that his eyes were not bad—his arms were just too short for him to see small things clearly at close range—we all knew he needed glasses. Vanity made him put off wearing them. And now that I thought about it, I was positive that the iron sights on his rifle must fuzz up when he aimed, so he had to have them set very coarse to use them at all. Thus, when I pulled the front sight of his rifle down into the V of his buckhorn rear sight, the gun was bound to shoot low!

I advanced this defense heatedly, but without results. Sympathy lay with Norman's position, and he stoutly maintained that the sights on his rifle were adjusted in the standard fashion.

The argument had gone full circle several times when one of the bunch got up in disgust, grabbed Norman's rifle and said, "See that knothole near the left-hand corner of the outhouse? I'm going to aim squarely at it and settle this damn fool argument once and for all!" Without waiting for comment or assent, he threw the gun to his shoulder, and splinters flew as the high-speed load slammed into one side of the outhouse and out the other.

The crack of the rifle hung in the air as the outhouse door burst off its hinges and Dolores catapulted out in high gear with superchargers on. Her flour sack skirt was a blur of color as she made for parts unknown in a sprint that would have measured up well in Olympic competition.

We were all so exhausted by the time we brought our laughter under control that no one had the energy to walk down the slope to see where the shot had hit. And we never had time to check it out later because we were too busy doing all the kitchen and camp work ourselves for the rest of the trip! The worst part was we ran out of rapadura—the kind only Dolores knew how to make in her backyard kettle.

Monkeys

Ocie and Norman got out of the pickup and walked to the river's edge with expressions of puzzled disbelief. When they were close enough to see that nothing serious was amiss, they burst out laughing, without waiting for an explanation for our presence or posture. We were in no mood for humor and responded with unseemly suggestions, delivered in uncultured language and punctuated with a barrage of inexpertly thrown river bottom mud. It occurred to me there were some who could throw better than others, a thought that did nothing to improve my disposition.

I guess we did look silly sitting in the middle of the creek scrubbing ourselves with sand. Undoubtedly, we had brought it upon ourselves. After all, you really couldn't blame the monkeys. I'm not sure any of us knew exactly why we wanted to catch that damned monkey in the first place.

It was a beautiful morning and Chuck, Clark and I had driven as far into the Jamastrán Valley as we could go before setting out on foot down a trail etched into the jungle floor by generations of wildlife. Each of us carried a high-powered hunting rifle, but this was more habit than serious intent, as we had no specific fauna in mind and were out more than anything to take in the many sights and sounds of early morning in the heavily forested Central American valley. Parrots were everywhere, ranging in size from tiny green puffs of down, to multicolored, king-sized macaws with three-foot tails. The air was crowded with their screamed chatter.

We reached a small clearing and escaped into the relative tranquility of open skies. It was then that we saw the mother monkey. A tiny offspring clung to her breast as she swung up into the great tree that stood near the center of the clearing.

I realize now that had we stopped to think at all, it would have occurred to us that a baby monkey is much better off in the custody of its legitimate dam than it could possibly be in the custody of three itinerant Jungle Jims who didn't know when to leave well enough alone. But we didn't know nearly as much about monkeys as we were to learn within the hour, and set about the task of catching this one with the unthinking dedication that usually accompanies the launching of any fool's errand.

When we explored the situation from the base of the tree, it developed that instead of a single mama monkey and her baby, we had managed to tree a whole family of howler monkeys. They had retreated to the upper reaches of their tree upon being surprised feeding on the ground when we came into the clearing. Although they could not escape their isolated haven without coming down, they showed no sign of concern about our presence, which was understandable enough, considering the size of the tree and our inferior climbing ability. Our problem was to get the mother and her baby down on the ground.

The Central American howler monkey, known in Honduras as the Olingo and in Nicaragua as the Congo, is slender with a long tail. A full-grown male stands a little over 30 inches tall. His name does not do justice to his roar; if his size were equal to his howl, he would dwarf the African gorilla.

The Olingo is a family man and, as we discovered, sticks by his kin in an emergency. As we debated the most productive approach to taking possession of mama Olingo's offspring, we gave no thought to the bull monkeys in the band, who gathered on a high branch by themselves, seemingly oblivious to our presence. I now think this was a ruse to throw us off guard while they held a council of war. But at the time, we paid them no attention, concentrating instead on developing a strategy calculated to outsmart mama monkey.

After much debate, we decided we would have to split the branch that our monkey was perched on with rifle shots and then take advantage of the confusion to snatch the baby monkey when the branch hit the ground. We lined up three in a row and took turns blazing away. The branch was thick, but we were making good headway when the trouble started.

While we focused on shooting down mama monkey's branch, the bull Olingos quietly maneuvered to strategic positions above and behind us. Each one had an assigned target, and before we knew what was going on, we had been liberally pasted with globs of excrement of the exact consistency to throw well but splatter effectively. Our retreat was humiliating—as one, we turned and fled out of range.

In telling this story since, I have had experts deny that monkeys laugh. But as we sat in the river washing our clothes that morning, the howls we could hear coming from the direction we had just left had a distinctly mocking pitch. Or maybe we imagined it sounded like laughter, being understandably sensitive about just having made monkeys out of ourselves.

Aboard the *Mary K*

If there was one thing certain about my life in the Foreign Service, it was uncertainty. I guess that was one of the attractions. But it had its drawbacks, too—at times it was sort of like living on an elevator: there were ups and downs and never any way to be sure what floor you would be on when it stopped. The day after my son John Kennedy was born at Hospital Viera in Tegucigalpa, the chargé sent for me.

"Crockett, I want you to go over to La Ceiba for a couple of weeks to have a look at the situation there. An Air Force plane is leaving this afternoon and you can catch a ride on it. Don't worry about Mary. We'll watch out for her." I packed and went. The two weeks turned into six months.

La Ceiba was a sleepy little port on the Caribbean where a Standard Fruit Company boat docked once a week to load bananas. The other six days nothing much happened, as a rule. But these were unusual times and the town was very much alive when I arrived. It was said that General "Bravo," commander of the local military garrison, harbored ambitions to become the country's president.

Since there were no elections in the offing, President Tiburcio Carías understandably took a dim view of General Bravo's ambitions. An interesting coincidence of developments had evolved because of this situation.

First, the Honduran Air Force selected a spot just offshore of the military garrison for target practice. Several partially filled gasoline drums were dropped into the Caribbean in front of General Bravo's headquarters, and then spectacularly exploded and sunk by bombing and strafing runs. Next, General "Guerra," who was loyal to President Carías, called on General Bravo to inform him that his garrison was to be "inspected," requesting that General Bravo run on home so he wouldn't be "inconvenienced by the process." Impressed with the Air Force's demonstrated competence, General Bravo went. But he failed to call in the bulk of his loyal troops who were maneuvering in the mountains where the Air Force couldn't practice.

That's where things stood when I arrived. General Guerra had been inspecting General Bravo's garrison for some weeks, while the latter stuck close to his house across the street from the consulate and received a constant stream of callers from dusk to dawn. Meanwhile, his loyal troops up in the mountains never seemed to get General Guerra's repeated orders for them to come down and be inspected like everybody else. I observed and reported, but it soon got to be damned slow business. Every time it was rumored General Bravo was tired of staying home and planned to come out, the Air Force would have more target practice, and General Guerra would send word he had not yet completed his inspection.

Things would quiet down for a couple of weeks and then the cycle would be repeated. I found I could count on a week or so of stalemate during each cycle, which gave me the opportunity to get out and around the consular district. I saw places that hadn't been visited by an US consul since the American writer William Sydney Porter, best known by his alias, "O. Henry," roamed the area 50 years earlier and got the inspiration for his novel, *Cabbages and Kings*.

Bishara Kawas was my closest friend in La Ceiba. His wife was named Mary, so his *goleta* was named the *Mary K*. A goleta is a double-ended motor schooner, used mainly for coastal and island trade, but seaworthy enough to make the trip to Florida, which Honduran goletas often did. Bishara had invited me to make a trip on the *Mary K* and see parts of Honduras that couldn't be reached any other way. One day I found a break between banana boats and insurrections and went along.

We were to deliver supplies as we sailed down the coast to Tuci on the Brus Lagoon near Cabo Gracias a Diós, where Columbus first set foot on mainland America, and then load coconuts as we circled back through the Bay Islands. We should return to La Ceiba in five days—if the weather held. I was excited. Brus Lagoon and the Bay Islands were isolated areas where the people, customs and way of life were different from anywhere else.

The *Mary K* was strictly a work boat, built for cabotage in these waters. Every inch of space was planned for efficient work use, with very little regard for the comfort of those who worked her. Passengers were incidental, and bunk space was limited.

Eighty-two feet long, eighteen feet wide and drawing five feet fully loaded, its pointed stern was intended to facilitate backing off an unexpected reef or sand bar. It also made possible the ingenious design of sanitary facilities. There were two of these, one overhanging each side of the extreme aft portion of the deck, extending out over the water. Thus, there was always running water in these seagoing outhouses.

Lem Ebanks, Jr., was our captain. A 31-year-old black man, he stood six feet tall and weighed over 200 pounds. There was not an ounce of fat on him. He was quiet, intelligent, and very much the master of the vessel. I liked him from the start. As I came to know him better, I also developed a great respect for his natural leadership ability.

We cast off on a windy afternoon with a choppy sea, running east along the coast several miles offshore. Around La Ceiba, the jungle-covered mountains rise sharply near the coastline and are spectacular when viewed from the sea. Two heavy lines with feather jigs were trolled astern and produced a steady catch of mackerel and barracuda, which were later fried on the *Mary K's* wood-burning stove in a galley so tiny the cook could reach any corner without taking a step. I spent that night stretched out on the hatch of the small forward deck, glad to be alive, glad to have come to Honduras, and glad to be at sea under a tropical moon.

By first light we were off the Mosquitia coast. The rugged mountains were a faint blue outline against the horizon, and the shoreline was flat for miles inland. Row on row of coconut palms grew along beige beaches outlined in frothy white surf. We were approaching Juan Lafitte's coconut plantation, which stretched for miles along a narrow strand between the Caribbean and Brus Lagoon.

We dropped anchor outside the breakers in 10 feet of water and watched the activity on shore. Outboard powered cayucos, sturdy boats hewn from a single log and sometimes over 40 feet long and six feet wide, were launched in the surf to bring out loading crews of indigenous Miskitos. The women carried coarsely woven sacks of 20 hulled coconuts each down to the beach, where the men took over, wading into the surf armpit deep to load the cayucos while others struggled to hold them in place against the churning surf.

Once the boat was fully loaded, two men scrambled aboard and jerked the outboard engine into life. The men in the water steadied the cayuco until a wave crested beneath, shooting it straight toward the next swell. No one seemed to pay any attention to the occasional triangular fin that cut the water beyond the breakers. I was eager to get ashore but less than enthusiastic about the way it had to be accomplished. Those triangular fins were also circling the *Mary K*, and the thought of a cayuco capsizing somewhere between her safe deck and the dry beach did things to my stomach. But the Miskitos knew how to handle them and had me ashore in short order, although wet below the waist from wading the last few yards.

Juan Lafitte met me at the water's edge, and we walked together across the narrow strand to where his house stood on tall stilts over the lagoon. I watched the Miskitos work from his thatch-roofed porch. There were perhaps 50 natives involved in the carting and loading of our coconuts. Six outboard powered cayucos plied between the shore and the *Mary K*. We would take on some 80,000 coconuts in all, and Juan estimated that loading would be completed in about five hours.

The Miskito, quite different from their neighbors, the Maya, were no longer a pure strain. They had crossbred with the Caribs, of African origin, and were virtually pygmy-sized. The women were mostly under five feet and the men not much taller. They all smoked something. The women favored homemade pipes with bamboo stems and corozo nut bowls. The men smoked home-rolled cigars for the most part, although some had store-bought pipes.

They were jolly, and there was much laughter, although they worked hard and steadily. Juan said their earnings for loading would go for supplies from his commissary. No cash would change hands. It felt like time had moved back a hundred years en route from La Ceiba.

We raised anchor late in the afternoon and set a course for Guanaja, the easternmost of the Bay Islands, where we were to load another 40,000 coconuts. As we headed away from the mainland, we took the sea bow on, creating quite a pitch. I borrowed Lem Ebanks' bunk in the pilot house and spent the night braced as best I could to keep from being thrown out.

I was glad when the new day dawned. Our entry into Guanaja's harbor was breathtaking, my first visit to a typical Caribbean island. Coral keys and reefs afforded protection from the open sea, and the surface of the harbor was as smooth as a millpond. The town of Guanaja, also known as Bonacca, was not built on the island proper, but on a small key, several hundred yards offshore where such breeze as there might be scattered the swarms of mosquitoes and sandflies common to the area. The village had long since outgrown the small key, and half the population lived in houses built on stilts out over the water. They were connected one to another by a crazy quilt maze of wooden walkways, none of which had railings.

The Bay Islands were originally British, as many of the early settlers were English pirates. It was said that Morgan had one of his home ports on the neighboring island of Roatán. Toward the end of the 19th century, the United Kingdom ceded the islands to the Republic of Honduras. But some 70 years later when I visited there, the language in general use was still English, and most official records were kept in English.

It was not English as we know it, but much closer to Elizabethan, and the African influence was also noticeable. My ear didn't become immediately attuned to the mixture, and I frequently found myself a sentence or two behind in comprehension. A typical sentence might go, "I can't see no how to fix this one engine, man," all with a little Scottish brogue thrown in. It was fascinating.

The *Mary K* had loaded the 40,000 coconuts we were to pick up at Guanaja. Benches in the mess had been stowed and the entire area was filled with coconuts to the height of the counter. The same with the crew's quarters. The walkways along each side of the vessel were loaded to the height of the railings with coconuts. As a result, we crawled on coconuts to get from here to there. We sat on coconuts to have our meals, and we slept on coconuts for the most part, too. I never have cared much for coconuts since then.

The Bay Islanders were noted for their parties, and the locals threw a good one for us that evening, featuring music, food and drink of many varieties. This was no cocktail reception but a foot stomping, high swinging, Bay Island dance.

There were few men, compared to the number of women present. At any given time, most of the men from the Bay Islands were at sea. Thus, the males on hand made sure each of the eager ladies had equal time on the dance floor. By midnight, I was exhausted and thought it might be up to me to leave so the party could end. None of that! The dancing, drinking, singing and eating continued until human endurance reached its limit around three in the morning.

In that climate, before the days of air conditioning, we were drenched with perspiration from dawn to dusk. Now came the climax of the evening's entertainment. The party adjourned en masse to two tiny beaches separated by a rocky prominence. The men bathed on one side and the women on the other. Clothing was optional. I didn't know the water and was afraid to get in too deep, but out there in the dark, beyond the rocky divider, there was a lot of laughter.

The *Mary K* sailed for Oak Ridge on the island of Roatán before daylight. The waters on the lee, or south, side of the Bay Islands are calm and smooth. I found a spot over the pilot house and stretched out to look at the stars.

These waters are, I am sure, among the most beautiful in the world. Innumerable small, coconut-lined keys guard the entrances to countless magnificent harbors. The waters are crystalline, permitting a clear view of coral reefs 40 feet down. Greens of the foliage on shore match the greens of the depths. Looking down, you can see brightly colored coral and fish. Looking up, it is brightly colored flowers and shrubs. When there is a breeze, it is truly lovely. When there is not, the combination of heat, humidity and clouds of stinging sand flies and mosquitoes can make life hellish.

It was early morning as we entered the harbor at Oak Ridge. The passage through the reef was narrow but the harbor itself was large and protected. Word of our impending arrival had gone ahead of us and Captain Joe Gough was on the dock as we moored. He and his brothers operated a local shipyard and were engaged in coconut and other island trade. In addition to building island schooners, they operated a fleet of their own. I spent the day touring Captain Joe's shipyard while he told me about business activity in the area.

My last day on Roatán was reserved for exploring, and I headed for Captain Morgan's hideaway. The pirate chose the location for his stronghold with great skill. The harbor is about three miles long and a mile wide. There are three entrances through the reef from the open sea. Within the harbor lies St. George's Key (now known as Fort Morgan Cay), which Morgan chose as the site for his citadel. His fortifications were built to command with his cannons defending each of the three entrances to the harbor. The key would have been difficult to storm. Except for a shallow and narrow channel, it is surrounded by shoal water and shallow reefs that extend several hundred feet from the shore.

The day was rounded out with a cruise along Roatán's south coast to Coxen Hole and French Harbor, each with a beautifully protected harbor and small settlement. Along the way we passed one-man cayucos with ingenious sails. The Caribs had learned that a single coconut palm frond, held at a certain angle, would catch enough wind to save a great deal of paddling. I wondered how long this island paradise would go undiscovered. I hoped I could come back to stay before it was—dreaming is what life is made of.

I returned to La Ceiba to find the town fairly bubbling with rumors that the standoff between Generals Bravo and Guerra was about to come to a head. One rumor had General Bravo ready to call his loyal troops in from the mountains to lay siege to the local garrison, still under the command of General Guerra. Another version had General Guerra ready to arrest the locally popular General Bravo and ship him off to Tegucigalpa. There were several other versions of what was about to happen, and new stories were hitting the street at frequent intervals.

I also learned that during my absence the wise men of the Potomac had decided that Paul Daniels, who had been sent to Honduras as United States ambassador three months earlier, was urgently needed in Washington to head the office of American Republic Affairs and would be arriving in La Ceiba within the week to board the S.S. *Cefalu* and sail north with the weekly load of bananas.

This little piece of intelligence upset me more than the problem of Generals Bravo and Guerra. No one could remember the last time a US ambassador had visited La Ceiba—if ever. We had to give the locals an opportunity to meet him—even if that same function would also serve as an opportunity for those same people to bid him goodbye. Washington couldn't have picked a worse time to put me in such an untenable situation.

In working out the guest list for Ambassador Daniels' reception, I gave some thought to pretending General Bravo and his numerous local supporters just didn't exist. I decided I couldn't do that because despite General Guerra's presence in La Ceiba and the common knowledge that General Bravo was all but under house arrest, he was technically the senior Honduran official in the region, and he also enjoyed local popularity. I bit the bullet and invited everybody. There wasn't anything else I could do. I couldn't consult with Ambassador Daniels, given the sluggish communication between La Ceiba and Tegucigalpa.

The ambassador arrived in La Ceiba late on the afternoon before the S.S. *Cefalu* was scheduled to sail. He knew I was having a reception in his honor that evening, and he knew about the problem of Generals Bravo and Guerra. He looked a little startled when I told him I had invited both generals and their entourages but shrugged it off mumbling that it was a helluva late date to be getting his feet wet on this one.

Fully an hour before the reception was scheduled, I saw General Bravo's supporters arrive one by one at his house across the street. Their white linen jackets did not conceal the bulges of side arms underneath. As I made my final check to see that all was ready, they marched forth from General Bravo's house en masse, crossed the street, and filed into the consulate's reception area. They looked grim as they shook hands with the ambassador and then found places to sit or stand in a group at one end of the room, clustered around General Bravo.

General Guerra arrived precisely at the indicated hour, accompanied by a sizeable contingent of his own officers, all in uniform and all looking somewhat deformed because of the bulges created by side arms underneath their dress jackets. They, too, looked grim as they were introduced to Ambassador Daniels and then gathered at the opposite end of the room from General Bravo and his men. The rest of the guests straggled in one or two at a time. Hardly a man failed to blanch and mop perspiration from his brow as he crossed the consulate's threshold and sized up the two groups at either end of the reception room.

Soon the waiters began to circulate, and after a round or two of drinks, things had loosened up. By then it was clear neither side intended to start trouble—both were merely prepared in case the other side did. Ambassador Daniels circulated, and when he came to General Guerra, he took the General's arm and led him into my office. After a while they emerged, on noticeably cordial terms. Next it was General Bravo's turn. Again, he and the ambassador emerged from my office arm in arm, laughing at some shared joke. A short conference with General Guerra ensued, after which the ambassador accompanied both General Bravo and General Guerra into the privacy of my office. Conversation in the reception area came to an abrupt halt. Undoubtedly, every soul there would have given a farm to hear what was being said beyond the closed door.

Nothing happened for what seemed like an age. The only sound in the room was made by the waiters circulating with drinks and the clink of glasses being drained in a single gulp to be replaced before the waiter moved on. At last, the ambassador emerged, one arm flung over General Bravo's shoulder and the other thrown over General Guerra's. All three smiled as if this were the happiest occasion ever.

I never knew what went on in my office that evening. There were three reasons why I did not. First, Ambassador Daniels boarded the S.S. *Cefalu* that same night and the ship sailed early the next morning. Second, General Bravo was also aboard the S.S. *Cefalu* when it sailed, bound for a vacation in New Orleans. And third, General Guerra returned to Tegucigalpa before I could find a graceful opportunity to query him.

When everything had quieted down and things returned to normal, I decided to have my first try at what we know as "economic reporting" in the Foreign Service. I prepared a dispatch about what I had learned on my trip aboard the *Mary K* entitled, "Trade and Industry in the Bay Islands of Honduras," and sent it to the State Department in Washington.

Months later the bureau of foreign and domestic commerce reacted with a restrained but complimentary evaluation. It was thrilling enough to know that someone in Washington had read my report—that it had been found useful was beyond my fondest hopes. I had taken the first step toward developing a new skill in the Foreign Service.

La Ceiba

La Ceiba wasn't exactly the end of the world, but it was the end of the line. There were three ways to get there from the outside world: take a steamer from New Orleans; catch a C-47 from Tegucigalpa; or ride a mule over the mountains. Mail service was slow and there was no telephone service except within town.

These factors, and one other, combined to make the consulate a rather independent operation. The final consideration was that under normal conditions nobody much cared what went on in La Ceiba. Thus I was not the least bit disappointed when my "two week" detail stretched past two months. With no end to the assignment in sight, I asked Mary—always game for an adventure—to lock up the house in Tegucigalpa and join me in La Ceiba with Laura and Jack.

The old frame building that housed the consulate's combined office and living quarters stood on nine-foot stilts across the corner from the central plaza. La Ceiba's hotel also faced the plaza, as did the post office, the Palacio de Gobierno, and the town's one nightclub. It was a straight shot down the street to the end of the Standard Fruit Company dock, which stuck out into the Caribbean without benefit of harbor or breakwater.

A railroad spur ran from the far end of the dock, down the middle of the street, to the front of the consulate. When a ship finished loading bananas, the purser boarded a locomotive out at the end of the dock and came steaming through town to the consulate, where he would rush inside, collect the signatures and documents he needed before sailing and then steam back through town to board his ship and sail away. It was picturesque. It also served to keep everyone in town up to date about what was going on. The locomotive engineer made sure of that, by frequent loud toots on his whistle as he came and went.

Unlike Puerto Cortés, La Ceiba was a delightful little tropical town. Although hot and humid during the day, there was welcome relief at night. The Cangrejal Mountains (now known as Cordillera Nombre de Dios) rose five thousand feet merely a few miles inland, and a cooling breeze swept down from the heights after dusk to make the nights reasonably comfortable.

Our house was a vintage model of the type common to fruit company towns throughout Central America at the time. It boasted ceiling fans inside and many tropical fruit and shade trees in the garden, ranging from coffee bushes to an enormous and prolific avocado tree. This was something of a mixed blessing. The avocados were delicious, and the bearing season was long. But the fruit fell on the galvanized iron roof day and night with a great whang on impact and an uneven thumping down the steep pitch. We never did get used to it, and when a large avocado fell from a high branch in the dead of night, it was enough to bring a mummy upright in bed.

La Ceiba had other advantages over Puerto Cortés. Black sand flies were relatively scarce, and the Bay Islands far offshore provided protection for the beaches, which were quite tranquil. At Boca Vieja, where we often enjoyed an afternoon swim, tall trees grew to the edge of the beach and extended their shade out over the sand and into the water.

We had no transportation of our own, but when the Naval liaison officer closed shop after World War II, he had left behind a 4x4 Dodge Command Car, number USN-138744, that was parked under the consulate when I arrived, immobilized for lack of spare parts. There were no roads leading into or out of La Ceiba, but I wanted the command car to at least get us back and forth to the beach. With a little tinkering and a lot of improvisation, I had it about ready to start, except for two problems. The fuel pump diaphragm was ruined with age, and there was no muffler. Neither part could be found in La Ceiba. As a last resort, I made a diaphragm out of a piece of leather and decided to let the muffler go.

Grudgingly, USN-138744 backfired into action. The din was startling. Dogs barked, roosters crowed, and donkeys brayed. In time, we got used to the noise, although I'm not sure if the rest of La Ceiba did. Certainly, not the dogs, roosters and donkeys, who never failed to take note of comings and goings.

The run from La Ceiba down the beach to Boca Vieja soon got boring and we began to venture farther and farther. Then we discovered how to cross the rivers that emptied into the Caribbean by either turning inland through the jungle until there was a rocky ford or, alternatively, circling out into the ocean and around on the shallow bar formed where the current and the waves met. The command car was quite at home in water up to three feet deep. We were soon into territory where no motor vehicle had ever been before, and the day came when we worked our way as far as the bamboo and thatched village of Salado. It was quite an event for everyone. Village children had never seen a car before and peeked at us wide-eyed from behind the coconut palms.

La Ceiba offered other attractions. There was an occasional birthday party, but there were no cocktail parties, receptions or black-tie dinners. Socializing was strictly informal, usually incidental to a game of golf on the little course the fruit company maintained on the hospital grounds, or a foursome of bridge in the evening. This idyllic life was nearly perfect, except for one thing: my dealings with the Standard Fruit and Steamship Company management at La Ceiba left much to be desired.

Part of the trouble undoubtedly stemmed from my earlier service at Puerto Cortés, a United Fruit Company town. There, no effort had been spared to make life comfortable. Whatever I needed from the fruit company was mine for the asking, and I often got things I didn't need or didn't ask for if the management thought it might make a hostile environment more bearable for us. Ships carrying bananas need to sail when loaded and this often meant taking care of their paperwork in the wee hours of the morning, or on weekends, or both. I didn't mind, and the company people were careful to limit the inconvenience by keeping me fully informed of loading and estimated sailing times. It was a different story at La Ceiba.

The division manager at the Standard Fruit and Steamship Company in La Ceiba was of the old school, having come up through the ranks and proved himself by fighting jungle and disease out on the plantations. He had learned the hard way and he believed in the direct approach to things. When he sliced a tee shot on the golf course, he had been known to wrap his driver around the trunk of the nearest coconut palm. When things went wrong at bridge, he relieved his tensions by tearing a full deck of cards in half. He was one tough hombre.

The people who worked for him were afraid of him, and nothing happened in his jurisdiction without his approval. My only problem with all that was the way it affected my duties, a major one being meeting the company's needs for consular services. And here I seemed to be frustrated at every turn, but mostly where shipping was concerned.

I was familiar with the complexities and problems involved in shipping bananas. The tens of thousands of stems required to fill a ship were usually harvested from different areas of the division, served by different spurs of the railroad. Carloads of bananas had to come in from these farms to make up the train that would bring them to shipside for loading. Several trainloads were involved. It was a complex process and required lots of planning and coordination.

I always marveled that all the pieces fell into place so that loading was completed at the precise time to get the ship to port in the United States when the bananas were exactly ready for marketing. But it was old hat for the people who did it, and always seemed to come off without a hitch. And when the ship was loaded and ready to sail, it was time for me to do my part.

At Puerto Cortés, I was always kept abreast of the harvesting and the train schedules and the loading as each step in the process evolved. I knew within an hour or so when the ship would be loaded and when to expect the ship's purser to arrive at the consulate with his papers, so they could be processed, and the ship could sail. I was ready and waiting for him, at any hour on any day. Taking care of the fruit company's business was an important part of my duties, and I was eager to do it the best I could.

At La Ceiba I always knew when a fruit company ship docked; there was no way to miss such a major event in the town's life. But from there on, I found it impossible to get any information on plans for the ship's loading or its departure. Company officials didn't refuse to give me the information I asked for, but they consistently and uniformly put me off when I tried to get it. Consequently, I found myself hovering around the consulate 24 hours a day for several days at a time when a banana boat was in port.

My advance notice was limited to how far away I could hear the steam engine chuffing and tooting up the single track toward the consulate's door with the ship's purser aboard. This was often on a weekend and usually in the dead of night, and it was very frustrating.

I brooded over my problem. If it had been one or two of the lower level people who wouldn't cooperate, I could have found a way around them. But I was stonewalled everywhere I turned, and this was clearly a consequence of instructions from the top. I couldn't escape the conclusion that the division manager thought of me as just another underling who would do what he was told and shut up, or else. It could have been company policy from New Orleans, and that thought bothered me even more.

Although I would not have admitted it then, there is no doubt my dignity was injured. I thought I was a rather important person who deserved better treatment. Otherwise I couldn't have taken the pride I did in being the representative of the government of the United States of America in La Ceiba, Honduras. Eventually the time came when I decided enough was enough.

The ship I had been waiting for made port on a Thursday. It was the company's newest boat and it brought a cruise party, guests of the D'Antoni family who then owned the Standard Fruit and Steamship Company and one of whose members was aboard as host. I called the company's shipping agent, noted that a banana boat had docked and inquired if he could tell me when it was expected to sail. He could not, and he didn't know when he might be able to give me an estimated time of departure. When the purser called to deposit the ship's registry documents, I asked him the same question and got the same answer. I knew from experience I couldn't expect more, but for my purposes I had to go through the motions.

On Friday, I again called the shipping agent and asked the same question. I got the same answer. During our conversation I mentioned that he, of course, knew the consulate was closed from Friday afternoon until Monday morning but assured him I would be available on any day and at any hour, *provided* (and I stressed the provided part) I had some idea when my services might be needed. Yes, he knew that. End of conversation.

On Friday afternoon, I walked down to the dock where loading was in progress and located the purser. I went through the same routine with him, with the same results. Now I was ready.

There wasn't much room in the command car for passengers after the camping gear, ice chest and grub box were loaded on Saturday morning, but we managed to squeeze in. It was a lovely morning for our drive down the beach toward Salado. We stopped for a swim and lunch at the mouth of the Cangrejal River before working our way on down the coast to a spot where a beautiful grove of trees towered over a white sandy beach. Here we pitched camp, and here we stayed until late Sunday afternoon. It was dark before we thundered our muffler-less way back into town and pulled into the consulate's driveway. As was customary, dogs barked, roosters crowed, and donkeys brayed. The quiet was startling when I switched off the engine and the din subsided. All La Ceiba knew we were back home.

The consulate's messenger/janitor was waiting. Yes, the company's shipping agent and the ship's purser had been by on numerous occasions but not for the last several hours. The great, white ship loaded with Honduras' green gold was still tied up at the dock. He was uneasy about it all. I was too, but I had done it and was determined to stick to my guns.

The purser was grim as I returned the ship's registry papers, certified his consular invoice and visaed his Crew List. When he had all his papers, he said, "You know, we have been loaded and waiting for 24 hours. I am to tell you that you have just lost your job." I was ready and shot back, "You can tell them that if they can get it, I wouldn't want it anyway."

Things were rather tense around La Ceiba that week. The whole town knew what had happened, although not exactly why. I had no idea who I would hear from first, or what I might hear. The fruit company people in town steered clear of me and of the consulate. It was not until Friday afternoon that I knew I had won. First the company's shipping agent called to tell me there would be a banana boat in port the following Monday and she was expected to sail by Wednesday; he would keep me posted. Next, we had an invitation to dinner and bridge with the general manager, which I accepted with pleasure. It was a delightful evening. Neither he nor I mentioned the weekend incident, and I never knew how far the threat to get my job had been carried. All I knew was that my dealings with the Standard Fruit and Steamship Company had become cordial and productive. Life in La Ceiba was perfect.

And then we were called back to Tegucigalpa.

Invitation to Dinner

The small-town atmosphere of Honduras provided a hospitable environment for Mary and me to begin to learn about the Foreign Service. One of the advantages was that because there were so few of us assigned there, we were included in everything, despite our junior status. I had the pleasure, and the honor, of a day with General Jimmy Doolittle. Mary danced one night through with actors Cesar Romero and Tyrone Power.

Together, we won the Country Club scotch foursome golf tournament one year and we were always near the top in the ongoing contract bridge competitions. Professionally, it had been good for me, too. I came to Honduras at Class FSS-12 and left at Class FSS-9, thanks to one regular and one double promotion during the two-year tour. All of this was nice, but two years was by far the longest either of us had ever been away from home, and we were homesick long before we were eligible for home leave.

We still had no intention of making a lifetime career out of the Foreign Service and discussed at length whether we should take home leave and one more assignment or resign and go home for good. After mulling over the proposition at breakfast, lunch and dinner for months, we decided to try to have the best of both worlds. We would ask for a transfer to Mexico where we would be much closer to our parents and our home. If it came through, we would have our leave and go on to our next post. If not, we would call it quits, with no regrets.

I phrased my transfer request with much care in the hope that the person in Washington who decided those things would conclude I was precisely the vice consul the DOS needed at Mérida, or Mazatlán or Guaymas, or some other small post on the ocean in Mexico. I was careful not to close the door on any post, except Mexico City. I asked not to be assigned there and gave what I thought were good reasons for my request. Overall, I thought it was a persuasive presentation. The response came with the department's usual due haste—in some months, that is—and I was informed that I would be transferred to Mexico City. We decided to take it.

No sooner did word of our impending transfer get around than friends began to plan despedida parties for us. We were soon booked up solid, except for the last night before our departure. I steadfastly refused to give up that night, knowing we would desperately need the time to do the many last-minute things that would have accumulated by then. And we needed every minute we could get. There were no packers or moving companies in Honduras—we had to pack our own things, or they wouldn't get packed.

As time grew short, it became a real race against a hard deadline. I had my regular work at the office, the nightly program of despedidas and the packing and crating, too. How thankful I was to at least count on one free night before we caught the plane north. Otherwise I wouldn't be able to pack my own clothes.

With less than a week to go, the pace was frantic. I found myself crating furniture after we got home from parties in the evening. More and more things turned up at work that I wanted to finish before I left.

The morning had already been hectic when the ambassador's secretary called and said I should come down to his office right away. We had a new ambassador, Herb Bursley, who was newly arrived. I didn't know him very well and was a little gun-shy around him. I hoped he didn't have a project for me; I didn't have time for anything else. It was a relief to find that all he wanted was to invite Mary and me to have dinner with him and his wife. I thanked him profusely, explained that we had commitments for every evening except our last night at the post, and pointed out that this had to be left open for those last-minute things that always had to be taken care of on a move such as this.

Ambassador Bursley gave me an odd look and let it be known that I was dismissed. I wondered if he knew about my transfer, but I was too busy to give it much thought. That evening, as we were getting ready to leave the house for our nightly despedida, the ambassador's chauffeur delivered a small envelope containing a card confirming our invitation to dinner with the ambassador and his wife in honor of the foreign minister and his wife, for the evening prior to our departure. I had been taught one more lesson in the Foreign Service. Some people must learn the hard way, but I didn't much like being one of them.

Somehow, I managed to stay awake during the ambassador's dinner party. After coffee, he made a nice little speech about how valuable I had been to the embassy. The foreign minister, who was my neighbor and friend, made a nice little speech, too. All I could think of was how much I had left to do and how little time I had to do it. I started work on the last of the packing as soon as we got home. By seven in the morning I was finished. By eight I was back at my desk in the embassy doing the final chores there. By eleven I was ready to drive to the airport. The plane took off at noon. Somehow, we were on it.

I was too exhausted to enjoy the flight home. We overnighted at both Guatemala and Mexico City. There was no plane service to Laredo in those days, so the last leg of our trip was from Mexico City to Monterrey and then to Nuevo Laredo where we would drive across the Rio Grande to our home. By the time we boarded in Mexico City I had rested enough to generate some enthusiasm, and we were an excited family as the plane took off from our stop at Monterrey.

The familiar brush country of northern Mexico spread below in the bright, summer sunshine. I tried to recognize landmarks but there was little to distinguish one panorama from another. I was intrigued by a creek in the distance that was overflowing with muddy water. Probably a flash flood upstream—they did happen in that country. We began our descent to Nuevo Laredo and the creek grew wider.

Suddenly I realized I was looking at the Rio Grande in full flood. I was concerned, but not alarmed. After all, the international bridge at Laredo stood over 60 feet above the riverbed and had withstood flooding before. The Nuevo Laredo airport came in sight, and the pilot circled to come in against the wind. It was then I saw the long line of cars on the highway stretching miles back from the river toward Monterrey—and the international bridge under water.

Our dismay was acute, profound and complete. We had looked forward to this day of reunion with our families for so long. We had a son over a year old who had never been seen by his grandparents. How long would it take for the waters to recede? Where would we stay meanwhile?

We were dejected as we waited for our baggage, wondering what to do next. Then, beyond the barrier separating us from the waiting room, a familiar face stood out in the crowd: a shock of white hair, a hand-rolled cigarette under a bristling mustache, dancing brown eyes and a crinkly grin: Mary's father!

I should have known he would anticipate our dilemma. I should have remembered there were small planes that could ferry us home. I should have had faith and confidence everything would work out. I was ashamed that I had not, but I never let anyone know we had expected anything less than to be met and flown over the flooded Rio Grande as if it were an everyday occurrence.

Mexico
1949

Mexico City Visa Mill

In the late 1940s when I reported for duty there, the United States embassy at Mexico City employed over seven hundred souls. Most of these labored at the chancery on Avenida Insurgentes or at the annex on Avenida La Reforma. The ambassador dealt with the Mexican foreign minister and sometimes the country's president; the economic counselor maintained liaison with local bankers and the captains of Mexican industry; the political counselor was involved with the chiefs of both the Partido Revolucionario Institucional and the Confederación de Trabajadores Mexicanos; the cultural counselor spent his time with the nation's artists, poets, university professors and sometimes the princes of the Church; the consul general was the lead man in the embassy's dealings with the large US colony; and so on. But sooner or later, every one of the Mexicans, their families, or closest friends had to come to the visa section for documentation to travel to the US.

The visa section entertained hundreds and hundreds of Mexican callers daily. Long lines of applicants formed on the sidewalk before the opening of business, and there were still lines when the offices closed for the day. The visa section dealt with more Mexicans every day than the rest of the embassy put together and multiplied by ten. They came from all walks of life asking for something they urgently wanted, or in many instances vitally needed—documentation allowing them into the United States to spend their money or get medical treatment or visit their relatives. It would seem like a natural place for the United States to make friends, the ideal situation to demonstrate what we were and what we stood for. And maybe it was, and maybe we did. Then again, maybe we did not.

The visa section did not have its offices in the chancery or the annex. It was housed apart, in a run-down converted residence on Calle Londres. No career Foreign Service officers worked in the visa section. The officers were all commissioned clerks, or vice consuls not-of-career as they were then known. Visa work was considered a nuisance by those who did not have to do it and, unfortunately, by some of the twenty-odd employees who did. What the powers that be most wanted from the visa section was not to be bothered by it, and this lack of concern was clearly why responsibility for supervision of this work was entrusted to a vice consul who was not yet 30. I took charge of the visa section shortly after my 29th birthday.

Youth, so often, is innocence. But sometimes this is for the best. I took on the visa section impressed with its importance and determined to make it the most efficient and effective operation in the embassy—if not in the entire Foreign Service. The first order of business was to take better care of the public. To do this, we had to find some way of getting more of them through our machinery each day. We didn't establish quotas, but we started keeping records of individual production and posted them regularly. This helped. We developed flow charts, and found ways to streamline the mechanics of the operation. This also helped. Gradually we cut corners by changing the time-honored way of doing things and were able to increase our production.

Eventually, the section's output increased by over 50 percent, but long lines continued to form each morning before opening and lasted throughout the day. We struggled mightily, and we handled more and more people month after month, but we never got ahead of the game. It became obvious that there were enough people in Mexico who wanted to go to the United States to keep us busy issuing visas day and night, 7 days a week and still not catch up.

Despite the heavy caseload and endless repetition, we had a high number of willing workers on the staff, and though we often had to stay after hours to clean up after a long day, there were always volunteers for the job. Alice Mahoney was our most able visa officer, but Roberta Meyerkort knew her business well and carried her weight day in and day out.

Joaquin Godoy and Bob Prieto, our star clerical employees, could always be counted on to hang in there as long as it took—as often as it took. Both had been born in Mexico to US citizen mothers, both had seen active combat duty as US Marines in World War II, and both were bright. Between them, they did the work of any other four people on the staff. One day, Bob came into my office and closed the door behind him.

"Boss, there's something fishy going on out there. Come have a look." At the window, he pointed out two men working their way back along the line of applicants on the sidewalk. We could see that some sort of transaction was going on between them and one or another of the people waiting for visas. We picked a man who appeared to have done business with the pair and waited for him to work his way inside. When his turn came to be interviewed, Bob brought him into my office, and we started to probe.

Like many of our applicants, he only wanted to go to the United States to sightsee and shop. So did millions of other Mexicans, but most couldn't afford it and all too often applicants who said they wanted to go up for a visit really wanted to look for a job. This was understandable, but against the law. The test here was to find out whether an applicant was financially able to make the trip for fun and shopping. Thus, money had to be a criterion.

When we came to this part of the interview, our applicant confidently pulled out of his pocket a roll of US bills big enough to choke a goat. He didn't look like a typical tourist—but then who does? I approved his visa and we kept a close watch on the sidewalk for him to come out. The same two men who had spoken to him before were waiting for him now. Our customer produced the roll of US bills and handed it over to them. He then took out his wallet and counted out additional bills. We wondered what the interest rate might have been for his short-term loan. If he was legitimate, we had helped victimize him. If he wasn't legitimate, we'd been had—but there was no law against it and not a damned thing we could do!

A couple of months after this incident, Joaquin Godoy came into my office late one afternoon scratching his head. Could I help him with a nice old man from Tehuantepec who insisted he needed talk to the Jefe? I said, "Sure, bring him in." His customer had an enormous handlebar mustache and was dressed in his Sunday best. He could have stepped out of a Pancho Villa movie set. His suit was once blue serge but had long since aged to shiny green. The string tie at his collar was threadbare from many knottings. His coarse cotton shirt had certainly never seen a Manhattan label, and I judged was probably homemade. He held a sweat-stained sombrero in his gnarled hands. New huaraches could not hide enormous, splayed feet that had clearly never known shoes. He was a typical, work-worn peasant dressed up to go to town, and I guessed that he had never been so far away from home.

Campesino he may have been, but it was obvious he was a proud and dignified man. His black eyes held steady as I tried to evaluate him and wondered why he wanted to go to the United States. He opened the conversation by apologizing for taking my time. He understood that I had many responsibilities and was very busy. But his business was important, and he had come a long way. There was a certain danger, too. He did not trust bankers. He much appreciated my giving him of my valuable time. Then, in the fashion of country people in Mexico, he went over the entire preamble again to make sure neither he nor I had missed any of the details. Eventually, it came out. He wanted to go to the United States to buy four or five new trucks.

Trucks cost six to eight thousand dollars then, and I was sure there was no way he could afford one. But I didn't want to offend him, so I skirted around hoping for an opening to give him a gentle letdown. How did he happen to be in the trucking business? It was a long story, he explained. His father and grandfather had been *carreteros*, ox-cart drivers. He, too, had been a carretero for many years, but by working hard and saving his money he had been able to buy a small truck. His business had steadily prospered and when his first son was old enough to drive a truck, he had bought another. Now he had four grown sons and each of them drove a truck. In addition, his first son's first son would soon be old enough to drive a truck. There were other grandsons coming up. His trucks were old, and now that the war was over he wanted to buy replacements in the US.

Our customer knew a lot more about trucks than I had guessed. But having come this far, I plunged on. Did he know how much a new truck cost this day and time? Oh, yes, he said, a good one for his business cost about $7,000.00 in the States and then he would have to get it back to Tehuantepec. Now my opening had come. You know, I asked him, that under our regulations you will have to show you have the money before we can give you a visa? Oh, yes, he understood, and he had the money with him. Could he call his woman in from the waiting room?

Tehuana women are often quite tall, and this one was no exception. She wore the traditional, regional dress of many petticoats, ruffled skirt and an ornate, loose blouse. Her hair fell to her waist in long, black braids.

Her angular face was expressionless, but her dark eyes were alert. Although her hands showed evidence of much heavy work, they were slender, and the fingers were long. Somehow, those graceful hands and thin, composed face seemed out of place—her body was bulky and overweight.

"El dinero," the man said to her. "Enséñale el dinero," (Show him the money). Without hesitation, the woman lifted her blouse to expose a slip beneath, decorated with colorful ribbons. One by one she untied these and from pockets inside the slip began to pile neatly tied bundles of large bills on my desk. Next came the petticoat beneath the full, ruffled skirt. There were more ribbons and more pockets. The pile on my desk grew with each new bundle of bills, while the woman became slender and agile. For the first time, she smiled.

By the time she finished, there were over 30 bundles of bills, each neatly bound with homemade henequen cord. We did not count it all, but a random check proved that our applicant would be able to finance his trip and purchases. They got their visas.

Protection Duty

Ten thousand US expats were permanent residents in Mexico City; and at any given time, there were another ten thousand US visitors in town. The residents knew how to stay out of trouble for the most part, or at least how to get out of any trouble they might get into. But, oh my, the tourists! There seemed no end of trouble they could get into, all too often of their own making, although not always.

Rightfully, they turned to the embassy to help them out, and the way they told it they were never at fault. One old-timer put it in pretty good perspective when he said, "It's true the authorities can occasionally be abusive, but I have yet to run across a protection case where anyone was put in jail for praying in church."

There was at the embassy an officer who had a law degree from the National University at Mexico City. For many years, he had been assigned fulltime to helping expats in trouble, and he could be quite effective. But there were expats in trouble 24 hours a day, seven days a week—far too many for any one man to handle. As a result, several officers with other regular duties spelled him on a rotation basis after hours and on weekends. For over three years I was one of these, and my turn to take night and weekend protection duty came around every third or fourth week.

I looked forward to protection duty with mixed feelings. The work week was always busy; there was no time left for personal activities, and staying up half the night in a traffic court or a hospital emergency room after 10-12 hours in the visa mill was not a pleasant prospect. Still the work involved people and people's problems and seemed important to me because those in trouble truly needed our help. It was the one place we could perform a useful service for the taxpayer. Of course, it was not always possible to be of much help. But I could at least offer assurances things would look brighter in the morning when a way could be found to set things straight. Meanwhile, I could usually arrange for detention outside a common criminal's cell and that counted for a lot in the wee hours of the morning when a hangover was beginning to take hold, and remorse was setting in.

Another thing that attracted me to protection duty was the opportunity for ingenuity. There was no limit to the range of situations US citizens ended up in, some truly bizarre.

This Saturday had been about par for the course. There were the usual number of yanquis arrested for drunken and disorderly conduct. Disagreement had to be mediated between a visiting deacon and a lady of the night who had failed to negotiate a fixed price beforehand. I agreed her fee seemed outrageous, but what are you going to do, when you're a deacon? There were a few traffic violations thrown in for good measure but, thankfully, no serious accidents.

I was back home and in bed before daylight Sunday morning, but soon called out again when a demure Midwestern couple were caught sneaking out of their hotel room without first having settled their bill. They hadn't been satisfied with the service, the food was terrible, and they didn't see why they should pay for being treated so badly. Some US expats are something else! At least I got back home in time for a late Sunday lunch and it stayed quiet long enough for a nap afterwards.

Things were looking up by late afternoon when a call came in from the guard on duty at the embassy. He reported a telephone message from a caller who would not identify himself but who wanted to report that several US girls traveling together had run over a Mexican out near the pyramids and had been hauled off by the local authorities. He gave no other details.

My first reaction was that they must have worked out their problem on their own or they would have called the embassy themselves. But I knew I was tired and that was wishful thinking. The little village of Teotihuacán was quite primitive, and it was in such places that US expats in trouble were likely to be given the hardest time. If I didn't check it out myself, my conscience would never give me a minute's peace. Mary agreed to go with me, and we pulled up in front of the old colonial building that housed Teotihuacán's municipal offices as darkness fell.

The windows were shuttered, and the doors closed. No one was to be seen anywhere around the building. There was a sedan with US plates parked outside and I wondered if it belonged to the people I had come looking for. There appeared to be no damage except that both windows on the driver's side were shattered.

Music and laughter filtered through the dust hanging in the light of an open doorway down the street. It had to be the local cantina and I walked toward it knowing that whatever action there had been around town on that day, or any other day, would be the subject of conversation there tonight. But conversation stopped when I entered. I was conscious of how out of place I must look in a jacket and tie. Some of the patrons wore shoes, but there were many wearing huaraches, and more than a few bare feet. No jackets and no ties were in evidence, although there were a couple of short riding jumpers. Ponchos and serapes woven from native wool shielded the rest from the chill of the evening.

I asked if someone might tell me where I could find the Jefe Politico or the Jefe de Policía.

"No está," came the reply.

I wanted to ask if anyone knew anything about the girls but felt so uneasy and out of place that I inquired instead where I might find the local jail. The directions weren't very precise, but the village wasn't very big, either. We found it quite easily.

I suppose there aren't many attractive jails anywhere in the world. Certainly, I never ran across any. And I don't want to criticize Mexico for its jails, but it is true they left much to be desired. Teotihuacán's jail must have been among the worst. It was a one room building located behind the Palacio Municipal and seemed to have been dug or built into a hillside. There were no windows; light and ventilation came through the one door. It was unguarded.

Four girls were pressed against the iron bars of the door, and it did my heart good to see their reaction when I identified myself. They seemed even happier to see Mary. They had been in the cell for several hours. There was no light and judging from the stench, the sanitary facilities were primitive, if they existed at all. They told us their story about what happened.

The girls were classmates in college and their trip to Mexico was a graduation present from their parents. They had been treated well everywhere they went and theirs had been a wonderful vacation until that afternoon. When they started back to Mexico City after a day exploring the pyramids, a man walking along the edge of the narrow pavement had unexpectedly lurched onto the road as their car drew abreast. The right front fender had sent him sprawling.

They immediately stopped and rendered first aid. The man was covered with sores, but except for scratches and bruises had not been injured. They were sure the car had not run over him and there were no broken bones. A crowd had gathered. They became nervous and got back in their car and rolled up the windows.

A man wearing a pistol but dressed in civilian clothing appeared, took one look at the injured man, and became furious. The girls tried to explain they were fully insured but he didn't understand or didn't care. They locked the doors. The man beat at the windows with his pistol. They panicked and attempted to drive away. Fortunately, they stopped when they realized the man was about to shoot. He got in, directed them to where the car was now parked, marched them to the cell, and locked them in. He hadn't been around since. I told them he must be the local law, the man I would have to find if I were to get them out.

There was a chorus of dismay at the thought I would leave them. They had been terrified for hours. They spoke no Spanish. One started sobbing. It was too much for Mary. She volunteered to wait with them while I looked for the Jefe. I wasn't too happy with the plan, but the girls were delighted and there didn't seem to be any way around it.

I left my car in front of the jail and headed off on foot to look for the chief of police. The cantina seemed to be the place to start but I disliked the idea of going there again. As I hesitated at the door, an old man sitting in the shadow on the porch said, "Buenas noches, Señor." It was only "Good evening," but I knew it was an invitation to talk, and I grabbed at the straw.

"Buenas noches," I replied, and asked if he knew where I could find the Jefe de Policía.

"No," he told me, "the Jefe has been here, and he knows you are looking for him, as does everyone else in Teotihuacán, but he doesn't want to see you. He is mad because his brother has been injured. His brother is a lazy and syphilitic drunkard. The Jefe has never cared much for him before, but now. . ."

The implication was clear. The shakedown was on and the girls were being softened up. The same method was used in some rural towns back home. I thanked the man, wondering what to do next.

The prospects for getting anything done in Teotihuacán at that hour on a Sunday evening seemed remote. I was tired and discouraged. I would not be able to find the chief of police if he didn't want to be found. In a small town such as this, I couldn't expect much help from any other municipal authority, had I been able to locate one.

But I couldn't leave the girls where they were. Suppose the Jefe decided to throw a drunk or two into the tank with them to hasten the softening up process? No, I had to think of something. There had to be a solution. My subconscious had something but I couldn't quite grasp it.

Suddenly I realized what it was. In the distance the final note of a bugle call faded into the dark. There had to be a military garrison nearby! And I had long since learned that the ultimate authority in rural Mexico was the Comandante de la Guarnición.

The comandante was a major somewhere around 40. The neatly pressed khakis fit his erect frame perfectly. The ring told me he was an Academy graduate. I knew my luck had turned, although he had not changed expression after a brief smile when I introduced myself. When I had finished my story, and asked if he could, his response was a quick, "But of course, Señor Vice Cónsul, how could I not?"

In quick succession, a lieutenant was dispatched to find the chief of police and bring him to the jail; an orderly was sent to the major's quarters to inform his wife there would be guests for dinner—and we were off for the jail.

I had hardly finished introducing the major to Mary and the girls when the lieutenant arrived with the chief of police. He was one tough-looking customer and I felt some relief that I hadn't been able to find him on my own. There were no formalities in the major's orders to the chief: "I assume responsibility for these prisoners. Unlock the door."

The chief said nothing, and did exactly as he was told, but I didn't like the gleam in his eye as he cast a sidelong glance my way. I hoped I would never have the misfortune to run across him again.

The major's quarters were brightly lit, and his wife was most gracious as he introduced us. She might have been expecting us all week. She invited the girls to wash up while the servant brought refreshments. The major explained he could not go so far as to let the girls leave his jurisdiction, but he would be honored to make them comfortable pending resolution of the charges against them. He thought he might be able to be of some help to this end, as well. He asked if I could arrange for the insurance adjuster to be there by 10:00 in the morning? I sure could!

"Very well," he smiled, "then it is all arranged, and we shall have a pleasant evening together."

He was as good as his word.

Detail to Washington

After I had overseen the Mexico City visa section for about a year, we were visited by George Stewart and Ed Harding out of Sam Boykin's Office of Consular Affairs in Washington. They were interested in improving consular operations in general, and specifically visa operations, so they paid special attention to what was going on in my shop. I was glad they had come; I had several suggestions about what the people in Washington could do to improve things. Ed and George said it hadn't been exactly their charter to find out what was wrong in Washington—they were supposed to find out what was wrong in Mexico. Didn't I have some suggestions about what could be done there?

I did—I had several, in fact, starting with the lack of funds to physically rearrange the visa section. I showed them how, with an expenditure of a few thousand dollars to save steps, and speed up the flow of work, we could save tens of thousands of dollars each year in personnel costs. They were impressed, and they got me the money. When the work was finished, the statistics backed up my claim of increased efficiency. In fact, the before-and-after flowcharts I drew for them ended up as teaching aids in the Foreign Service Institute's administrative officer's training course.

Ed and George were sufficiently impressed with our operations in Mexico that a few months later, when a small team of experts was gathered in Washington to prepare the first draft of the Foreign Service Visa Handbook, I was one of the three specialists recruited from the field to do the job. My detail to the DOS for this job lasted from January until April of 1950.

It was my first exposure to work in Washington. And it was worth every sacrifice it involved.

I had known the names of the technicians whose knowledge guided visa operations worldwide for years, and now I got to meet them personally. It was a thrill to discuss my trade with the best, to hear from their own lips the what and the why of many points I had pondered over the years. It was also flattering that they were willing to give me their time when I came to them for guidance or background on some point. It was more flattering when one of them asked my interpretation of an obscure section of the immigration law or some long-unused rule or regulation.

I thoroughly enjoyed the work I had been brought to Washington to do, but much less so my life outside the department, in the dead of winter. I had never been alone before in a big city. It did not suit my temperament. I looked for diversions—movies, dinner at various restaurants, long walks in the snow. Nothing worked. I was ravaged by loneliness. Time hung heavily on my hands.

In addition, when I left Mexico City for Washington, Mary was already well advanced with her third pregnancy. My concern about being away when she might need me didn't help. I longed mightily to be back home.

It was a great relief when my work was finished, and I could be on my way. How much I anticipated seeing Mary and the children again. There would be time to catch up with friends, too. We would have to invite all of them over to celebrate my homecoming.

As so often seems to happen, the day selected for my party was one of those days when everything seemed to go wrong at the office. I had hoped to get home early to help with the last-minute details, but as the afternoon wore on, I could see I would be lucky if I got home before the guests arrived. When I finally thought I had everything finished and could lock up, the messenger from the embassy of an unfriendly power showed up with diplomatic passports to be visaed. He was a dour KGB-type and I knew he would give me an argument if I tried to put him off. There was nothing to be done but take care of him.

Now, there are people in the governments of most world powers who entertain a burning curiosity about the passports of people in other world powers—where they have been, where they are going. The government of the United States of America has its share of these. I maintained, in my big, double-door safe, a box containing a strong light and a good camera, mounted so that on short notice I could take excellent pictures of passports or other documents of interest that happened to cross my desk. I'm sure that wouldn't come as a surprise to anyone sophisticated in these things, but we chose not to advertise.

After hurrying through the last-minute passports, I rushed back out to the waiting room and handed them to the messenger who had brought them. "All done," I told him.

He looked down at the passports in his hand and then back up at me, shaking his head, and said, in heavily accented English, "Too much hot. Overexposed." Then he grinned.

I put everything back in my safe and swung the double doors together, throwing the bolts into place. A hurried look around to be sure nothing had been overlooked in my rush, and I was off for the big party I had looked forward to on my way home. I managed to get a thin smile out of old Roberts, the civilian guard, as I signed out of the building—no mean feat.

The party was outstanding. In fact, I was wondering if the last dozen hangers-on were going to go home at all, when Mary took me aside and whispered it was time to head for the hospital. When I announced that the Crocketts were sorry, but we had to say goodnight and be off to receive our third child, the stragglers piled into cars and came right along with us. We made a rather impressive cortege as we drove together toward the hospital.

The maternity section of the old American-British-Cowdray Hospital was a delightful place. Doors to the private rooms opened onto a hallway that led to the delivery room, but French doors on the opposite side of the rooms opened onto a screened veranda with comfortable chairs and couches where those in attendance could take our ease while waiting for the guest of honor, as it were, to appear.

I was considerably relieved to have Mary there in good time. When our first child was born while we were at Nuevo Laredo, Mary got a little excited and we ended up walking the halls of Mercy Hospital for thirty-six hours before Laura decided the time had come to make her debut. When our second child was born at Tegucigalpa, Mary was determined not to make the same mistake again and ended up waiting so long to start for Hospital Viera that the head nurse delivered Jack before we could get Mary into her room, much less arouse Doctor Nutter from his midday nap. Things looked much more promising this time around.

Waiting, in any context, is tedious. But waiting under this context, after a night of partying was unbearable. Soon, someone went out for more refreshments. Someone else went out for the next round. By the time Mary was wheeled off to the delivery room, a renewed warm and rosy glow had settled over us all. Mary was back in what seemed like no time to report that Judy was doing fine and so would she, as soon as someone handed her a scotch and soda.

It was hours before the hospital administration suggested that the celebration had gone on long enough and a little rest for all might be in order. I guess they had a point—the first rays of daylight had come without our notice. The group dispersed with everyone agreeing it was one of the nicest birthday parties, ever.

I was too excited to go to bed, much less to sleep. I drove down to the office, thinking to get a leg up on my work so I could take off in good conscience later to check back at the hospital. There was no sign of old Roberts as I let myself in. Probably making his rounds, I thought. But when I got up to my office, I was horrified to find Roberts there, slumped on the floor, his back against the doors to my safe, his head lolling to one side at a crazy angle. His revolver had slipped from his fingers and lay on the floor beside his open hand.

On closer examination, I could see he was breathing. There was no sign of a wound, and no evidence of a struggle. Maybe a heart attack? At this point Roberts started to snore—a loud, hearty snore. Any man who could snore like that couldn't have been seriously hurt. I shook his shoulder and he came to right away, grabbing at his holster for his revolver.

"It's on the floor beside you, Roberts," I said.

He scooped it up, glared at me, and fairly shouted, "Don't come near the safe. Don't touch the safe. Go call the security officer."

I thought it best to do what Roberts said. He was too agitated for me to try to reason with him, and I was more than happy to have someone else take on the job. I went downstairs to the phone on Roberts' desk, and got John Ford out of bed. He wasn't too cheerful about it but said he would be down as quickly as he could.

Once John was there, the mystery unfolded quickly. When Roberts made his rounds, he found my safe closed, but the combination hadn't been spun, so all anyone had to do was throw the bolts to open it. His instructions in such an eventuality were to touch nothing before the security officer could check things out. However, to call the security officer, Roberts would have had to go down to his desk at the entrance. There was no way he could do that and keep an eye on the safe. He had opted to stand guard at the safe until someone showed up, and when I found him, he had been there some 10 hours.

John went as easy on me as he could, given that there were files in my safe that were classified, not to mention several tens of thousands of dollars' worth of Fee Stamps and a thousand or more in cash. I got a reprimand and a warning in my personnel file, and I sure hated that to happen. It was my first, and I suppose I need not add, my last. But, you lose some and you win some—that day's mail from Washington brought me a copy of a letter from Sam Boykin to Ambassador Walter Thurston, commending my contribution to the Visa Handbook.

It was a real boost to my morale. In fact, I began to wonder if I wasn't one of those bright young men you hear about from time to time.

The Fourth of July

There is a lot of obligatory social activity at any embassy, especially for the senior officers. At large Embassies in major capitals such as Mexico City, mandatory social can be onerous. For instance: A new ambassador must pay individual courtesy calls on each of his foreign colleagues, maybe a hundred in all. Then, each of them must return the ambassador's courtesy call. Next, the ambassador from, let's say, "Paramaya" will express his wish to honor his colleague, the new ambassador of the United States, with a formal dinner. The ambassador of the United States has no alternative but to accept. To decline would be an insult to the Republic of Paramaya.

No matter that the ambassador of Paramaya hopes to enhance his own prestige in the process. And no matter that he has, not so far in the back of his mind, the thought that he, in turn, will be the guest of honor at a return black tie dinner hosted by the ambassador of the United States, which the US ambassador must offer, whether he wants to or not. Failure to do so would be an insult to the Republic of Paramaya. Figure out for yourself what happens when you get on that kind of a merry-go-round a hundred times. There are any number of other occasions when a large reception, a cocktail party, or a black-tie affair is required for the furtherance of international diplomacy.

In Mexico City, Mary and I were occasionally called upon to help senior embassy officers carry out social responsibilities. The ambassador's Fourth of

July reception for senior Mexican government officials and diplomatic corps in 1950 was one such occasion.

This annual affair is traditionally and inescapably the largest reception hosted by a US ambassador. Even when the guest list was held to the barest minimum, it was a struggle to keep the total below a thousand. Because there was no way to squeeze so many guests inside the ambassador's old residence on Calle Génova, it was the practice to rent a large tent to accommodate the overflow in the garden.

On any given Fourth of July, the sun could easily be so strong that standing around outside without cover would be unbearable, or it could rain torrents, a likely prospect given that the founders of our Republic chose a date to issue their proclamation that falls at the height of the rainy season in Mexico City. The fact that both host and guests prayed fervently for a dry afternoon seemed to have little effect on the weather. I am reliably informed it rarely does elsewhere, for that matter.

We were proud to be invited to help with this affair. No matter that our job would be to see that the important guests didn't stand around with empty glasses or find themselves in the awkward position of not having someone to talk with. We put on our Sunday best and presented ourselves at the embassy gate well in advance of the appointed hour.

The heavens opened and the rain came down in sheets before we could get from the gate to the front door of the ambassador's residence. It was a bad beginning to what would turn out to be a very gloomy afternoon.

As more and more drenched staff members took refuge in the ambassador's living room and dripped on his rug, we assured each other that at least the crush of guests we had anticipated would fail to materialize. None but those required to attend would venture out in a chubasco such as this. Evidently, everyone on the guest list felt required to attend, as more and more people waded into the living room despite the intensifying storm, all dripping on the ambassador's rug.

It seemed impossible for the storm to get worse, but it steadily did. No one was interested in the tent out in the garden, because the entire lawn was flooded several inches deep, both inside and outside the tent. The house became so congested, the waiters couldn't circulate and the guests who weren't already in the dining room had no chance of sampling the buffet. Those near the bar fared best.

The entire house became a steam bath, smelling heavily of wet wool. The severity of the storm and its poor timing was the topic on everyone's lips. The deluge continued until the last guest had braved the rain to go home. Thereupon, it promptly stopped, as if a spigot had been turned.

Mary and I drove home through flooded streets, greatly relieved to have such an unpleasant afternoon behind us, eager to get out of our wet clothes and into a dry martini. Neither of us had been able to get so much as a glass of water during the reception. It was slow going, and the closer we got to our neighborhood the more severe the flooding. We started to worry about the children long before we had to abandon the car several blocks from home. The water was too deep to drive any farther. We pulled off our shoes and waded the rest of the way. The flooding was knee-deep on Calle Amsterdam as we turned into our gate, but we were relieved to find that the water had not reached the level of our front door.

Our relief was short-lived. Inside, the house was an unbelievable mess, although everyone inside seemed to be fine. Son Jack, a three-year-old toddler, sat happily in a puddle of white plaster, dribbling it through his fingers onto his lap. Newest daughter Judy, less than three months, laughed and cooed in her nana's arms, blissfully unaware that anything was amiss. Older daughter Laura, nearing six, seemed to think it was all her fault and wept copiously.

The servants, native stock all, stood stoically awaiting whatever might come next. They had experienced disaster all their lives. The story came out as we surveyed the damage.

French doors provided access from the upstairs bedrooms to second story balconies, edged with solid masonry parapets. Drainage conduits had been inadequate for the torrential rain, and the overflow had come through the French doors, flooding the second floor, seeping through the ceiling, and cascading down the stairway.

Plaster on inside walls had given way and fallen in great sheets, covering everything on the first floor with a gooey, white paste. The legs of every piece of furniture showed water marks to several inches, from when the flood was at its height.

We spread things to dry for days, polished furniture legs with oil to remove the water stains as best we could and waited for the ceilings and walls to dry enough to allow the plasterers to restore them. At the height of the rainy season, it was a losing battle. We gave up and moved to a newer, more spacious place.

Just Following Orders

I confronted my first serious problem with Washington from the vantage point of the visa section at Mexico City. The dark cloud of McCarthyism hovered over Washington and this was a period of acute security consciousness. A new immigration law had been enacted. I had recently received Instruction No. 323 telling how the new law was to be applied. We were to take appropriate action immediately.

I had studied the law and followed the hearings when it was adopted by Congress. I felt satisfied Congress never intended this new law to be applied in such a callous and unjustified manner. But the rule of the road in bureaucracy is do what you're told by Washington. Still, I could see the new rules had not been thought through and would not stand the test of day-to-day application.

I wished my boss, Consul General Carl Strom, was not out of town. He would be away for weeks and if I went to his stand-in, I knew I would be told to do what the instruction from Washington said and forget about it. Carl, on the other hand, was a think-through kind of man with broad Washington experience and the gumption I needed to have on my side if we were to avert a catastrophe in the operation of my section. I wondered what Ed Maney would have done in my situation.

I was a secret admirer of Edward S. Maney. Ed came from Pearsall, Texas and had served at many of the posts I coveted in Mexico. His sense of humor was well-honed, and his wit was boundless. He was often compared to Will Rogers and looked a bit like him as well. He had the reputation, well earned, of being fast on his feet when it came to working his way out of a tight spot.

Ed had overseen visa work in London after the invasion of Poland and before our entry into World War II. England was crowded with refugees from continental Europe, all of whom wanted to go to the United States. Each day's mail brought bags and bags of letters from friends and relatives in the US inquiring about them. The staff was inadequate for the volume of work suddenly thrust upon it by the outbreak of war.

There were boxes and baskets of unopened letters stacked in every nook and cranny of the visa section when the new ambassador, Joseph Kennedy, made his first tour through Ed's section. It is said the ambassador was horrified when he saw the piles of unopened mail, and his orders were precise and clear-cut. He told Ed he would be back in two weeks and wanted to see the mess cleared up—everything was to be taken care of in a businesslike manner by then.

True to his word, the ambassador was back in a fortnight. He found Ed's offices in perfect order. The piles were gone, desktops were clean, everything was in order. His words of commendation for Ed were profuse.

What had Ed done? He had shoveled the works into the incinerator. He reasoned that at least half of the unopened letters were follow-up inquiries. Probably half the cases had already been taken care of. Where there was interest or reason enough for new follow-up inquiries, they would come along in due course and at least the decks would be cleared to take care of them. Ed had made good use of a clear instruction which, on the face of it, would have been impossible.

Thinking about Ed helped. My instructions were clear enough, but I had focused on the word "immediate" rather than the word "appropriate." Now I saw the light. I immediately tossed the instruction into the pending box and did nothing more about it until Carl Strom got back several weeks later. That seemed entirely appropriate to me.

By the time Carl got back, major newspapers everywhere carried stories about the inequities of the new Immigration Law. Washington was deluged with pleas for relief. And soon the whole damned thing was suspended and replaced by a workable system. It took months for the major overseas visa offices to get back to normal. All of them except Mexico City.

Transfer to Tampico

Three years at Mexico City passed quickly. Despite our reservations about living in a large city and working in a large embassy, we had enjoyed ourselves and learned a great deal about the Foreign Service. We learned about protocol, and despite our dislike for the concept, came to understand why it was necessary. I was fortunate to have an unusually able chief. The work of the visa section involved long hours and frequently, thankless responsibility. There were daily opportunities for me or my staff to make a wrong decision that would create serious problems, but somehow the sailing had been smooth all the way. My climb up the promotion ladder had continued uninterrupted. From Class

FSS-9 when I came to Mexico City, I was promoted each year and had reached Class FSS-6 three years later.

Our personal life in Mexico City was most pleasant. We had a congenial circle of friends. The city was beautiful and there were many places of interest within easy reach. We had access to some of the best restaurants in the world, and to some of the world's best entertainment at a cost we could afford. Both the tennis courts of the French Club and the excitement of the bull ring were within walking distance of our house. We were young enough to take full advantage of it all—and we did. But three years in one place in the Foreign Service is long enough, and one day the urge came to move on, to see and do something else—the fever of Foreign Service wanderlust.

I still coveted a post of my own. It was presumptuous, but I knew I had done a good job in a difficult and tricky situation and decided to have a go at it. To my surprise, instead of the anticipated raised eyebrows, I was given a choice between Tampico and Veracruz—both in Mexico. It should have been an easy choice.

The consulate at Veracruz was beautifully located, overlooking the harbor and the open sea. There were furnished government quarters in the same compound and a small swimming pool in the garden. The city of Veracruz was charming, with many excellent sidewalk cafes and a great deal of local color. At Tampico, on the other hand, the consulate was located downtown in old and crowded quarters. There was no government housing, and houses on the local market were scarce and far from adequate. Nor did Tampico offer the attractive ambience of Veracruz. But there was more to it than that.

The man I would replace in Veracruz was energetic and extroverted. His vivacious wife was of Latin descent and both spoke fluent Spanish. He had been president of the local Rotary Club and a leader in civic affairs. Together, they were much sought after and had been very active socially. The man at Tampico, on the other hand, had more of an intellectual inclination and his previous service had been mainly in the European area. His wife was a charming person of Scandinavian stock but quite reserved. Neither of them spoke adequate Spanish, and they had not enjoyed their assignment at Tampico.

All things being relative, and comparisons as important as they are insidious, it seemed to me that I could at least look a lot better at Tampico than I could at Veracruz. By temperament and background, I would fit into the rough-

and tumble atmosphere of an oil town like Tampico much better than I would in the rather staid and formal life of historic Veracruz.

I asked for Tampico, and I got it.

At last, the despedidas were behind us, our household effects were crated and ready for the moving van, and we had finished packing the things we thought we needed to have close at hand. We must have been a sight as we pulled away from the house on Calle Texas with three small children, a maid and two white rabbits in the back seat, followed by a trailer loaded down with luggage on which was stacked a travel crate with our dog inside. But we were happy and excited and ready for the future. My title of full consul had come through and I was on my way to take over my own post. My ambition in the Foreign Service had been realized. I was 31 years old.

Tampico
1951

The US Consul

It was with a great deal of pride and at least a small measure of awe that I first sat down behind the desk in the principal officer's suite at Tampico, Mexico. The chair seemed rather large, but I knew I would get used to it. The position I would fill for the next several years looked equally big, but I was confident I could handle it. I knew the hardest part would be to get on top of the job before it got on top of me.

In the center of the green blotter on the desk before me was a large manila envelope left by the man whose place I had taken. It was addressed: "To My Successor." On top of the sheaf of papers inside was a blue sheet with the letterhead of the American Council on Education. The text described "The Ideal Consul" as one who:

> Creates good-will and common understanding, and, with restrained and critical leadership born of mature experience and profound knowledge of men and affairs, uses these as instruments for enhancing international confidence and cooperation among governments and people.
>
> Adapts himself, his conduct, and his mode of living appropriately to climate and surroundings in the country to which he is assigned.
>
> Learns to speak the language of the country in a manner that reveals a background of intelligence and cultivation.
>
> Comprehends his own country, and with unremitting endeavor comes to understand deeply the foreign country where he is stationed.
>
> Furthers accurate knowledge and friendly understanding of the United States in foreign countries; and, also, of the foreign countries in the United States.

It sounded like a tall order. Maybe the chair I sat in really was too big for me. Time would tell, but I would at least start out from the right place. I wanted very badly to be the best US consul there was—anywhere. I had yet to test many of the qualities and qualifications called for, but I did have a start. I knew the language and I knew a great deal more than most people in the Foreign Service about Mexico and the Mexican people. The climate and surroundings suited me fine. I intended to work hard on the rest.

Tampico offered plenty of opportunity for me to test my wings. The consular district was large and important both politically and economically. There was another officer to take care of day-to-day work and a half-dozen experienced clerical employees to take care of the housekeeping chores. I would be free to get out and around where the action was. I had some well-formed ideas about improving public relations. And the Foreign Service needed a constituency—as many people as I could develop, both Mexican and US nationals who thought we were useful and productive, rather than an obstacle to getting what they wanted or a burden on the taxpayer.

One of the consulate's responsibilities that I felt could be developed in this way was protection work. The Pan American Highway traversed the consular district for hundreds of miles and tens of thousands of US citizens drove over it each year. Some of them inevitably ran into trouble along the way—the kind of problems a responsive and ingenious consul could help solve and, hopefully, demonstrate in the process how important and useful the Foreign Service is to Mr. John Q. Taxpayer.

To make the most of this opportunity, I needed to set up a system that would alert me to US citizens with problems without delay. I visited every town and a good many villages along the Pan American Highway, recruiting as many people as I could who were willing to let me know as soon as they got word of US citizens in trouble. I had nothing to offer in return, but I felt sure I would get cooperation. After all, the more remote the place, the more important a consul from Tampico seemed. Soon enough, my plan started to bear fruit.

The call from the Motel Medianoche in El Tomaseño came during the late afternoon. The connection was bad, but I could understand enough of the message to know that a US couple had been in an automobile accident there. I promised to get on the job immediately. No matter that El Tomaseño was well over 200 miles from Tampico and a good five hour drive. No matter that I couldn't hope to get there before the sidewalks would be rolled up for the night. Duty called, and I would answer.

It took a little while for the sleepy night clerk at the Motel Medianoche to understand who I was and why I was there. No one had told him to expect the United States Consul from Tampico. But I kept after him and got the information I wanted. Mr. and Mrs. Tom Smith from the small West Texas town of Pecos had overnighted at the motel, and when they headed south that morning their car ran off the road outside of town. Both the car and the Smiths were pretty banged up. The cause of the accident had not been established. It seemed that Mr. Smith had been distracted somehow and had driven off the highway and over a steep embankment. The Smiths were at the local infirmary.

The nurse on duty at the infirmary told me both Smiths were asleep, having been given a sedative to ease their pain and the shock of the accident. I would not be able to see them until the next morning. She assured me their injuries were not serious and they should be able to travel in a few days. With this encouragement, I decided the next thing I needed to do was find out whether there were any charges against them.

At that time of night, it took a good bit of probing to find the right local official, but I managed to get the one I wanted out of bed. In typical Mexican fashion, he was courteous and cooperative, despite my intrusion into his household at an ungodly hour of the night. He was pleased to assure me that since neither of the Smiths had been seriously injured, no other vehicle had been involved and no damage had been done to the highway, there were no charges against either of them. They could leave El Tomaseño and Mexico as soon as they were well enough to travel.

"Well," I thought, "this is going to be an easy one!" The Smiths probably hadn't needed my help after all, but how was I to know? At least I had checked on them, and they would be grateful for that. I wondered what else I might do and thought of something. What if their family in Pecos had expected a call from them this evening? What if they were sick with worry? I could at least put their minds at ease. I could also let them know the US consul from Tampico was on the job and looking after everyone's interests.

El Tomaseño didn't have nighttime telegraph facilities, which meant I would have to drive 50 miles back down the highway to Ciudad Victoria. No matter— my duty was clear, and I would discharge it fully. I was tired by the time I got to Ciudad Victoria, but I had composed my message mentally and was ready to send it. It went something like this:

> To: The Family of Mr. and Mrs. Tom Smith, Pecos, Texas.
> Regret to inform you Mr. and Mrs. Smith have suffered automobile accident near El Tomaseño, Mexico. Injuries not serious but will be unable travel for few days. I am here to assist in any way possible.
> United States Consul, Tampico

I stayed to make sure the telegrapher sent it that night. It took him quite a while because of the English and possibly because of the hour. I was plenty tired but very pleased with myself when I finally went to bed after midnight.

Mr. Smith was asleep when I got to the infirmary the next morning, but the nurse showed me into Mrs. Smith's room right away. A lovely young woman, she was bruised and bandaged, but seemed a little vague when I told her who I was and why I was there. I figured she was suffering from the shock of it all and got out of her room as quickly and gracefully as I could.

Mr. Smith was soon awake, and the nurse took me in to see him. He was undoubtedly twice Mrs. Smith's age. His carefully trimmed moustache was white, and while there was a dapper look about him even in the hospital bed, he wasn't what I expected after meeting Mrs. Smith. "Well," I thought, "you never can tell about some of these old geezers."

As quickly as I could get it all out, I told Mr. Smith how much I had done the night before to be helpful, making sure to stress the trouble I had gone to in the process. I wanted him to be properly impressed with the zeal and dedication of the Foreign Service of the United States of America.

Mr. Smith's reaction wasn't exactly what I expected. At first his expression seemed to be one of shock. Then his face began to turn red. By the time I had finished my account, it was purple. I didn't understand until Mr. Smith spoke. "You goddamned busybody," he shouted.

"My wife is in Pecos and thinks—or thought until you butted in—that I'm on a business trip to Houston!"

The Body

Not all my efforts to develop a constituency for the Foreign Service turned out as disastrously as my first try at El Tomaseño. And going beyond the call of duty to help someone in real trouble gave me a great deal of personal satisfaction. Protection work often involved US citizens in tragic situations. All too frequently there were serious accidents on the Pan American Highway. Loved ones lost their lives, and sometimes those who survived were so badly injured they could not take care of themselves, much less handle the many details involved in returning the body of a friend or relative to the United States. The extra effort I put into these cases was fully rewarded by the response I got from those I was able to help. The serious protection cases didn't bother me. It was the inevitable US citizen with a minor problem who thought he shouldn't be subjected to the laws of a foreign country that gave me trouble.

At first, I tried reasoning, but I quickly found out it wasn't possible to reason with someone who was unreasonable to begin with. Eventually I developed two strategies for dealing with this type of person, using whichever best suited a given situation. The first consisted of simply agreeing with the complainer. No matter that he had killed a burro on the highway that he should have been able to see for a half mile down the road. No matter that he had barely missed the old man walking beside the burro, whose livelihood had depended on his faithful animal. No matter that the authorities were prepared to let my client off without charges if he would pay the old man what the burro was worth. No, I agreed that a burro would never have been found walking down a road in the United States and it was a crime and a shame this was allowed in Mexico. Sometimes I could nearly be moved to tears during one of these sessions, but in the end, the man paid. After all, if it was easier for him to do it that way, what did I have to lose?

It took a little longer to develop my alternate strategy. There were always a few US citizens who couldn't be satisfied with anything less than a confrontation between the United States consul and the traffic judge, or whomever. These types usually had something to say that went, "Why do you think I'm paying your salary? That's why you boys are down here—to see that these foreigners don't abuse us. I'm a citizen and I know my rights."

These people wanted to see me do a little pounding on the desk of the chief of police. And when I could, I gave them satisfaction. What they didn't know was that I had long since explained this type to as many of the officials I dealt with as I could. I had asked their forbearance if I had to come in and make a speech on behalf of a client. I told each one that if I thought a US national was getting a raw deal, I would come to see the official alone and tell him so, and why. But he could be sure that if I came in with a client and made a fuss, I thought the US citizen with me had coming to him exactly what he had gotten.

Mexicans have a good sense of humor, and I never found one who didn't play along with this strategy with pleasure. But in the end, it was always, "Pero, no hay remedio" (But there is nothing I can do about it). Everybody went away happy.

There was another problem with protection work that gave me trouble—until I hit on a solution. A sizable colony of old-timers lived in Tampico, left over from the oil boom days of the early 1920s. One or another of them passed on from time to time, and many were returned to the United States for burial in veterans' cemeteries.

It takes a lot of documentation to ship a body out of Mexico. Individual state authorities are charged with granting the necessary permits and it shouldn't have been much of a problem to get the documents in Tampico—located in the State of Tamaulipas—for shipment of a body to the port of exit, which was Nuevo Laredo—also in the State of Tamaulipas.

The trouble was with the State of Nuevo León, which the Pan American Highway passed through between Tampico and Nuevo Laredo. The Nuevo León highway inspectors at the border between Tamaulipas and Nuevo León insisted that for a body to pass through Nuevo León, it had to be accompanied by a complete set of documents issued by the authorities of Nuevo León. This was a problem. There was no reasonable way I could meet this requirement from Tampico.

But I couldn't help brooding. And this time, brooding did help. I remembered a comment from an old-time protection officer years back. He used to say, "Nobody but the family of the deceased wants a body—and sometimes even they don't want it." I thought I had the solution to my problem. All I had to do was wait for the next old-time-oil-man with no known relatives to depart for that big rig in the sky, and I could test it out.

When I got the body I wanted, I had the undertaker send the driver of his hearse to me for instructions. I went over exactly what I wanted him to do when he got to the Nuevo León inspection point—what he should say, and the expression he should keep on his face. He was a bright young man, and I felt confident he could carry the thing off. I told him to call me if he ran into any problems.

He was back in my office on the third day. The broad grin on his face told me the plan had worked. I couldn't suppress a chuckle as he told me the story.

The officers at the Nuevo León border inspection point had been adamant that he could not pass through the state without the documents required for transporting a body. His argument that he had all the documents required, issued by the authorities of the State of Tamaulipas, was to no avail.

"I shrugged, like you told me to, Señor Cónsul, and then I started to back up very slowly. The guards looked puzzled when I stopped right across the Tamaulipas state line. They watched as I went around behind the hearse and started to unload the casket on the roadside. I could hear them talking to each other, getting more and more excited by the second. When I had the casket out on the ground, I got back in the hearse, like you said. Slowly, I turned the hearse around to head back the way I had come. It was then that they began to run toward me. Like you told me, I moved slowly enough for them to catch me. Ah, it was wonderful to see the expressions on their faces when I told them my instructions were to leave the casket right there if I couldn't take it through Nuevo León. They said that was absolutely prohibited. I told them the casket was in Tamaulipas, not Nuevo León, and they had no authority. After all, I had my instructions and they had theirs. A few minutes passed before the one in charge said, with much profanity, 'Son of an ox, take your casket and go on.' He was extremely unhappy."

We shipped many bodies north through Nuevo León after that, but we never had another problem with the boys at the inspection point on the highway.

American Pirates

Tampico was a small town in the early 1950s, and it didn't take long for me to become well acquainted—and well known. I was active in Rotary, the promotion of US interests, and local social events. My picture appeared in the papers regularly. I made it a point to speak to anyone who looked my way, and in response was usually addressed as "Señor Cónsul."

Against this background, it didn't surprise me when the crowd that filled the street and blocked traffic in front of the US consulate opened to let me through and many greeted me with a friendly "Buenos días, Señor Cónsul." What surprised me was that a large crowd had gathered there at all, much less before the consulate was open for business.

The reason didn't remain a mystery for long. Several of the demonstrators held up copies of the morning newspaper for me to read the black headlines:

"Glorioso Ejército Nacional Captura Tres Barcos Piratas Yanqui" (Glorious Mexican Army Captures Three Yankee Pirate Boats). The shrimp wars were headline news once again. It wasn't the first time and it wouldn't be the last. At least things had been reasonably quiet on that front long enough for me to get settled in my new job.

I worked my way through the mob to the consulate's front door, returning greetings as I went, and climbed the stairs to the second-floor suite. Pedro stood ready to let me in, bolted the door behind me, and went back to tidying up, oblivious to the insistent demands of the telephone.

His job was to run errands and keep the offices neat, not answer the telephone. No one else had come in—maybe because it was early, or maybe because of the mob blocking the street below. I had a suspicion that whoever called today would want to speak to me, so I answered the phone.

Our man in Tuxpan, where the US shrimp boats had been brought in, wanted to make sure I knew what had happened. No, he had no idea how it came to pass that the Mexican Army, rather than the Navy, had captured the American boats at sea. He would try to find out.

There was another call as soon as I put down the receiver. This time it was the Brownsville Shrimp Producers Association wanting to know if I knew. I gave assurances I was on top of things. It was good the caller didn't think to ask what I planned to do about it—which saved me the embarrassment of confessing I had no idea. Calls from the DOS and the embassy at Mexico City followed. The message from each was the same. "Do something." I finally had to respond that if I could get away from the telephone, I might be able to get busy and *do something.*

The balcony of my office overlooked the street below where the *manifestación,* as they were called in Mexico, was going strong. A few participants with placards had joined the crowd. "Yankee Pirates Stop Stealing Mexico's Patrimony," read one. Another called for "Death to the Yankee Pirates." The mood of the crowd was agitated, but not ugly. I raised my hand in greeting and was surprised at how many waved to me in response. True, a few shook fists—but not many. I must have jumped in surprise when my secretary, Rosa Pelaez, spoke at my elbow. There was a murmur of laughter from the crowd below.

"What are you going to do, Ken?" Rosa asked.

"Do you have any suggestions?" I responded. "I suppose I'll drive down to Tuxpan and see what's going on."

"Aren't you afraid to go out through the crowd?" Rosa wanted to know.

"Not really. I came in through it just like you did. These people aren't mad at me. They're mad at the shrimpers. Has anyone else come in?"

"No, and I'm afraid no one will until this crowd goes away," Rosa said. "You're the consul and I'm a woman, so we're safe. The others aren't so sure."

The drive from Tampico south to Tuxpan was less than 100 miles, but the narrow, rough road left much to be desired. As I worked my way between mud holes, I thought back about my aerial survey of the coast a few days earlier, when a friend had taken me up in his little Cessna.

Not a single cloud broke the solid blue canopy stretching across the horizon. We took a wide swing north, then headed south. As we flew at 500 feet, every detail of the panorama below stood out in the clear morning light.

White beaches were washed by white foam that crested on breakers rolling in from the shimmering Gulf of Mexico. There were many shrimp boats—some working their way north, others headed south. They flew no flags, but it was easy to pick out their home ports painted in bold letters across the stern of each boat—Brownsville, Aransas Pass, Rockport, Grand Isle, Tampa, and others. These were the US "pirates" the Mexicans complained about so bitterly, which caught the white shrimp in much demand in the US

Three shrimp boats trawled behind the breakers between Cabo Rojo and Lobos Island, hidden from the sea by the island, and from the land by the expanse of Tamiahua Lagoon. Remembering these vessels, I wondered if they were the same boats now held in Tuxpan.

This wasn't the first time US shrimpers had been seized by the Mexican authorities. My predecessor had spent much of his time on the problem and had been called to testify before a Congressional committee about it.

The port of Tuxpan wasn't much in those days. A few thousand people lived along the banks of the Tuxpan River, earning a livelihood from the sea. Our man there ran the ice plant. I found him in his cubbyhole of an office. I wanted first to know what he might be able to tell me before I went anywhere else. It was quite a story.

The day before had been Army Day in Mexico. After the parade was over and the speeches finished, the local comandante had entertained his officers with the traditional Mexican barbecue and toasting session. The US pirates were on every man's mind these days. The newspapers were full of nothing else. And what news had Pimporro, the lighthouse keeper at Isla de Lobos, brought to Tuxpan when he sailed his small dinghy in that morning to join the celebration? Nothing less than word that three pirate ships were stealing Mexico's national patrimony off Cabo Rojo. They trawled by day but in the late afternoon they anchored close inshore on the sheltered side of the island to rest overnight.

The comandante had an inspiration. How more gloriously could the Army detachment under his command do special honor to their annual celebration than to capture US pirates? It would be a feat the Mexican Navy rarely accomplished. The longer he thought about it, the better the idea sounded. A man of action and no mean strategist, he explained his plan to the assembled officers. They, too, thought it well-conceived, and after a toast, or two, or three for the success they would achieve and the glory they would bring to the nation, they set out to get the show on the road.

Our man at Tuxpan said he didn't know exactly what had happened except that the three US shrimp boats had come into port after dark, unescorted and under their own power, with a contingent of Mexican soldiers aboard one of the boats. They were now tied up at the municipal dock with military guards onboard. The crews were in the town lockup, pending instructions from Mexico City about what to do with them next. Local feelings were running high, and unless I had real need of his help, he would rather be left out of it from here on in.

I thanked him and left. After all, he had tipped me off before anyone else got to me, and the help he had given the consulate over the years was on a strictly voluntary basis. He never got more than what I gave him now—thanks and a handshake.

It took a little talking to see the crewmen, but I finally found the right man. Knowing Mexican jails, I understood why he insisted on having the men brought out to see me, rather than allowing me to go back to see them.

They were nine in all, one captain and two crewmen for each boat. They worked for shares of the catch and, hoping to make good money, made do with as small a crew as could manage the work. They were not terribly impressive, just tough. One of the captains stepped forward and spoke for the rest.

"All right, what happened?" I asked.

He was ready with the answer. "Nothing. We were anchored behind Lobos Island to get out of the weather and these bastards came aboard with their guns and said we had to go in to Tuxpan."

"You weren't fishing?" I asked.

"Well, we had been fishing about eight miles offshore earlier, but we were fixing supper when they got us."

"Have you caught anything this trip?" I asked.

"Yeah, we got over 20 barrels of white shrimp on ice, and if they keep us here much longer, we'll lose it. How soon you gonna get us out?"

"I've heard you only catch whites around here in fairly shallow water—not eight miles offshore," I said. "By the way, do you remember the little plane that circled your boats several days ago off Cabo Rojo? I took some pictures out of that plane and I'll have them tomorrow. Was that you fellows? If I'm going to be able to help you, you're going to have to level with me." He didn't answer, but the expression on his face told me he knew I had him.

"Tell me, Captain, how the hell did you let yourself get caught like that? There's no patrol boat here at Tuxpan."

The captain hung his head for a minute and then looked up with a sheepish grin. "Because I was a damned fool, that's why," he said. "They pulled a real smart one on me and I got caught with my pants down!" That was closer to the truth than I anticipated.

All three boats were at anchor behind Lobos Island right before dusk while they processed the day's haul. As they were finishing up, a small Mexican trawler approached from the direction of Tuxpan. They knew the boat and the crew quite well. They had shared their fresh food with the Mexicans, so there was no alarm as the trawler drew near.

But there was a lot of excitement as it drew near enough for the shrimpers to see several females on deck. One of them smiled and waved a bottle in a most friendly fashion. The men noticed the Mexican captain jerking his head and rolling his eyes to one side, but their thoughts were on other matters as they lashed his boat tightly alongside, so the ladies could come aboard without danger. It was then that the Mexican soldiers threw open the hatch and scrambled out, Mauser rifles at the ready.

It was hard to suppress the grin that welled up inside me. I knew the boys would see the funny side in time—but I realized that right then wasn't the time. I told them to stick to their story and promised to see what I could do about getting them out of the pokey first thing in the morning.

Then I hurried off to dispatch my report to the embassy in Mexico City, the DOS in Washington and the Owners Association in Brownsville, letting them all know the boats and crews were safe and their man at Tampico was on the job. I wished I could have reported that everything was under control, but I wasn't quite sure how I was going to get there from here.

For lack of a better idea, I headed for the comandancia first thing in the morning. The officer who received me was courteous but said he could tell me nothing about the charges against the US fishermen. He said capturing pirate fishermen was not exactly in the normal line of duty for the Mexican Army. The general had decided to report to Mexico City and request instructions. No reply had come yet, and nothing would be done until one did.

I decided to ask the embassy in Mexico City to inquire at the Mexican ministry of defense, and loped off to the telegraph office. The telegram I drafted put the monkey squarely on the embassy's back. I sent a copy to Washington, and asked the department to repeat it to the shrimp boat owner's association. Then I headed back to the comandancia to see if I could get the shrimpers out of jail.

I had to work my way up the rank order from the captain I had talked to earlier, through the major he reported to, and finally to the general in command through his adjutant, the colonel. They knew something about passing the buck, too. This exercise gave me a chance to hone my arguments, and by the time I got to the general I had developed a pretty good case for letting the men go back to their boat, where they would be under guard until it was decided what should be done with them.

The general was most gracious. "Why of course, Señor Cónsul, I understand your concern for your people. For me it is a simple matter: You are a man of honor and your word is more than enough for me. Just promise that the men will not attempt to escape, and it is done." He had me.

The men were elated to get out of jail and back to their boats. Each gave me his pledge not to attempt escape. But to be on the safe side, I had the captains remove a key piece from the main engine and the auxiliary generator of each boat. I warned the shrimpers that the Mexican military guards onboard would shoot.

How much this impressed these guys was clear when a diminutive corporal with a Browning automatic rifle pointed it at one of the crew who walked too close to him. The big Cajun grinned, stuck his index finger into the business end of the barrel and said, "Bang!"

I spent the next three days preaching to anyone who would listen in Tuxpan, Mexico City or Washington that there had been no basis for the detention. The boats had merely taken safe haven in Mexico's territorial waters. They had not been caught fishing. They had been taken into custody illegally while at anchor. There was no way to prove where their shrimp had been caught.

It bothered my conscience some, but I stuck to it. The time came when the shrimp in the holds had to be taken off the boats or lost. I knew it was lost to the shrimpers, but I insisted it should be paid for by whoever took it. I realized that would never happen, but it was a good line. Stay on the offensive as much, and as long, as you can. It might not help, but it couldn't hurt.

I never knew whether my strategy worked, or even helped, but at the end of three days, the comandancia suddenly notified me the shrimpers were free to go and I should get them out of Tuxpan and Mexican territorial waters as quickly as possible.

I took the engine parts back to the boats and they were ready to cast off in nothing flat. As I watched them leave the harbor, I wondered if they had learned their lesson. I doubted it.

The next time we stopped by Lobos Island to drink some of Pimporro's coconut water, he told me the boats were all back fishing off Cabo Rojo the same day they sailed from Tuxpan. I wasn't surprised. I wouldn't have been surprised to find them dragging their nets up the Pánuco River through Tampico's harbor if there were shrimp to be found. They were a tough bunch. If I was to keep US shrimpers out of Mexico's territorial waters, I would have to do something more than preach to the crews. In time, I did.

***

I made it a point to stay current on the ongoing US-Mexican debate about how much territorial water a nation could claim under international law. The United States held to the traditional view it was three miles from the coast. Mexico asserted her right to six miles.

As the inevitable captures occurred, the owners' associations appealed to the DOS and congressional representatives for protection from what they felt was arbitrary and illegal detention of their boats by the Mexicans. State backed them up. The consul was expected to "do something about it." The consulate at Tampico hadn't been able to do a lot, but I was determined to change that—the problem I faced was, how?

I knew there were not more than a dozen Mexican shrimp boats working the northern Gulf, about half of them out of Tuxpan and the remainder out of Tampico. Yet I had seen hundreds of shrimpers fishing close off Mexico's coast to the north of Tampico on my aerial survey.

I didn't intend to question the claims of the owners' associations that their captains were explicitly forbidden to fish in Mexican territorial waters. But it seemed possible the captains didn't always follow the owners' instructions. I had to learn what was going on out there if I was get out from between the rock and the hard place where I found myself.

I started nosing around the commercial fishing dock when Mexican shrimp boats were in port. It wasn't hard to get acquainted with the Mexican captains over a few tequilas and tacos. Inevitably, the talk turned to shrimping, how it was done, how white shrimp were caught during the day and brown shrimp at night, how deep a given type of trawler could work, and much more. I began to have a feel for shrimping. It was interesting, and I enjoyed it.

When I thought I had become well enough acquainted with my new friends, I started asking questions about where the gringos fished. I expected the Mexican captains to be indignant over the pirates' abuse of Mexico's territorial waters and to criticize the Americans' activities. Not so. The Mexican captains immediately became vague and wanted to change the subject.

One captain told about losing his rudder in a storm and how two US shrimpers worked for hours rigging up an emergency rudder so he could get back into port. Another had lost his last net on a snag while fishing far to the north. A US shrimper had loaned him a spare, so he would not lose fishing time. All of them had been given cigarettes, fresh milk and other supplies by US shrimpers when their own had run low and the fishing was too good to return to port.

I quickly got the picture. The Mexican captains weren't about to say anything that might hurt their friends and fellow seamen. I would have to think of something else.

One of the shrimp boats that worked out of Tampico belonged to Wendell Cox, a friend of mine, and I thought he might be able to help me get the information I needed. He gave me the go-ahead to go out with his crew as often as I liked. It was the season when brown shrimp were being taken at night and the catches had been excellent just a couple of hours cruising time from Tampico.

During the next few weeks I had some of the best times of my life. I went to sea. Cox's boat left port in the late afternoon each day and came back a couple of hours after daylight each morning to unload and let the crew rest.

I didn't go out every night—I still had to work—but I made a lot of overnight trips, and I did find out what I needed to know.

US shrimpers fished wherever the fishing was good. They knew all about territorial waters and the dispute between Mexico and the United States, but territorial waters meant nothing to them, and they fished where they pleased.

I started keeping notes on each US shrimp boat I could identify; date, time and place sighted, whether fishing or changing locations, and anything else that might be pertinent.

I was amazed at how easily I could get the information I needed out where the action was. No one paid any attention to me, although we often spoke to US shrimpers a mere few yards apart. Also, the americanos were great talkers, and the air was full of their radio chatter from dusk to dawn. Before I was through, I had a list of over a hundred violations of Mexican territorial waters with full specifics as to boat, captain, time and place. Now I was ready.

It wasn't hard to promote an invitation from the Brownsville Shrimp Producers' Association to come up and address their group. After I laid the groundwork with a generalized speech about the ramifications and dimensions of the problem, it was easy to get the attention of the individual owners in smaller private meetings. I had on my list at least one boat belonging to each owner, and I gave each of them specific data to check against their boats' logs and to discuss with their captains.

I had no way of knowing whether the owners had ever before known what their captains were doing, but that didn't matter. I wanted them to know that I knew, and before I got through, there was no doubt in their minds that I did. Now the shoe was on the other foot.

We continued to have regular seizures as long as I was at Tampico and I continued to do everything I could to defend the American's interests and get the crews and boats released quickly. I don't think I did any better job afterwards than I had done before, but I didn't have any more complaints from either the Department of State, Congress or the owners' associations. On the contrary, I got nothing but thanks.

Sam

Every human who loves animals has had a favorite dog, cat, horse or hamster—an animal like no other, anywhere. I too, had such a friend: a short-haired pointer named Sam. Sam wasn't actually mine—my buddy Wendell Cox let me have him for a hunt one afternoon and Sam ended up staying with us until we moved on to our next assignment. He was mine while I had him, and over those years I couldn't have loved him more. He was the best dog I ever had.

Sam was a natural around the house—a gentleman indoors, although he mostly preferred to be outside—and there was never a kinder or more tender companion to our wee ones. They pulled his ears, explored his teeth, fell asleep resting on his flank and sometimes rode him like a horse. Sam bore it all in good spirit.

Hunting dogs quickly learn what signs to watch for when a hunting trip is in the making, and Sam often knew we were going out in the field as soon as I did. But it didn't really matter to Sam whether we were going hunting or not. What mattered to him was that we were going. Hunting he liked best, but he was happy to be taken fishing, or to the beach where he could practice his pointing on sandpipers and seagulls.

Sam and I first hunted together at the time of year when bobwhite quail were full grown. If we had time, we took the ferry over the river and explored the pineapple fields between Tampico Alto and La Mesa. The bobwhites loved the sandy ground there, and we always found lots of coveys down that way.

When our time was short, we could always find a few coveys up toward Altamira, although neither of us liked that country too much because of the heavy tick population. Still, it was better than no hunting at all. As I came to know Sam well, I understood that his passion for hunting quail was, if anything, greater than my own.

When duck season rolled around, I took Sam with me for two reasons. First, I wanted to see how he worked at retrieving ducks, and second, there was no way I could get out of the yard without him. Whoever trained Sam had done a magnificent job: he was perfect in the blind, waiting quietly until he was told to go. But once he got the word, he was as aggressive a retriever as anyone might wish for. Wounded birds did not get away from Sam. It was a wonderful quality, but one that very nearly broke up the close friendship we had developed as only two dedicated hunters can.

There's a lot of water around Tampico, and where there's a lot of water, there's a lot of ducks. I worked out a system where I could get in a little hunting every day. This meant getting up and out to where the ducks were before first light. I could often find puddle ducks sitting in range of the road that ran through the many sloughs and swamps surrounding Tampico. Sam would sit beside me on his canvas until I got off my shot, and then I would let him out to retrieve my duck. Often, we were back in town before breakfast with a half dozen pintails or teal.

One of our favorite spots for this sort of shooting was the road from Tampico to Pánuco. There was lots of water near the roadside and it was shallow enough to make for both good feeding, which pleased the ducks, and good footing, which pleased Sam. It was easier for him to splash through the shallows than swim through the deep.

Sam understood I didn't always get a duck every time I fired. If I missed, I didn't open the door for him, and we drove on until I stopped and fired again. If I made a hit, I opened the door and Sam was out and after my kill before I could say, "Go get him, boy." Each of us fully understood how this worked and there was never any trouble between us about it—until the day I broke the rules.

We had already picked up a brace of cinnamon teal when we came upon a nice flock of gadwall. They were at extreme range, but I had at them anyhow, emptying my shotgun without so much as loosening a feather. With all that shooting, it's understandable that Sam anticipated there would be something to bring back. When I decided the time had come to relieve myself and opened the door to step outside, Sam hit the water in a blur, ignoring my whistling and calls, in his determination to make a good showing. He was going strong when I lost sight of him in the distance.

There was nothing to do but wait until Sam was convinced he wasn't going to find the duck he was so sure I had shot and returned to the car. I knew he would come in with his head down and his tail trailing. Sam hated to admit defeat. How was I going to get across that there had been a misunderstanding and it wasn't his fault there was nothing to bring back?

Sam was gone for a long time. When he returned, I could hear him splashing through the swamp before I could see him and was looking in his direction when he first came into sight. Head high and tail erect, he fairly strutted toward me holding a bird in his mouth. I couldn't imagine where he had found it, my shots had all been clean misses. Proudly, Sam came to me and sat, waiting for me to take the prize he had brought back with so much effort.

Even before I had Sam's retrieve in my hands, I realized it was a mud hen, a common coot. How he managed to catch it, I'll never know, but a careful check failed to reveal anything wrong with it, and when I tossed it high, it flew off cackling with delight. It was then that I realized I had made a grave mistake.

Sam stared at me in utter disbelief. After all the effort he had put into finding and bringing in my game, I had thrown it away. He simply couldn't believe what he had seen. Slowly, he turned and crawled into the car, curling up on his tarpaulin with his back toward me. I knew we were through hunting. I wouldn't have dared send Sam out again after that. He didn't need to be able to tell me what was going through his mind. I could guess.

Many days passed before Sam would look me full in the face again. His eyes and ears drooped like a bloodhound's when he turned his gaze my way, and he made none of the moves that meant he was wondering if we shouldn't go hunting together. He had many ways of getting his messages to me, and the message was always the same. Sam felt betrayed. He wanted me to know things may never be the same between us again.

In time, Sam forgot how I had treated him—or at least found it in his heart to forgive. We enjoyed many more hunts together, but we never again hunted the swamps on the road to Pánuco. That would have been too painful for both of us.

Transfer to Washington

In each life and career, there are turning points. Our destiny is shaped by these watersheds. I always tried to keep control of my destiny, but I doubt I had much more success than most people. At least I knew when a turning point was reached and tried to make the best of it. During my tour at Tampico, there were several.

Although I started out as a clerk in the Foreign Service, I was soon an officer of the Foreign Service, and I was fortunate enough to move up the ladder very quickly. However, to be an officer of the Foreign Service is not the same as a Foreign Service Officer (FSO). Officers of the Foreign Service were members of the staff corps and "not-of-career." They did what was called "non-substantive" work. The elite—those who were called upon to do substantive work—were Foreign Service Officers. I may sound odd, but that's the way it was. The difference between the two personnel categories was great in every way—except that there were good, bad and indifferent officers in each category, as there are in all walks of life.

Even before my assignment to Tampico, the DOS had decided that since many officers of the Foreign Service were actually doing substantive work, they should be blanketed into the Foreign Service Officer category. This would also hold true for officers of the DOS and civil servants (yet another personnel category) who likewise were concerned with substantive foreign affairs matters. All would be united under one personnel system. All would be promoted on the same basis and all would be subject to selection out of the Foreign Service if they failed to measure up to their peers. Foreign Service Officers are supposed to be the most able men in the service of the United States government. The competitive examination process by which they are selected is the most rigorous and exhaustive of any government service or agency. I had my reservations about competing with that bunch, and besides, I was happy where I was.

Another factor crept into the equation during my tenure at Tampico. From the very beginning my goal in the Foreign Service had been to be a full consul and have my own post. Having attained that goal, it was obvious I would have to establish another one or go stagnant. The next step up would be consul general. But there was a hitch. Staff officers were granted the title of consul but were not eligible for assignments as consul general. That was reserved for Foreign Service Officers. It set me to thinking.

Although I had no intention of making a lifetime career out of the Foreign Service, I hadn't done anything about finding something else to do. I liked living abroad, and I had enjoyed everything I had been given to do in the Foreign Service. There seemed to be no rush to do anything different.

All of that changed around the time of my thirty-fifth birthday. An executive of a major United States manufacturing concern, visiting Tampico to look over a prospective site for a Mexican branch plant, asked me to consider going to work for his company. We talked about it at length, and when we came to the part about remuneration, my interest perked up measurably. The figure he mentioned as a starting salary was well over twice my government salary. The allowances were at least as good, and some of the other fringes were better. I began to give it some serious thought.

To my good fortune, we decided about that time to spend a couple of weeks in Laredo visiting family. During the visit, I went to see the father of one of my boyhood chums who was killed during World War II. The subject of my possible change of jobs came up and we discussed the pros and cons. He, more mature and wiser than I, brought up the question of relative retirement benefits. He had a point. Counting my pre-World War II time with the U. S. Army Engineers and the Department of Justice, plus service at hardship (extra-time) posts, I already had close to fifteen years credit toward retirement from government service.

My friend's father said he could help me check it out thoroughly. One of the insurance companies he represented had a machine called a computer at its central office, and it was available for complicated calculations. If I wanted, he would send in the basic data and ask the computer to calculate how much of my prospective salary I would need to save over the years in order to match the retirement benefits I could anticipate from my government job should I work fifteen more years until age fifty. The number that came back was astounding. I realized my decision had already been made—not by me, but by a machine I had never seen or heard of before.

If I stayed in the Foreign Service, and that seemed to be preordained, I would have to come to a quick decision whether I wanted to stick with the Foreign Service staff corps and take my chances, or go ahead with conversion to the Foreign Service Officer corps and take my chances.

There were other things besides the competition that concerned me about converting to the Foreign Service Officer category. The rules for them required that a certain percentage of their years in service be spent working in Washington. I didn't like that at all. I was a country boy and my place was in the field. My brief exposure to the DOS on detail from Mexico City had already confirmed my earlier conclusion that I wanted nothing of it. I thought my mind was made up, but this conflict, like others before it, was to be resolved by factors beyond my control.

Scott McLeod, administrator of the Bureau of Security and Consular Affairs (SCA) of the Department of State, attended a conference of the principal officers in Mexico around the time I struggled over the issue of my future. We saw each other frequently during the conference—at formal sessions and social occasions. I didn't find him nearly as fearsome as he was reputed to be.

My shock couldn't have been greater when a few weeks later I got word that I would be transferred to Washington. My assignment would be Staff Assistant to Scott McLeod. Another decision had been made for me. It was clear that: If 1) I had to serve in Washington, and 2) I couldn't afford at this stage of my life to leave government service, and 3) I hoped to move on to my next goal of being a consul general, then 4) I had better get busy and convert to the Foreign Service Officer category.

I went for it. What else could I do?

Washington, DC (I)
1955

SCA

I realized there would be changes in my personal circumstances when I took up my new duties as a staff assistant to Scott McLeod in the Bureau of Security and Consular Affairs (SCA). I may have been a pretty big fish at Tampico, but Tampico was a small puddle, while Washington was the biggest of them all, and I would be a small fish there. All of this I knew and understood. But I wasn't prepared for the reality.

The administrative people I reported to on my first day in the department were courteous enough, and the required paperwork was quickly completed. Then someone then took me down the hall and pointed out my desk, crammed in one corner of a room that would have been small for my secretary at Tampico. This I would share with another officer. Neither of us would have a secretary, which was a good thing, because if there had been one, we would have had to take turns at the two desks. There was no way another one could be squeezed into the room.

It was easy for me to understand my status, although I can't say I appreciated it. But in the months and years to come, I would realize how fortunate I had been to get that small desk in that little office. Orson W. Trueworthy was my officemate. Mild-mannered and affable, Trueworthy held an M.A. and an Ed.D. from George Washington University. He had worked on the Hill before coming to the department, and along the way, had acquired extensive knowledge of how Washington and its bureaucracy worked—what button had to be pushed to get a given response, who mattered in our organization and why. In short, how to get things done.

Just as George Winters taught me how to survive and prosper when I started out in the Foreign Service, Orson Trueworthy taught me how to survive and prosper in the Department of State. Perhaps, in time, I would have learned without him. But being able to turn to him for answers to my abysmal ignorance day after day made the difference between fighting an uphill battle and smooth sailing from the beginning. No man could have had a more able mentor. And no man could have had a better friend.

From the beginning, my duties in the Bureau of Security and Consular Affairs were both ill-defined and unusually varied. I seemed to get those jobs no one else wanted. It was good training. One day a letter from the senior senator from Utah was routed my way, marked "Take appropriate action." The senator was irate.

A young Mormon missionary working in Germany had voted in a Bavarian election and thus lost his US citizenship. The senator said he would not have such a thing and we should do something about it immediately. First, I would have to find out how a Mormon youth came to vote in a Bavarian election.

If the consequences hadn't been so serious, the story would have been worth a good laugh. The young man boarded with a German family, and his name had been given, along with everyone else's in the household, when the census was taken. This would have created no problem, except that when the voter registration list came out sometime later, his name appeared on it, too. Nor would this have created any problem except that the youth thought to have a good laugh at the expense of the usually meticulous Germans by showing up at the polls. It was here that he got into trouble.

Sizing up the fierce-looking inspector at the polling place, the young missionary had second thoughts about his plan, and decided it would be best to just move right along and vote. He would get his laugh later, when he told his fellow missionaries how he, a citizen of the United States, had voted in a German election. But when he did, someone suggested he read the warning in the back of his US passport. It was then he discovered he had forfeited his citizenship when he cast his ballot.

Being an honest and honorable man, the young missionary had gone immediately to the US consulate and explained what had happened. The consul promptly canceled his passport and informed him he was now a man without a country. From there the matter had come to the senior senator from Utah, who also happened to be an elder of the church—and now I was supposed to do something about it.

The passport office had jurisdiction over such matters, and since it was one of the offices that made up Scott McLeod's bureau, I expected to get a sympathetic hearing when I told them about the problem at hand. Not so. For the passport office, it was an open and shut case. Too bad the young man hadn't read the warning in his passport. But that was his responsibility. There was nothing to be done about it. The law was the law.

I talked my problem over with Trueworthy, who, as always, set me on the track to a solution. Orson pointed out that lawyers at the passport office might be the top dogs in our league, but they weren't in the majors when it came to the department as a whole. The legal advisor to the secretary of state could override any lawyer in the passport office. I took it from there.

The assistant to the assistant legal advisor had a well-developed sensitivity to matters of concern to senior senators. He was also a very bright young man. He had already figured out what to do by the time I finished telling him the story. All that had to be done, he said, was establish that the missionary hadn't really voted in a foreign election in the first place. This could be done if it were established that because he had been ineligible to vote, his ballot was invalid. If he hadn't cast a valid ballot, he hadn't voted—in a legal sense.

The German embassy was most cooperative. Clearly, the US missionary had not been eligible to vote in a Bavarian election—the inclusion of his name on a register of voters had been a simple and understandable mistake. They were pleased to give me a note to that effect. They were glad to include a statement that the ballot was categorically invalid. I had what I needed.

The next step was to get the passport office to state its position on paper. I drafted a request for a review of the case that went out over McLeod's signature. When the answer came back, I drafted a request for the legal advisor's opinion on the correctness of the passport office's ruling. My new friend, the assistant to the assistant legal advisor was ready. His brief, over the signature of the legal advisor, ended the matter right there. The Mormon missionary got his citizenship—and his passport—back by return mail.

I learned two things from this exercise. First, that the law is not always the law, but rather what a given lawyer says it is; and second, I discovered who the real enemy was in Washington. It wasn't those foreign governments who threatened our security from abroad. It was the other bureaucrats who were continually getting in the way of what I had to do.

Historical Footnote

When we came to live in Washington in mid-1955, Davy Crockett was the center of national attention. There was a Davy Crockett movie, a Davy Crockett television series, a Davy Crockett song, and Davy Crockett merchandise. Our children become minor celebrities and they wanted to know if they were related to Davy, and if so, how.

My knowledge about the relationship between Davy Crockett and my own ancestors was skimpy at best, but I'd heard there was a family book, so I called the Library of Congress.

"We have all kinds of calls for information on Davy Crockett these days," said the voice on the other end of the line. "Our most popular reference is Volume V of *Notable Southern Families,* entitled *The Crockett Family.* I'll send one over to the State Department for you."

When it came, the book more than fulfilled my expectations. The authors, Mrs. J. Stewart French and Miss Zella Armstrong, had done a thorough job, starting back in 1643 and carrying through to my grandfather's generation. His name and those of his siblings were listed. Most important, so far as the children were concerned, Davy Crockett was there too. Our common ancestor was Joseph Louis Crockett, who was born January 9, 1676 in Ireland and immigrated to the United States around 1716, along with his Irish wife, Sarah Stewart of Donegal. Joseph Louis was Davy's great-great-grandfather—and my great-great-great-great-great-grandfather. To put it a different way, Davy was a third cousin of my children's great-great-grandfather. It didn't seem to me like much of a connection, but it was enough to satisfy the children.

I had always understood the Crocketts were Irish. What I hadn't known was that they were originally French Huguenots named Croquetagne, who fled to Bantry Bay, Ireland, in 1672 and changed the family name to Crockett to help lose their French identity.

There were other interesting tidbits. Colonel Hugh Crockett, from whom I am directly descended, was on the staff of General Green during the American Revolutionary War. His son Samuel, born in 1775 and married to Margaret Reyburn, moved from Virginia to Tennessee and then on to Missouri where my father was born. I wasn't any different after I learned these things, but like the children, I felt I now had a much better idea where I came from.

Washington Wonderland

Many junior officers complain that a first assignment to the department is a real drag—nothing interesting or important ever comes their way. That could not have been farther from the case in my own experience in the Bureau of Security and Consular Affairs. Besides being the utility player on Scott McLeod's team, my regular responsibilities were expanded considerably. Among my duties were two that were quite sensitive. I was designated as the liaison for FBI consultations with the DOS in cases where a planned FBI activity might involve a foreign diplomat, or diplomatic establishment in the United States, including the United Nations. I was also assigned to a team that would help relocate the seat of the United States government outside of Washington in the event of an atomic attack on the nation's capital.

Both responsibilities required special security clearances involving an updated, full-field investigation. I was warned that FBI agents would be asking questions about me and my family. I didn't give it much thought—I had nothing to hide.

It's not easy to get acquainted in a new neighborhood in a large city, and we considered ourselves fortunate to have met the neighbors who lived in the house adjoining ours on Middlesex Lane in Bethesda. They were a congenial couple and we seemed to strike it off well, until the morning the wife burst into Mary's kitchen in a state of great agitation to tell Mary she had been visited by a special agent of the FBI who asked all sorts of questions about us. She thought Mary would like to know. Mary might also like to know that the FBI man would return in the evening to talk with her husband.

We lived at the house on Middlesex for many months after that, but we rarely caught a glimpse of the neighbors. I never could figure out when they did their gardening because there was never a sign of life at their place when I was out in my yard. Such was life in Washington during the McCarthy era for a State Department employee the FBI was asking questions about. I don't think it would have surprised me if the next door neighbors had picked up and moved.

At the time all this happened, investigations were also being made in Laredo, our hometown. Digging back into old files, the FBI had turned up a job application I had submitted while still a teenager. One of the references I had given at that time was Frank R. Campbell, a well-respected man I was exceptionally fond of. We had hunted and fished together on many occasions, and he was almost like a father to me.

When the FBI agent arrived to interview Mr. Campbell, he learned from his son Dick that Mr. Campbell had died several years earlier. The agent asked Dick if he knew me and when Dick said yes, set about interviewing him. Dick told the agent I was the most loyal, trustworthy, industrious, intelligent man he had ever known. He heaped praise on praise. He answered every question the FBI agent asked with glowing accounts of what a wonderful and able person I was. Dick did not tell the agent we were brothers-in-law. The agent didn't ask that question.

As FBI liaison, I came to know a lot of things most people never imagine. I found out how determinedly unfriendly regimes were (and, I'm sure, still are) working to subvert our system of government. I also learned what we were doing to hold them at bay as best we could, given the constraints of our democratic system. My daily meetings with my FBI counterparts quickly came to be the highlights of my work in SCA—if not of my work in the DOS during my first assignment to Washington. Both the FBI and I came to know a good deal about one another. This would be of invaluable help to me 10 years later when someone with access to high places in the US government raised a question about my integrity.

In time, my responsibilities with the group planning the relocation of the seat of government in case of an atomic attack brought me to the chairmanship of what was called The Washington Liaison Group (WLG). This group—composed of a State Department chairman, and members of the CIA, the Army, the Navy and the Joint Chiefs of Staff, was also charged with coordinating worldwide planning for evacuation of citizens of the United States and friendly powers from war zones in case of armed hostilities. Our primary interest at the time, which was at the height of the cold war, was Europe and the Eastern Mediterranean—particularly Lebanon.

The more I learned about plans being developed under the auspices of the WLG, the less confidence I came to have in them. Eventually, I suggested we scrap the whole business and start over from scratch, not a popular approach in any organization. I still believe it would have been the best thing we could have done, but I was to move on to other work before I could sell the idea. Meanwhile, I visited planning groups in London, Dublin, Paris, Frankfurt,

Wiesbaden, Vienna, and several other centers whose locations I will not mention as they were classified at the time and, for all I know, may yet be. The WLG planning may have been unrealistic, but the travel involved in finding this out made the effort entirely worthwhile.

Yet another area of interest during my stint in SCA was the Immigration and Naturalization Service (INS), then supervised by Commissioner and retired Army General Joseph Swing, who happened to have been a classmate of then-President Dwight D. Eisenhower. This relationship should not have caused any problems in dealings between SCA and INS, and it would not have, except that General Swing thought his organization should take over the visa issuing function of the State Department, a responsibility falling under Scott McLeod's jurisdiction. Anyone at all familiar with the bureaucracy will understand how McLeod took a dim view of General Swing's ambitions. It is also easy to understand why McLeod was obliged to exercise finesse in fending off Swing's attempts to take over a sizable piece of his turf.

General Swing selected the place where he hoped to get his foot in the door with consummate skill: Cuba—within quick and uninterrupted plane access from and to the US. It is possible General Swing felt it worked to his advantage that our ambassador to Cuba was a political appointee who was much more likely to support General Swing in any test with the State Department regarding his prestige. There were other advantages that came to light as events unfolded.

The INS plan involved a scheme in which INS inspectors would be assigned to Havana, where they would perform their function of clearing aliens applying for admission to the United States before embarkation. Thus, an applicant cleared by INS to board his transportation to the US was to be simultaneously "admitted" so that on physical arrival in the States, all the traveler needed to do was clear customs and be on his way. This system would result in a savings of manpower and money, according to General Swing, because it would eliminate the need for travelers to bother the embassy for visas.

On the face of it, that made sense. But on closer examination it was evident that security considerations would require the INS to conduct exactly the same checks regularly made by visa-issuing offices of the State Department, and all the change would amount to as far as the US government was concerned would be to substitute an inexperienced agency (INS) to do the same job already being performed by one with decades of experience in the work (DOS). In addition, a quiet visa refusal conducted within the confines of the US embassy was one thing. It would be quite another for United States officials to refuse a Cuban citizen permission to board an aircraft at the airport in Havana. It was on this latter point that we in SCA decided we could best make our stand.

The Bureau of Security and Consular Affairs was not without an ally in its efforts to protect its vested interests. J. Edgar Hoover, director of the Federal Bureau of Investigation, had his own reservations about any change in the status quo. His people located at our embassies abroad had long since established productive working relationships with State Department people, and many safeguards in place to screen out subversives had been implemented on FBI recommendations. The director was reasonably satisfied with current operations. He saw no reason to change something he was satisfied with for something that wasn't the least bit familiar. As was his custom, he played his cards close to his vest. What counted was that we who were on the frontline knew where he stood.

In keeping with Washington tradition, General Swing's desire to set up shop with his "pre-inspection" plan for Cuba resulted in endless meetings between his representatives and Scott McLeod's. The memos prepared by INS participants recording what happened in these meetings were so far from factual that I began taping the sessions with a hidden microphone in my lapel, and a recorder no larger than a package of cigarettes—a marvelous innovation for the mid-50s. I was able to hold my own, but our meetings got nowhere.

The day came when General Swing met directly with McLeod to make a proposal aimed at breaking the deadlock. Why not ask the Cubans whether they would object to INS inspectors enforcing United States laws at the Havana airport? That should answer the question once and for all, the General said.

"We can go down there together and talk to them ourselves," he told McLeod. "What better way to find out the exact lay of the land?" Since our people in Havana had been repeatedly told by the Cuban foreign ministry that INS inspectors were not wanted in Cuba, McLeod saw no reason not to accept. The deal was on.

As plans for the meeting in Havana developed, General Swing told McLeod that he and his INS advisers would travel from Washington to Havana in an INS aircraft. McLeod and his people were welcome to come along in the same aircraft.

"In fact," Swing suggested, "since there's plenty of room and no additional cost, why don't you bring your wives—get them out of the Washington weather for a few days?" McLeod took Swing up on that one, too.

Something kept nagging at me as I prepared for our meeting in Cuba. I got the embassy in Havana to recheck with the Cuban foreign ministry to make sure their opposition to the INS plan was firm. The reply came back, "Firm as a rock."

I rechecked with my mother in Laredo to make sure she could come to Washington to watch the children—there were four now including little Linda born in Texas in 1953 while Mary was home for a visit. "No problem at all, son," came the reply.

Still, I was bothered, and I couldn't resist calling a strategy meeting of our team to talk it over. I think what worried me most was that we had not heard a single word from General Swing or his people since we agreed to the Havana meeting. The whole bunch had dropped out of sight. We held our strategy meeting on a Thursday afternoon. I felt a little silly pulling everyone together to talk about some vague feeling I had that all was not right. But McLeod was sympathetic.

"Kennedy," he said, "our meeting with the Cuban foreign ministry people is not until next Monday. Why don't you fly down to Havana tomorrow morning and check things out on the ground? If something is wrong, you can let us know by phone. If everything seems OK, we'll bring Mary down with us Monday in the INS plane." It sounded like a good idea and I went.

My principal contact in the embassy at Havana wasn't anyone in the Foreign Service, as might have been expected. The man I trusted most in Havana was Clark Anderson, my old friend from our time together in Honduras in the 1940s. He had become the embassy's legal attaché, the special agent in charge of the sizable FBI contingent in Havana. I knew I could count on Clark's help, both because of our strong friendship and because I knew where his boss stood on the problem at hand.

By Saturday afternoon, details of what had happened were pieced together. None of the evidence would stand up in a court of law, but there wasn't going to be any court of law. I called McLeod to make my report.

Briefly, General Swing and a couple of his senior aides had quietly flown into Havana several days earlier to meet with senior officials of the Batista government. It wasn't hard to guess who had set up the meeting for the president's classmate. General Swing had an opportunity to outline his plan to the Cubans under most favorable conditions and to stress how important it was to him that the Cuban government find the "pre-inspection" plan acceptable. Either someone in Swing's party had suggested, or someone on the Cuban side had concluded independently, that General Swing would be a strategically-placed friend for the government of Cuba when the time came for the annual revision of worldwide sugar quotas. Who better to put in a quiet word for Cuba than one of the president's oldest comrades in arms?

Mcleod asked what I thought we should do. I told him it seemed to me the best course would be for him to come down with such a bad case of the flu that the trip would have to be called off. And so it was. There was no point in taking a hand in a game where we knew the deck had been stacked ahead of time.

This little story would end here except for two additional details. My mother did not like to travel by air and was already halfway to Washington by train when our trip to Havana was called off. Rolland Welch, director of the department's visa office, didn't like to travel by air either and he was already halfway to Key West on the train before the trip was called off.

My mother enjoyed her visit to Washington notwithstanding. I never had the nerve to ask Rolland if he enjoyed his trip to Key West.

Employee #131300

In planning our transfer from Tampico to Washington, we had kept in mind that things would be a lot different for us in the United States. Losing one's allowances and the use of a government automobile at the same time that costs go up is not to be taken lightly. We fully expected to skimp in order to make ends meet. As it turned out, we were not realistic.

Both Mary and I had been raised in households where it was normal to have servants. Many middle-class families living along the border with Mexico at that time did, and we continued to after our marriage. After much discussion, we agreed we would have to make do with one servant when we moved to Washington. It was quite the come-down after a staff of three to four in Tampico, but we would manage.

We couldn't afford to buy a house in the Washington area, and were determined not to go overboard on rent. We settled on what we felt was a modest, two-story Cape Cod on a quiet street in Bethesda, Maryland. It had a full basement with a game room and large oak trees scattered around the yard. The house gave us enough room for our family of six, plus a separate bedroom and bath for the maid. The rent was more than we had planned on, but we did have a nest egg we could draw on.

I quickly found that getting to work presented a problem. I did not rate a State Department parking space, and besides, Mary needed the car to take care of household chores. I lucked into a carpool made up of old-timers from the Bureau of Inter-American Affairs, including Ed Jamison and Henry Dearborn, who did have a parking permit. Over the long haul, I learned more about Latin American affairs and the workings of Inter-American affairs riding to and from work than I did during formal office hours. What would otherwise have been a tedious commute alone was converted into a discussion period I looked forward to with much anticipation every working day of the year.

Meanwhile, back at the Department of State, the office of personnel continued to grind out its endless stream of papers, and I was instructed to go up and be sworn in as a full-fledged Foreign Service Officer, Class 4. I think it was also about this time that the Department of State decided that each of its employees needed an employee number. I don't know who it was in personnel that had a grudge against me, but I ended up with number 131300. In the end, it turned out to be a pretty lucky number.

Entry to the hallowed ranks of Foreign Service officers marked a turning point in my career. The way was now open for me to go after my next goal, the title and job of Consul General of the United States of America. On the flip side, I was now in direct competition for promotion with as select a group of officers to be found in the federal government—and by the rules of the game, if I couldn't establish my eligibility for "promotion up" when measured against my peers, I could look forward to prompt "selection out." I still couldn't see all that much difference between being Foreign Service Staff Officer, Class FSS-4, and Foreign Service Officer, Class FSO-4, however.

I had suspected from the beginning that we were living too far beyond our means in the house on Middlesex. My suspicion was confirmed before the end of our first year. The nest egg we brought to Washington had shrunk at an alarming rate, and I realized we would have to cut expenses. The maid was first to go. We were able to place her with a nice family that had served overseas, but it was like losing a member of the family—Juanita had come to work for us in Tampico when she was barely sixteen and had been with us nearly five years. It was hard to let her go, but worse, it wasn't enough.

I knew what the next step must be, but I hated to tell the others. We loved the Cape Cod on Middlesex and living there was convenient in so many ways. No matter—what had to be done, had to be done. We were able to find a smaller house in Kensington—twice as far from the department—and we moved as quickly as we could. It was a disappointment at the time, but I doubt it made any difference in our lives since. The important thing was we were solvent again!

The other shoe fell rather quickly. In one of the interminable tinkerings with the Foreign Service Act, it was decided that the number of classes of Foreign Service officers would be increased from six to eight. It was obvious some of us would have to be set back and it was also obvious FSO class 4 was where the split would have to come. My morale was pretty low when personnel announced the formula for splitting the class. I couldn't help regarding the moved back to FSO-5 as anything but a demotion. It hurt!

My year in the Bureau of Security and Consular Affairs passed quickly, but despite some interesting assignments, my enthusiasm for the work flagged. Interesting as it was, it was still Washington bureaucracy, not foreign affairs. I was a Foreign Service Officer, and I wanted work involving the Foreign Service.

Scott McLeod tried to perk me up by suggesting he would nominate me for the slot SCA had in the State Department contingent to the National War College. It sounded great until personnel informed us no one below the rank of FSO-4 could be considered under any circumstances, and they much preferred that all nominees be classified at least FSO-3. I was far enough down in the dumps that I really hadn't expected the deal to work out, so I wasn't disappointed when it didn't. I knew things were getting serious when I realized I hadn't tried to put up a fight.

There was one thing I could do and that was travel. The Washington Liaison Group had a requirement for a trip to the Far East—Tokyo, Hong Kong, Manila, Singapore and Jakarta. Since there seemed to be no reason why I shouldn't go, I worked up my itinerary, got my tickets, packed my bags and was within 48 hours of leaving when everything changed.

In casting about for someone to take over the Office of Mexican Affairs, the Inter-American Affairs somehow developed an interest in me. Their assistant secretary asked McLeod if he would release me for the assignment if I were selected. Scott knew how much being a desk officer meant in the career of any

FSO and agreed to let me go. The interviews went well, and instead of going halfway around the world the following Monday, I went down the hall and around the corner of the old State Department building to sit at the desk of the Officer in Charge of Mexican Affairs.

OIC/Mexican Affairs

The desk officer for any country is the focal point for all substantive contact between the embassy/ambassador abroad and the secretary of state in Washington, not to mention the White House and the president. I could hardly have been more poorly prepared for the job by way of experience. My line of work had always been consular and administrative. But I knew I was selected because there wasn't anyone more qualified available. It was a comforting thought for me, although a sad commentary on our personnel system.

I had barely found the in-box when the assistant OIC/Mexican Affairs suffered a heart attack. He would be out of the office for months. I often wonder if it wasn't brought on because he outranked me by two grades and had been my boss in the not-too-distant past. Whatever, I was sorry about his infirmity, both for his sake and for mine. He knew how to do what there was to be done. I didn't. But I quickly found out my luck had held. T. R. Martin, who handled the international boundary and water commission work in the Office of Mexican Affairs had extensive experience and knew what to do and how to do it. He also knew the background of Mexican-US problems from year one—by heart! I couldn't have made it without him. I have since realized that many an OIC/Mexican Affairs before and after my time relied on T. R. when the going got tough.

With Dwight Eisenhower in the White House, John Foster Dulles in the State Department and Francis White in the embassy at Mexico City, Mexican-US relations came in for a lot of high-level attention. The presidents of the United States and Mexico met regularly. It is impossible to explain the detailed planning and preparation that goes into such a visit—you have to live it to believe it. As the focal point, I was deeply involved. These meetings never became routine, but they did follow a pattern, and after the first it was a little easier, for no other reason than I knew from experience how hard it was going to be.

The hardest part of preparing for my first meeting was a single, letter-size sheet of paper entitled "The Chamizal Dispute." My instruction from the White

House was to prepare a briefing paper for President Eisenhower on this territorial dispute between Mexico and the United States to consist of no more than three paragraphs, each paragraph no more than five lines, both left and right margins to be one-and-one-half inches, and so on. The difficulty was that the Chamizal dispute dated back more than 100 years and was sufficiently important and complicated to take up most of a three-hour international law course my junior year at University of Texas. Fifteen lines, indeed! But we did it—how, I cannot now remember.

My job in the bureau of SCA had been pretty much nine-to-five. The issues we dealt with seemed important and I'm sure they were. However, they were hardly ever urgently important. The Mexican desk was different. People up the line wanted answers—now! And the people up the line became very important, very quickly.

I got my first taste of direct calls from the White House—not so many in the Eisenhower administration as later, but enough for me to know that the business I was supposed to keep abreast of was important to people concerned with the actual running of our country. My office hours stretched correspondingly, as there always seemed to be at least one problem that needed urgent attention—and sometimes there were a half dozen or more. I didn't want to find myself in the position of having someone up there call me to ask a question about anything in my bailiwick that I couldn't answer. So, I regularly came in well before office hours and stayed on well after the close of business. The hours were long, but I didn't mind. I didn't know it then, but I already had a mild case of Potomac Fever—that malady suffered by some in Washington that makes them think the government can't go on unless they are there to see that it does.

There were compensating factors for the long hours. Mary and I were the subjects of much interest to the Mexican ambassador and his wife, as well as the senior members of his staff. And why not? I could help make their jobs easier or I could foul them up in any number of little ways. They all but killed us with kindness. We really had no time for social activity at the Washington diplomatic level, not with four kids at home, no servants and an extremely strained budget. However, we accepted invitations because it was expected of us—part of the job. In truth, some of the sparkling functions we were invited to were exciting, and if Mary's evening gown happened to be homemade and my tuxedo rented, no one knew or cared.

Once I figured out how to keep things going in the Office of Mexican Affairs/Washington, it wasn't hard to find a good reason for frequent travel to Mexico. There were always topics to be discussed with the senior officers of the embassy in Mexico City that were better not committed to paper or hashed out over the telephone.

Tactics for the many ongoing negotiations between the US and Mexico were subjects Ambassador White and I regularly consulted on personally. The ambassador was a hard-nosed representative of US interests, but experienced enough to know the iron fist worked best when covered with the velvet glove. He fully understood how sensitive Mexican government officials were to anything that might remotely be interpreted as "undue pressure" from the Colossus of the North. He developed a system for getting around this prickly problem that made his point quite firmly but involved no offense or loss of face for the Mexicans.

For example, let's say the matter under negotiation with Mexico is renewal of our aviation agreement governing what airline of which country can service a given route. The Mexicans want route X, which the United States is absolutely unwilling to give up. However, to retain route X for a US carrier, we are willing to let Mexico service routes Y and Z. We are confident they would take routes Y and Z, if fully convinced that we, in the long run, are not going to give in on route X. We must break this stalemate in order to move on to discussion of other points in the negotiations.

After a face-to-face meeting with White in Mexico to discuss tactics, Crockett returns to Washington on Sunday night. On Monday morning, White calls Crockett to press for favorable consideration of Mexico's insistence on route X. The conversation is barely getting started when there is an interruption. The operator in Mexico City asks for patience—there is a technical difficulty. When the connection is reestablished, White pleads masterfully for Washington's understanding of how important it is for Mexico to have route X. Crockett says he fully understands both White's concern and Mexico's insistence, but there can be no give in the US position due to a variety of factors, some of them very important from the domestic political standpoint. White insists. Crockett goes over the ground again. Finally, White realizes there is simply no way. He is most discouraged as he ends the conversation.

In the next formal session of the aviation agreement negotiation, the Mexicans concede the United States position on route X. Things again move forward. It was as if someone had been listening in on what Crockett and White said over the phone.

There were also personal advantages to frequent travel between Washington and Mexico. When I felt I could afford a day or two of annual leave along the way, it was easy to work up an outing with Carter Gaston, my favorite hunting and fishing companion at Tampico. How nice it was to return to Washington with a good bit of frozen quail or robalo.

Then, too, Laredo wasn't far off the most direct route, and I was able to get in a long weekend with my parents at regular intervals—something that was always important to me. Over all, the Mexican Affairs assignment had a great deal to offer, and I took as full advantage of it as I could.

The Secretary of State

The Mexican desk officer is frequently sought out for one function or another involving Mexico—mostly in Washington but often elsewhere, such as along the border. I participated in my share of these, many of which turned out to be anything but what I had anticipated. The most notable involved an unexpected invitation to stand in for the secretary of state.

In the late 1950s, arrangements were completed for the purchase of natural gas from Mexico's field at Reynosa. Ceremonies were planned for opening the pipeline uniting the two countries, and invitations to participate were extended to senior officials of both the Mexican and the United States governments. For some reason, the secretary of state could not attend, nor could the under secretary, the assistant secretary or the director of middle American affairs. At the last minute, that left me. I was assured that all I had to do was get myself to Houston. After that, the large, private US corporation organizing the event would take over my care. I got my travel order and ticket for a seat in economy class. I told someone who called from Houston what flight I would be taking. The voice at the other end of the line assured me I would be met.

My flight taxied up to the terminal at Hobby International late in the afternoon of the day before the inauguration. As we came to a stop, the captain's voice boomed over the intercom, "We have been informed from the tower that the secretary of state is on board. You are requested to kindly keep your seats until he and his party have disembarked." I thought, "My God, someone didn't get the word! What do I do now?"

The best thing seemed to be sit tight—maybe it would all go away. Regrettably, it did not. When minutes dragged by and no one moved, flight attendants began walking up and down the aisle, looking for John Foster Dulles. I got one of them to lean down so I could whisper in her ear that I represented the secretary of state and perhaps if I got off that would solve the problem. In a loud voice she said, "Please follow me, Mr. Secretary, they are waiting for you at the ramp." I felt every eye on me as I struggled to my feet and stumbled into the aisle—there was no way to hide the hot flush that crept up from underneath my collar.

At the foot of the ramp stood a group of three: a tall distinguished-looking gentleman in chauffeur's livery, a middle-aged lady with a clipboard in one hand and pencil in the other, and a rather rotund type who had PR written all over him. All three had their eyes focused beyond and behind me, evidently looking for John Foster Dulles. I cringed at the thought of letting them down.

It wasn't easy to get PR's attention, but I managed to communicate that the secretary of state couldn't make it and I had been sent instead. I wanted very badly to say, "He sent me instead," but I didn't feel it would be honest to stretch things that far. PR's face fell, but he quickly regained his composure in keeping with the code of good PR types who are always prepared for any kind of surprise. Clipboard was clearly disappointed as well, but she dutifully recorded for posterity everything that was said as the conversation progressed. It soon became obvious we should move along. The other passengers were crowding off the plane and glaring at me and my group.

As we walked, PR told me about the arrangements he had made for me (read: *the secretary of state*). I need not worry about my luggage—just give Clipboard my claim checks and she would see that it was delivered to my suite. Chauffeur would drive me to the Shamrock Hotel and stand by to take me wherever I might like to go during the evening. He would also pick me up in the morning for the trip to Reynosa. Everything had been taken care of at the hotel, and while in Houston, I would be the guest of the company. There was no room for argument, so I climbed into the back of the limo and tried to relax.

As we pulled up to the main entrance at The Shamrock, a uniformed doorman stepped forward smartly and let me out with a cheery, "Welcome to the Hotel Shamrock, Mr. Secretary." It occurred to me that someone had gone to a lot of trouble coaching everyone along the line. A man of impeccable dress and deportment emerged from the shadows and peered into the back of the limousine, expecting to greet John Foster Dulles. Finding no one there, he turned to me with a look of reproach and waited for an explanation. I introduced myself and repeated my story. He identified himself as "*In Charge of Special Operations*" and said he would be pleased to show me to the suite reserved for the secretary of state, which he was sure the company would want me to occupy since, after all, I represented the secretary of state.

When the elevator doors opened we stepped into a private foyer facing carved double doors. As my friend, In Charge of Special Operations, swung the doors open, it was all I could do to swallow a gasp!

A room, the dimensions of which I couldn't estimate, stretched into the dim distance. It was handsomely furnished with groups of divans and lounge chairs, mahogany cocktail and end tables, and period buffets along the walls. An archway on one side gave access to a room furnished with several small tables and Louis XIV straight-backed armchairs, and a bar with at least a dozen upholstered stools spread along its length. I would have poured myself a drink, except that as if by magic a dapper young fellow dressed in black trousers and a white jacket appeared to pour one for me. He disappeared through a door to one side and re-appeared within moments carrying a tray of hot canapés. I began to realize this was going to be a rather pleasant evening.

Before taking his leave, In Charge of Special Operations showed me through two bedrooms, each with a bath large enough to accommodate a sizable cocktail party and assured me that whatever I might want in the way of food, drink or entertainment was mine for the asking.

It seemed sinful to waste the facilities, and I set about calling first one and then another of my old friends in Houston. No answer on the first call. Sick child at the second. Lodge night at the third. When I had exhausted my list of friends, I started calling acquaintances, but struck out there too. I ended up in all that elegance watching Davy Crockett on TV and eating a club sandwich for supper.

Chauffeur was waiting the next morning to take me to the airport for the trip to Reynosa. No one took notice as I climbed into the back of the big black limousine—apparently, word had gotten around that I wasn't really John Foster Dulles.

Another surprise awaited me at the airport when we pulled up to a private hangar emblazoned with the name of the sponsoring company. Parked outside was a twin-engine aircraft lavishly furnished with half a dozen overstuffed armchairs and chaise lounges. An attendant made me comfortable while her associate inquired if I would prefer coffee, breakfast, a bloody Mary, or all three. The captain came back to introduce himself and outline our flight plan. No one called me Mr. Secretary, but everyone continued to treat me as if I were. I was the sole passenger on the flight from Houston to Reynosa.

At Reynosa I thanked the pilot and crew, explaining I would not be returning to Houston, but finding my own way to Laredo once the formalities were over. Quick on his feet, the pilot said that if I was not going back to Houston, his instructions were to take the plane to El Paso. He would drop me off at Laredo, which was right on the way—no trouble at all. I started to object, but not very hard or convincingly. As soon as the ceremonies were finished, we were back in the air and on our way to Laredo. I was still the only passenger.

As I approached the old frame house at 1602 Washington late in the afternoon, I realized it was smaller than the suite in the Shamrock. I could hear my father's power saw going full tilt out in his garage-shop. Instinct must have told my mother I was coming home—she stood in the doorway drying her hands on her apron, not daring to believe it was really me. How much I looked forward to a weekend in that old house! No matter where else I ever went, this would always be home, as long as my parents lived. I wouldn't have traded my weekend there for a dozen in the Houston Shamrock!

The Birthday Present

I tried to keep my mind off it, but the "demotion" from FSO-4 to FSO-5 rankled. I had good prospects for promotion back to FSO-4 when the promotion board next met, but then I would back where I was before and couldn't realistically expect another promotion for several years. It was damned discouraging but even more so when I discovered that except for a hang-up in the handling of my papers by personnel, I would have been above the cut-off line and remained in Class FSO-4 when it was split. But when things seemed darkest, there suddenly came a tiny ray of hope.

There were other discouraged FSOs who had been set back. Several of them banded together and managed to present their case to Loy Henderson, then deputy undersecretary of state for administration—and well on his way to becoming Mr. Foreign Service. Agreeing that the injustice needed correction, he worked out a plan whereby all FSO-5s who had been set back from FSO-4 would, on a one-time-only basis, be eligible for consideration for promotion by the board reviewing Class FSO-5 candidates, and *then* the board considering Class FSO-4 candidates. That made it theoretically possible that an officer set back to Class FSO-5 could be found eligible for promotion to Class FSO-3.

Openly, my attitude toward the whole business was laid-back—who realistically could hope to make the grade for what amounted to a double promotion? But secretly, there was no way I could keep from hoping. In my heart-of-hearts, I hoped and prayed as the months passed and the selection boards deliberated. To make sure I could hide my disappointment if things didn't work out, I did not tell anyone. It always seemed bad form to me for others to know your reach exceeded your grasp.

As Thanksgiving approached, the members of the selection boards finished their work and returned to their regular duties. December came and passed, but no promotion list. Personnel continued in its own way and at its own pace to process the work of the selection boards. The excitement of the New Year dimmed as the cold of January tightened its grip on Washington. It was hard to stave off depression. Nothing good could come at this season of the year. Funny I should feel that way—my birthday falls on January 18th, and this year would be my 37th.

As important as it seemed from the standpoint of correcting an injustice, there were other considerations in hoping to be one of those selected for promotion to FSO-3. Entry into Class FSO-3 marked a threshold for Foreign Service Officers. At FSO-3, I could carry the title of first secretary of embassy when again assigned abroad. In all but the largest of missions, I would be a section chief. In the smallest, I could hope for assignment as deputy chief of mission, the second man on the totem pole.

These were all important considerations, but mostly I wanted this promotion because at Class FSO-3, I would be in a much-enhanced position to go after my next goal, the job and title of Consul General of the United States of America.

Finally, the day came. The telephone started to ring the minute the news was out. A crowd gathered in my office. There was much light-hearted banter.

In the good cheer and warmth of the occasion, we all but forgot it was a work-day. To me, it seemed sort of unreal. There were eight names on the list of those selected for promotion from Class FSO-5 to FSO-3. One of them was mine. What a day Friday, January 18, 1957 turned out to be!

Transfer to Guatemala

The Crockett family took little joy from living in Washington. True, Mary and I were not plagued with social obligations as was always the case in the field. On the other hand, my office hours were longer and my schedule much less flexible than in Tampico. Then, our plans had evolved around the next family outing, a fishing or hunting expedition, or a day at the beach. There was always something exciting to do, and besides having the time, most days we also had the weather.

In Washington, plans evolved around my work, first and foremost. I wanted to be available whenever needed, and this made it hard for us to plan an outing of any kind. We did make the zoo and the museums regularly. The children were into winter sports, but not with the passion of those reared in the cold. We never managed a single day at the beach. True, there was some fishing at certain times of the year, but hunting was too expensive, not to mention it took more time than I had to spare. And then there was the weather. If it wasn't too rainy or too cold, it was almost certain to be too hot. We all longed for a return to life in the tropics.

There was another, more urgent reason for me to want to get back out in the field as quickly as I gracefully could. Despite our frugality—and we had learned to conserve our money—it cost more to maintain the six of us in Washington than I earned. We needed to get back the fringe benefits of assignment abroad without delay. When I figured my reserves would last a scant six months, I thought it best to start looking for a way out.

The Foreign Service encouraged officers to seek assignment to various areas of the world during a normal career. The consequence has at times resulted in an officer going to a job he is not prepared for, in a country he knows next to nothing about, and whose language he neither speaks nor understands. I always suspected that the Old Boys who headed up the Washington bureaus fostered, or at least condoned, the policy out of self-interest. They, too, enjoyed making a career out of world travel and didn't want anything to stand in the way of continuing to do that when it came time for them to go back out in the field.

I didn't agree with this policy for several reasons. I believed that an officer who knew something about the history of a country, who could speak the language with fluency, who understood the historic and current relationships between that country and its neighbors, and who had previous experience in the area, would do a better job than an officer of equal or superior intellectual talents who did not. In other words, I believed—and still do—in specialization for all officers on the way up. When an officer's rank and talents reach the point where they cannot be fully utilized in a single geographic area, it's time to think about generalization.

I figured it best not to declare my conclusion too loudly. When competing for promotion with such an elite group, I would have an edge if I knew more about the area and spoke the language more fluently than the run of the mill. Latin America was obviously my bailiwick and I never made any attempt to work my way into another.

I started looking for an assignment as consul general somewhere in that area. The prospects were not as good as I had hoped. I didn't want the job of consul general at an embassy, where I would be just another flunky for the ambassador and the deputy chief of mission. I wanted my own post. Most independent consulates general were located in Mexico. I couldn't aspire to one of those yet. It was considered bad form for a desk officer to be assigned to the field in the country he had recently been responsible for in Washington. This made sense to me. There were several consulates general in Brazil, but the language there is Portuguese, and the posts were mostly in large metropolitan areas, which I preferred to avoid.

This narrowed the field considerably. In fact, there was one post in all of Latin America that seemed to meet all my requirements—Guayaquil, Ecuador. It was due to come open at a time that meshed with my plans for escape from Washington, and no one else seemed to want it. I went after it.

Things seemed to go smoothly. Dick Rubottom, then Assistant Secretary for Inter-American Affairs, agreed to release me for reassignment to the field. He did say he thought I would be wasting my talents in a consular assignment and was gracious enough to try to talk me into staying in Washington. There seemed to be no problem with personnel, and in due course I was told the assignment could be considered firm enough for me to go ahead with the formality of writing our ambassador in Quito to tell him of my prospective arrival and how pleased I was to have the opportunity to work under his direction, etc. I figured things should allow us to get in a couple of weeks to visit with our folks in Laredo en route, to coincide with the opening of deer season. Great!

I guess I should have figured things were going too smoothly to work out, because they were. Career planning didn't think the assignment was a good one for me and raised an objection. They thought I should have more experience in diplomatic vs. consular work. Although hardly anyone ever paid attention to the career planning people in that day and time, on this occasion their objection was sustained by the assignments board. My transfer to Guayaquil was not approved.

Normally, this would not have presented a problem. The administrative people in the geographic bureaus controlled the money, and while it might involve a minor skirmish with personnel, I had every confidence our people could force the transfer through the assignments board. What I didn't reckon with was that the administrative people in Inter-American Affairs were perfectly happy to have me continue as officer in charge of Mexican Affairs—indefinitely.

Their boss, the assistant secretary, was in no rush to see me go, so why should they bother trying to swing personnel around? After all, I had only been there a year, and they expected to keep people at least two. While they made the right noises when I pressed them to do something, nothing seemed to happen. Meanwhile, time passed, and I could see I was, at the least, going to miss the opening of deer season in Laredo.

At about this time my good friend Bayard King, then serving as officer in charge of Guatemalan Affairs, asked if I would like to have the job of first secretary and chief of the political section in the embassy at Guatemala City. He pointed out that ever since our man, President and Colonel Carlos Castillo Armas, was shot and killed a couple of months back, things had gone from bad to worse in Guatemala, and an assignment there at this time could be interesting, lively and possibly rewarding. He said he could swing it if I wanted—just say the word. I told him thanks, but no thanks. I wanted my own consulate general.

Fall came with a burst of color and delightfully crisp weather. The countryside was beautiful at exactly the time I had planned for us to be on our way to Texas. But here we sat in Washington. I continued to press the administrative people to get after personnel, and they continued to assure me they were doing everything possible to break my assignment loose—yet nothing happened.

Meanwhile, Bayard continued to mention from time to time that the opening in Guatemala was mine for the asking.

The day came when I realized that if we didn't get moving soon, we wouldn't make it home for Christmas. I began to waiver. The clincher arrived in the form of a great ice storm that hit the Washington area in the early winter of 1957. I had trouble getting up the steps to my own front door. That did it! I went to Bayard, hat in hand, to ask if I could still get the job in Guatemala City.

The assignments board acted in record time and my orders were cut and in hand in less than a week. I was released for the transfer with instructions to report for duty in Guatemala City no later than the first working day of 1958. It was all so easy. I knew I'd been had, but what the hell, at least I was getting out of Washington. The consulate general would have to wait.

Stretch of Pan American Highway, northern Guatemala, 1957.

**Volcán de Fuego, Guatemala (Crockett station wagon and
trailer in the foreground), 1958.**

Guatemala
1958

Off the Beaten Path

With the change in transfer plans from Guayaquil to Guatemala City, we decided that instead of going by air as planned, we would drive. Our Ford Station Wagon was still rather new and in good condition, and we had our faithful homemade luggage trailer to transport our always mountainous pile of baggage and paraphernalia. The immediate problem was the weather. Snow and ice storms had made most highways to the west dangerous if not impassable. Things weren't any better toward the southwest, where we needed to go. When I asked Mary what she thought we should do, she said, "Go straight south as fast as we can until we sight our first palm tree. Then we can think about where we go from there." It sounded like a good idea to me.

From Washington to Richmond to Savannah, the land lay frozen in winter's grip. But when we spotted a magnificent row of stately palms in the Savannah suburbs, we knew it was time to head west. Our route took us to Valdosta, Thomasville and Tallahassee. It was here we hit Interstate 10 and warm weather.

Someplace along the highway between Biloxi and Gulfport we came to the spot we had all been longing for ever since we left Tampico—a broad stretch of sand, sparkling white against the deep blue of the Gulf of Mexico, and deserted in late December. In no time at all, the children were in bathing suits and Mary was busy getting sandwich makings ready for lunch, while I mixed a scotch and soda. We didn't make much time on that day and we did suffer from sunburn in December. But there was nothing any of us would rather have had than a day at the beach after the better part of three years and two winters in Washington.

We never seemed to have enough time at home in Laredo. The busy days before Christmas passed quickly and soon it was time to gear up for our trip through Mexico if we were to arrive in Guatemala City, ready for work on Thursday, January 2, the first workday of 1958.

Packing was much more difficult now than it had been in Washington. We left the DC area with more than we could easily haul but now had to somehow accommodate mountains of Christmas gifts and last minute shopping as well. Our trailer was piled high when we had everything loaded and the canvas cover lashed down. Lastly, on top of the whole bundle, I tied the antlers of the white-tail deer I bagged out at Mil Ojos hunting with brother-in-law Dick Campbell. As we pulled up for inspection at the customs station in Nuevo Laredo on the first leg of our trip south, the Mexican official on duty took off his cap and scratched his head in disbelief. I can't say I blamed him.

The interval between Christmas and January 6, the day of the Three Kings, is always festive in Mexico: two weeks of processions, fireworks and tequila. It was a good time to travel—we found men of good cheer everywhere. We drove from Ciudad Victoria to Puebla (I can testify that the loudest fireworks in Mexico were made in Puebla) to Tehuantepec.

By the late 1950s, Mexico had completed a good road from Tehuantepec to the border with Guatemala, but there was no reliable connection for travel on the Guatemalan side. Work was underway to stabilize that segment of the Pan American Highway known as El Tapón (the stopper), but landslides there were dangerously frequent and unbridged river crossings were unpredictable. The alternate route was not inviting either—the last leg in Mexico involved loading your vehicle on a railroad flatcar and travelling a full day thereon to reach the Guatemalan border at Tapachula—but that was the route we chose.

We got an early start and made good time from Zanátepec to Tapanátepec. There, we turned off the main road onto the dirt track leading into Arriaga, where we expected to load the station wagon, the trailer and ourselves onto the train to Tapachula. After asking for directions, I was persuaded to drive on to the village of Tonalá and loaded up there. Not knowing any better, we did.

Tonalá turned out to be merely a wide spot in the road, so it was no trick to find the station master and rent space on a flatcar. For a small extra fee, it was possible to arrange for loading early the next morning instead of the night before.

At the end of December, the dry season was well established and the roads and trails around Tonalá were deep in dust. A steady wind began to build up in the early afternoon and by dusk it blew a lively gale, heavily laden with pulverized limestone. It was too warm to close the windows of the station wagon and too dusty to leave them open. We began looking for a place to overnight. There wasn't much to choose from in Tonalá.

We settled for a large room in what passed locally for a motel on the outskirts of town where there was nothing to break the force of the dust-laden wind. Many of the windows of our room were broken, and we discovered the thin coverlet on each bed was all the bedding we were going to get. At about this juncture one of the girls found that the last tenants, unaware of the marvels of modern-day plumbing, had chosen to use the shower stall instead of looking for an outside privy. We spent a miserable night.

Loading onto the flatcar was simple, but risky. The station master leaned two heavy planks against the end of a flatcar and told me to drive up. When the tires skidded because the grade was too steep, a group of onlookers pitched in and pushed the car and the luggage trailer onto the deck of the flatcar with such gusto we nearly went off the other end.

Once situated, we were blocked, tied down, and ready to go. Although we were told our fare included the right to a wooden bench in the train's passenger car, we decided to stay in the station wagon.

The distance between Tonalá and Tapachula is about 130 miles. We made 54 stops. As I look back on it now I know that can't be possible, even if it is true. Despite our early morning departure from Tonalá, we arrived in Tapachula near midnight.

At each stop, vendors rushed forward carrying baskets laden with whatever the local economy happened to be producing that time of year—mostly foods prepared for immediate consumption. There were bananas, boiled eggs, fried chicken and fish, pastries, mangoes, coconuts (both eating and drinking), many varieties of homemade candy, chalupas and *nacatamales*. Although we had our own food, we couldn't resist trying what was offered locally and found everything exceptionally tasty. Drinking coconut water again after our years away from the tropics was delightful and we all had more than was prudent, given the lack of facilities on our flatcar.

The train's stops were brief and always in the center of each little village we passed through. There were no stations at any of the stops and certainly no restrooms. Things were barely short of critical when the train slowed and came to a gradual halt deep in the jungle. In unison, the male passengers got off one side of the passenger cars and headed for the bushes, while female passengers got off the other side and did likewise. It took us a minute to realize this was a scheduled rest stop—the only one we would have during the entire trip.

We had to rush to take advantage of it, too. In no time at all, the engineer gave a couple of toots on his whistle and started to roll while passengers scrambled back onboard, still arranging their clothing. I don't think we had anything more to drink until we got into our hotel room in Tapachula many hours later.

I spent the last leg of our train trip worrying about how we would manage to get the car and trailer off the train and into a safe place once we reached Tapachula. As things worked out, once the train arrived we were switched onto a rail siding and promptly forgotten. Leaving Jack to keep an eye on things, Mary, the girls and I walked to the local hotel, a lovely old timer built for the tropics. Our rooms were large with high ceilings and wooden louvers covering the windows and opened onto a large central courtyard planted in tropical vegetation and decorated with a splashing fountain in the center.

We located the man who would help us unload the station wagon and trailer, quickly came to terms on the charge, and headed off to the siding to get the job done. Upon our return to the flatcar, though, we discovered an unexpected problem. We had been switched against a boxcar, and behind us stretched what appeared to be an unending string of empty flatcars. My man assured me there was no problem—all I had to do was back off. He would carry his planks and set them up for me to back onto from one flatcar to the next. It was clear he had never tried to back up with a trailer hitched behind on the narrow confines of a row of flatcar beds in the dark of a switching yard in the middle of the might. Neither had I.

On the map, it appeared fairly simple to make the trip from Tapachula to Guatemala City in one day—only 185 miles. How naive we were. No sooner had we gotten all six tires on Guatemalan soil than the first problem arose. There were many trails, but there was no highway—nor were there any markers to set us on the road to Retalhuleu, where we hoped to hit pavement.

We started asking directions. That turned out to be much more complicated than we thought. There were plenty of people around, but getting their attention was no simple matter. They passed us with heads down, indicated they did not speak Spanish, or ignored our calls. The first one we managed to engage and ask what road to take to Guatemala City, answered quite simply: "All roads lead to Guatemala City," and promptly went on his way, head bowed to keep the wide strap across his brow from slipping and the burden on his back from hanging too low.

We decided to go on to the little town of Coatepeque and were soon headed up a steep mountain on a partially cobblestone but mostly dirt track, which we had been assured was *la carretera.* Narrow and steep, the switchbacks were so tight I had to back-and-fill to get the trailer around. On one of the tightest turns, about halfway up the mountain, the trailer bed came down onto one of the tires.

The wheels were buried in dust to the hubcaps, but by nestling my head in the dust, I could see the axle and make out the spring on the bad side, splayed out like the fingers on a hand. We began unloading the trailer onto the side of the mountain, so I could make repairs. A steady stream of locals on foot passed us during this operation, some going up the mountain and some coming down. Not one looked to the right or to the left, or in any way acknowledged our existence. It was a new experience for me after years in Mexico where everyone wants to get into the act, whether you need him or not.

We were no sooner on our way again, when the road split, each track appearing equally well-traveled and no road sign of any sort. A passerby gave a broad sweep of his arm in the general direction of the east when asked about the road to Coatepeque. I pressed him for a more direct answer before he could duck his head and walk away. His response was, "Por carretera o transloma?" (By road or across the mountains?)

On being assured we planned to drive, he suggested the right-hand track would probably be better, and again moved on. "How long from here to Coatepeque?" I insisted. After a minute's contemplation, he responded in all gravity, "Tal vez tres cigarrillos transloma." (Maybe three cigarettes over the mountains.) I was dumfounded, and he escaped before I could ask him to elaborate. How were we to know he meant that traveling over the mountains one would arrive at Coatepeque by the time he had consumed three cigarettes?

It was dusk when we reached the narrow ribbon of pavement stretching from Retalhuleu to Mazatenango, Escuintla and Guatemala City. The exhaustion of our hard trip on dirt and cobblestone roads over rugged terrain dropped away at the prospect of finishing up the trip on good old beautiful black asphalt. Someone started singing *99 Bottles of Beer on the Wall,* and we all joined in.

The full moon outlined the beautiful cones of Guatemala's volcanoes as we turned north toward the glow in the sky over Guatemala City. Our trip was at an end. Tomorrow, we would start a new chapter in our lives. We all looked forward to it.

General Miguel Ydigoras

Although I did not pick the Guatemalan assignment, I could not have chosen a better one for me to get my feet wet in the diplomatic business.

General Jorge Ubico, who took power in Guatemala in 1931, still operated a classic Latin American dictatorship in 1940 when I was majoring in Latin American government at University of Texas. His textbook operation was a subject of special study for my class.

The Ubico dictatorship was ended by the Revolution of October 20, 1944, which brought left-leaning Juan José Arévalo to power. Two years later, I was assigned to Honduras, right next door, then under the rule of Don Tiburcio Carías, another classic Latin American dictator, who had been greatly concerned about Guatemala's swing to the left under Arévalo's rule. We in the embassy at Tegucigalpa had followed developments in Guatemala very closely in order to be able to contend with repeated warnings from the Honduran foreign ministry that the communists were coming to Guatemala and we had better do something about it. We observed, and we reported.

But it was not until Arévalo was succeeded by Colonel Jacobo Arbenz—whose rule became clearly communist infiltrated—that the United States got around to doing something about it. It was then that we backed Colonel Carlos Castillo Armas in his 1954 revolt to overthrow Arbenz. When Castillo Armas triumphed, we strongly supported his presidency in order to make his administration a ringing success (we called it a "showcase of democracy") when measured against the communist leaning government of Arbenz.

Things seemed to go well until mid-1957 when someone shot Castillo Armas. The house of cards collapsed with his death. From that point forward, I had followed day-to-day developments in Guatemala from my front row seat next door to Bayard King, the Guatemalan desk officer in Washington. So, I hit the ground running when I reported for duty at the embassy in Guatemala City on Thursday morning, January 2, 1958. It was a darned good thing, too, because there was plenty of action.

There was no disposition on the part of the US government to walk away from the investment of time, energy and money that had gone toward making a showplace for democracy out of a country that had been selected by international Communism as its prime target in Central America. Every effort was directed at picking up the pieces and moving ahead as best we could. The man we chose as a successor for Castillo Armas was a young Guatemalan colonel named José Luis Cruz Salazar. He had been attached to the Guatemalan embassy in Washington and was known to the people directly involved in supporting Castillo Armas. The fact that he spoke English was, I fear, one of his most attractive attributes. When I arrived on the scene in Guatemala, he was our man and we were backing him both morally and materially to succeed Castillo Armas. This seemed to be his main claim to fame, the young colonel being all but unknown otherwise in his native land.

Aligned against Cruz Salazar was a throwback to the dark, pre-Arévalo past by the name of General Miguel Ydígoras Fuentes, who had been director general of public works during the Ubico dictatorship. Ydígoras Fuentes had been keeping an eye on the Guatemalan presidency for a long time but had been inhibited over the years by a series of events—not the least of which was many years of exile designed to kept keep him from making trouble for those he would have replaced, a standard practice in Latin America. But this time around things were different. We were going to have free, democratic elections and the best president for Guatemala that money could buy. Ydígoras Fuentes was welcome to enter the contest—and he did so with a vengeance.

Although we took the official position that the United States was impartial and could live with whichever anti-communist candidate emerged victorious, we advised and financed Cruz Salazar and missed no opportunity to badmouth Ydígoras Fuentes. The rhetorical question of the day was, "How could anyone expect a man who was formed during the odious Ubico dictatorship to be capable of heading an enlightened democracy?"

We thought that would be a real clincher and played it loud and long. What some of us didn't realize until it was too late (and some never realized at all) was that there were many Guatemalans who didn't give a hoot about the niceties of democracy. What they wanted was the peace and order and stability that had characterized the Ubico dictatorship—regardless of other considerations. In short, they longed for the *mano dura* and saw in Ydígoras a hope for a return to what now looked like the good old days, when measured against the instability that had plagued Guatemala since Ubico's downfall 14 years earlier.

As election day drew near, it was generally agreed that the outcome was too close to call. Our people who were concerned with such matters called meeting after meeting to discuss possible clandestine tactics that might be used to insure victory for our candidate. It was generally conceded that the rural vote would swing the election. In rural Guatemala back then, voters from the various fincas and coffee plantations were hauled to the polls by the truckload and voted as a block. Sometimes, the same truckload went from one polling place to another and voted any number of times. The uncomfortable truck ride between polling places was greatly improved by locally-made firewater, furnished by a given candidate's political hack. Thus, the secret for success was to have more political hacks, trucks and *guaro* than the opposition.

Although it was considered bad form (not to mention, illegal), for any candidate in a democratic election to use government-owned trucks, the government was the sole source of a large number of trucks on short notice. In desperation, it was there that our people in charge of such activities turned their attention on the eve of the election. And since it was all or nothing at this stage of the game, they put everything into the effort. The man they went to was high in the ranks of the provisional government. So was his price. But having come this far, there was no turning back. The deal was struck, and the price was paid.

Election results had not yet started to come in before we knew our man wasn't going to make it. One after another, our people in the field reported that while government trucks had been conspicuously active on election day, they had not been at the disposition of men backing our candidate, but instead by his opponent! As it turned out, our highly-placed collaborator and Ydígoras Fuentes had been friends for many years. Surely, no one expected him to betray his old comrade-in-arms to benefit some young upstart.

Ydígoras Fuentes ended up with a plurality of the votes, but not the majority needed for clear-cut victory. The election was thus thrown into the Guatemalan Chamber of Deputies for resolution. There, we thought, our man would definitely win. Castillo Armas had enjoyed a majority in the Chamber of Deputies, and Cruz Salazar was his heir-apparent. But we didn't count on the resourcefulness of Ydígoras Fuentes or the mood of the people—two rather important miscalculations.

Ydígoras Fuentes organized his people to pressure Chamber members. As we watched those we had counted on began to waver, we tried to stiffen their resolve with the all-powerful US dollar. Despite our best efforts, it became clear that Ydígoras Fuentes would get the votes he needed.

It was at about this point that a man who said his name was Karr appeared with an oversized briefcase stuffed with large-denomination dollar bills. He didn't try to hide that he had come to buy the election—he openly boasted about it. I never found out who Mr. Karr was or who he represented. No matter—as a powerbroker Mr. Karr was a dismal failure. I was glad that I could honestly deny any knowledge about the whole thing.

Word got around that Mr. Karr had been in contact with various influential politicians, but no one blew the whistle on him until he made the mistake of visiting Ydígoras Fuentes. Ydígoras Fuentes promptly went on radio and television to report that the mysterious Mr. Karr had stacked a half-million in cash on the table before his very eyes, and said it was his for the taking if he withdrew from the race for president. The candidate's indignation was palpable. He would not sully his honor nor that of Guatemala for any sum of Yankee dollars. He had ordered Mr. Karr out of his sight, never to return. That was enough to assure his victory when the vote was taken in the Chamber of Deputies. Ydígoras Fuentes was elected president of Guatemala.

Thus passed the initial days of my assignment to Guatemala, and my full immersion into the world of diplomacy as practiced in Central America. It was an interesting and instructive time, if you will forgive the understatement.

As a footnote, I want to emphasize the obvious. I have used the collective "we" and "our" throughout this condensed account in order to avoid any complications over exactly who was responsible for which instance of poor judgment in this episode. The several agencies and individuals involved had diverse ideas about what we should have done at any given time, but none of us had the luxury of making a choice between what looked good and what looked bad. Our choices were inevitably made between undesirable, if not entirely unacceptable, alternatives. That was the nature of diplomacy in those latitudes.

Despite the disaster for US interests that resulted from the election to the presidency of Guatemala of a man we had opposed with every tool available to us, the exercise paid off both for me and for the United States in the long run. The lessons I learned in Guatemala in 1958 were to stand me and my country in good stead when we needed to come up with the right man for the presidency of the Dominican Republic in 1965.

The Market Women

Before my assignment to Guatemala, I held jobs that involved management and administration. Now I found myself in a completely different environment. The chief of the political section is responsible for his own staff of three or four souls. He has no ceremonial or protocol responsibilities except on those infrequent occasions when he may be asked to stand in for the ambassador. His job is limited to observing, understanding, interpreting and reporting political developments. I chafed at this a little at first, but quickly learned that in order to understand and interpret what was going on politically, I had to do a lot more than read the morning newspapers.

Getting acquainted with Guatemalan politicians and political observers was not difficult. The prestige of the first secretary of the US embassy opened nearly every door. And in a country like Guatemala, politics is the lifeblood of the educated community, notably that segment attending college. Back then, these tended to be hyperactive as compared to students in the US.

There was no lack of motivated people with whom to discuss politics—theirs, ours or anyone else's. The problem I ran into was that every one of them had his own ax to grind. I understood that there is no such thing as an unbiased political opinion, but I needed to find a source close to the people that was as unbiased as possible. I found it in the most unexpected place.

Back near the beginning of my Foreign Service career, I learned that one of the best ways to get the feel of a new town in Latin America was to nose around the central market. The central market in Guatemala City was near the embassy, and it was a simple matter to remove jacket and tie and walk over for a quick tour whenever things got unbearable up on the fourth floor where the ambassador, the deputy chief of mission and the chief of the political section had their offices.

The central market in Guatemala City was the most interesting I had ever visited. The variety and quality of produce was outstanding, and the marketplace was cleaner and more orderly than most I had seen. Many market women wore distinctive native costumes, unbelievably colorful in their varied designs.

It was after several strolls through the marketplace and many a tentative approach, that I was able to strike up a conversation with one of the market women. Like many of her counterparts, her face was dark brown and deeply seamed. But also, like many others, her black eyes were bright and alert. Her curiosity had been aroused.

"For whom do you search, señor?" she asked.

"And why do you think I search for someone?" I replied.

"Because, señor, you come often but you buy nothing. If you were searching for something, you would have found it long before now." Thus started an association that was to prove quite rewarding for the remainder of my tour in Guatemala.

My circle of acquaintances among Guatemala City's market women never numbered more than a dozen. But there were hundreds of them, and they were well-organized. They were exceptionally well-informed about what was going on in the country and they were genuinely anti-communist. The reasons for this were multiple: they were indigenous, and they were catholic, but above all, they'd had a taste of communism under Jacobo Arbenz and that was more than they wanted ever again. They suited my needs.

My talks with the market women served me well in many ways besides providing insight on how the masses viewed any given political development. As they came to know me and have some confidence in me, they became an unusually reliable source of intelligence. When heavy bombs blew out the main entrances to the embassy and the archbishop's palace within the space of a few minutes, it was the market women who pointed the finger at President Ydígoras' people, rather than the communists. They understood that the "Ydígoristas" wanted both the Church and the US embassy to take the communist threat more seriously than it really was. They were also in a position to pick up the whispered accounts that passed from mouth to mouth about who actually drove the car and who made the hit. We had suspected as much, if for no other reason than because the first man on the scene after those blasts in the middle of the night—all decked out in fatigues with machine gun in hand—was none other than the president: General Miguel Ydígoras.

There were other occasions when the market women were most helpful. When President Eisenhower decided to send his brother, Dr. Milton Eisenhower, on a fact-finding and goodwill tour of Latin America, relations between the United States and the Ydígoras government were so strained that someone in the embassy remarked we were going to have a goodwill visit even if we had to shoot our way in. The market women's organization was willing to go out and get people interested in cheering and waving US flags along the route of Dr. Eisenhower's entry into Guatemala City. It was they who shoved and pushed the anti-American agitators, helping to drown out the taunts and insults from the sidelines.

At one point during my tour in Guatemala City, crowds of anti-American demonstrators gathered before the embassy for several days, blocking access to the building and generally disrupting operations. When the local authorities protested that they could not control the troublemakers, the market women launched counter demonstrations that quickly brought the entire exercise to a halt. All in all, the ladies in their colorful costumes came to be a source of special satisfaction for me.

Before I moved on to my next assignment, I was able to get an invitation for a representative group of four or five leaders of the market women's association to tour the United States as guests of the US government, despite the protests of the Cultural Affairs people that they didn't wear shoes. The State Department escort officer who shepherded them across our country reported that they made a tremendous impression wherever they went, comporting themselves with quiet dignity and accepting the attention heaped upon them with graceful courtesy.

The Junket

It doesn't take long for the newcomer in the Foreign Service to get acquainted with congressional junketeers. They go everywhere, any time, and it takes a heck of a lot of preparation to get ready for one of their visits, no matter how briefly the distinguished congressperson may decide to stick around or how little interest they may have in the program prepared for them. Usually, they have their own fish to fry or worse, their own ax to grind.

Sometimes an officer of the Foreign Service is designated to go along as an escort to make sure things go the way the legislator wants them to. I always envied those guys—they had it as good as the elected officials! At least that's what I thought until my turn rolled around.

The call from the very senior official in Washington came as a surprise. After all, high ranking government officials don't ordinarily call secretaries of the embassy—they call the ambassador. I was all aflutter and said any number of inane things before I finally shut up and listened.

It developed that a senior senator from the South had decided to make an overland trip through Central America—no minor undertaking in the 1950s. Given the senator's well-earned reputation as a difficult person, the very senior official in Washington had selected me to go along. It was emphasized that all concerned were anxious that the senator from the South should come through the exercise pleased as punch. It was a tall order, given his renowned ill temper.

Then, as an afterthought, he closed the conversation with, "Of course, since you will be the control officer for the senior senator's visit to Guatemala and, since he likes to see how the staff lives, he will plan on staying at your house. Details will be confirmed by telegram."

I wondered why I wasn't quick enough on my feet to point out that Mary was eight months pregnant and we already had four children under the same roof, but I wasn't.

Being the control officer for a senior senator's visit entails a lot of responsibility. Senior senators are inevitably chairmen of important committees—such as those dealing with State Department appropriations and other sensitive matters. It is incumbent on control officers to see that their visits come off smoothly—no matter what the hell kind of machinations may be required. I put all I had into it.

First, Mary crammed the two older children into the same bedroom with the two younger children. Then we moved into the bedroom of the two older children, thus freeing our own bedroom for the senior senator. It wasn't that much trouble, really. At the same time, I put a lot of effort—and more than a little ingenuity—into finding out what the senior senator liked to eat, at what time, and under what circumstances. Together, Mary and I searched out ingredients and begged, bought, or borrowed them from whatever source we were fortunate enough to locate. It was no trouble at all, really.

Meanwhile, endless meetings were held in the embassy to program the senior senator's time during the three days he had allotted to find out all there was to know about Guatemala and see the country's major points of interest. This took some doing, but we did it with enough time left over for the senator to get in a few hours' sleep each night. I can't say this was no trouble—it was a pain in the neck—not because the major sections of the US government operation in Guatemala competed for the senator's time, but because they vigorously sought to avoid him. The senator's reputation was widely known and understood.

Thus, on the eve of the senator's arrival, we stood poised and ready for whatever might come. I felt rather proud of myself. The schedule was tight enough to keep the senator fully occupied during his waking hours and hopefully, too busy to make trouble. After all, he was pushing 70 and what I had lined up for him would tax the energy of a man half his age. Little did I know!

I got my first look at the senator late in the afternoon. The two Bureau of Public Roads (BPR) officials who drove him down from the Mexican border arrived completely done in. For his part, the senator seemed lively as a cricket. His face was seamed but his frame was lean, his belly flat—and he exuded energy. I started doubting the adequacy of the program I had designed to keep him too busy to give us any trouble while he was in Guatemala.

Although it was well past 11:00 p.m. before we made it home from that evening's social engagement, the senator was up, dressed, having his orange juice and going over the schedule by 7:00 a.m. the next day.

At the chancery I led off the morning briefing with an overview of the situation in Guatemala, the problems we faced in attaining US objectives there, and the programs we had in place to that end. I then took my seat beside the senator and relaxed. From here on in it was up to the others. I was rather pleased for having arranged to get off the hook early in the day. But I noticed the senator kept glancing my way as the others took their turns at the podium. Finally, he leaned over and asked, "Aren't you going to take any notes?" I promptly scrounged a piece of paper and a pencil, and diligently scribbled throughout the remainder of the morning. When the senator asked a question—and he asked many—he would turn to me and say, "Did you get that?" making it clear he wanted his inquiry and the response to become a matter of record. I had no doubt who he expected would keep the record.

We were behind schedule before the midday break and had to cut short a delightful luncheon to pick up with the senator's plans. The afternoon involved visits to various endeavors sponsored by one US government agency or another near Guatemala City. Along the way to the first of these, the senator opened a large case containing equipment for 16 mm movies and instructed me how and when to use each piece as I made a documentary of his travels around the country.

I was to be the photographer for his documentary—and the senator would star in and direct it! He fastidiously instructed me to "Stand here and don't pan," or "Take this one from ground level, the angle will be better." I was exhausted by the time we got through the heavy schedule I had programmed for the afternoon to keep the senator from making trouble.

What a relief to get home and under a steaming shower for a few seconds. We barely had time to dress and make it to the cocktail party I had arranged for the senator to meet the clerical staff. I was ready to drop in my tracks before both hands of the clock on the mantle pointed straight up and the senator was ready to call it a night.

As we said goodnight, he added, "I think it might be a good idea to go over your notes first thing in the morning. Unless we keep up with things on a day-to-day basis, we're going to get behind!" A surge of rebellion welled up from deep inside me, but I was too exhausted to give it birth. Somehow, I managed to type up two dozen pages of notes before our breakfast meeting.

No one could say the senator wasn't kind and considerate. As he read through my notes, he kept looking up at me with an expression of mild concern. Finally, he smiled faintly and asked, "Didn't you sleep well last night? You seem tired this morning."

With no briefings on the second day, there were fewer notes to be taken. My main duties were to see that we kept up with our schedule and my obligations as cameraman for the senator's production. In that effort he continued to be helpful. His two favorite words were, "Don't pan!" I heard them a thousand times during the next two weeks, despite my best efforts to do my panning when the senator was looking the other way.

A single thought kept me going during the remainder of the senator's stay in Guatemala: Once we hit the road, things would be easier. I would no longer be both control officer and escort officer. Each post along the way would furnish its own control officer who would see to all local arrangements. Then, too, there would be long intervals of simply riding along, dozing. I could rest in between capital cities. As it turned out, and as usual, I underestimated the senator.

We got off early for our drive from Guatemala City to San Salvador. November was the best time of the year to travel in Central America—the rains were all but over, the countryside was lush and the weather temperate. That day of travel was to be informal with a box lunch somewhere along the Río Los Esclavos. The senator's dress was appropriately informal. That is, he took off his suit jacket but kept his collar buttoned and his tie in place.

My hope of getting in a catnap or two proved unrealistic. The senator was interested in everything and there was no end to the questions he could think of. I wasn't supposed to say, "I don't know," so I answered whether I knew or not. I didn't always get by with this tactic, though—the senator was an expert at ferreting out inaccuracies.

We had hardly cleared Guatemala City when we came to a rural school where children played in the schoolyard. He insisted we stop and climb through the barbed wire fence to interview the students, and the teachers. I filmed and translated as we went along. At last, we climbed back through the barbed wire fence and drove on.

We soon stopped again and climbed through another barbed wire fence to interview a man plowing a field with a team of oxen and a crooked tree branch. It went like that all the way from Guatemala City to San Salvador.

After Guatemala, El Salvador seemed easy. We heard briefings in the morning and toured in the afternoon. There was the inevitable evening reception lasting well past 11:00 p.m. When that had come to an end and the senator had gone to bed I was able to write up notes from the morning's briefing, so that he could go over them before we started on the next day's round of events. The pattern was set, and we stuck close to it for the remainder of the trip through Honduras, Nicaragua, Costa Rica and Panama.

The pace may have been hectic, but the experience was a once-in-a-lifetime opportunity to see a great deal of Central America in a fairly short period. The senator wanted to cover every inch of ground he could.

From San Salvador we drove to Tegucigalpa, Honduras, and when our business there was finished, we drove south toward Managua, Nicaragua. At each border crossing we were met by the next embassy control officer, and after he cleared the way through customs for us, I found an opportunity to give him the word on what the senator liked and disliked.

In Nicaragua, arrangements had been made to meet the ambassador at his residence outside of Managua. The senator had been looking forward to this for days. The State Department's office of foreign buildings had constructed the embassy residence back in the 1930s, and they had pulled out all the stops. The grounds encompassed more than 50 acres, and the ambassador's residence encompassed some 42,000 square feet on three floors—not to mention another most adequate residence on the same property for the deputy chief of mission.

In between the two homes were a large swimming pool and bathhouse. Then there was the caretaker's house, the gatehouse, the greenhouse, and so forth. The property was notoriously out of proportion to the importance of Nicaragua and the fulfilment of our objectives there. The senator intended to raise a number of questions about it all. In fact, he could hardly wait.

Our ambassador to Nicaragua was a political appointee named Thomas E. Whelan. In the career Foreign Service, people tended to brush him off as a country bumpkin who had bought his appointment with contributions to the Republican Party, by no means a new or novel route to an ambassadorship. He took pride in identifying himself as a potato farmer from North Dakota.

I could see the senator, a partisan Democrat, licking his lips in anticipation of meeting Ambassador Whelan. He would eat this Republican country bumpkin alive, taking the first warm-up bites with a rant on the scandalous cost of maintaining a residence like this in a country where many people didn't have enough to eat. The deeper bites would come when he demanded to know why someone hadn't gotten rid of the place long since.

But Ambassador Whelan was way ahead of him. He bounded forward to grasp the senator's hand in both of his and pump it up and down until I felt sure it would come loose at the shoulder before he stopped.

"Senator," the ambassador said, "Am I glad to see you! I've been hoping to talk to someone in a position of influence about getting rid of this monstrosity where the missus and I have to live. It's a shame and a disgrace for the United States to flaunt a place like this in poor little Nicaragua. It's absolutely inappropriate to our needs here. Why, you wouldn't believe. . ." The ambassador was fully prepared to go on for hours.

The senator's jaw slackened. His mouth all but came open. A pained expression spread across his face. He knew he'd been had, and there wasn't a thing he could do about it. Tom Whalen may have been a simple potato farmer from North Dakota, but he didn't just fall off the turnip truck. He had disarmed the senator before the battle was joined. I tucked this beautiful little ploy away for future use, should an occasion arise. Little did I dream I would one day use it in the exact same setting!

When we came downstairs to join the ambassador and his wife for breakfast the next morning, Mrs. Whelan so thoroughly charmed the senator, he didn't even look at his morning notes. And as the time came for us to go on to other things, Mrs. Whelan turned to the ambassador, said, "Tom, you take care of the senator today. I'm sure he won't mind if I keep Kennedy here, will you, senator?" She suffused him in one of her radiant smiles. The senator was dumfounded, but what could he say?

As they left the room, Mrs. Whelan turned to me. "Why don't you go up and put on a bathing suit so we can get some sun by the pool. You look like you need a day off!" I could have kissed her.

When the senator was ready to move on, we drove south from Managua to Diriamba, then Rivas, just north of the Costa Rican border. We stopped for our brown-bag lunch at a BPR camp called La Virgen on the shores of Cocibolca (Lake Nicaragua), across the water from the island of Ometepe. Concepción, the higher of the two volcanoes that dominate the island, had been putting on a show for months. At precise three-minute intervals, it spewed a double column of ash and smoke from its steaming maw in two explosions, one immediately after the other. It was spectacular. We were so engrossed with Concepción that I paid little attention to Lake Cocibolca, nor did I give much thought to the sharks and sawfish that inhabited its fresh waters many miles from the ocean. Fifteen years later, I would water my horse at that same spot on my way home from the ranch.

Once we hit Costa Rica, the drive became unpleasantly rough. It seemed there was some sort of message to be gleaned from the best highways in Central America being in Nicaragua, the most notorious dictatorship, while the worst were in Costa Rica, which boasted a model democracy. After a few miles, we gave up in favor of flying to San José in a United Fruit Company Cessna 310 that was standing by. Our landing at La Sabana International Airport on the west end of San Jose was uneventful, despite the unpaved runway.

The next day we again went through the familiar routine: long, drawn-out, boring briefings, visits to pet projects, coffee fincas, concrete block factories, and more. And, of course, the making of the documentary as we went along.

I was relieved to load our gear onto the same Cessna 310 and lift off La Sabana for the flight to Palmar Sur. As we leveled out and headed south, the pilot asked the senator if he had any instructions. The senator said he had come to Central America to inspect the Pan American Highway and he wasn't going to see much way up here on top of the clouds. Our pilot grinned and started looking for a hole in the thunderheads. I knew what he was thinking: "I'll give these greenhorns a trip to remember—as soon as I can find a place to get underneath." Greenhorn I may have been in many ways, but I had been flying in

Central American weather for more than 10 years and I knew what was coming. I wasn't nervous—I was scared.

Finding no hole, he plunged into the clouds. I protested but he assured me he knew exactly where we were going to come out. I braced for the crash. We broke out of the murkiness at about 500 ft., within sight of Cartago. I breathed again. The pilot found the goat trail that passed for the Pan American Highway in Costa Rica running south through the mountains. He flew 200-300 feet above it while the senator peered out his window on the copilot's side and I cowered in the rear. The clouds above us extended in a solid mass from the mountains on our right to the mountains on our left. There was no margin for error. Despite the cool air, I was sweating bullets in near panic. The senator was clearly enjoying himself.

Somehow, we made it over the mountains and past San Isidro de El General. I had almost stopped trembling by the time we landed at Palmar Sur. I could have throttled the pilot once we were on the ground, but unfortunately, our schedule called for us to fly with him again further down the road.

From Palmar Sur, we took the United Fruit Company's narrow-gauge railroad to Golfo Dulce on the Pacific. We traveled in an open motorcar nearly identical to the one I used on the north coast of Honduras more than 10 years earlier. We stopped along the route whenever the senator wanted to look at something, and there was much to see. The rail line connected the plantations with the port of Golfito, and much of the time we traveled through Costa Rica's principal banana-growing region. But the highlight of the trip was examining several of the massive stone spheres carved and rolled into the area during some prehistoric period—how, by whom, and for what purpose, no one knows. There were hundreds, possibly thousands, in varying sizes—some weighing tons and measuring six feet or more in diameter—all perfectly spherical, hewn out of rock not to be found anywhere near their current location.

When the time came to leave Golfito, we again boarded the Cessna 310, but much to my relief, we had a new pilot. On our way to Panama, we had a good view of the route the Pan American Highway would someday take, although it wouldn't be finished for many years to come. Our BPR engineer told us the area often had over 300 inches of rainfall a year, and sometimes there were barely six weeks in the year when it was dry enough to work the heavy dirt-moving equipment.

At Davíd, we left the Cessna and got back into ground transportation for the final leg of the trip into Panama City. It was then that I first caught a glimpse of the light at the end of the tunnel. Boy, did it look good! I lived through the next couple of days in a fog—too tired to know exactly what was going on but too near the end to give up. Finally, the last day was behind me. Tomorrow morning the senator and I would say goodbye. I sat at my typewriter trying to put into words what it was he might want to remember for the record of that day's activities.

The knock on my door at that late hour startled me. Finding the senator standing there brought me wide awake. I asked him to come in and join me for a drink. He took a seat but declined the drink.

"Crockett," he said, "I know you haven't planned to go on with me, but I've gotten used to working with you and I sure would like it if you could finish out the trip with me. What do you say? I'll call Washington in the morning and set it up."

For a moment I was tempted. I had sort of come to like the old buzzard—or at least admire him. But the thought of Mary alone at home, with less than two weeks left before the baby was due. . . I told the senator I couldn't do it. He understood, and we shook hands with real warmth, for the first time.

Back in my office on the fourth floor of the embassy in downtown Guatemala, I wondered how much of a report I should try to write up for the very senior official in Washington. After the hundreds of pages I had written for the senator, I had little interest in extensive narrations.

The senator's stamp of approval for our services came at Christmastime that year, and for a good many years after that, in the form of a box of excellent pralines—made in his own kitchen.

The Nightmare

It had been the same every night for months, now. The nightmare started with a view of the ocean in agony—the waves fierce and frothy as conflicting currents fought for dominance where the great swells rolled in from the open Pacific. It was a scene of wild, white water, a riptide of the most vicious sort. Next, I could see the boy, struggling to regain his footing as the undertow pulled him deeper and deeper into the ocean's grasp. His arms waved crazily above his head and he shouted some unintelligible plea. I struggled mightily with the crosscurrents, but my efforts were not enough—the gap between us widened. I could see the look of stark terror on the boy's face as the waves closed over his head. My state of panic peaked—I was not going to be able to save him.

It was at that point that I sat bolt upright and came wide awake, gasping for breath, drenched with sweat, cold horror cramping my belly into a great knot. In time the panic would subside, but every night the nightmare took its toll—and sometimes more than once!

It had been Jim Compton's idea that we all go together to Barra Ahumado. He was the warrant officer in the Army attaché's office in Guatemala City. He loved Ahumado and never missed a chance to camp in the coconut grove on the beach where the Chiquimulilla Canal empties into the ocean. I suppose it had been a mistake for us to go along. Mary's fifth pregnancy was well advanced, and at 38 it could have been risky. Still, we had never let pregnancies (or infant offspring) interfere with our regular country outings. Then too, I was eager for Mary and the children to know Ahumado, they were eager to make the trip and finally, it would likely be a long time before there was again a coincidence of a four-day weekend and a quiet spell at the embassy. We decided not to let the opportunity pass.

In addition to Jim Compton, his wife Caroline, and daughter Patsy, there was the Crockett tribe and son Jack's friend, John Berry, Jr., the Army attaché's son. It took three station wagons and two trailers to get all of us, Jim's boat and our mountain of camping gear down to Iztapa at the end of the highway from Guatemala City to the Pacific Ocean. That part of the trip was simple enough, but the remaining 25 miles to Barra Ahumado had to be traveled by water over the winding course of the Chiquimulilla Canal—an adventure we all looked forward to!

We launched Jim's runabout and loaded it with as much of our gear as it could accommodate, in addition to Jim and Caroline. The rest would have to go on the 40-ft. cayuco I had rented for the trip. It was a sturdy craft, six feet wide, with lots of freeboard, hewn from a single log floated down to the coast from the great forest at the foot of the Cordillera Central. We were an excited bunch by the time everything was loaded, and we cast off.

The Chiquimulilla Canal isn't really a canal, but a winding, narrow, brackish lagoon that parallels the southern coast of Guatemala for over 100 miles from Sipacate to Las Lisas against the border with El Salvador. It is a beautiful, natural waterway, fed by the many streams that tumble down to the Pacific from the Cordillera Central. From time to time, the combined waters of these rivers force an opening, or *barra* into the Pacific. The one near Iztapa was a favorite of ours for fishing and swimming, but so conveniently located that it was sometimes crowded and, always one of those taken for granted places you can visit any time. Barra Ahumado, on the other hand, was far from any overland access, and remote enough to be pleasantly isolated except for the most adventurous.

The cayuco proved to be a worthy craft for our purposes. Designed to haul rice, beans and other produce in from the outback, it was spacious, sturdy, and steady. The greater part of its length was covered by a roof or top, strong enough to hold all the children at once, and it was here that they traveled, high enough to have the best view as we plowed our way through the jungle toward Ahumado. My old Mercury sixteen outboard motor kept us moving at a satisfactory clip. We had sandwiches for lunch as we cruised along, and all too soon to suit any of us, we rounded the last bend and pulled into the shore at the coconut grove on the narrow strip of sand separating the Chiquimulilla Canal from the ocean. Here we would make our camp.

The kids were all for suiting up and heading for the beach right away, but we insisted they hold off until we could set up camp and have everything ready for the night. There were jungle hammocks to be hung between the coconut trees, and tarps to be spread over our dining area. Wood had to be gathered for the evening fire and our food boxes had to be slung from overhanging branches to be safe from land crabs. A latrine had to be dug back in the undergrowth and we needed a good-sized pit for burying our trash, so our campsite would be as clean when we left as it was when we came. There were other chores and the kids became increasingly impatient before we were ready to set off across the sand dunes for a late afternoon at the beach.

Before starting out, we gathered the children and laid down the ground rules for safety. The ocean here was often rough and the bottom shelved off rapidly. Also, there were uncertain current conditions caused by the Chiquimulilla Canal emptying into the Pacific. The children were warned that under no circumstances was anyone to get into the water before we had all gotten down to the beach.

With that, they strung out ahead of the adults, Jack and John Berry, Jr. leading the way, each with a large black inner tube under his arm. As the boys crested the dune separating us from the beach, I felt the first twinge of apprehension. Somehow, I knew they weren't going to wait for us before going in. I hurried to catch up, shouting into the ocean breeze for them to wait up. If they heard me, they gave no sign.

I was already breathing heavily by the time I managed to plow my way through the loose sand on the uphill side of the dune and gain the crest. The boys were at the shoreline, racing ahead to see who would be the first in the water. I screamed for them to wait as I ran after them, vaguely aware that Jim was not far behind me. I might as well have saved my breath.

The boys plunged into the rough surf, delighting in the cool water after the sweaty job of setting up camp. I could hear their laughter as a wave broke over them. Finally, I gained the water's edge and managed to make myself heard. Jack and John looked at each other in the realization they had failed to heed our warnings and clear instructions. Dejectedly, Jack turned toward shore, trailing his inner tube behind him, but John had already flung his inner tube toward the shore and dived into a wave that rose up to break over his head. He did not come up.

Grabbing Jack's inner tube as I raced past him, I plunged into the heavy surf toward the spot where I had last seen the boy. Jim Compton followed close behind. I knew Jim's strength was limited—he only had one lung—but I needed his eyes. Without my glasses, I couldn't distinguish anything more than a few feet away.

The boy popped to the surface not far beyond the breakers as Jim and I reached water deep enough to require that we swim. We could see John struggling to get out of the grip of the undertow, but he wasn't scared. He still hadn't realized how much danger he was in. Neither had I!

John was a fair swimmer for a boy of eleven, but this water was too much for him to do more than keep his head above the surface. The chop seemed to go in every direction, slapping him first in the face and then on the back of the head. The current was unbelievably strong. Jim and I would manage to maneuver our inner tube within a few feet of the boy, and inevitably the gap between us would widen as the cross-currents pulled him one way and us another. At the same time, we all drifted further and further from shore.

There was terror on the boy's face now, and there was terror in my heart. It was clear we were not going to get to him with the inner tube, and there was no point in trying to get to him without it. That would have been the end for all three of us.

A great wave crested above us, and when Jim and I managed to surface behind it, the boy was gone. The sensation that swept over me as I tried to spot him in the choppy foam was one of unbelievable horror. A few seconds before he had been there so close, and no matter how desperate our situation, there was still hope. Now, he was gone—there was no hope. I felt an urge to loosen my grip on the inner tube and let my own weary body slip below the surface. And well I might have, I was so spent, except that it was then Jim looked at me with desperation in his eyes and gasped, "Kennedy, I'm not going to make it." There was an immediate surge of energy from some hidden reserve I never knew I had. The boy was gone, but I wasn't going to lose my friend too.

There was no way for me to measure how long we had struggled to reach John Berry, Jr., much less how long it took for Jim and me to make it back through the riptides and the surf to shore. It wasn't easy. Jim was so fatigued that at times I had to hold him against me to keep him from sliding under while he got a new grip on the inner tube. We would gain a few feet toward the safety of shallow water then lose it all at the whim of an errant current. How could we fight against it? We hadn't been able to win over the currents when we were fresh and strong. Still, the instinct for survival is fierce, and somehow the time came when my feet touched bottom. The surge of a wave pushed us a little closer to shore and all at once we were walking.

Again, I seemed to be drained of strength when we reached the shallows and the children were able to wade in and help us out of the water. They were frantic, and insistent that somehow, we had to save John Berry, Jr. They hadn't given up at all. Their confidence that there was still something we could do gave me a new boost from that unknown inner source. I told them to get on the high ground along the crest of the dunes where they could better see out over the water, while I searched from along the shallows. If they were able to spot the boy, they could tell me where to look.

Horror welled up inside me again as we worked our way westward, the direction of the current. What if we couldn't find his body? What would I say to his father? Worse yet, what would I say to his mother? And how the hell could I explain my failure to myself? I should have been able to save him. I hadn't gone about it right. If I had, we wouldn't be in this unbearable situation. God have mercy!

Even in my exhausted daze and overpowering anguish, I could detect the excitement in the girls' voices as they shouted something unintelligible from the top of the sand dune. I couldn't see them well through the haze of myopia, but I could make out the outstretched arms, pointing out to sea. I lunged into the churning surf, ready for the steep shelving so common along this shore. But the water remained shallow—there was some sort of sandbar here where the riptides from the mouth of the Chiquimulilla Canal slowed and formed an eddy. Instead of getting deeper, the water became shallower, hardly up to my waist. It was then that I saw the flash of white skin against the green water. With the strength of a madman, I raised the boy in my arms and struggled for the shore. He felt limp and cold—utterly lifeless. Why did relief flood through me? To recover the boy's body was, after all, a hollow victory.

My uneasy relief turned to welling joy as I put the boy down on the sand and he twitched. Thank God—he was alive!

John Berry, Jr. was a pretty sick boy that night, retching saltwater, trembling uncontrollably, unable to speak—but he was no sicker than the rest of us. The ordeal had drained us all. The children finally fell asleep in their jungle hammocks, but the adults didn't even try. When the first glow of approaching dawn lightened the eastern horizon, we switched from Scotch to coffee. When there was good light, we started repacking our gear and loading the boats.

We were back home in Guatemala City before lunchtime, physically and mentally exhausted, but immensely relieved to deliver John Berry, Jr. back to his parents, safe and sound.

Terremoto

Life in Guatemala in the late fifties was extremely pleasant. We never felt unsafe roaming around the country. Since this had always been the rule for us, we saw nothing exceptional in it. Little did we realize the peaceful circumstances we enjoyed would someday come to an end—and may never again be duplicated in Central America.

Our house in Zone Nine was spanking new and, thanks to the magnificent climate, the yard was a virtual garden of Eden. Lush green grass provided a perfect background for a profusion of flowering plants and shrubs of an endless variety of colors. An unusual feature made the house especially attractive. There was a lovely sunroom on the second floor, with spectacular views. Here Mary and I had our coffee each morning. When the weather was good, which is often in Guatemala City during the early morning, we moved out to the open veranda around to the sunroom. It's no wonder our days in Guatemala City were so pleasant when they began with a quiet hour soaking in the ever-changing panorama of green and blue mountains encircling that enchanted valley.

My friend Walt Spangler, who headed up Standard Oil's geological team exploring the Petén Territory, found us a delightful place to rent on the shore of Lake Amatitlán, some 25 miles from our house in town. It boasted a large, landscaped lot, a double boathouse and a swimming pier. In addition to family outings, we used the place for informal entertaining when we wanted something relaxed.

It wasn't long before both the Spanglers and the Crocketts had ski boats there ready for use at a moment's notice. Ours, which we named the *Blue Goose,* was designed to serve multiple purposes. The 17-foot mahogany lapstrake hull was built in British Honduras, both because there were quality boatbuilders and quality mahogany readily available. We flew the bare hull to Guatemala City on a freight plane and hired a local carpenter to fill in the blanks.

When completed, the *Blue Goose* had seats running lengthwise on each side for over six feet, which could be used for bunks. The open cockpit aft was spacious enough for a couple of comfortable canvas chairs for trolling, while the midsection, behind the front deck, was roofed with an open cabin strong enough for the children to ride topside. Our 35-horsepower Evinrude was big for that day and time. The *Blue Goose* was a great family boat, but it was also a means of inconspicuously visiting leaders of the political opposition who owned or were guests at lakeside villas.

Our favorite place away from Lake Amatitlán was Iztapa on the Chiquimulilla Canal. A Guatemalan friend made his beach house available and we went as often as we could, hauling *Blue Goose* behind one of our Ford station wagons. There were other places to launch along the Pacific, including the lovely esteros at Sipicate and Santa Marta del Mar, to the west of San José. Once, son Jack and I hauled the *Blue Goose* north to Puerto Barrios on the Caribbean and camped over a long weekend among the cays in the Bahía de Amatique. The *Blue Goose* earned her keep.

Water sports didn't occupy all our recreational time. We took in many of the major indigenous markets and visited most of the places where ruins of colonial construction were still found, mainly Antigua, which to me remains one of the most fascinating places I have ever been. The thrill of Chichicastenango's indigenous culture was hardly less.

Some tend to think of Guatemala as a place of lush green mountain highlands or lush green jungle lowlands. But there is another Guatemala—the northeastern province of Zacapa, on the Honduran border, where the climate is arid, and desert plants and cactus abound. Here, Mary and I were reminded of home—cactus, rattlesnakes and mourning doves—and we visited as often as we could during hunting season. We spent many hot afternoons pass shooting there, and when we could stand the heat no longer, the Río Motagua provided many excellent places for a cool swim and plenty of clear running water to prepare our game.

Thanks to Walt Spangler, I had the opportunity to visit Tikal, the major Mayan ruin in the Petén Territory. What an adventure to explore those towering structures, most still covered with jungle growth. How impressive had been the civilization that thrived there. It was impossible to leave unawed, or to suppress a yearning to return someday to walk the avenues where Mayan God Princes had strolled with their retinues, over a thousand years before.

There are many reasons to remember Guatemala, but the most salient was the birth of our fifth child, a girl, at the end of November in 1958. Almost immediately a series of earth tremors began that was to continue for days.

The tremors increased in intensity until there came a full-fledged earthquake on the day we brought Mary and the baby home from the hospital. It was strong enough to evacuate us from the house, and we spent several hours out in the center of the lawn, baby basket and all, until we felt the danger of another temblor had passed. No sooner had everything been hauled back inside and upstairs than along came a stronger earthquake, opening a crack along our stone staircase with a bang loud enough to be mistaken for a cannon shot. Rumbling and shaking persisted long after Mary, the baby and all the related paraphernalia had again been carted downstairs and out into the middle of the front yard. Mary was never one to take an adamant stand if she could avoid it—unless, that is, her children were involved.

Having had to evacuate the house twice was every bit enough for her. She announced that she would stay out in the yard until the earthquakes were over—and she did. We set up a tent, got out bedrolls and built a campfire. The cook prepared meals in her kitchen and we ate them on our folding table out in the yard. It was kind of a lark for us, and the baby didn't mind at all. In fact, it seemed to me that she tended to smile each time there was a rumble from down deep in the earth, followed by a good shaking of her basket.

The little girl was given the name Teresa Alice, but her nickname from the beginning was *Terremoto*. In many ways, as she grew over the years, she lived up to it.

Cookie Pushers

The sun was not yet three hours old, but the coarse black volcanic sand common to much of Central America's Pacific coast was already uncomfortably hot on my bare feet. I dug them a little deeper below the surface where it was moist and cool as I scanned the horizon for the hundredth time. The flight was slowing down and I knew the morning's shooting was about over. What a shame!

The month was November, and our location was Iztapa, east of Guatemala's principal Pacific port, San José. Our birds were in migratory flight to wintering spots in Central and South America. There seemed about as many mourning doves as white wing doves, with a few blue rock pigeons thrown in for good measure. They flew down the coast in flocks numbering from 50 to several hundred, and for two or three hours each morning and evening the flight was nearly continuous. During the past two days, we had seen tens of thousands of birds go by.

Since the children had been left at home for once, Mary and I decided it would be fun to camp in the *Blue Goose*. All our gear was packed aboard when we launched into the Chiquimulilla Canal to make the run from the highway down to where the estuary empties into the Pacific at Iztapa. The spot was one we knew well. We had often thought of making an overnight mooring there to take advantage of the early morning fishing at the bar. To the east of the bar the narrow strand separating the Chiquimulilla from the open sea was bare of vegetation, and thus the immediate area was relatively free of the lively insect population of tropical Guatemala, which is at its peak in November, the end of the rainy season.

Before launching, we had stopped on the highway east of San José to pick off enough birds for supper from the afternoon flight along the cleared pastureland paralleling the coastline. The flight had been good, and we had a mess of birds within a half-hour. I specialized in mourning doves because they are better eating. Mary reached for the white wings because they are bigger, and she had an odd theory this made them easier to hit.

As we cleaned the birds, lying at anchor near the mouth of the Chiquimulilla, we congratulated ourselves on having picked a perfect time for our trip. The incoming tide would be reaching its peak during the early morning hours, making for ideal fishing conditions. We could run up the canal in the *Blue Goose* to within walking distance of a point where we could shoot the afternoon flight. Our only concern was that between fishing in the morning and shooting in the afternoon, we might be short on time for swimming and the luxury of a midday siesta afloat, under the cool shade of overhanging mangroves that lined the inland shore of the estuary.

Even cooked in an aluminum skillet over a one-burner gasoline stove on the cockpit deck of the *Blue Goose*, our supper that evening was far tastier than any of the meticulously prepared and elegantly served formal dinners we had been privileged to attend over the years by reason of our professional obligations. This was living, the way it should be done!

We crawled into our bunks early to reminisce about our day's activities but were soon lulled into deep sleep by the combination of a hunter's supper, the soft tropical breeze and the ripple of the tide along the sides of the *Blue Goose*.

I awoke with a start. It was broad daylight, and I had slept 10 hours straight. For a full minute, I couldn't recall where I was. Mary was still sound asleep. I rolled out, pulled on a pair of Bermuda shorts and stooped out to the cockpit for a stretch. It was a beautiful, clear morning, but we had slept through the best fishing. I really didn't care. I felt too good to feel bad about anything. I took another long, lazy stretch and wondered if I should rouse Mary to try a little fishing with me . . . or let her sleep. Then I came fully awake with a bang. A flight of roughly two hundred mourning doves was passing directly over the *Blue Goose*, in reasonable range!

I lunged back under the canopy and started rummaging for shotgun and shells stowed under Mary's bunk. She opened one eye a crack, asked if I had given the baby her bottle, then turned over and resumed that soft peculiar sound she made while sleeping which she indignantly denied was snoring. I found my gun but couldn't find the shells. I hit my head trying to look under the bunk and repeated several words my mother had forbidden me to use. It didn't help my head a bit. The flight was still passing, and I demanded that Mary tell me where she had stowed the shells.

She said they were where they always were, on the right-hand side of the top shelf of the refrigerator. I repeated the forbidden words again, but I still couldn't find the shells. Mary sat up and asked if the coffee was ready. I could see the tail end of the flight passing out of range.

But all was not lost. Another flock was already in sight coming down the coast headed south. This put the birds directly above a 150-yard stretch of open sand immediately adjacent to our anchorage. We decided to let our morning coffee go and defend ourselves against this invasion of our fishing area by these feathered intruders. We found ourselves obliged to continue this defense during succeeding mornings to the detriment of our fishing but to the benefit of our insatiable appetites for broiled, fried, baked or roasted doves.

Now we were within a few hours of the end of a wonderful mini-vacation from the formality that typifies much of the professional diplomat's life. As always, I tried to soften the thought of returning to it by recalling that it is a necessary part of relations between sovereign states. But as always, recognition of the validity of this argument did little to make the prospect any more attractive.

The morning's flight had slowed. I shifted my shotgun to the other arm and looked back to where Mary had taken her stand a hundred yards to the east. She was gingerly making her tenth round of a small area where she had lost a downed bird in the uneven grey-black sand which so closely matches a dove's coloration. I laughed in spite of myself. The sand was already hot enough to be uncomfortable on her bare feet, and she would take a few quick steps, then abruptly plop down to let them cool while she scanned the immediate area. One leg of her slacks was rolled up to the knee and the other was wet to an equal height where she had waded into the surf to retrieve a bird. She was sunburned and windblown. She was a mess, by all standards except those of the outdoorsman—and to me she was beautiful.

I was suddenly conscious of my own appearance. Bare footed and bare backed, wearing a pair of faded khaki Bermuda shorts and a game bag, I could have been a beach bum on any tropical island in the world.

People in our business had been taking a hell of a thrashing from the public's spokesmen recently. Some of it was warranted, but much of it was not. It is always unpleasant to be the butt of uninformed criticism, but it is doubly so when telling rebuttals must remain undelivered in the best interests of all who make up this nation we serve.

Mary's shout snapped me back to the present just in time to get set for a flock of stragglers that were coming at us across the channel. I shot too quickly at the first bird. A clean miss. The second bird hit the sand near my feet, but the third fluttered crazily and fell in the estuary a dozen yards from shore. Wonderful! I realized I had been hoping for some reason to dive into that inviting water. I dropped off my gun at the *Blue Goose* and went after my bird before it was swept to sea by the outgoing tide. Right before I hit the water, I heard a plaintive, "Hey, wait for me!"

The trip was over. It was time pack up and return to the life of the first secretary of the embassy of the United States of America and Mrs. Crockett. This evening it would be a black-tie reception in honor of the foreign minister, and I dreaded the thought of a stiff shirt on my sunburn. Mary was already protesting that unless we hurried, she wouldn't have time to do her hair.

I recalled the work that had gone into preparing the guest list for this evening's function. To include all of those who should be invited to this particular affair in the interest of our mission had been impossible. When one longtime resident discovered he had not been included, his injured dignity prompted him to visit the embassy and lodge a vigorous protest. My explanations about space limitations fell on deaf ears, and he responded with the charge that there was no space for him because the place would be jammed with "you cookie pushers who neither have nor want to do anything else." I wished that I could have let him go in my stead. But he would never believe me. His impressions of the inner workings of professional diplomacy were based on traditional misconceptions shared by much of the public.

As we drove back toward Guatemala City, the absurdity of it all continued to bother me. If I could write a book about what the Foreign Service officer does and how he goes about it, maybe it would help dispel some of the unfounded and unflattering ideas of what he is like. I didn't have a firm idea how I might go about it, but I vowed to tackle the job someday.

Transfer to Tijuana

From a career standpoint, Guatemala was a stepchild of an assignment. I took it to get out of Washington, although I came to love Guatemala and my work there as much as if the assignment had been of my own making. Things often turn out that way.

Although I had to put up with a couple of less-than-inspiring DCMs (deputy chiefs of mission), once Les Mallory took over as ambassador not too long after my own arrival, life at the embassy became quite pleasant. Les and I had a lot in common. We liked to hunt, we liked to fish, we enjoyed carpentry and we had sons of the same age who were very compatible. We spent a lot of time together outside the office as well as inside it. I might have stayed on there for two full tours (four years) but for two of those unforeseen developments that are so common in Foreign Service life.

First, Les Mallory was transferred to Washington after a short tour in Guatemala. The second shoe fell when his replacement turned out to be one of the few people I was to come across in nearly 30 years of public service to whom I could not relate. What bothered me about the new ambassador most was his exaggerated mannerism of the strong, silent type. He couldn't commit himself on anything, and often remained silent after hearing a complex presentation that required some sort of directive response from him. Very disconcerting! Every time I dealt with him I was reminded of one of my father's favorite maxims, "You don't have to be very smart to get along in life if you're simply smart enough to keep your mouth shut."

The silent treatment would have been enough to drive me elsewhere, but the process was greatly speeded up when word got back to me that the new chief frowned on the possession of firearms and intended to see that anyone under his command who had them get rid of them immediately. I had no intention of being separated from my hunting equipment, much less the keepsakes that had gone everywhere my father had gone for the better part of his long life. I quietly set about lining up a transfer.

If I was to leave Guatemala, I wanted a post that met my requirements. Doesn't everybody? First, I didn't want to go back to Washington. Second, I still had uppermost in mind my long-range goal of heading up my own consulate general. And finally, I hoped I could swing an assignment along the Mexican-US border where the children could attend school in the States, while I would be assigned abroad. These considerations narrowed my options to two posts: Ciudad Juarez, across the Texas border from El Paso, or Tijuana, across the California border from San Diego. I would have much preferred Ciudad Juarez, being a Texan and all, but the incumbent there had held the assignment since the cow died, and we were old friends, anyway—I wasn't willing to try to dislodge him. That left Tijuana, which happened to be coming open. I went for it.

Mindful of the problems I had run into the last time I tried to move into a consular assignment from a foreign affairs officer position, I planned to slip this one by the folks in personnel. Les Mallory agreed to help from his strategic position of deputy assistant secretary of the Bureau of Inter-American Affairs. As it turned out, my transfer was a "within bureau" change of assignments and personnel was not, at that time, powerful enough to block it—but that didn't keep them from trying.

Personnel took the position that a consular assignment wasn't in the best interests of "The Service," or "The Department," or "Career Planning," and if that wasn't enough, I didn't have the seniority (at FSO-3) for assignment as a consul general in the first place! We were still hung up at that point when I became eligible for home leave. It looked like I was headed for the same kind of a cliff-hanger I had lived through during my last change of assignments.

I need not have worried. This time, I held the high cards. Les Mallory provided support in the bureaucratic pushing and shoving—and he held tough. I suspect personnel's position was undermined by our new ambassador, who must have said he would prefer that I be sent somewhere else. Whatever the reason, personnel at last relented to my assignment as principal officer at Tijuana, Mexico. But they held fast to their contention I was not senior enough to be granted the title of consul general. That didn't worry me as much as it might have. I had an ace up my sleeve which I fully intended to play when the time was right.

Clemente Marroquín Rojas

As anyone who knows Latin America can tell you, there isn't a capital in the area that doesn't have its virulent and often violently anti-American newspaper editor. The man who filled this role in Guatemala City for over a quarter century was Clemente Marroquín Rojas, editor and publisher of Guatemala's leading daily, *La Hora*. Don Clemente did not single out the United States for his criticism—he was ready and able to take on anyone at any time and often did. This included the Guatemalan chief of state, regardless of who happened to hold the job at any given moment, and Don Clemente's caustic editorial missives were so devastating that every effort was made by all and sundry to keep out of his line of fire. President Ydígoras' tactic was to have Don Clemente elected first designate to the Guatemalan presidency, the equivalent of our vice president, and to name him minister of agriculture as well. It didn't work—Don Clemente gave Ydígoras hell exactly as he did everyone else.

If there was one talent I brought to the business of diplomacy that I had confidence in, it was the ability to get along with anyone. To me, Don Clemente was a challenge. His knowledge of the intricacies of Guatemalan politics and the background of so many current problems could be invaluable to me in understanding and reporting on what was going on in the country and why—my prime responsibility as chief of the embassy's political section. Early on during my assignment, I decided I was going to get to know and be the friend of Clemente Marroquín Rojas. But I was careful about mentioning this around the shop. It tended to provoke gales of laughter when I did, and no end of derisive comments about how cheerfully Don Clemente would cut me up into small pieces and then gleefully roast me over the white heat of his hatred for all things connected with the United States.

The first thing I had to do was meet Don Clemente. That, of itself, seemed a formidable task. How does the first secretary of the US embassy go about getting acquainted with the leading critic of the United States in his country of assignment? After giving the problem some thought, it seemed to me that the most natural thing would be to tell Don Clemente I wanted to meet him and to ask for an appointment to call on him. I figured Don Clemente would want to know what this fool gringo, young enough to be one of his own children, thought he was about in braving the curmudgeon in his own den. The appointment I asked for was granted without delay.

Sitting there in Don Clemente's waiting room, I had no idea how I would go about managing the conversation. In addition to Don Clemente's brutal editorials, it was reported on good authority that he had felled his own son with a piece of cordwood when he came home tipsy once too often. I thought again about being young enough to be Don Clemente's son. It was not reassuring.

The wiry gentleman with closely cropped grey hair who emerged to escort me into his office was rather smallish, but it was not his stature that provided the first impression; it was his intensity. He seemed to be surrounded by a field of energy—directly concentrated on the object of his attention at any given moment—that radiated as if it were a strong electric charge. I was almost reluctant to shake hands, for fear I would get a shock.

Don Clemente did not wait for me to open the conversation. He immediately launched into an explanation of his frequent criticism of the United States. It was in no way an apology. On the contrary, it was, if anything, a challenge to refute the points of US vulnerability he enumerated. And the list he rattled off was lengthy, indeed. I thought it best to limit my rejoinders to "Very interesting," or "I see your point," or simply "Ummm." That was all Don Clemente needed to keep the "conversation" going.

It was difficult, after close to a half hour, to find an opening for my thank-yous and to express my hope that we could discuss politics again some time. Don Clemente would hear nothing of it. "Why," he said, "we have barely scratched the surface of the many things I have wanted to tell the North American embassy for so many years," and launched into another discourse on the fallacy of United States policy in Guatemala. Many of his points were uncomfortably close to the mark.

Over the months, I found occasion to listen to Don Clemente on a regular basis. The time came when I dared try to explain the reasons behind a given US course of action. I found that Don Clemente could listen, although he was reserved when it came to agreeing. Still, we were getting to know one another, and I dared to be increasingly bold in my supportive presentations.

The day came when I realized we were debating as one friend to another. Don Clemente was as critical as ever, but he was no longer strident, at least in his presentations to me. Our friendship and mutual respect reached the point where it was inevitable that my presentations should assume the character of justifications, as contrasted to explanations. I never realized, except in retrospect, when that milestone had been passed.

As we came to know one another better, I wanted very much to sip cognac and talk politics with Don Clemente before my own hearth, as we had before his. But I was reluctant to invite him to my house. Many times he had vowed publicly that he would never set foot in the US embassy or the ambassador's residence, under any circumstance. Did this extend to the residence of the first secretary of embassy? It was a long time before I felt confident enough to ask that question of Don Clemente. When I did, he threw his arm across my shoulder and had a hearty laugh. "Just try me," he said. Our friendship was cemented.

I'll never know if I changed Don Clemente's attitude toward the United States. I do know he was always ready to listen to reason after we came to know each other. And I can remember no instance after that when he published a criticism of one of our actions or initiatives when I had had an opportunity to explain beforehand why we were doing whatever it was that we did, provided, always *provided*, there was some valid rationale I could fall back on—which all too frequently there was not. The one thing I can say for sure is that getting to know Don Clemente well enough to be his friend didn't in any way hurt us or impede the attainment of our objectives in Guatemala. Quite the contrary, I like to think it was helpful.

Our last evening in Guatemala was like most last evenings before transfer in the Foreign Service. After the final despedida, Mary and I sat among the packing boxes stacked in our living room, shoes off, savoring the warmth of our friends' last goodbyes and wondering how we would ever manage to get up, get the kids ready and get on the road early enough to cover the ground we had scheduled for the first leg of our trip home the next morning.

The timid knock on the door came as a shock, but not as much of a shock as it was to find Don Clemente and his daughter Marina standing there with sorrowful smiles on their faces. Inside, they presented us with a pair of beautiful upland blankets, hand woven by Quiché Indians, as a going-away present. Then Don Clemente produced a bottle of fine, vintage cognac for our final toast and we relaxed in the warmth of valued companionship.

Tijuana

1960

Consul General

Robert C. Hill was ambassador to Mexico when I took charge at Tijuana in the summer of 1960. We had known each other for several years, and while we weren't necessarily friends, we were cordial colleagues. I had checked with him before I set out to get the Tijuana assignment—it would have been foolish to go after it without his blessing—but I hadn't involved him otherwise. Now that I had assumed charge of the consulate general, I wanted the title of consul general to go with it. My plans called for Bob Hill to take care of that little detail for me.

If there ever was one of a kind, it was Bob Hill—he made a career out of the Foreign Service without ever being career Foreign Service. Bob tried it out the hard way first with assignments as vice consul to Calcutta and New Delhi in the wartime Foreign Service Auxiliary. He found that slow going and looked for greener pastures once World War II was over. It didn't take him long to find an easier way to the top. A good marriage helped, and Bob quickly rose to be assistant vice president of W.R. Grace, a major company long and intimately involved in Latin America. Appointment as ambassador to Costa Rica followed in 1953 when he had reached the ripe old age of thirty-six. Bob Hill had found his greener pastures.

I first met Hill in 1955 when I was assigned to Scott McLeod's Bureau of Security and Consular Affairs. By then, Bob had added the ambassadorship to El Salvador to his trophies and was holding down the job of special assistant for Mutual Security Affairs in the Department of State. He and Scott McLeod were both protégés of Senator Styles Bridges (R-New Hampshire) and close as fleas on a dog. Soon Bob managed to switch into yet another job, the prestigious and influential assistant secretary for congressional relations. And by the time he was 40, he had managed appointment as ambassador to Mexico.

Bob had a certain talent for getting ahead. He also had political clout, and he never hesitated to use it. He rode roughshod over more than one bureaucrat, and neither he nor they forgot. It was this circumstance that I felt sure could be worked to my advantage in getting from where I was to where I wanted to be.

I hurried through the inescapable routine of taking charge and getting acquainted at Tijuana as fast as I could. I wanted to get to Mexico City and see Bob Hill—soonest. As it worked out, Bob was in the United States attending the 1960 Republican National Convention, and his return to Mexico City coincided with my arrival there for consultation. The evening Hill got back happened to be the evening I had dinner with Supervisory Consul General Bob Cartwright, whom I had come to know well during our time together in the Bureau of Security and Consular Affairs. Hill joined us for brandy, and we spent the evening listening to his account of how the convention had gone.

The occasion could not have been more propitious for my purposes. We were three old cronies from Washington days, and the evening became more mellow as the level of the cognac bottle decreased. By the time Hill had talked himself out and asked how things were going with me, I was ready. He couldn't believe personnel would assign me to oversee the consulate general at Tijuana and then withhold the title of Consul General. How could that happen?

"Well, Bob," I replied, "you know you *do* have enemies in the Foreign Service—but it sure seems like a sneaky way for them to get back at you." That was all it took!

Swearing In

I felt oddly disconnected and vaguely aware of a tableau before me. The room was much larger than any office I had ever had. A leather divan and two overstuffed leather chairs were grouped around a long, hardwood coffee table at one side. An oversized swivel chair stood with back to the window before a walnut double pedestal executive desk. A bust of Lincoln graced a small table, along with a shiny carafe and spotless glasses. A conference table and more chairs were clustered at the far end of the room, near a door giving access to a small restroom. Although there were perhaps 15 US staffers gathered here, we were not crowded. It gave me a thrill to realize this was the office of the Consul General.

Poised and debonair as always, Joe Cicala presided over the ceremony as if it were a daily event. *"Raise your right hand and repeat after me,"* he said. *"I, Kennedy M. Crockett, do solemnly swear. . ."*

My voice repeated the words, but my mind was far, far away, 24 years back in time, to that day in the 1930s when a skinny 16-year-old boy with thick glasses first slid behind the wheel of a Pure Oil Company tanker truck. It was the boy's first real job—a man's job in the Depression years. It was the attainment of a secret dream: to have a man's job in a man's world. Let the other fellows jerk sodas.

". . .that I will defend the Constitution of the United States against all enemies, foreign and domestic. . ." It hardly seemed possible that 16 years had passed since a still wet-behind-the-ears clerk first repeated those words when he took the oath of office as vice consul of the United States of America. That, too, had seemed like a dream. How proud the new vice consul had been—how sweet it had been to have taken such a giant step forward. The world of the Foreign Service was his oyster.

". . .that I will bear true faith and allegiance to the same; that I take this obligation freely, without any mental reservation or purpose of evasion. . ." How strange those lines had sounded to me when I took the oath of office as consul of the United States of America eight years earlier! Mental reservation or purpose of evasion, indeed! This was what I had worked for. This made up for those long stretches away from home, friends and family. This made the endless hours of overtime and the dreary tasks worthwhile. A burning ambition had been realized. I had managed to make the grade. There was deep satisfaction and pride—certainly no reservation, much less purpose of evasion. I had gone as high as I could go, according to the rules of the game at that time. It was when the rules were changed that I began to wonder if someday, somehow, I might go one step higher.

Now that day had come. I had dared to dream, and once having dreamed, it turned out to be an easier road to travel than I had anticipated. I savored each word as I repeated after Joe, *". . .and that I will well and faithfully discharge the duties of the office of consul general of the United States of America on which I am about to enter. So help me God."*

It was done. If I retired at first eligibility, that was still 10 years down the road—time enough for a full tour of duty at Tijuana, a consulate general in some other part of the world and a last assignment as consul general at Monterrey.

All of that was for the future. The job immediately ahead of me was to make the operation of the consulate general at Tijuana the best in the Foreign Service. I had no doubt I could do it. I could hardly wait to get started.

Baja California

I didn't expect to find any surprises in my new job as principal officer at Tijuana. I had served on the Mexican-United States border before, and I had served as a principal officer before. Tijuana would be more of the same.

To begin with, the staff was larger than that of a good many embassies, and some were unusually competent. But we had more than our quota of dead wood, has-beens and never-weres. The personnel problems that are inherently part of any management job were multiplied accordingly. We carried those who tried but couldn't and looked for ways to work around those who might have but wouldn't.

The volume of work at the post resulted from Tijuana being at the end of two funnels. The wide opening to the south funneled visa applicants from the interior of Mexico up to our visa mill in countless masses, while the wide opening to the north funneled fun-seeking gringos down to Sin City by the millions—a fixed percentage of whom ended up getting into trouble and becoming protection statistics for the consulate general's sizable section devoted exclusively to the task of trying to help them out.

The visa workload didn't bother me. There was adequate staff and I knew that end of the game inside out. True, it took a while to work around the "old visa hands" who were determined to continue doing it the hard way, but I had faced and overcome that problem more than once in the past.

Nor was I concerned about the large numbers of US nationals who got into one kind of trouble or another every day of the year. What caught me by surprise was the realization that my out-of-the-office responsibilities would not be limited to Baja California, my official beat. There were many groups in Southern California that found it convenient, for one reason or another, to include me in their plans. There were times I wished I had been born twins.

In Mexico, the chief representative of the United States government in any community is included on the guestlist of most special occasions. In Mexico, the number of special occasions is astronomical—Mexicans like to celebrate. The consul general at Tijuana went, whether he felt like it or not. To do otherwise would have been discourteous to his hosts.

There weren't as many functions on the US side of the border, and thankfully they did not all produce invitations for the US consul general to put in a personal appearance, but more than enough did. The Eleventh Naval District Headquarters are located at San Diego. Many US Naval affairs called for invitations to be sent to Mexican counterparts. When that happened, I was rung in too. Ditto for the Marine Recruit Depot at San Diego.

The sister cities programs often produced special invitations from cities and towns in San Diego County, as well as from many cities and towns in Los Angeles, Orange and Riverside counties. The Newport to Ensenada Yacht Race required an appearance at both Newport and Ensenada. The Greater Los Angeles Press Club wanted to grill the new US consul general. The list went on and on and on. It extracted a heavy price in wear and tear on the liver and the digestive system.

However, this aspect of my official duties at Tijuana was certainly not all blood, sweat and tears. For the confrontation with the Greater Los Angeles Press Club, Mary and I were housed in a magnificent suite and showered with courtesies and considerations of every sort from the moment we arrived until the time we left. I was made honorary chief of police of Redondo Beach, badge and all! The Newport Beach Yacht Club put us up in a villa fit for a king and took us out to see the race start in a yacht that must have belonged to royalty.

From time to time there was satisfaction to be gained, too, from accomplishing something more than simply putting in a ceremonial presence. I like to feel that my participation in joint meetings between the Mexican Confederation of Labor and the San Diego chapter of the AFL-CIO contributed to better understanding and more productive relations between the working men of Mexico and the United States. These occasions were out of the ordinary. There was another I remember fondly.

A group of nice ladies from somewhere in Southern California had graciously sponsored a public library in La Paz, Baja California, at the southern end of the peninsula. They had managed to gather several tons of used books in their respective neighborhoods to fill the La Paz Library's shelves. But then they ran into a problem: how to get the books from San Diego to La Paz in a day and time when there was no usable road between the two cities.

At about that same time, work was completed on the conversion of the USS *Nereus*, a World War II ship of some 500 feet in length, to be the Navy's first nuclear submarine tender. The Eleventh Naval District wanted to send the *Nereus* on a shakedown cruise before she sailed for her duty station in the Pacific. Unfortunately, the office of the chief of naval operations (CNO) in Washington couldn't provide funds for that purpose.

Enter the US consul general. The State Department was asked to request the Navy's cooperation in transferring the books from San Diego to the La Paz Library—a contribution to good relations between the United States and Mexico. CNO agreed to cooperate. The Eleventh Naval District had a ship ready to make the trip, the USS *Nereus*. Everybody was happy—there were funds available for good neighborly relations. But most exciting to me was being invited to go along on the *Nereus'* cruise from San Diego to La Paz. Since La Paz was in our consular district and I needed to make a "get acquainted" visit there anyhow, I accepted. I couldn't think of a more impressive way to put in my first appearance at La Paz. As it turned out, I couldn't have picked a nicer way to go.

I knew that submarine tenders were designed to go anywhere in the world and set up shop as floating bases, able to service and repair submarines and thus keep our fleet at sea and ready to go. All I knew about the *Nereus* was that it had been outfitted to serve as flagship for the admiral commanding the Pacific Submarine Force and his perks were to be assigned to me for this voyage. I figured I'd be comfortable.

As I arrived at the gangway, a junior officer in spotless whites saluted sharply and introduced himself as my aide. At an unseen signal, a row of sailors, also dressed in white, formed a corridor at the top of the gangway on the main deck. As I ascended there was much blowing of pipes, which ceased after I had been ushered aboard and acknowledged the welcome. To say that I was impressed would be a gross understatement.

Next, my young friend took me up several flights of steps to the quarters I would occupy. My billet was austere, but complete and comfortable. It included a galley attended by a young man in white jacket

Next came the flying bridge, where I met Captain McGinnis and his officers. They made me feel at home, and said I was welcome to remain topside while we got under way. The sun shone brightly, the wind was light, and the sky was blue as we worked our way free of the dock and headed out the channel toward the open Pacific.

The cruise south was near perfect: bright sun, smooth seas and quiet hours to do nothing but bask. When the spirit moved me, I enlisted my young friend to escort me through the labyrinth of the ship's innards and explain the intricacies of her extensive facilities. I was surprised to find she boasted such a large crew, and impressed with the facilities they were afforded to make life at sea comfortable despite the restricted space they had to live in.

The bridge was always a busy place, interesting if not exciting. At one point, I was as startled as anyone when without warning, bells sounded, and sirens wailed. The shout of "man overboard" blared over the speaker system. We started a sweeping turn, and it was then that I first caught sight of a form in the ocean rapidly falling behind in our wake. It was a helpless feeling, but even as I watched, a small boat was lowered over the side and launched despite our headway. Someone handed me binoculars. I watched with fascination as the rescue boat found that tiny form in the far distance and pulled it aboard as we continued our circle to come abreast of the spot where the accident had occurred. When the rescue boat was again alongside, and the victim was being hoisted to the deck I discovered it was a dummy and we had just witnessed a drill.

We rounded Cabo San Lucas at the bottom of the Baja California peninsula early on the day we were to arrive at La Paz. Except for a small fishing village, the crescent-shaped beaches, separated by rocky outcroppings, were deserted. Progress had not yet come to Cabo San Lucas. The shoreline was as God had made it—white sand and white foam against a backdrop of arid desert where man had yet to try his hand at improving the perfect.

It was exactly 10:00 a.m. as we dropped anchor in La Paz Bay. The Navy planned to put me ashore at precisely 11:00 a.m., the hour I had stipulated when I notified local authorities of my visit. I went below to put on my seersucker suit and find my Panama hat.

By the time I had dressed and made my way back to the main deck, the sailors were lined up and the bosun stood ready with his pipe. At the foot of the gangway was moored a beautiful boat of a type I had never before seen. Perhaps 40 feet in length, she was all varnished mahogany and teak woodwork with highly polished chrome and brass fittings. Her two deckhouses were outfitted much as the inside of a carriage, complete with white seat covers. Sailors in white stood at the ready on her deck and there was a bosun's mate at her helm. I was to learn my carriage was called an Admiral's Barge. It was a thrill to see the consul general's flag flying from the mast at the bow with Old Glory at her rightful place on the stern.

Many years later I was told some of the old timers at La Paz still remembered the day the new consul general came to make his courtesy call. It was an impressive show.

Chino Actor

It was hard to tell Ray Cannon was eating crow. He finished off his second piece with gusto and speared a third from the serving plate. "Best fish I've had in months," he grinned at me.

When it came to fishing the waters of Baja California, Ray Cannon wrote the book, literally. He covered Baja for *The Western Outdoor News* for years and besides his regular column, published several books and a double handful of pamphlets about fishing along both coasts of the peninsula. No one dared question his word when it came to talking about the subject of his life's work. I wouldn't have, either—except I didn't know who Ray Cannon was.

I had finished what I came to do at La Paz by mid-afternoon on a Saturday and managed to hitch a ride down to El Chileno, where the Cabo San Lucas Resort was being constructed. The men supervising the building had offered to put me up in their bunkhouse for the weekend. I planned to devote Sunday to fishing along the rocky promontories and sandy beaches I had seen from the bridge of the USS *Nereus* when I first came this way. I could hardly wait.

There were three guests at the construction company mess table on Saturday night. I was one, and Dr. Boyd Walker, a scientist, was another. I didn't catch the name of the third man. He was a wizened fellow with a grey goatee who always seemed to have a cigarette dangling from his lips and who wore a yachting cap at a rakish angle. Although he spoke with authority about any subject bearing on Baja, I didn't find him very impressive. Apparently, he was not impressed with me either. When I said I planned to spend Sunday morning spin fishing off the rocks, he guffawed and cut me short with. "Well, you can try, but take it from me, you won't catch anything." The others nodded to one another as if God had spoken—and that was that.

The cliffs leading down to the water at land's end on Cabo San Lucas were steeper than I anticipated. But once I got down, it wasn't too hard to move about. The rocks that projected out into the water shelved off sharply. Large areas of foam and spray washed in and out as the waves broke against them. It was deep even close in. It was there that I cast my Tony Accetta #5H spoon.

I knew I had made a find when I felt a heavy strike before I could retrieve my first cast. It took a good, hard tussle to gaff a brightly colored fish I had never seen before. I was to learn the locals called it *chino actor* because the brightly colored mask-like design on the face resembled the makeup of a Chinese actor. The scientific name of this fish is *Cirrhitus rivulatus*, and it is also called *mero de roca* by native fishermen.

Any fisherman worthy of the name could have known it was going to be good eating. I thought of the fellow with the yachting cap and couldn't suppress a silent grin. I'd show him!

An hour and a half later the sun was high enough to beat down on my rocks with authority. I found shade along the cliff and sat leaning against it. I wasn't sure of the count, but my stringer was so heavy I had to strain to lift it. Besides the chino and several of his brothers, I had trigger fish, a couple of parrot fish, some *sierra* and a *cabrilla* in addition to a good selection of tropical reef fish I could not identify. It was early, and I hadn't tried the beaches yet. It felt good to know there would be enough fish for everyone at Sunday dinner.

A shadow cast from above came into view below me. I recognized the outline of a yachting cap and nonchalantly walked to where my stringer was tied. The gasp from above as I lifted the fish out of the water was audible even over the rush of the waves. The old man was impressed. It was a nice feeling.

Several weeks later, I got a clipping of Ray Cannon's column from the latest issue of *The Western Outdoor News*, describing my catch of that day with plentiful praise.

Cannon and I were to meet again as we both covered Baja California. In fact, we became rather good friends. I never dared give Ray any advice about fishing his waters. And he never gave me any more advice on that subject, either.

Four Great Shots

For 50 years, guns were an important part of my life. I can't remember when my father still carried a gun to work, but the old single-action Colt .45 with yellowed ivory grips that he carried for many years is among my earliest memories. He kept it in his top bureau drawer, loaded with five cartridges, and on special occasions I was allowed to examine it under his watchful eye. I knew someday I would get to shoot it, and I hoped I would be able to shoot it well.

In the place and time that I grew up, men were supposed to know how to shoot, and one of the greatest compliments a man could be paid was to have it said, "He's a good shot."

My father's sidekick, Blaze Delling, was such a man. He had grown up a cowboy, using the butt of his pistol to hammer a missing staple into a fence post or the barrel to take a tightening turn in a slack strand of barbed wire. He had also learned how to shoot and used that skill often in the years he spent as a Texas Ranger and border guard. Delling was an old man when I knew him and had long since given up carrying a handgun. Although he taught me much about shooting and hunting with both the shotgun and deer rifle, I saw him fire a pistol just twice. Both were great shots.

As Officer in Charge of the Immigration and Naturalization Service in Laredo, my father oversaw several small ports of entry along the Rio Grande both upriver and downriver from Laredo. He visited these regularly on what he called inspection trips, but which I suspected were often excuses to get out of the confinement of his office in the federal building and visit with Blaze Delling, who was chosen to accompany him more often than anyone else. They had shared many pleasant hunting and fishing experiences over the years and these trips afforded an opportunity to remember good times past or to plan others for the future. Sometimes I was asked to go along, and on one occasion when World War II was in the making, my father also took along a new colonel from the cavalry troop stationed at Fort McIntosh who wanted to get better acquainted with the area he might someday have to defend.

The little crossing at San Ygnacio, south of Laredo, was served by a one-car ferry and a four-man rowboat for those who entered or departed legally. Many more crossings were made at the rapids downstream, without benefit of inspection. While that was illegal, no one paid too much attention as there wasn't much that could be done about it. There were more rapids than there were border patrolmen, customs guards and immigration inspectors put together.

As we drove through the undergrowth over the dirt trail that led out of the river bottom, a large rattlesnake stretched across the road in front of us. We scrambled out of the car to kill it. A rock or a stick would have served, but the colonel quickly drew his service .45 automatic and got off a shot at some 15 paces, which kicked up dust beyond the rattler's head. We watched as he took careful aim and fired again. He was closer but still missed. Alarmed, the rattler coiled and raised his head a foot off the ground. How close the next three shots came I do not know, but the rattler remained unscathed, neck arched for a strike and rattles whirring furiously.

The colonel was the picture of dejection. His arms hung at his sides and the .45 dangled in his hand. Aware that his shooting had been less than impressive, he turned to Mr. Delling and said, "Would you like to try your hand?" Mr. Delling looked at the colonel and at the snake and back at the colonel. A coiled snake's head at 15 paces isn't an impossible shot for an expert, but it is far from an easy shot for anyone.

Mr. Delling took the gun. His movements were neither casual nor deliberate but rather matter-of-fact. He raised the gun to aim and it seemed to go off before he was ready. Certainly, neither the colonel nor I expected the shot and we both flinched. Mr. Delling handed the gun back to the colonel. The rattler writhed, headless in the dust. The colonel had little to say during the trip home, and Mr. Delling and my father courteously avoided any mention of the rattle-snake.

***

The port at Dolores, to the north of Laredo, was smaller than San Ygnacio. There was no ferry here and the rowboat that brought people back and forth across the boundary on the one day a week that the port was officially open had room for two passengers at a time. Dolores had once been a coal mining center, served by the Rio Grande and Eagle Pass Railroad. The RG & EP never went to Rio Grande or to Eagle Pass but hauled coal from Dolores to Laredo before the first World War.

In those days, the border was a wild region where smuggling was an important part of the local economy and bandit raids from Mexico were an ever-present threat. Mr. Delling had been the only law in Dolores then, and in true Texas Ranger fashion he kept such peace as there was without asking or needing help from anyone. Now the mines were long since closed and the town had all but disappeared. But those who remained remembered Mr. Delling and treated him with great respect.

The Rio Grande at Dolores was deep and rather swift. We stood on the high bank overlooking the river, watching the boatman pull hard on his oars as he brought his passengers across from the Mexican shore. A soft breeze rippled the river's surface and made the boatman's task more difficult. A small, slender man approached, hat in hand, the late afternoon sun glistening on his wrinkled, dark brown skin. There was an old flour sack slung over his shoulder. With a slight bow he asked, "Do you remember Tomás Martínez, Mr. Delling?"

After greetings had been exchanged, Tomás untied the flour sack and drew out an enormous .44 caliber Colt single action with at least an eight-inch barrel. Even then it was nearly old enough to be a museum piece, and it had obviously seen much service during its long life. Tomás explained he wanted to buy it. Would Mr. Delling have a look and tell him whether it was worth the $15 the owner was asking?

Mr. Delling took the gun and spun the cylinder to make sure it was unloaded. It rattled loosely. He cocked the hammer, which fell with a great clack the minute he touched the trigger. Either the sear had almost worn away or someone had worked on it with a file. He handed the pistol back to Tomás and said. "Offer $10 and don't go over $12—if it will shoot."

Tomás' face lighted up. Reaching in his pocket, he produced three cartridges. The lead slugs were corroded white and the brass cases were tarnished to a velvety green. "Please, Mr. Delling, you tell me if it shoots good." Mr. Delling accepted the cartridges reluctantly and looked at them dubiously. But he put them in the cylinder, although not without some difficulty. Then he looked for something safe to shoot at.

On the surface of the river, 50 feet below us and perhaps a hundred feet downstream, a snapping turtle paddled leisurely, craning his neck in search of something good to eat. His back was no broader than the span of a man's hand. Again Mr. Delling raised the pistol matter-of-factly, and again the shot came before I expected it. There was a boil of water and a stain of blood. The turtle floated along the bank, belly up.

Mr. Delling handed the gun to Tomás, who quickly tucked it back in his flour sack and, all smiles and bows, hurried off to close the deal, confident that he would soon be the proud owner of an exceptionally accurate weapon. My father said, "Blaze, that was a right good shot." Mr. Delling grinned, "Frank, I think that old gun went off before I was ready, and from the way it popped I know the powder was bad. But you got to admit, Tomás is satisfied."

***

These were great shots, but they didn't involve any risk to life or limb. It was 25 years before I saw another great shot. This one ran the risk of crippling a man for life—not any man, but a man who was himself a great shot.

It was a strange setting for a pistol match. Our party had been quail hunting south of Ensenada, in Baja California. The morning's hunt had been difficult. Although the quail were plentiful, they were wild, and we had raced through the heavy manzanita thickets and up the steep hills to the point of exhaustion. Our bags were heavy, and we were played out when we reached the rendezvous with the pickup that brought our lunch and refreshments. Gratefully, we found places to rest on the soft sand of the dry wash. The iced beer quenched our thirst as we regained our wind. The thick sandwiches brought back our strength. Soon we were again a congenial bunch of hunters, reliving a great morning's shoot, satisfied in the knowledge that we had game to show for the shots we had fired.

I had looked forward to this hunt for many months, not because it was a new experience for me to shoot quail in Baja, but because it would be the first hunt I would share with Harlan Carter, a friend from my youth and a man whose father had been the friend of my father. More than that, Harlan was a world class shot who held many national and international titles, mainly with the pistol and rifle. I was eager to test my shotgun against his. Such is a man's ego, even when it comes to his friends.

The group lounged and reflected on the morning's shoot, not knowing whether the greatest satisfaction came from the success of our hunt or the relief we all shared that the afternoon would be all downhill. As often happens in a gathering of men who like guns and know how to use them, before too long someone produced a .38 caliber Smith and Wesson revolver. He was a young Mexican official whose name I have long since forgotten but whose skill remains fresh in my memory. Moving away from the group, he rolled a tin can along the ground with a series of quick shots. He knew how to use the gun—he was accurate, and he was fast. After a few more outstanding shots, he invited Harlan to try his hand, in effect, to try to match his skill. He did not taunt, but the challenge was there.

I have no doubt Harlan could have matched or bettered the younger man's skill. I will never know whether he hesitated because of modesty, or because he was as unsteady as the rest of us from the morning's exertions, or because it would have been misguided to best a Mexican's bravado on his own turf. But he turned the challenge aside by making a counter challenge of his own. Harlan raised his empty beer can and said, "Show us one more shot, compadre." Then from his reclining position against a rock, he put the can on his raised knee and held it there with the palm of his right hand. "Try this one, amigo," he said. "It is different to shoot at a man than to shoot at a can."

The Mexican official stood some distance away, but hardly farther from Harlan than he had been from the can he had bounced along so skillfully. There was doubt in his eyes, but he raised his pistol and took careful aim. Then, slowly, he lowered the gun and looked from one to the other of us, an unspoken question on his lips. Clearly, he wasn't keen to try a shot that could, with the slightest miscalculation, leave a man crippled for life. Still, he could not back down without losing face. He obviously hoped someone would caution him not to try it. Harlan spoke before anyone else. "Go ahead," he said, "The shot is an easy one for a man of your skill. Why don't you move back another 10 paces?"

Strain showed on the young man's face and his brow glistened with a thin film of sweat as he took the pistol in his left hand and wiped his right palm on his trousers leg. Very slowly, he again raised the pistol and sighted with great care. Finally, the shot came. It was a perfect bull's-eye in the exact center of the circular label on the beer can. Harlan got up and came forward to shake hands, but the man would have none of that. Instead, he seized Harlan in an emotional embrace and buried his head on Harlan's shoulder. He had made a great shot—but he had lost the match, without Harlan having fired a shot.

***

Great as these three shots were, it was the fourth great shot that gave me the most satisfaction—because one of my children made it.

I wanted all my children to know how to shoot, and I started them at it as soon as they were old enough to understand the need for safety and the things one should or should not do with a gun, loaded or unloaded. I cut down the stock of a little bolt action .22 caliber Winchester rifle which each child had to master as a beginner. Then I used a .22 caliber Smith and Wesson revolver on a .32 frame for beginner's pistol instruction. The round butt fit comfortably in even the smallest hand. Next, they learned how to handle a shotgun and finally a high-powered hunting rifle. Usually, the heavy handguns were left until they were at least in their teens.

As is the case with any group, some of the children learned quicker and shot better than others. The star pupil of our family was our daughter Linda, who always excelled at any sport requiring good coordination and concentration. By the time Linda was eight, she could outshoot any of the others with the .22

caliber firearms. One day when we were target shooting, I asked if she would like to try the .45 Colt automatic. I was amazed to find she could shoot it nearly as well as the .22 Smith and Wesson, although she didn't like the noise or the heavy recoil.

A few weeks later we were guests at a friend's beach house outside Ensenada in Baja California for a typical Mexican barbecue. As is customary, the men kept apart from the women, talking and joking with one another while the meat sizzled on the coals and the collection of empty tequila bottles grew. Spirits were high by the time the meal was served, and the food did little to dampen the group's enthusiasm. Many of the guests were Mexican officials, both civilian and military, and after the formality of eating had been observed, someone suggested a little target shooting, as so often happens at Mexican parties in the country.

A variety of handguns appeared from jacket pockets, shoulder holsters and automobile glove compartments, predominantly .45 caliber automatics, a favorite with Mexican officials. Tequila bottles emptied during the pre-dinner happy hour were collected, and the group set off for the sand dunes out back with much good-natured boasting about accuracy, sidearms, and skill. Tequila is a great ego-builder and we had all consumed enough to be feeling downright cocky. A row of bottles was lined up atop a low dune, and the bunch started banging away. Given the number of shots fired, someone should have hit at least one bottle, if nothing else, by accident. But guns had been emptied, reloaded and emptied again without a single hit.

As has been the case much too often during my lifetime, I couldn't keep my mouth shut. Before I knew it, I blurted out, "Hell, I have an eight-year-old daughter who can shoot better than that!"

Immediately the challenge was taken up. There was no chance to back down and I went off to look for Linda, much more sober now. What if Linda was afraid to shoot the .45 in front of so many strangers? What if she missed her shots? After all, the range was substantial, and Linda had not had all that much practice with a .45 automatic. I would look the fool for having made the boast, but worse, Linda would be embarrassed. I knew I would be in for a good ribbing if she missed—knew I would deserve it, too.

I found Linda and we walked to the car to get the old Colt .45 automatic that Blaze Delling had passed on to my father and my father had passed on to me. Linda had never fired more than two or three rounds at a time with the heavy gun, but her curly blonde head was erect and her blue eyes steady as we walked back to the dunes where the others waited.

Linda seemed terribly small in that crowd. It was very still as I jacked a round into the chamber and she sat down on the ground, knees up, ready to shoot. The automatic looked big as a cannon in her small pale hands. I could hear the whispers behind us as she carefully rested her elbows on her knees and stretched her arms far forward, the pistol rock steady in her two-handed grip.

Linda had always been a methodical shooter, no doubt one of the reasons she was so accurate. But now she seemed to be taking forever. I could hear heavy breathing behind us, but otherwise there was absolute quiet except for the steady rumble of the ocean in the distance. I felt sure Linda must be tightening up, and if she did she would never be able to hold a steady bead.

Abruptly, the .45 bounced in her hands with a great roar. I had been so intent on Linda that I had not looked toward the line of bottles that seemed so far away. But I knew she had scored a hit from the cheer that went up behind us. I took the gun from her steady little hands, and for the first time since I had gone to bring her out to the dunes, there was a bright smile on her face. One of the men lifted her from the ground and carried her on his shoulders as we all marched back to the house with much cheering, back slapping and expressions of disbelief.

That shot was the main topic of conversation for the rest of the afternoon—but not one of the men suggested he might have another try at breaking one of the empty bottles.

Tijuana Consular District

The Tijuana consular district extended from the northwest corner of the State of Baja California on the Mexican-US border for over 750 miles, as the crow might fly, to land's end at Cabo San Lucas on the southern end of the peninsula in the Territory of Baja California Sur. By road, and such trails as existed in 1960, the trip overland between the two extremes measured about a thousand miles. Even before I arrived at Tijuana, I planned to make the trip from one end to the other.

When the Spaniards first came to the area 400-odd years before, they found large settlements of natives scattered throughout the peninsula. The padres built their missions among these people long before they ventured as far north as what is today the state of California. But something changed a couple of centuries back. Baja California dried up. The indigenous settlements disappeared. What had once been a populated area became a vast, barren wasteland, all but deserted except for a few scattered villages where sweet water still flowed.

By 1960, modern man had managed to develop the northern fringe of the Baja California peninsula: agriculture in the Mexicali Valley; business and industry at Tecate and Tijuana; tourism and fishing at San Felipe and Ensenada. There was corresponding development at the extreme southern end as well, although to a lesser extent. But in between, for some 500 miles, there had been little or no development during at least the last 200 hundred years. In some places, what man once built had been abandoned and left to crumble. I wanted to see all of Baja California, but mostly, I wanted to see what I could of the vast in between— that 500-mile stretch where few had ventured before me and certainly no US consul general had ever set foot.

I had been at Tijuana for well over a year before the signs were right for my trek through the consular district. We had received a new Chevrolet Carryall which, although not four-wheel drive, did have lots of room for extra gas and gear. I had picked Don Olliff as the junior officer who would accompany me, and I had things well enough in hand around the office to feel comfortable about getting away for a few weeks. We set forth right before Thanksgiving 1961.

I figured one pass through the "in between" would be an interesting experience, but once down and once back would be a strain. We left Chula Vista going east on Telegraph Canyon Road headed for Mazatlán on the west coast of the Mexican mainland. From there we would ship the Carryall across to La Paz, and then drive north along the length of Baja California, ending up back home.

As it turned out, I gave thanks time and again that we had the foresight to do it that way. To have made that run over the "in between" twice in one trip would have been something more than a strain. There was no freeway over the Laguna Mountains east of San Diego in 1961. Telegraph Canyon Road connected with Route 94 through Potrero, Campo, Manzanita and Boulevard. Old Highway 80 East from Boulevard Junction wasn't too bad, once the descent into the Imperial Valley had been navigated. From there to Calexico the road was at least level. After crossing into Mexico at Mexicali, the highway on to Sonoyta was newly completed.

The sun had set by the time we came to Pitiquito in the Sonora desert. Here we found a track leading away from the highway. Once out of sight, we managed to gather enough dry shrub and cactus for an evening campfire and spread our bedrolls under the early November nightfall. We had started our trip.

Morning outside Pitiquito brought a surprise. The tarpaulins covering our bedrolls crackled with a heavy coating of ice. It was too cold to dawdle. We loaded up and got under way at first light. We would have to find a place to dry things out before we could go to bed that night.

At Santa Ana we hit Mexico 15, the main highway from Nogales south to Mazatlán and Guadalajara. South of Santa Ana, outside the village of Benjamín Hill, a flight of white winged doves flew low across the road ahead before dropping into a milo maize field less than a quarter mile to the east. Who was I to defy Providence?

We pulled off the road and spread the tarpaulins to dry over the low bushes while we worked the field for jump shots. By the time the sun had done its job on our tarps, we had done ours, too. When we headed on south toward Mazatlán, our ice chest held two dozen plump white-winged doves that would make a meal fit for a king—make that a couple of kings.

Art Metcalfe, the US consul at Mazatlán, helped us arrange for shipment of the Carryall across the mouth of the Gulf of California to La Paz. We were to have it ready for loading early Friday morning. That left Thursday free, and which happened to be Thanksgiving Day. Don and I found a deserted beach outside Mazatlán with large rocks to protect our campfire from the wind. We had a delightful swim in the surf while the mesquite wood fire burned down to perfect coals for the heavy Dutch oven. Our Thanksgiving dove dinner was entirely appropriate for such a special occasion.

After an overnight at La Paz to get organized, we headed south through Rancho Buenos Aires, Santiago and San José del Cabo to Cabo San Lucas. The ocean and the beaches were nothing short of terrific. We made camp on the shore at El Tule, and I had fresh fish ready for the pan before breakfast the next morning. Everywhere there were signs of "progress." New resorts and new resort facilities were being laid out or were under construction at each turn in the road. I knew these things had to come before the tourists from the north would bring their dollars to Baja. Still, it disturbed me greatly. Deserted beaches against a background of natural desert would soon be replaced by palm thatched cabanas and beachfront hotels. Progress?

At Cabo San Lucas, we took a deep breath and started out on the trip we had come to make—a 1,000-mile run the length of the Baja California peninsula. As we left San Lucas town limits, a covey of quail hurried across the road ahead of us, obliging the first of many such stops we were to make in the days ahead. By the time we moved on a half hour later, there were quail enough in the ice chest for a couple of meals.

There was no way to avoid La Paz on the trip north, but we hardly slowed as we drove on to Santa Rita and Villa Constitución, where the pavement ended. A long, straight stretch of graded road through cultivated lands led to Pozo Grande. It was here we edged into the "in between." The transformation was complete. Cultivated fields quickly gave way to stark desert. Sheer buttes rose from the desert floor to form isolated mesas. Much of the sparse vegetation bore little resemblance to the desert growth of California and Arizona. There were saguaro-like cactus trees, called cardón, but there were other bushes and plants we could not identify at all.

At Comondú, we found a two-mission town, San Miguel de Comondú and San José de Comondú. Grass grew on the main street and the rows of low, flat-topped adobe buildings that bordered it must have dated back to colonial times. If a person wanted to find the quiet life at a leisurely pace, Comondú would have been the place to look. The most notable thing we saw there was a citrus tree that grew grapefruit shaped like pears—a strain introduced by the padres centuries earlier, according to local legend.

Beyond Comondú, there was even less evidence that civilization had ever passed this way. There were no houses, no ranchos, no livestock and precious little game, except quail—of which there were more than enough to make up the difference. I had never given any thought to there being such a thing as having too much quail to eat, but I found out there is. I considered giving some of it away, except there was no one around to give it to. We were as isolated as if we were visiting another planet.

At Canipolé junction we turned toward the coast for a look at Loreto, the oldest settlement in Baja, dating from 1697. Here, too, we found the oldest mission in Baja, Nuestra Señora de Loreto. It was well worth the bad road we had to travel to find this colonial settlement nestled behind Isla Carmen at the edge of the Gulf of California. Late in the afternoon, we found ourselves on the beach, where local fishermen invited us to join them for a supper of *cahuama* on the half shell. The cahuama or green sea turtle, had been cleaned in a way that left generous chunks of flesh clinging to the upper shell. The half shells were then tilted over the coals and roasted until the meat was done to individual taste. It was a welcome change from quail.

There was no way out of Loreto except to double back through Canipolé. But we soon forgot the winding dusty road as we came in sight of the spectacular panorama of the lower end of Bahía Concepción. This 30-mile inlet was unquestionably the most beautiful body of saltwater I have ever seen. We found an ideal place to pitch camp under the shade of a spreading mesquite tree set atop a peculiar mound close by the water's edge.

Bahía Concepción proved to be as beautiful up close as it had seemed from afar—white sand beaches and clear blue-green water. There were first-rate campsites everywhere. Some day there would be a paved highway leading here from the United States. I looked forward to that time. But for now, I was glad to have come while things were still as nature had intended.

Before we moved on the next morning, we made two interesting discoveries. The mound we had pitched camp on was an enormous shell pile, undoubtedly left there by untold generations of natives who had harvested shellfish from Bahía Concepción over the centuries and shucked them on that spot. As we explored for shellfish at low tide, we found a species of clam completely new to me. Locally known as *almeja callo de hacha,* or hatchet clam, these unusual and enormous bivalves clung to rocks and mangrove roots that were entirely exposed at low tide. Shaped much like a hatchet, some were a good eighteen inches long. The meaty part was small, compared to the size of the shell, hardly larger than a good-sized scallop. But the quality of the flesh was excellent. These clams were mild and tender when fried, and they made excellent ceviche. I have never tried better seafood—anywhere, anytime.

We had come over some rough and dusty roads to reach Bahía Concepción. But we hadn't come across anything that was dangerous. That was about to change. As we drove north above the western shore of the bay, the road climbed higher and higher and became narrower and narrower until we found ourselves on a one lane track, the left side of the Carryall all but scraping the mountainside while the roadbed threatened to crumble under the right wheels, which all but hung out over the water far below. What we would have done had we met oncoming traffic I have no idea. Regardless, the drive was spectacularly beautiful.

About 10 miles north of the mouth of Bahía Concepción is the village of Mulegé, a settlement founded by the padres long before the thirteen English colonies dared declare their independence from the mother country. The Misión Santa Rosalía de Mulegé which the padres completed in 1766, is an impressive structure. But for me, the outstanding feature of Mulegé was the Río Santa Rosalía, a beautiful flow of fresh water that worked its way to the Gulf of California through citrus groves, olive orchards and row upon row of date palms. Mulegé is an oasis worthy of the name. Here we found primitive accommodations at Hacienda Mulegé and decided it was time to break up our trip. No one can truly appreciate a good hot bath and a real bed until you've slept on the ground and bathed out of a jerrycan for a few days.

Although we had planned to stay close to the Gulf of California coastline on our way north, after passing through the mining community of Santa Rosalía, there was no way to avoid going inland. Not even a trail led up the rugged coastline from that point on. Reluctantly, we swung west toward San Ignacio. The road climbed sharply at a steep grade many vehicles would have been hard pressed to make. As we made the ascent we came to a cactus-covered plateau that stretched to the slopes of three volcanic cones—Las Tres Vírgenes. Arid and barren as the countryside had been along the coast, here it was more so. There was a noticeable nip in the wind. Gone was the tropical warmth of the Gulf of California.

Our first view of San Ignacio was like looking into another world. Here, at the bottom of an arroyo, was water and a forest of date palms, citrus, figs and grapes. It was a classic oasis. The magnificent Misión San Ignacio was more impressive than any we had yet seen during our trip. Over 200 years old, the original structure was well-preserved and serving the spiritual needs of its parishioners.

From San Ignacio north, one day of spectacular but hard travel blended into the next. Difficult trails were the rule, except where they got worse. We passed through the country of cirio trees, tall and candle-like, and we passed through the country of elephant trees, squat and gnarled. Always, there were high buttes standing against the skyline. When we crossed the 28th parallel north, leaving the Territory of Baja California Sur behind as we entered the North Territory of Baja California, we knew we were finally on the downhill side of our journey. It was a good feeling. There are limited thrills to be gotten out of one stretch after another of rough, barren desert and stark, rugged mountains.

As we worked our way back across the peninsula toward the Gulf of California, we came to Misión San Francisco Borja. Even deserted and all but in ruins, it was a magnificent sight after so many, endless miles of nothing. Although more than 4,000 natives lived in the area when the padres built San Borja, it was now too arid for any type of agriculture, and no one lived there when we passed that way. Two magnificent bells hung in the mission belfry. Within a year I heard that one had been carted off by someone passing through.

Our return to the Gulf of California at Bahía de los Angeles was a welcome relief. The desert is always more pleasant where it meets the sea. It was now December, and there was a marked chill in the air. The warmth of the evening campfire on the beach facing Isla Angel de la Guarda was most welcome. The setting would have been awe inspiring had it been our first camp on the Gulf instead of one of our last. We were eager to finish our trip, although we hated to see it end.

The maps we had used as general guides on our trip showed the main trail swinging west from Bahía de los Angeles toward El Rosario and San Quintín on the Pacific. According to one map, there was no road connecting Bahía de los Angeles and the pavement at San Felipe. But we knew from word of mouth that there was a way to get through to Bahía San Luis Gonzaga, Puertecitos, San Felipe and Mexicali. We were determined to find it and finish our trip along the shores of the Gulf of California as planned.

It's good we were optimistic, for the trail turned out to be difficult. More than once we came to places where our track divided into two, with nothing to mark which way to go. When we asked the occasional driver coming our way, we learned there were far too many splits in the road ahead to be remembered. And on top of everything else, we had to cross several dry lakebeds where for miles on end the powdery dust was almost axle deep. There was one day we traveled 10 hours to cover 90 miles!

It's been many years since Don Olliff and I made our run through Baja California. Looking back, I ask myself what Uncle Sam got out of our adventure. Don did write a report on economic progress and prospects for the peninsula which must have been of interest to someone in Washington. I'm sure the half-dozen rolls of 35-mm film I exposed were developed and studied by someone, somewhere. Maybe there was some notoriety of having a US consul general at Tijuana, Mexico, who knew more about his consular district, firsthand, than any Mexican who lived in it. Make that any two Mexicans who lived in it.

Hechicera

I don't remember how it was we first came to Hechicera. It may have been on one of the exploration trips we always made when we were getting acquainted with a new post. Or perhaps Mary and I just wandered off the beaten path while looking for a good place to hunt quail in Baja California. But I clearly recall our first glimpse of pine treetops after traveling up a dusty dirt track through low brush. Almost simultaneously we spotted a faint trace of an overgrown road cutting off between a compact oak and the rocky shoulder of a small hill. We needed a rest and we needed water, so we turned off.

Less than a mile over a low hill we came to a beautiful little cup in the mountains, completely hidden from the outside. There were tall ponderosa pines and enormous oaks scattered at random across the floor of the little valley. Winding through the trees was a crystal-clear stream of mountain water. We called the spot Hidden Valley, and we returned there many times to camp and have our fill of crisp mountain air, pure sparkling water and the enormous solitude of this place so far from turmoil.

It was only after we had been to Hidden Valley several times that we learned it was part of Rancho Hechicera. We had noticed the large ranch house perched on a hilltop just off the road into the valley. It was kind of spooky because we never saw a living soul there, no matter how early or how late in the day we happened to pass.

There were always horses nibbling at the sparse grass in the pasture that spread below the house, and occasionally we caught a glimpse of a wisp of smoke rising from the chimney of a smaller house built among the oaks, up against the mountain on the far side of the pasture. But we never saw anyone until the day a horseman rode into our camp leading a couple of saddled geldings, and introduced himself as the foreman of Rancho Hechicera.

"I have come," he said in Spanish, "on the instructions of my jefe, Don Juan Rodríguez. This ranch is his property. Don Juan wishes me to tell you that you are welcome at Hechicera. It would give him great pleasure if so illustrious a person as the consul general of the United States of North America in Baja California would do him the honor of making use of not only his house but of all the facilities Hechicera has to offer, whenever and as often as it may be your pleasure."

It was obvious he had been carefully coached or had long practiced his speech—probably both. I have no idea how Juan Rodríguez knew who it was that came to camp on his property. At the time, I had never met him, although I knew his father, General Abelardo Rodríguez, a former president of Mexico and the principal benefactor of Baja California. But Juan knew who we were, and in typical Mexican fashion, nothing would do but that we should be made as welcome and as comfortable as it was within his power to make us.

I was fascinated with the name Hechicera and always intended to ask Juan how his ranch came to be known by it. But like so many things I always intended to do, I never got around to it.

The *Velásquez Spanish and English Dictionary* defines the word as: witch, charmer, enchanter. To many, Juan's ranch was known as Agua Hechicera—and there was no better way to describe the enchanting little spring-fed stream that flowed through Hidden Valley.

Juan Rodríguez rarely visited his ranch, although he had once taken a great interest in it. Not only had he built the house on the hill with its great circular fireplace in the main living room, he had also built a landing strip so he could fly in at will in his Aero Commander. Water was always scarce in Baja, and Juan had bulldozed up a series of earthen dams across the course of the stream to form long, narrow ponds.

These he had stocked with black bass. Raised in that cold mountain stream, they were about as good eating fish as I have ever tried—and they were plentiful! We were often torn between making our camp under one of the great oaks along this string of ponds, or back in the privacy of Hidden Valley, our first love.

No matter where we camped, Mr. Ruiz—as the children came to know Juan's foreman—always showed up within an hour or two, leading a couple of horses for us to enjoy. But before anyone could take off on a ride we had to finish setting up camp—unloading the trailer, pitching a tent for the adults and younger children, hanging Army surplus jungle hammocks for the others to sleep in, hoisting a canvas shelter over our picnic area, and starting a campfire. There was never a shortage of chores and activities, and we always feasted on fish or quail, and occasionally a skillet of Mary's fried rabbit stew.

Our appreciation of Hechicera was enhanced by many factors—the music of quail calling to each other at dusk, waking at dawn from the best sleep ever, the thrill of seeing a deer or a rare covey of high-country partridge feeding in the draw just beyond our campground, the excitement of watching one of the children hook into an old granddad bass—one of the initial stock. And always, our pleasure was compounded by our children's enthusiasm for the kind of life Mary and I enjoyed the most.

Turning Point

September of 1962 should have been a good month for me. It marked the midpoint in my anticipated tour at Tijuana—two years behind me and two more to go. It was a time to look back on what I had accomplished during the first half of my tour. It was also a time to plan how I would take care of those things I wanted to do before I moved on two years down the road.

The wheel of Foreign Service fortune had stopped on my number when the 1961 selection board drew up its list and was included among those favored few to be promoted to Class FSO-2. It had been five years since my last promotion, a long dry spell, and I was delighted.

I was pleased with the change that had been made in the operation of the visa section, which involved 50 percent of our staff. Without adding personnel or requiring overtime, we practically doubled our output. Fees collected exceeded operation expenses by $159,267.46 my second year at Tijuana. Perhaps this is as good a place as any to mention that an inspection of the consulate general after I left suggested I must have operated a sweatshop. I hadn't.

The Kennedy administration had brought about renewed interest in promoting good relations with our neighbors to the south, primarily Mexico. I worked hard on both sides of the border to make a meaningful contribution.

One of the accomplishments that gave me the greatest satisfaction was the relationships I was able to establish with the movers and shakers in Baja California—those in government, business, the media and the Mexican military. When there was need to seek a favor, the way was clear to the person who could grant it.

I was satisfied with my work over the past two years. I don't know what I might have visualized had I looked ahead, but it would not have been what the future held in store for me. On a Friday afternoon early in September 1962, I received urgent orders transferring me to Washington, where I was to report for duty the following Monday morning. I was devastated.

I didn't give up without a fight—but struggle as I might, the die was cast. I went back to the substantive end of the business as deputy director of the office of Caribbean and Mexican Affairs, about as far removed from consular work as a Foreign Service officer might get. Among other troubled spots, Cuba, Haiti and the Dominican Republic would be in my bailiwick. The 1962 Cuban Missile Crisis was to become the supreme test of our national willpower before I had a chance to get my feet on the ground in my new job.

I hated to admit it, but I knew I had reached a defining moment in my career. I had realized my ambition in the Foreign Service and seen my accomplishment slip away like sand between my fingers. There would be no return to consular work, no matter how much I might hope.

But I reminded myself the world hardly ever comes to an end. I would have to play the hand I had been dealt. I resolved to set a new goal for myself—and attain it!

Briefing President Lyndon B. Johnson on the disposition of US troops in Santo Domingo, Dominican Republic. May 14, 1965.

Kennedy Crockett, Director of Caribbean and Mexican Affairs, US Department of State, 1965.

Washington, DC (II)
1962

JFK

There have been two events in my lifetime catastrophic enough for me to remember exactly where I was and what I was doing when I learned about them. On December 7, 1941, I was driving my sister to the train station in Austin, Texas, after a football weekend when I switched on the car radio and heard a live broadcast of the Japanese attack on Pearl Harbor. On November 22, 1963, I was having lunch with José Antonio Bonilla Atiles, the foreign minister of the Dominican Republic, at a Georgetown restaurant when the headwaiter whispered in my ear that President Kennedy had been shot and I was to return to the State Department immediately.

It had been over a year since my forced transfer from Tijuana to Washington. I had not wanted to make the move, and developments since my arrival had done nothing to convince me I had been wrong. The Kennedy administration was populated with bright people, but by and large they seemed determined to build a new world rather than learn how to get along in the admittedly flawed one we already had. There were too many idealists in positions of power. We may have all spoken English, but we by no means spoke the same language.

I suppose it was old-fashioned of me, but I found myself concerned about the striking lack of on-the-spot experience in my chain of command. John Crimmins, director of Caribbean and Mexican affairs (CMA) was my immediate supervisor—an intelligent, dedicated and hardworking trooper. However, his field experience in western hemisphere affairs was limited to a single assignment as an economic officer at Rio. His boss, Assistant Secretary of State for Inter-American Affairs Edwin M. Martin, a brilliant man and consummate bureaucrat, was basically an economist with no service at all in the area he was responsible for. No one could question the dedication of either man, but I would have felt a lot better if my orders had come from someone who had a little more hands-on experience.

I need not have worried about John Crimmins. The Cuban Missile Crisis of 1962 came to a head within weeks of my arrival in Washington, and before it was over John had been transferred to Miami where he concentrated full time on Cuba, which was moved out of the office of Caribbean and Mexican Affairs and virtually into the White House. I filled in behind Crimmins as acting director of Caribbean and Mexican Affairs. I was to remain in an acting capacity for as long as the Kennedy administration lasted. Ed Martin knew I did not want the job, but he had no one better to replace me. I stayed on doing the best I could, but I was not a happy camper.

If I had been concerned about lack of hands-on experience in the direction of CMA before I took over, my own incumbency was no occasion for celebration. I boasted years of firsthand experience with Mexico but had never been in any of the Caribbean island republics except for a short visit to Cuba years earlier. Very quickly I began to pay the price for my lack of knowledge about the area I was responsible for. When Ralph Dungan, special assistant to the president, called to discuss Haiti, I had to plead ignorance to his first three or four questions. I cringed when Dungan asked, "Are you sure I have the right number?" There's always something to be thankful for—at least we weren't face to face.

Haiti and the Dominican Republic dominated my day-to-day work during my year in the Kennedy administration—Haiti because the Kennedy liberals wanted to get rid of Papa Doc Duvalier, and the Dominican Republic because Leonides Trujillo had recently been assassinated and the country was struggling to find its way to democracy after decades of brutal dictatorship. At the time of John Kennedy's death, my attention was focused on the Dominican Republic because of a coup d'état, which had left us in the position of not recognizing any government there. But for the most part, Haiti had been the focal point for my efforts.

I could hardly have been less equipped to deal with Haiti. I had never served there. I did not speak, read or write the official language (French), much less the more commonly used Haitian Creole. I did not know or recognize the names of many of the major players in the game of Haitian politics. And all these shortcomings were well-known to people both up and down my chain of command. Still, I had to play the game, and I found myself largely on the other side when it came to the most popular issue: how to get rid of Papa Doc. I wanted to know who or what would come next if he should relinquish power, for whatever reason. I usually got a scowl when I raised this point in senior-level strategy sessions.

The day came when a plan had been hatched whereby Papa Doc would be forced to relinquish power. We were to present it to President Kennedy for his approval. It called for frightening Papa Doc into resigning his Presidency for Life. Imagine frightening a man who consorted with the devil himself!

Our group met with President Kennedy in the Cabinet Room at the White House. I sat quietly while the pitch was made, wondering how I would manage to get my reservations across without mashing too many toes. I never got the chance. The first thing President Kennedy asked after hearing out the pitch-man was, "Who have we set up to move in afterwards?" No one had an answer for that. The meeting adjourned shortly afterwards.

I had come to Washington prepared to dislike President Kennedy. I could not forgive him for failing to provide the backing that might have made it possible for the Bay of Pigs invasion to succeed. I had been against the Bay of Pigs plan from the beginning. I felt we could not sell it to the rest of Latin America—there would be too much concern over who might be next. But I felt that if we were determined to go ahead, then we should be prepared to do whatever might be necessary to insure the success of the invasion. Nothing succeeds like success—even something as distasteful as seeing the United States openly abandon its popular and long-standing policy of non-intervention in Latin America. President Kennedy had made both mistakes: he approved the invasion attempt, and he allowed it to fail by refusing to permit our armed forces to provide back up when it became essential for success.

My first meeting with President Kennedy took place in the Oval Office. Jamaica had just been granted independence, and I was designated to accompany her first ambassador to the United States when he presented his credentials. No one else was involved except the Jamaican ambassador, President Kennedy and myself. The president didn't know who I was other than someone from State, but he was careful to greet me courteously and include me in the brief informal conversation whenever appropriate. His presence was commanding, his grin infectious. There was no way not to be impressed. My resolve not to like him crumbled.

Now it was all over. Telegrams were rushed to all United States Missions informing them of President Kennedy's death and the Constitutional succession of Lyndon B. Johnson to the office of president of the United States, along with instruction to pass the message to the host government. Reassurances that all was well were to be given informally—in case anyone had any doubts. We went about our tasks of preparing for the state funeral in an atmosphere of deep gloom and depression.

Several of us from the State Department were detailed to the White House to help with the large contingent of visiting dignitaries. We ushered and answered questions and tried not to be obtrusive. It was, I hope, a once in a lifetime experience—enormously solemn and impressive. Mrs. Kennedy was prominent at all times. I marveled that she could carry through so gallantly.

The delegation from Nicaragua was headed by ex-President Luis Somoza. It fell to me to act as his aide on various occasions, and I found him a charming person to deal with. How different history might have been were it not for his massive heart attack in 1967 at the age of 44, when he had so much to offer and his wise counsel was so badly needed by his younger brother, Anastasio, as he became president. That thought would occur to me often in the years ahead.

Finally, it was all finished and President Johnson got down to establishing his own administration. He tried to carry on with Kennedy policies and Kennedy people wherever he could. The notable exception was the Bureau of Inter-American Affairs and the Alliance for Progress in the State Department. That was my bailiwick, and it was there that things got a thorough going over—and I got a new lease on my professional life.

New Beginnings

John F. Kennedy's funeral cortege had hardly passed out of sight of the State Department when it became evident I was not alone in my concerns about the direction of our hemisphere policy. There must have been hundreds of things that needed doing with the greatest urgency in those first days of Lyndon B. Johnson's presidency. Among those, the one that came near the top of the list was finding a new assistant secretary of state for Inter-American Affairs. The man who got the job was President Johnson's first appointee.

We in the office of Caribbean and Mexican Affairs (CMA) were probably the first to know the president was shopping for a new man to take over hemisphere foreign relations. We knew because the president had turned to

Thomas C. Mann, then serving as ambassador to Mexico. There was no way Tom Mann could come to Washington and headquarter in CMA without Bob Sayre (then Officer in Charge of Mexican Affairs) and me knowing something was up. Tom took us into his confidence during his negotiations with LBJ, and we both respected that confidence—scrupulously.

Johnson could not have selected a more able and experienced man for his Latin American chief. Tom Mann's service in Latin America dated back to 1942 when he represented the Board of Economic Warfare in Montevideo, Uruguay. He had also served in Caracas, Venezuela, and Guatemala, and had worked his way up the ladder in Inter-American Affairs during tours in Washington before being appointed ambassador to El Salvador at the age of 43. His more recent experience included a stint as assistant secretary of state for Inter-American Affairs.

Although I had never worked directly with Tom in the Foreign Service, we had been raised within a few blocks of each other and had been friends as far back as I could remember. We got together regularly to catch up on each other's activities during the 20 years we had both been in the Foreign Service. I knew how he felt about his Foreign Service career, and that he had long since decided to retire rather than take another assignment after his 50th birthday. Above all, he had no interest in another Washington assignment. Tom had just celebrated his 51st birthday when Johnson called him to Washington. I wondered what he would do.

I'm sure Tom must have known how futile it was to say no to a request from Lyndon B. Johnson, but I know he tried. When it became clear Johnson refused to take no for an answer, Tom's tactic was to get a presidential commitment for full backing in exchange for accepting the assignment. In addition to becoming assistant secretary of state for Inter-American Affairs *and* coordinator of the Alliance for Progress (where the money was controlled), Tom was named a special assistant to the president. For once he would have the clout it took to move things along through the State Department bureaucracy. We in CMA were euphoric. I suspect the liberals among the Kennedy carryovers were hardly as pleased. Tom was a pragmatist, and they had no use for anyone with his feet firmly planted in reality.

There were many changes in the way things were done in the Bureau of Inter-American Affairs during the initial days of Tom Mann's incumbency. Among the first was splitting off Mexican Affairs from CMA—a move I had favored ever since serving as officer in charge of Mexican Affairs in the mid-1950s. Now Bob Sayre became director of the Office of Mexican Affairs—equal status with the director of Caribbean Affairs—in recognition of Mexico's influence in the hemisphere and her special status in the order of things as far as the United States is concerned. Simultaneously, the "acting" was removed from in front of my title, a move I felt was long overdue.

These adjustments were nice—even important—but in no way as momentous as Tom Mann's injunction to all his office directors to "take responsibility for your own actions and move along on your own authority instead of bucking everything upstairs for clearance." That instruction was music to my ears. During the Kennedy administration, I had spent hours. . .days. . .even weeks in conferences and rewriting plans trying to please everyone. How nice it was to have some independent authority for a change. I couldn't wait to use mine—and I was surprised how many of my associates were afraid to use theirs.

I was to remain in Washington throughout the first two years of the Johnson presidency, and they would prove to be the busiest and most productive of my Foreign Service career. That was in no way the result of my own planning or strategy. Fate dictated that I should be where a great deal of the action was in Latin America from the fall of 1963 until the fall of 1965.

John Bartlow Martin | Dominican Republic

The Jackal of the Caribbean, Dominican dictator Rafael Leonides Trujillo, met his death at the hands of assassins on a dark country road the night of May 30, 1961, ending over three decades of cruel subjugation of the Dominican people. His timely demise provided an ideal situation for the Kennedy people to demonstrate how a showcase of democracy could be built by the right people, doing the right thing, at the right time—always, of course, with the support of the Alliance for Progress and the Peace Corps.

The man chosen to supervise on-the-spot implementation of this ambitious project was John Bartlow Martin, a freelance writer who presented his diplomatic credentials as United States ambassador to the Dominican Republic on March 9, 1962. A supporter of Adlai Stevenson for many years, Martin had joined the Kennedy campaign staff as a speech writer after Stevenson withdrew from the race.

From the moment of my arrival on the Washington scene in the fall of 1962, John Martin was the principal architect of US policy in the Dominican Republic. His dedication to establishing a thriving democracy on Dominican soil was complete—and no man could have put in longer hours of dedicated effort to that end. I came to admire him and value his friendship.

He had more ideas than a dog has fleas, and if one thing didn't work (and it usually didn't) he could always come up with something else. The policies he crafted were probably as good as any others and I usually followed his lead, if for no other reason than because I didn't have any better ideas of my own. (Martin's book, *Overtaken by Events*; Doubleday & Co., 1966, is must-reading for the serious student of developments in the Dominican Republic from Trujillo's assassination in 1961 through the revolution of 1965.)

Only once did I take strong exception to a policy line espoused by Ambassador Martin. He and others close to the White House feared that former Trujillo front man Joaquín Balaguer would bollix up our plans if he returned to the Dominican Republic. Balaguer, then residing in New York, was consequently prohibited from departing the United States. I had two problems with this policy. First, we couldn't enforce it. In our free society, there were a hundred ways Balaguer could leave the country without detection any time he chose. Second, my experience with Miguel Ydígoras in Guatemala had convinced me that a man like Balaguer could quite easily become prominent once again in Dominican politics. I could see no reason to alienate him for no practical purpose. I authorized lifting the departure controls on Balaguer and other Dominican exiles we were theoretically keeping from returning to their country.

It wasn't long before I had one of my regular telephone calls from the president's special assistant, Ralph Dungan, wanting to know why I had done it. He didn't use the president's name, but suggested he was annoyed and wanted me to justify the "unauthorized" action I had taken. I hadn't counted on a reaction that high up, but I had my arguments ready. In fact, the memorandum Dungan wanted was already in all-but-final draft. I cleaned it up and sent it over. It was the last I heard about that matter. If President Kennedy was involved, he apparently agreed with my reasoning. When it came time for Balaguer to again take an active role in Dominican politics, we at least started off on friendly terms.

After an unending series of cliff hangers, elections were held, and a poet-turned-politician named Juan Bosch was inaugurated president of the Dominican Republic on February 27, 1963. He was clearly not the right man for the job, nor was the time ripe for such pure democracy in the Dominican Republic. As Rómulo Betancourt of Venezuela was to comment, when it came to politics, Juan Bosch was a good short story writer. His presidency was terminated by a military coup, less than seven months after his inauguration.

At his own request, Ambassador Martin was recalled to show United States' displeasure. His intention was somehow to make the Dominican military undo what was irrevocable. That process was ongoing when the Kennedy presidency came to an end on November 22, 1963.

As it became clear that Juan Bosch could never be returned to the Dominican presidency—and probably didn't want to anyway—I started trying to pave the way for John Martin to understand that his days as United States ambassador to the Dominican Republic were over. I warned that given the way things are done in Washington, he would wake up one morning to read in the *Washington Post* that so-and-so had been nominated as the new United States ambassador to Santo Domingo. If John heard, he didn't give any sign. He had to find out the hard way.

One of Lyndon Johnson's first official acts as president of the United States was to visit the State Department. He addressed us in the main auditorium, pledging to continue Kennedy administration policies. Afterwards, all United States ambassadors present were invited to meet the president in one of the seventh-floor reception rooms. As John Martin stood in line waiting his turn to be introduced by Dean Rusk, the secretary presented the man standing in line right ahead of John as "...your new ambassador to the Dominican Republic." Such is life in top-drawer politics.

But John wasn't through with the Dominican Republic. When the going got tough after the 1965 revolution, one of President Johnson's first acts was to bring him back to Washington from his fishing camp in the Michigan woods and send him to the Dominican Republic as a special representative of the president of the United States. Johnson needed someone who could talk to the political left in the Dominican Republic, and Abe Fortas convinced him John Bartlow Martin was the best man for the job. I tended to agree—more so when Martin insisted he would have to take Harry Schlaudeman along to help out. Of course, that left me without a Dominican desk officer when I needed one most. It worked out for the best in the long run, although it was rough going over the short haul.

Benson E. L. Timmons III | Haiti

Having carried the life-long burden of three last names myself, I could sympathize with Benson E. L. Timmons III—who those of us who came to know him well were allowed to call Lane. Not having a first name can be hell.

Lane Timmons' career was as extraordinary as his name. Born in Georgia and a graduate of the University of Georgia, he went on to earn both BA and MA degrees as a Rhodes Scholar at Balliol College, University of Oxford. World War II came along between the BA and the MA, but Lane didn't waste any time while in the Army. He was promoted to the rank of lieutenant colonel before peace came.

Timmons first signed up with the State Department in 1948, working as an economist at the embassy in Paris. Doing one important job after another in the economic or related fields, he managed to stay in Paris, or close by, until 1961 when he was assigned to New Delhi as Ambassador J. Kenneth Galbraith's deputy chief of mission. After Galbraith had enough of India, Timmons was named as ambassador to Haiti.

Timmons' main qualification for his new assignment was fluent French—possibly more fluent than anyone else in Haiti. Lane did things that way. I liked him from the beginning. He was a dedicated and determined officer.

Every officer assigned to the US embassy at Port-au-Prince during Papa Doc Duvalier's long reign came to despise him very quickly. Lane Timmons was no exception. A running feud quickly developed between them, which would have been OK with me except that the relative importance of the Timmons-Duvalier spat quickly got out of proportion. To Lane, it was the first and foremost thing I should devote my attention to, and at least one of the most important problems which the entire State Department was faced with at any given time. While it was true that Papa Doc's antics drew some attention in the immediate Caribbean region, in Latin America they were hardly worth a yawn—and in the world at large, it was "Papa Doc who?"

The only meaningful threat Papa Doc could make was to declare Timmons persona non-grata and send him packing. He didn't make these threats openly, but he was an expert at leaking them where they would be most audible. Timmons sought to counter Papa Doc's threats with threats of our own to take punitive action in retaliation. For some reason, things always seemed to come to a head in Haiti when we were in the midst of delicate negotiations in the Organization of American States (OAS), striving to sell a point vital to our interests or build a fig leaf to cover our intervention in the Dominican Republic. Worse yet, it was usually at a time when Haiti held the swing vote.

Lane's tactic was to send us lengthy telegrams reviewing Papa Doc's shortcomings back to year one and recommending what we should do to straighten Duvalier out. The courses of action he favored were designed to get at Papa Doc where it would hurt the most. My responses, which tended to become as lengthy as Lane's presentations, were designed to convince him we could not do what he wanted at a time when we badly needed Haiti's OAS vote. This kind of a debate was much to Lane's liking. He inevitably came back quickly with well-reasoned and persuasive arguments to counter my every point.

I had no problem with these intellectual exercises, except that in my order of priorities, Lane's difficulties with Papa Doc came close to last in line. This meant that I could get around to drafting my responses between 10:00 p.m. and midnight, after a grueling day taking care of more important problems. Still, out of elementary courtesy to the president's personal representative in Haiti, the effort had to be made—until I'd had enough.

My day had been an exceptionally demanding one in a series of demanding days. There had been no opportunity to go home for a couple of nights, and it looked like I wasn't going to make it home for a third night in a row when Lane's most recent epistle came in. His telegram must have been about five single spaced, letter-size pages. There was no way to know when I might find time to read it, much less react. It was more than a man could stand. In response, I dictated the shortest telegram ever sent out of the State Department. It read, "NO" and was signed, "Rusk." There was no way to know how the secretary of state might react to my use of his name, but I was tired enough not to give a damn.

Shadow People | Washington, DC

Not everyone with whom I maintained contact during my second tour of duty in Washington held an official position. There were people in the shadows, or along the sidelines if you prefer, who could and did influence developments in my area of interest. It was impossible to ignore them and carry out my responsibilities as productively as I thought they should be discharged. But on the other hand, there were also dangers in getting too intimately involved.

Irving Davidson was already mixed into Haitian affairs when I first came to the office of Caribbean and Mexican Affairs. I never was able to learn much about his background, although it didn't take me long to conclude that he lived—quite comfortably—by his wits. Not long after we first met, Irving casually mentioned that he was associated with interests owned by a Texas millionaire of my acquaintance. I checked his story out and discovered he was, indeed. The evaluation I got back was, "He's always done right by us."

Davidson was also in contact with Benson E. L. Timmons III, our ambassador in Haiti. He knew about the disputes between Papa Doc and Lane Timmons and was helpful—possibly more than once—in smoothing things over when Papa Doc was about to send Timmons packing. Eventually, Davidson's dealings with—and representations on behalf of—Duvalier became frequent enough that we insisted he register as a foreign agent.

From the beginning, I recognized the dangers inherent in dealing with Irving and was always careful to maintain a written record of our contacts. These I circulated to my associates who had a legitimate interest in what Davidson might be doing at any given time.

During my Washington tour, Davidson played a major role in Haitian-American relations as a go-between who could say things to Papa Doc that no US official dared. But Davidson's most vital role was in developments involving the Dominican Republic. Early on, Davidson had come to the same conclusion I had—that Dr. Joaquín Balaguer could again become a factor in Dominican politics. By some means which I never learned, Davidson managed to meet and establish a strong relationship with Dr. Balaguer while he was an impoverished exile in New York. The two were about the same size, and Balaguer was able to clothe himself rather splendidly in Davidson's castoffs. The relationship was so tight that Davidson could produce Balaguer when and where I might need him, when I didn't dare set up a meeting on my own.

This handy situation was ready-made for some of the delicate undertakings that would be mine during what came to be known as the Dominican Crisis of 1965. It also brought forcefully home how big a risk my dealings with Irving Davidson could entail. I once walked into the Davidsons' home in Maryland for a crucial meeting with Dr. Balaguer to find Teamster Union boss Jimmy Hoffa, his wife and his son seated at the table with the Davidsons. There was nothing to be done but join them. At least I could talk to Hoffa about having been a truck driver during the Depression years. I have no idea how I would have explained where I was to people in the Department of State if word had gotten out.

Davidson once performed a valuable service for me in a different context. Drew Pearson, senior muckraker of his day, had mounted a campaign in his syndicated column against Undersecretary of State Tom Mann. I felt sure Pearson would drop the matter if I could get to him and straighten him out on the facts. Davidson was well enough connected to set up a meeting for me with Pearson at his Maryland farm, where we spent a long lunch talking Dominican and US politics. All strident criticism of Tom Mann subsequently disappeared from the Pearson column.

Another of the people always nearby in the shadows at that time was Dr. Francisco "Pancho" Aguirre, publisher of the Miami-based Spanish language daily newspaper, *El Diario de las Américas*. Day-to-day direction of *El Diario* was in the hands of Pancho's brother, Horacio, who lived and worked in Miami. For his part, Pancho lived in Rock Creek Park and spent the greater part of his time dabbling in Latin American politics—notably Dominican.

Pancho knew more of the Dominicans active in politics than anyone else in Washington, and more about what they were doing—or planning to do—than anyone else I had access to. I could see him and discuss developments I was puzzled about almost any time of the day or night, and he invariably added something to my understanding of those developments during our conversations. As important as anything else, Pancho's house was a pleasant place to let down and speak a little Spanish when I needed it most. I never left his phone number as a place where I could be reached—that was the icing on the cake.

At no time during our association did Pancho ever attempt to take advantage of our relationship. But there were dangers. The risks entailed would be brought home to me at a time when I was least prepared to cope.

I don't want to leave the impression that working relationships between Foreign Service officers assigned to the Department of State and outside contacts like Davidson and Aguirre are commonplace. I suspect they were quite rare—there is too much risk involved for the Foreign Service officer. Unusual circumstances created the situations that brought about my involvement, and I knew I took risks when I decided to play the game.

Dr. Joaquín Balaguer

When I came to Washington in 1962 I knew virtually nothing about the Dominican Republic except that Christopher Columbus had landed there sometime back and more recently, the country had been liberated from the brutal dictatorship of Generalissimo Leonides Trujillo by reason of his timely demise from acute lead poisoning. I knew less about Dr. Joaquín Balaguer, who was titular chief of state when Trujillo was assassinated. I suppose there was some advantage to being uninformed. At least I was free of misconceptions. Clearly, some research was in order.

From the beginning, I was fascinated with Dr. Balaguer. I learned that he first served Trujillo in 1937 as interim secretary of Foreign Affairs. He had either been part of the government in one capacity or another, or waiting nearby in the wings, ever since. I could understand why the Kennedy people held him in such complete contempt. But I was also able to understand how that sort of thing could happen during the Trujillo dictatorship. It was well known that Trujillo forced virtually every able-bodied man in the DR to serve him, using some form of duress.

It was also significant to me that Trujillo's son Ramfis was the one who held real power at the time of the excesses following the senior Trujillo's death. There had to be some reason why Balaguer continued to preside over a bankrupt government when his fellow citizens booed him in the streets. Balaguer had been around a long time and knew how things worked in the Dominican Republic. He could well become an important presence again. I felt the need to get to know him on my terms before a situation developed where I would be obliged to get to know him on his terms.

Setting up a meeting with Balaguer was a delicate undertaking. Ambassador Martin would be violently opposed. Criticism could be expected from liberals on the Washington scene, both in and out of government, if I didn't do it right. Somehow the meeting had to be "casual," if there were any way on God's green earth to make it so. The key was Irving Davidson.

Davidson had missed no opportunity to assure me Balaguer was nothing like his public image and had urged me to get acquainted with him and find out for myself. Now I was ready. I told Davidson I could not take the risk of trying to meet him secretly, or of inviting Balaguer to the Department of State, which would raise a stink in many different quarters. However, ours was a free society (back then, anyone could walk into the State Department building) and if

Dr. Balaguer happened to knock on the door to my office, I would see him. That was all it took.

Dr. Balaguer was a smallish man. Grey-haired and bespectacled, he was nattily dressed in a cream-colored double-breasted suit I had once seen Davidson wearing, a proper cravat, and a white shirt with French cuffs. His smile was warm and his handshake firm. He was not at all the sort of person you would expect, given his background. I later discovered he wrote poetry and considered himself an intellectual. What I did discover very quickly was that we both spoke the common language of Latin American politics and were able to communicate without difficulty.

If anyone took note that Dr. Balaguer called on me in my State Department office from time to time, I do not know. Certainly, no one took exception. We did not meet regularly, but we met often enough to become well acquainted. I felt confident we could count on him to listen to our counsel should the occasion arise when he would again take an active part in Dominican politics. I also felt pretty sure that Dr. Balaguer had come to know me well enough to take my word at face value. Neither of us expected the other to do anything damaging to his own country's best interests.

All Hell Breaks Loose

Tom Mann's assumption of duties in the Bureau of Inter-American Affairs by no means ended the turmoil in volatile areas of Latin America. Rioting in Panama broke out almost before he had a chance to hang his hat. People on both sides of the Zone fence lost their lives. Nor did my bailiwick become suddenly peaceful and calm. What did change was the way we went about taking care of our problems. It was a welcome change for me.

With new ambassadors in both Haiti and the Dominican Republic, I found time to visit the Caribbean, my first of any consequence. It was love at first sight. I vowed to return at my leisure as soon as I could. Sadly, I never did find time.

One of the most interesting aspect of my visit to the Dominican Republic was the opportunity to get acquainted with Donald Reid, one of three men heading up an interim government. Reid was the dominant figure in the triumvirate and, for all practical purposes, Dominican chief of state. It didn't take me long to conclude that the best thing that could happen to serve both our interests would be for Reid to get the job on a permanent basis. Things didn't work out that way.

Pancho Aguirre had paved the way for us to get acquainted, and Reid and I hit it off immediately. The palace in Santo Domingo wasn't conducive to relaxed conversation, and as soon as formalities were observed, Reid led me down to the basement where he climbed behind the wheel of a nondescript old sedan, and we drove out the service ramp. We spent the rest of the day getting acquainted as we visited the poorer areas of the Dominican capital. At many of the places we stopped, people quickly recognized Reid and petitioned him for help or a favor of some sort. He listened carefully, took note of names, and generally handled his interviews skillfully. He had a way with his people. It's a shame he had no political base. Had he been able to survive in office until elections could be held, our intervention of 1965 might have been avoided entirely.

The embassy in Santo Domingo and those of us directly concerned in the Department of State labored mightily during 1964 to keep things quiet until Dominicans could work out their own system for selecting a new chief of state to replace the deposed Juan Bosch. Things did not go smoothly. One minor crisis followed another. Tensions were always high although, somehow, the lid never blew completely off. For me, it was day after day of cliff hanging and night after night of being awakened at home by urgent telegrams out of embassy/Santo Domingo warning that the end was near. Somehow, I thought I should do something about it—what, I had no idea.

When I'd had enough, I took the bull by the horns and planned a family trip to the beach for a change. Our old station wagon broke down before we were hardly out of town, and by the time I had traded for a replacement, I couldn't afford a trip to the beach. We tried picnics nearby in Virginia and Maryland, but my pager inevitably buzzed right as the steaks went on the grill.

Finally, 1965 arrived and winter gave way to a promise of early spring. We planned an outing to my cousin's farm in Maryland for the afternoon of Saturday, April 24. I labored mightily in the State Department Saturday morning to get everything in order so I might enjoy an uninterrupted afternoon in the country. But it was not to be. Before noon, winter returned with a vengeance, and by the time I skidded into our driveway in McLean, several inches of snow covered the ground. It felt like the last straw.

Mary and I mixed up a batch of margaritas, as was our custom when there was fresh snow, and tried to make light of our disappointment. We were both getting very tired of life in Washington. I couldn't help remembering how much pleasure I had once gotten out of the Foreign Service. All of that seemed so long ago and far away. The more I thought, the gloomier I got. The gloomier I got, the easier the margaritas went down. By the time we finished lunch and turned in for a nap, I was at rock bottom. I took the phone off the hook and shoved it inside a drawer. To hell with everything!

That afternoon, Donald Reid's provisional government was overthrown by a military coup d'état. There wasn't anything I could have done about it, but it's decidedly bad form for an office director to sleep through a coup in one of his own countries. My hangover lasted two days.

The Dominican Revolution

The palace revolt was a common occurrence in Latin America and rarely cause a raised eyebrow in the outside world. The Dominican coup of April 24, 1965 was different from the beginning. It was not bloodless as so many Latin American coups are. From the beginning there was extensive fighting, which quickly escalated to full-blown revolution. This was bad enough, but what drew the US president into the fray was the people who appeared in the rebel leadership. Many were Castro sympathizers, if not active collaborators. President Johnson did not intend to stand by while a clone of Castro's Cuba was born. From the beginning, he took personal charge of US initiatives designed to make sure that did not come to pass.

It took a day or two for the political risks of the 1965 revolt to become clearly apparent. Meanwhile, heavy fighting endangered the lives of many, including the large US colony resident in Santo Domingo. The need for an emergency evacuation quickly became evident. I had moved the aircraft carrier *Boxer* around the Caribbean often enough in minor disturbances to know what would be required and how it would have to be done.

Late on the night of April 25, I asked the Pentagon to position the *Boxer*, with its embarked Marines, beyond the horizon from Santo Domingo to await further developments. There it was when the president decided to order it in and prepare for landing Marines early on the morning of April 27. The Marines were to secure the evacuation of US citizens and protect embassy personnel and premises. Once they landed, we were engaged. None of us realized at the time how hard it would be to disengage.

For me, the Dominican crisis boiled down to coordinating the dozens of actions undertaken or under study at any given time. I was named Director of the Dominican Task Force—the unofficial job description was "do whatever had to be done."

I was expected to be at so many places and do so many things at the same time, my memory of much that went on is scrambled beyond any hope of recall. Strategy meetings at the White House were chaired by the president or his special assistant for National Security, McGeorge Bundy. Usually present were the secretary of state, secretary of defense, director of the CIA, chairman of the Joint Chiefs of Staff and assistant secretary of state for Inter-American Affairs, along with such aides as might be necessary, plus the guy at the bottom of the totem pole—me. When some sort of working paper was required, I was expected to prepare it. When an instruction was sent to Santo Domingo ordering an action that had been decided on, I was expected to draft it, get it cleared, and get it out before any of the senior officials involved asked if it had been sent. I was busy.

Only a few weeks before the Dominican crisis broke, President Johnson promoted Tom Mann to the post of undersecretary of state and replaced him in the Bureau of Inter-American Affairs with Jack Vaughn, formerly of the Peace Corps, but experienced as an ambassador in Latin America. I didn't know much about Vaughn, but my relations with him had been cordial. Vaughn had the same problem I did. When all hell broke loose in the Dominican Republic he was attending a meeting in Cuernavaca instead of home tending to the chickens. The president had turned to Tom Mann for advice and guidance, and our initial posture had been decided upon the afternoon before Vaughn's return to Washington.

I finished drafting and clearing the president's instruction to Santo Domingo in time to meet Vaughn's evening flight at National Airport. It had been an easy job because I had been there when the president decided, I knew what he had decided, and when it came to clearing the instruction, I wrote down the names of the Cabinet-level people who had attended the meeting and initialed them myself. I had annotated Jack Vaughn as authorizing the instruction on behalf of the secretary of state, which was his prerogative as assistant secretary for Latin America. I took the cable with me when I went to meet Jack's plane.

As we drove back to town, I brought Vaughn up to date on events in the DR, and what the president had decided to do about it. I then handed him the instruction to Santo Domingo which we would send as soon as we got back to the department. Jack read the telegram with great care and then said rather casually, "I don't agree with that and I won't sign it." I was dumfounded. I had no idea what to say next, so we completed our ride to the office in silence.

I had recovered from my shock by the time we got to Jack's suite and was prepared to reason with him. I pointed out that certain decisions had to be made and it was no one's fault he hadn't been around. I also pointed out that the president must take ultimate responsibility and therefore must have ultimate authority. I covered all the ground in between. Jack didn't budge an inch. Finally, I had to ask, "Well, what are we going to do?"

Jack's answer was ready. "Whatever you want but leave me out of it." I took the president's instruction out to a typewriter, x-ed out Vaughn's name, typed mine below where his had been, and signed the damned thing myself. Nothing ever came of it, as far as I know—except my respect for Vaughn's courage and his stubbornness went up a few pegs.

The Long, Hard Grind

There were so many things to keep track of during the initial days of the crisis that time lost its meaning except for White House meetings. For those, you damn well remembered the exact hour. But otherwise, day melded into night, which melded into the next day. Things did slow down late in the evening and Mary would drive in from Virginia so we could meet in the car across the street from the main entrance to the Department of State. There we stole a half-hour or so, catching up on each other's doings. We'd share a thermos of martinis and have soup and sandwiches for supper. The time to take the clean clothes Mary had brought and go back up to the Operations Center always came much too soon.

Governor Adlai Stevenson, our United Nations ambassador, had been told less than the truth about our involvement in the Bay of Pigs disaster in Cuba. His suspicions were immediately aroused when word went around that we would land troops in the Dominican Republic to safeguard US lives. He came to Washington to check things out for himself. The president and his senior Cabinet officials, along with the Chairman of the Joint Chiefs of Staff, plus White House and State Department staffers, met with Governor Stevenson in the Cabinet Room to answer his questions and reassure him as to the purity of our intentions. I got the job of providing the opening briefing, and after that he asked me up to New York at regular intervals to fill him in on developments. After all—I had plenty of time!

One of the principal problems we ran into early during the crisis was identifying new faces that turned up in the rebel leadership. Biographic files on the Dominican leftists were inadequate. President Johnson was quickly disillusioned when the CIA had to respond to his requests time and again that there was no background data available. As was his custom, he set about fixing things the way he knew best. He instructed J. Edgar Hoover to establish an FBI contingent in embassy/Santo Domingo—immediately, if not sooner—to tell him who was who.

The following day, a representative of the FBI met with the president to get his approval of the agent who had been selected to head up the new embassy/Santo Domingo FBI contingent. I recognized the candidate as my old friend Clark Anderson long before recitation of his biographic data had been completed. Terribly excited at our good fortune in having him on our team, I blurted out, "and he's an alumnus of the same school as the president of the United States." The president turned on me in a flash and demanded, "What's his name?" I was struck dumb—I could not get Clark's name out.

After what seemed like an eternity, but couldn't have been more than a few seconds, the FBI briefing officer took me off the hook. "Clark Anderson, Mr. President," he answered.

Still looking me straight in the eye, the president asked, "Well, is he the man we want?" I found my tongue enough to get out, "There isn't a better man anywhere, Sir." The president gave a grunt and the meeting was over. Clark Anderson had been approved.

Things did not go well in the Dominican Republic so often that it became the rule, rather than the exception. The Dominican military establishment was unable—if not unwilling—to contain the rebels and turned to the United States for help. Embassy/Santo Domingo was reluctant but decided to support the request when it became evident that to do otherwise was to risk losing the country to the Castroites.

When given the go-ahead, our military establishment quickly managed to transfer over 20,000 soldiers to the island of Hispaniola. The problem we then faced was how to get our troops out once things had calmed down enough to make that feasible. The first thing that had to be done was to get a government into office that could run the country.

President Johnson never did things halfway. If what we needed in the Dominican Republic was a government, then a government we would have—as soon as one could be built, begged, borrowed or bought. The president dispatched his first team to take care of the details. Not including Ambassadors William Tapley Bennett and John B. Martin who were already on the scene, the team was made up of Special Assistant to the President for National Security McGeorge Bundy, Undersecretary of State Tom Mann, and Deputy Secretary of Defense Cyrus Vance, who would later become Jimmy Carter's secretary of state—good men all.

The basic idea was to establish a provisional government of national accord to rule until a new constitution could be written, and a permanent government elected—no small undertaking. The first problem was finding someone able to rule who might be willing to serve in an interim capacity. Qualified candidates wanted the job permanently. Those who might take the job temporarily weren't strong enough politically to exercise the office. Someone had to be found who could, and would provide quiet, effective, behind-the-scenes support for an interim chief of state. That man was Joaquín Balaguer.

When the time came to seek Balaguer's help, President Johnson ordered me to see him on the double. It was after 7:00 p.m. and we were finishing a strategy session in the Cabinet Room. Dr. Balaguer was in New York, but where, I did not know.

When we got back to Jack Vaughn's office in the State Department, we tried to figure out how to start. The first thing we needed was enough money to get me to New York. That was in the days before credit cards were commonly used, and after the hour when government funds could be dispensed. Jack Vaughn took off his shoe and produced a $20.00 bill from the lining. Someone else fished a $10.00 bill from an inside pocket. Among us, we collected enough to pay my fare on the shuttle and cover the cost of a taxi from the airport to downtown New York. No one gave a thought as to how I would get home, much less where I would find a quiet place to go over details with Dr. Balaguer.

To reach Balaguer, I had to go through Irving Davidson. I took a chance and called his home. He was in, but he was coy about telling me how to find Balaguer. Irving wanted to go along so badly he could taste it. Later I learned Davidson also had to go through someone else to connect with Balaguer. There wasn't anything for me to do but agree to meet him at National Airport—or call President Johnson and tell him I would have to take care of his request some other time. It was late, and if Davidson and I were to catch the last shuttle, the plane would have to wait for us a few minutes. Reluctantly I made the call it took, and we boarded the flight 10 minutes late. As we took our seats, we got plenty of dirty looks from the other passengers.

All Davidson would say on the flight to New York was that Dr. Balaguer would meet us at the Regency. I didn't have time to grill him anyhow. We hardly reached cruising altitude when a flight attendant whispered in my ear that the White House was calling, and would I please come to the front cabin to take the call. I was dumbfounded.

The captain didn't know much more than I did except that there was a White House operator on his radio frequency asking that I be put on the line. He handed me his headset and I identified myself. I immediately recognized the voice on the other end as belonging to one of President Johnson's favorite lawyers—a man who was occasionally invited to sit in on strategy sessions, who liked to use a pseudonym and who thought himself a master of intrigue. His first question was, "Is anyone listening in on this connection?" I passed the question on to the Captain. Everyone in the cabin burst into gales of laughter. When he could speak, the Captain replied, "Probably not more than four or five thousand people around the world, would be my guess." I passed the word back and promised to call from a telephone booth after we landed. My caller thought that would be OK, "but make sure it's secure." As it turned out, there was no reason for the call in the first place. Maybe the man got a thrill from making calls through the White House switchboard to airplanes in flight. Some people are like that. But would you believe that one like that would become a Justice of the Supreme Court?

Dr. Balaguer sat in the hotel lobby waiting for us. I recognized his suit as another I had seen Davidson wearing. When we had exchanged greetings all around, I looked for a quiet corner where we might find at least a little privacy. Davidson motioned us toward the elevator. "Come along with me. I have a room." When and how he managed it, I don't know, but he had a key, and when he opened the door, we walked into an elegant suite, complete with bar and serving kitchen. Davidson took his leave, and Dr. Balaguer and I got down to business.

I didn't have to do much explaining. Dr. Balaguer was up to date on the situation in the Dominican Republic. It amused me to realize how government people often assume they know more than anyone else, when in fact, they often do not know half as much. He knew there was urgent need for an interim government in the Dominican Republic to hold things together until more permanent arrangements could be made. He understood that in order to survive, this interim government would need the support of the established political parties. And he fully appreciated that the Dominican military would have to be persuaded to go along with whatever could be worked out, or there would be no hope, regardless of other considerations. All there was left for me to say was what we thought he could do to help get where we all wanted to go.

President Johnson's special team had identified a candidate for interim Dominican chief of state who was willing to serve, but we weren't sure he could garner broad-based support, primarily among the military. Dr. Balaguer knew our candidate and found him acceptable. We quickly agreed on actions he might take from his base in New York to be helpful. Before the evening was over, he had recorded a speech which I took back to Washington with me for future use, should the need arise.

Laugh Until You Cry

The spring of high drama and momentous developments in the Dominican Republic degenerated into a summer of stagnation. There was a standoff on the military front and a vacuum on the political front. Everyone involved kept working at a feverish pace to find solutions to the unlimited assortment of problems we faced.

I continued to spend enough nights in the department that someone persuaded the general services administration to build a soundproof bedroom in a corner of the area assigned to the operations center. When the door was closed on the little cubicle, it was quiet as a tomb. When the light was turned out, it was as dark as the inside of a cow. About the time sound sleep was at hand, the red telephone on the bedside table often jangled. But it was much better than a leather office couch. And there was a dividend—it boasted a bar as long as I occupied it.

Our efforts to find an interim president for the Dominican Republic came to naught. The man initially chosen was found wanting, and the search began anew. When a substitute was located, I was asked to check the new candidate out with Dr. Balaguer. Don Joaquín had his doubts but agreed to endorse the man if we decided he was the best we could come up with. He taped a contingency speech and sent it down with Irving Davidson for me to have in case it was needed. I marveled at his trust. A recording like that could cause him great embarrassment should it fall into the wrong hands or turn up at the wrong time, especially since I still had his taped speech endorsing the first candidate that had been identified.

During a break in the commotion surrounding the Dominical Republic, I reached a point where I could no longer beg off participating in a US Navy program designed to update senior Foreign Service officers on its current capabilities. There has traditionally been a close working relationship between the Navy and the officers of the Foreign Service. At one time the Navy was the only uniformed service capable of coming to a diplomat's assistance at those isolated places around the globe where diplomatic establishments seem so often to be located. And the Marines were still the ones to come to the Foreign Service officer's rescue when the going really got rough.

The program involved visits of several days duration to aircraft carriers on the high seas, and I was included in one of the final groups around the middle of 1965. We were flown from Washington out to the carrier and landed on her postage stamp deck exactly like the fighter planes. Our quarters well below decks were quite comfortable, but without portholes or any other means of orientation. This made the sensation of the ship rising and falling eerie, to say the least.

Various exercises demonstrated what the modern Navy could do. One involved a simulated delivery of an atomic bomb. The Navy jet carrying the "bomb" skimmed the waves as it came toward the target. Just short of where the bomb was to impact, the pilot veered into a vertical climb. Simultaneously, he released his bomb, which continued to climb as he rolled his plane over to head back the way he had come. By the time the bomb arched down and hit the target, the pilot and his plane were far from the danger zone that would have been created had the exercise been real.

We also watched the firing of several heat seeking air-to-air missiles. A magnesium flare was dropped on a parachute to serve as the target. From an impressive distance, a Navy fighter fired a missile which unerringly sought out the flare and exploded on impact. There was a bombing demonstration using a target towed behind the carrier, and a show of antiaircraft gunnery, as well as search and rescue operations. We headed home via steam launch from the carrier's flight deck. It was all very impressive, and a refreshing break from the long, hard grind that had begun two years earlier.

On return to the department, I found my office swarming with security people going through files. My staff had no idea what it was all about. Security officers had barged in and told them the files were to be searched, and they would not have access to their own records until the search was completed. Initially, I wasn't much more successful, either. But when I threatened to go over their heads, the senior officer closeted himself with me in my office and confided that grave charges had been made, and I would be well-advised not to interfere with an investigation that had been authorized at a senior level of the US government. That I understood. What I did not yet understand was that the charges had been made against me.

After a couple of days, we were all consumed with curiosity, and finding it increasingly difficult to carry out our duties while denied access to our records. It had quickly become common knowledge around Inter-American Affairs that a major investigation was underway having something to do with the office of Caribbean Affairs. We were all becoming quite sensitive about it.

I had run out of patience when the senior security officer again closeted himself with me to tell me that his search of our records had been completed. Then he mentioned he would have questions ready for me to answer under oath in a day or so. It was then I realized I was the subject of the investigation. There are no words to describe the shock and shame that washed over me in one wave after another. What could I have possibly done to warrant something like this?

After what seemed like an eternity, the questions I was to answer for the office of security were hand-delivered to my office in a sealed envelope marked "SECRET—EYES ONLY." My hands shook as I drew out the papers inside. The suspense had been nearly more than I could bear. I was on the verge of tears.

I quickly scanned the list of questions and felt my chest heave with laughter. The charges were so ridiculous, I laughed until the tears flowed. Answering the allegations would be no problem at all. The challenge would be to find a way to let all the people whose suspicions had been aroused know there had been no basis for the investigation in the first place. It didn't take me long to hit on the way to do it.

My memorandum dated July 3, 1965, was addressed to the chief, special assignments staff, office of security, and read in part:

> Attached are my responses to questions posed in the enclosure to your memorandum of June 29. I have altered the format of the questions to produce a more orderly and organized presentation. I am prepared to attest to my answers under oath....
>
> Although your memorandum, and the attachment to it were classified SECRET—EYES ONLY, I have not classified this memorandum or my responses to your questions. I see no reason to exercise administrative control—you may use my responses to your questions for any purpose that may be of assistance in discharging your responsibilities.
>
> I would welcome the opportunity to respond to any additional questions you may have. Meanwhile, I am providing copies of this material to my superiors....
>
> Q: State whether you know or have ever met Bobby Baker[1].
> A: No.
>
> Q: Have you had contacts, either official or personal with Baker?
> A. No.
>
> Q: Did Baker or anyone on his behalf ever attempt to influence you with respect to recognition of the Dominican Republic late in 1963?
> A. No.
>
> Q: Did "Pancho" Aguirre, aka Francisco Aguirre Baca, attempt to influence the conduct of your duties in connection with the recognition of the Dominican Republic in late 1963?
> A: *I had various conversations with Francisco Aguirre Baca during the period September 25, 1963–December 14, 1963. I do not believe that anything said to me by Mr. Aguirre during this period was intended to influence the conduct of my official duties. I do not recall that Mr. Aguirre asked any action of me. Nor did he suggest any action I might take or consider taking. I cannot, of course, be certain what Mr. Aguirre may have had in his own mind at any given time.*
>
> Q: Did José Antonio Bonilla Atiles [Dominican Ambassador] attempt to influence the conduct of your duties in connection with the recognition of the Dominican Republic in late 1963?
> A: No.
>
> Q: Did Donald Reid Cabral attempt to influence the conduct of your duties in connection with the recognition of the Dominican Republic in late 1963?
> A. No.

Q: Did any other person of the United States government attempt to influence the conduct of your duties in connection with the recognition of the Dominican Republic in late 1963?

A: I received instructions and guidance in the normal course of day to day operations from a variety of my immediate superiors during the period in question. No person in the United States government attempted to influence the conduct of my duties in any way not entirely consistent with routine operating procedures. To the best of my recollection, there were no substantive differences of opinion between any policy officials of the United States government with whom I had contact about the course of United States policy in dealing with the Dominican Republic during the period in question.

Q: Did you receive any money or thing of value from any person... for the purpose of your influencing the United States government's policy regarding the recognition of the Dominican Republic during the period September 25, 1963 through December 14, 1963?

A: No.

Q: Specifically, did you receive amounts of money approximating $256,000 or $1,000,000 for the purpose of influencing such recognition?

A: No.

Q: State your financial position as best you can as of September 25, 1963, December 31, 1963, and now. This should include all assets, including bank accounts, real estate, stocks, bonds (purchase price), expensive jewelry, etc. Also set forth liabilities.

A: The question, as posed, is unduly broad in scope and would require me to undertake much research, obtain evaluation of assets, etc., in order to make a full response. On September 25, 1963, our worth was plus $859.54. On July 1, 1965 we were $3,490.00 in debt.

That put an end to the whole business and got my side of it broadly circulated within the Department of State. People I didn't know stopped me in the halls to shake my hand. Even FBI Director J. Edgar Hoover found an opportunity to write a laudatory letter to me, to make sure everyone knew where he stood.

I could again hold my head up and look everyone in the eye, but the strain of the whole incident took a mighty toll. How much longer would I be able to endure?

Right Man for the Job

Yet another of the candidates for interim president of the Dominican Republic had fallen by the wayside, and we sat with President Johnson in the Cabinet Room exploring alternatives for the next move. The president's Washington lawyer argued passionately for consideration of Antonio Guzmán, the minister of agriculture in the fallen Bosch government.

It concerned me deeply that no one argued against what to me was obviously a non-viable choice. I could not keep silent any longer. The president looked my way but made no comment on my objections. His Washington lawyer went right on as if he hadn't been interrupted. Again, I stated my reservations and the reasons for them. At that point, Tom Mann got up and walked around the table to whisper in my ear that I should take it easy—a decision had already been made. I immediately shut up.

I never understood why it was necessary to go through the exercise, but it wasn't until the president's counselor had argued himself out that we got down to the real business of deciding what was to be done next.

It boiled down to a consensus that the time had come for Joaquín Balaguer to return to the Dominican Republic. If there was to be an interim government, it would be necessary for him to be close enough to throw the weight of his stabilizing influence behind it. Time was running short.

"Can you get Dr. Balaguer on the morning flight to Puerto Rico?" I was asked. I should have said, "I'll give it my best." But I was so anxious it should come to pass that I answered simply, "Yes."

As I rose from the table and walked to the door of the Cabinet Room to get started on the task, President Johnson called after me in his deep southern drawl: "Lord help you, you don't do this right." What a way to start a job that could well prove to be impossible!

Once again, I found myself in the position of being sent off to New York long after government offices in Washington had shut down for the day. But having been caught short once, I had no intention of being caught short again. I had set aside money for an emergency and I had phone numbers where Dr. Balaguer could be reached. I jogged from the White House to the State Department.

It was easy enough to get the emergency funds out of my safe. But I drew a blank when I tried to reach Dr. Balaguer to tell him I would be coming. There was no answer at one of his numbers, and a consistent busy signal at the other.

Precious minutes were lost as I again tried each number. Time to catch the last shuttle to New York drew short. My anxiety was approaching panic level. Who could I find at this hour to keep calling while I went to the airport? Irving Davidson.

I found Irving at home. Yes, he would get a message to Dr. Balaguer that I was on my way to New York and wanted him to meet me at the Regency that evening.

"Anything else?" he asked. I thought it best to give Balaguer some warning.

"Irving," I said, "I can't go into details, but we may want Dr. Balaguer to take a little trip for us early tomorrow morning. Can you tell him that?"

"No trouble," came the reply. "Are you sure you don't want me to go along and help?" I thanked Irving, but thought it was a little late to be asking. I would regret that decision.

Dr. Balaguer awaited me in the Regency lobby. I registered, and we went up to my room to talk. When I voiced the reason for my urgent visit, Dr. Balaguer was not the least surprised. He always seemed to be one step ahead of me. Yes, he agreed that precious time had been wasted trying to bring back Juan Bosch. Yes, there was time to pull together an interim government of national concord. Yes, he was willing to return to the Dominican Republic to help. Yes, he would be ready to catch the morning Pan American flight to San Juan. In fact, he had a car available and would pick me up in front of the Regency to go to the airport. We understood each other completely. His trust in me seemed to be without reservation.

Early the next morning, a black sedan with two men in the front seat pulled to the curb in front of the Regency. The man on the passenger side got out and walked toward me. He looked vaguely familiar, but I couldn't quite place him. Then I realized he was a special agent of the Federal Bureau of Investigation. J. Edgar Hoover saw to it that all his men dressed identically without wearing uniforms: snap brim hat, white shirt, double breasted suit, dark, well-polished shoes.

"You are Mr. Crockett," he stated. "Dr. Balaguer is waiting." He motioned me to the car where Don Joaquín sat in the rear seat. If any of the three thought I might be surprised at this arrangement, no one gave a sign. And I never did find out how it had all come to pass.

Things went well at the Pan American counter. When I identified myself to the agent, he assured me space could be found on the San Juan flight. He wrote up the ticket and weighed Dr. Balaguer's bag. The problem came when he asked how payment was to be made. Dr. Balaguer didn't have enough money and neither did I. Between us we couldn't cover half the fare. The agent was courteous but firm in telling me he couldn't accept my assurance that payment would be made as soon as I could get back to Washington. No, I couldn't speak to anyone in the main office. It wouldn't be open until after the flight had departed. I began to feel desperate—until down the corridor I spotted a dapper little man striding toward us from the direction of the Washington shuttle. Once again, Irving Davidson had turned up in the nick of time.

I can't say with certainty that Dr. Balaguer played a key role in the establishment of an interim government under the provisional presidency of Hector García-Godoy, but I believe he did. What happened next is history. Joaquín Balaguer won a four-year term as president of the Dominican Republic when regular elections were held in 1966, and he was later elected to two additional four-year terms. Those 12 years were the most peaceful and prosperous in the history of the Dominican Republic.

The Investigation

Two seemingly unrelated developments combined to break the monotony of working in Washington. My mother wrote from Texas that my father's health was failing, and the Agency for International Development in Santo Domingo recommended recruitment of a US businessman to help get things going again in the Dominican Republic. I had a candidate in mind, and he happened to live within a hundred miles of my parents' home.

Harold Hauseman and I grew up together in Laredo. He played the violin in the high school orchestra and I played the cornet. We both graduated in the Class of 1937. Harold became a cadet at Texas A&M, where he earned a degree in chemical engineering before World War II caught up with him and he was called into the Army Corps of Engineers for the duration. After the war Harold returned to Texas, settling down in Eagle Pass where he prospered in both business and politics. He accumulated property and served for a time as Eagle Pass City Manager. His Spanish was fluent. He seemed ideally suited to our requirements in the Dominican Republic, but I had no idea whether he could be persuaded to take the assignment. Obviously, the thing to do was go see if he could be recruited. But first I would look in on my parents.

I found my father weak but cheerful, my mother catering to his every need. It was wonderful to be with them again. But it was also depressing to realize they approached the end of a normal life span. My father, past 80, was no longer able to drive, and my mother, in her seventies, had never learned how to manage modern cars. They jumped at the chance to get out and about when I suggested they go with me to see Harold Hauseman.

Harold and I hadn't seen each other since the end of World War II, but when we shook hands, the friendship of our youth bridged the gap of 20 years. Harold found a quiet room where my parents could rest, and we busied ourselves with catching up on those lost years. It was the most pleasant day I could remember in a long, long time. Most importantly, Harold agreed to give serious thought to taking on the Dominican assignment, which he eventually did. I think what brought him around was the prospect of working for Tom Mann. Tom was the ideal of every kid in Laredo when Harold and I were growing up.

The days that followed were devoted to being with my parents. There was nothing I could have done that would have pleased them more. Time to go back to the life I was beginning to hate came all too soon. But at least we'd had a little time to ourselves. It was to be the last. My father was gone in six months— my mother within the year.

Mary met me at National Airport. The minute I saw her face, I knew something was wrong. She would have put off telling me, had I not insisted. My first thought was the children.

"No," Mary said, "it's something to do with Irving Davidson. Several reporters have called asking for you, and about Davidson—if we're close friends of theirs, how often you see him, and variations of the same. I haven't told anybody anything except that you're out of town and I'm not sure when you'll be home."

My desktop was littered with yellow telephone messages when I got into my office the next morning. Most of them had to do with Davidson. There was also a clipping from the *Washington Post*, which asked, "Why was it necessary for the Department of State to go through Irving Davidson in its dealings with Joaquín Balaguer?" The message that impressed me most was a summons from the Seventh Floor—where the top brass held forth. It was then I began to fully realize I was in big trouble. Why put it off? I went upstairs to do my obeisance.

My reception was distinctly cool. There was dismay when I reported, "Yes, I've had occasion to see Irving Davidson numerous times over recent months, often with Dr. Balaguer." I didn't get a chance to point out that every meeting had been the subject of a written report, circulated to all who might have an interest. Instead, I was cut off with, "Well, the Government Operations Committee of the House of Representatives is incensed and plans hearings. I hope you know how to take care of yourself. This is going to be a rough one!" With that I was dismissed. The message was clear. You're on your own, and Heaven help you.

The whole business caught me by surprise. I knew Davidson lived by his wits. I'm sure some thought him an influence peddler, and he well might be. I hadn't brought him into anything—he had already been there before I came along. And as far as I was concerned, his contribution had been constructive. There had been no secret about my contacts with him. Why all the uproar now? It took a while, but I was able to learn that Davidson had once claimed during an open Congressional hearing that he had access to the presidency of the United States through an aide who had since been shamed and discredited. Whether that was true or not, I did not know, but it seemed to be the charge that caused the uproar in the first place.

You learn about the art of self-defense in the Washington arena if you are to last long. I never learned it all, but I did learn a lot, dating back 10 years to the days when I worked for Scott McLeod, a real expert. One of those was, "If they go after you, drag in as many others as you can, as high up as you're able to reach. There's safety in numbers."

I knew I had to lay my hands on our file copy of every memorandum I had written reporting on a meeting with Davidson over the past couple of years. I would need help. It would have to be done over the weekend. My help would have to be cleared for access to our classified files. The people I would have to turn to were our secretaries. I figured we could get the job done if four of them were willing to give me a hand. The first four I asked generously agreed.

We came in early on Saturday morning and started digging. I can't say we found every pertinent file, but we found more than I needed. All had been well-circulated around the Department of State and/or to the Embassies at Port-au-Prince and Santo Domingo. Most had gone to the office on the seventh floor where I had been given such a cold reception. Maybe the man didn't see them himself, but one or another of his aides sure had.

When we had all the ammunition I thought we would need, we prepared folders for each of the departmental offices involved, providing them with a set of the memoranda I had marked for circulation to that office. I covered each folder with a short "For Your Information" memo. On Monday morning, I hand carried each folder to the office it was intended for and personally told the aide who received it what it was all about, and what the implications were.

Long before lunch I had lined up a hell of a lot of support for whatever joust might develop between me and the Government Operations Committee of the House of Representatives. It sure was nice to have so much high-level company. In fact, the whole business seemed to fade away as quickly as it had boiled up. Along the way, however, I was instructed by one of the president's most senior assistants to discontinue my contacts with Irving Davidson. I did what I was told, but it didn't seem right to me. As Irving used to say, all he wanted was to serve his country and get a piece of the pie.

Enough is Enough

The incident over Irving Davidson depressed me much more than it should have. But it came after months of grinding pressure, long hard hours, and the investigation into charges I that had accepted a bribe to promote recognition of the government formed following the overthrow of Juan Bosch. There seemed to be no end to problems which should never have arisen—over missteps I was not guilty of. The fact that I was exhausted didn't make things any better. I had reached the point where I couldn't hold a piece of paper without it trembling violently. I didn't want to admit I was nearing the end of my rope, but I was. It took all the willpower I could muster to drag myself from one day into the next.

The last straw was a classic example of how well-meaning people can bring on the greatest problems. We had on our staff a lady coasting into retirement whose voice could cut steel, but who had little else noteworthy enough to remember now. She had worked long and hard. She needed a place to be until she reached her 30 years. I didn't have the heart to ask that she be moved elsewhere. We kept her on and found ways to work around her. It was she who greeted me with a message that an emergency meeting of the Special Group Counter Insurgency had been called on short notice and I should get myself over there to report on how things were going in the Dominican Republic. I didn't worry about making a report—I had been eating, sleeping and living the Dominican Republic for months.

The Special Group-CI was high-level stuff. Averell Harriman, then under-secretary of State, presided. Other members included General Victor Krulak, a four-star Marine, the attorney general or his alternate, the director of the Agency for International Development and an assortment of the same ilk. I walked carefully around that bunch. It was important for me to be on my toes.

I was escorted into the committee chamber and seated, appropriately, near the foot of the table. The head of the AID was talking about the Dominican Republic. His information was outdated, it had already been overtaken by events. When he finished speaking and I was introduced, I pointed out that there were recent developments in the area he had been discussing and started to explain them. With that, Averell Harriman exploded. "We're not interested in what you think about the Dominican Republic. You're here to tell us what's going on in Haiti. Confine yourself to the subject you're supposed to be informed on."

I was seized with an all-consuming fury. I was furious at the woman who had given me the wrong information. I was furious at the old goat who dressed me down with so little provocation. I was furious at myself for having lost my cool. I sat trembling, unable to speak. Someone poured me a glass of water. I had to hold it with both hands. Eventually, I was able to address the subject of Haiti. I really wasn't well prepared—it was the Dominican Republic that had consumed me for weeks on end, and now threatened to do me in.

I walked back to the department in a state of abject depression. I was certain, my career was over. I had broken under pressure—something no Foreign Service officer should ever do. I was through. There was nothing for me to do but resign. I'd see about it tomorrow.

By the next day, things looked a little brighter. Talking it over with Mary had helped, as always. A night with the telephone off the hook had allowed a good rest. The world hadn't come to an end. Maybe I wouldn't have to resign. After all, I would be eligible to retire in less than five years. But I had to get out of Washington—anywhere would do.

When I told Jack Vaughn that I'd had enough, he raised objection.

"We can't do without you at this crucial stage, Kennedy." I told Jack it was no good.

"Either I get a transfer, or I quit." Jack had a good heart but didn't dare agree on his own.

"Let me think on it," he said. "Let's have lunch tomorrow and see where we stand then." There was no reason not to agree. I knew I would get what I knew I had to have.

Deputy Chief of Mission at San José, Costa Rica, was the assignment Jack came up with. Not all that important, but not all that bad for an officer in my circumstances. I, too, asked for time to think on it, but I knew I would go along. Anywhere, anything would be enough—as long as it was away from Washington. I genuinely believed that otherwise I would be done for. It was that bad.

[1]A powerful influence-peddler and self-described "Capitol Hill operator," Bobby Baker was closely allied to Lyndon B. Johnson for much of his political career. Baker knew many of Washington's secrets and was linked to many Washington scandals. He was eventually convicted of tax evasion and other crimes, for which he served 15 months in prison.

Costa Rica
1965

The Good Life

Counselor of Embassy and Deputy Chief of Mission can be a very good or a very difficult job, depending in large measure on the man who represents the president in the country of assignment—the United States ambassador. In Costa Rica, our ambassador was Raymond Telles, former Mayor of El Paso, Texas, and a Kennedy appointee. We hit it off from the beginning. He enjoyed making speeches, going to social engagements and ceremonial functions.

I enjoyed keeping the work flowing in the embassy and coordinating the activities of the many US government agencies represented in Costa Rica, including the Coast and Geodetic Survey, Peace Corps, Agency for International Development, and the United States Army group engaged in developing antivenin for tropical snake bites in Vietnam, among others. We made a good team.

I also had a special assignment. Costa Rica had, for years, spent beyond its means and stood teetering on the brink of bankruptcy. Drastic austerity measures were urgently needed. The United States wanted to help, but there was no way unless the Costa Ricans were willing to help themselves.

A brilliant young economist named John Bushnell was sent along with me to Costa Rica to help the Costa Rican government find the way to fiscal solvency. It was my job to keep Ambassador Telles from hampering Bushnell in bringing the Costa Ricans around to understanding that they must take the bitter medicine of austerity. The assignment turned out to be fairly simple. Ambassador Telles was quick to understand what had to be done and why. That might have been because of Bushnell's great powers of persuasion and his unusual ability to state the most complicated economic problems in simple terms.

San José had been scheduled for a periodic inspection before I was assigned, and the inspectors turned up within a few weeks of my arrival—long before I had settled into the saddle, much less found the stirrups. Ken Wright, who I had known in Mexico City, was the senior inspector, and Bill Calderhead was the administrative inspector. They were breaking in but seemed to be going about the job in a professional manner. I didn't expect them to give the post a top rating—there were problems that hadn't yet been corrected—but I didn't anticipate they would find reason to be so strongly and consistently critical of every aspect of the post's operation.

I may have been surprised, but Ambassador Telles was indignant. His instructions to me were clear and unequivocal.

"I want that report withdrawn—declared null and void. I will not accept it. Do whatever is necessary to have it canceled." My attempts to dissuade him from giving me an assignment that I believed to be impossible were to no avail. His approach was Do or Die. Since I have always greatly preferred to do rather than to die, I gave it my best.

My initial reading of the inspection report had been undertaken from a somewhat detached perspective. After all, I hadn't been at the post long enough to bear responsibility for its shortcomings, and measures had been instituted since my arrival to correct most of the problems cited. Now, I reread it, carefully noting every criticism that might be rebutted. To have any hope of getting the report withdrawn, we needed to demonstrate it was biased or the conclusions unjustified by the facts, or both. Once I got started, I found there were plenty of loosely drawn criticisms—based on unsupported conclusions. Prospects for accomplishing what the ambassador had ordered looked brighter. I began to warm to the job.

It took months. I would draft a letter for Ambassador Telles to sign, telling the Department of State how unwarranted criticisms in the report were, and why. There would be a rebuttal from Washington that I would take apart in another letter for the ambassador's signature. There would be another rebuttal. We would repeat the process. After months of more of the same, the day came when we were informed that the Inspector General of the Foreign Service would be down to talk things over. Before we were through, the impossible had been accomplished. It had been agreed the inspection report would be declared null and void. As far as I know, that had never been done before.

Costa Rica was a quiet country, as close to a working democracy as could be found in Latin America. The pace of life was leisurely, and the nearest thing to a crisis in the normal course of events was the final game of a national soccer tournament. There was enough work to keep me busy at the embassy from nine to five, but almost always enough time to make it home for lunch and a nap at midday. My job was exactly what I needed after three stressful years in Washington dealing with the volatile Caribbean area. In retrospect, about the hardest work Mary and I were called on to do came after office hours.

Team spirit is indispensable to efficient functioning of any organization, but particularly a Foreign Service post far from home. Life can be lonely. New people must be made to feel welcome, and needed, and wanted. And when it's time to move on, it's important to leave knowing your efforts have been appreciated. The time and trouble that go into sending a person off with genuine thanks and recognition of a job well done isn't lost on those left behind, either.

At Foreign Service posts, the ambassador and his wife arrange for senior staff to be introduced and bade goodbye. It falls to the deputy chief of mission and his wife to take care of the rest. Mary and I knew from our own experience how important this was to good morale, especially among the more junior people. We took on the job at San José with eagerness and dedication. I never thought I'd see the day, but after the drab existence of work, work, work for three years in Washington, it was a distinct pleasure to get back into the swing of Foreign Service social life.

Our in-house entertainment was kept simple, mainly because the cost of food and drink came out of our own pocket. Government funds for entertainment were reserved for functions more directly related to foreign policy objectives. The usual fare at our house was finger food and refreshments to suit any taste. Of course, the house was paid for by Uncle Sam, who also helped pay for our servants.

The residence furnished by the US government for the deputy chief of mission in San José was functional, comfortable and elegant—in a conservative fashion. It was by far the most livable house Mary and I had ever occupied. The entertaining rooms downstairs were ample and well appointed. There were four bedrooms on the second floor—the master suite boasting a fireplace, his-and-her closets and a private dressing room adjoining the bath. There was a small table for coffee or light meals, overstuffed chairs, deep rugs and a gorgeous view of the valley below and the mountains in the distance.

Shortly after we occupied the residence in Los Yoses, the Department of State sent the widow of a once-prominent United States senator around to see about decorating the walls with oil paintings left over from the Works Progress

Administration (WPA) program for artists sponsored by the government during the Depression years. She was fascinated by the foyer, a two-story room boasting a circular staircase. She had exactly the right painting for that area.

In due course, the oil came. It was about the size and shape of a bathroom door, all red and black, with no discernable theme. But then, I've never been strong on modern art. The idea of having that monstrosity hanging on our beautiful spiral staircase, the first thing any visitor might see, was horrifying, but I knew we had to use it somewhere. It took a little thinking.

There was a small waiting and cloak room to one side of the foyer, with a divan and easy chairs. There was an ideal space for the oil above the divan. All I had to do was obscure the artist's signature and hang the bathroom door crossways instead of vertically. It didn't look at all bad back there in the dark.

Some months later the lady passed through San José to see how her selections looked on our walls. When she came to the black and red bathroom door, she all but swooned. "Perfect, absolutely perfect," she murmured.

The "Rich Coast"

Costa Rica may well have been the most pleasant place to live anywhere in Latin America during the late 1960s. The people were friendly and handsome, the climate was delightful, and the pace was easygoing. It may be a small country, but within Costa Rica's boundaries there's a wide variety of scenery and climate. Once we had settled in, we took advantage of any opportunity that came along to see as much of the countryside as we possibly could. The roads weren't much, and the accommodations were often primitive, but we never came home from a trip feeling the least bit cheated.

The banana plantations of the Standard Fruit and Steamship Company are located on the Caribbean coast, in an area that was isolated from the rest of the country. To get there, you could either fly from San José, a trip of an hour or so, or take the train, a trip of a day or so. We were never able to spare the time for the train trip, but we did fly in a couple of times and enjoyed the fruit company's hospitality as we learned as much as time permitted about the remote and undeveloped eastern half of Costa Rica.

The United Fruit and Steamship Company had its operations on the Pacific slope—bananas, oil palm nuts, cattle and related activities, including a first-class narrow-gauge railroad tying the whole together. When Mary and I really needed some time to ourselves, we could fly down to Quepos and make use of the fruit company guest house high on a hill overlooking the Pacific. A long weekend there was worth a month anywhere else. We always hoped there would be time to take a motor car on the little railroad from Palmar Sur to Golfito, but there never was. Mary had to settle for my stories about making that trip in 1958.

Puntarenas, a two hour drive by car, offered the best public accommodations. It could also be reached on the little electric railway, a delightful experience, even if the trip took twice as long. There were several isolated beaches within easy reach of Puntarenas, and uninhabited islands of all sizes to be explored in the Gulf of Nicoya.

The province of Guanacaste and the Nicoya peninsula offered an entirely different perspective. Arid and relatively flat, Costa Rica's northwestern corner is unlike the lush, mountainous central plateau or the tropical Caribbean coastal region. This is the realm of cattle and ranches and cowboys—the Texas of Costa Rica. Along the Pacific coast, there were innumerable lovely beaches, isolated and mostly deserted during our time—prime for swimming and fishing, or loafing. We didn't get up there often, but always came home vowing to return as soon as possible.

On my last trip through Guanacaste, I took son Jack and his friend Fernán Guardia for a week's camping right before they went off to college. We shot doves or caught fish, or both, every day which I cooked over the campfire in the evenings. We explored the Sardinal River, the bays at Brasilito, the beaches at Tamarindo, and the swimming at Playa Potrero and El Coco. Before the trip was over, the boys rounded up a bevy of girls they knew from San José. I learned something new on that trip. At 47, I was no longer able to keep up with a couple of teenagers. Heading home, I realized I was looking forward to slowing down for a change.

***

Possibly the most interesting US government program in Costa Rica at the time involved snakes. The war in Vietnam was being fought in jungles crawling with poisonous snakes like those found in Costa Rica. The US Army assigned a veterinarian to Costa Rica to develop antivenin for use in Vietnam—Major Herschel Flowers.

To say that Herschel was happy-go-lucky is a gross understatement. Herschel was as relaxed as anyone I've ever known. When he suffered from overindulging the night before, which he often did, Herschel wasted no time worrying about it. He found a bottle and solved his problem with the hair of the dog that bit him. It didn't seem to bother Herschel that the risk of getting bitten by one of his snakes was bound to increase the more "relaxed" he got. He walked among them, picked them up, and threw them down with the same wild abandon he did everything else.

Every spring the Diplomatic Corps in Costa Rica organized an outdoor fair known as the Feria de las Flores to raise funds for local charities. There were booths serving food and drink from far-away lands, and kiosks selling whatever appealed to the milling throngs that came to see what the foreigners would think up next. The most popular of these each year was the booth organized by Herschel where he handled and milked venom from several dozen of his most poisonous snakes, including the bushmaster, the fer-de-lance and the coral snake. A bite by any of them could be fatal.

There was always a line of people waiting to get into Herschel's next demonstration. It was a real money-maker. Herschel was proud of his popularity and always put on a good show for his customers—the later the hour, the better the show. Not unexpectedly, the night came when the ambassador decided Herschel was going too far, and I was instructed to shut him down. It wasn't easy, not in Herschel's condition, but I did it. For the first time since we came to know each other, Herschel wasn't happy with me when we parted to go home.

I worried all night about Herschel's snakes. Had he caged them properly? Was there any risk of one finding an escape route even if properly caged? What if they all got loose and spread throughout San José? At first light, I dressed and went out to the Feria to check things out. Sure enough, one of the snakes had escaped and the place was in an uproar. I had no intention of trying to capture the snake myself, but I did find it and herded it under a box, which I sat upon while someone went to rout Herschel out of bed.

An hour passed before Herschel staggered up to where I sat. He was still in a bad humor with me and apparently hadn't had time to loosen up properly at such an early hour. He had a young neighborhood girl with him who was interested in snakes. Herschel wanted to know what kind of a snake I had under my box. I had no idea what kind of a snake I held captive, but I described it in detail, making sure Herschel and the crowd that had gathered appreciated what a service I had rendered by keeping it confined until he should come to return it to its cage.

When I had finished, Herschel gave a disparaging snort, motioned to the girl, and turned to go home. The little girl lifted my box, picked up my snake, put it inside her blouse, and ran after Herschel without a look back. Herschel had his revenge.

***

Soon after our arrival in Costa Rica, I was invited to attend a conference of my Central America peers in Panama City. Bob Sayre represented the Department of State and surprised me during one of the sessions by presenting me with the department's Superior Honor Award for my work during the Dominican Crisis. The citation read:

> For superior service and untiring devotion to duty during the crisis in the Dominican Republic, from April to September 1965. His sound advice and guidance to all levels of the United States government and his good judgment in matters of both policy and operations reflect great credit on the Department of State and the United States government.

A medal came with the parchment. I suppose it was a nice gesture, but that episode of my career has never been one of my fondest memories. Maybe someday it might mean something to one of my grand- or great-grandchildren.

Changes and Challenges

There was no reason to think 1967 would be an unusually exciting year. Certainly, it started out inauspiciously enough. We were more or less recovered from the grind of our Washington assignment, we were familiar in the community, we were enjoying life again and we would be eligible for home leave in the fall. Best of all, in three years I could retire. If we were returned to San José after home leave, which seemed most likely, we might be able to stay on until my 50th birthday came along at the beginning of 1970. If I was to be transferred, then we might be able to get consul general at Monterrey, Mexico, for my last post—something we had looked forward to for years. It was time to sit back, relax and enjoy the good life to the fullest.

Around the time I was ready to lean way back in my chair and put my feet on the desk, things changed. Ambassador Telles was transferred to Washington and Clarence Boonstra was chosen to replace him. I was acquainted with Boonstra and felt sure I could get along with him. After all, in the Foreign Service you get along with the ambassador—or else. Still, breaking in a new ambassador is a pain in the neck and Boonstra was set in his ways. On the brighter side, he had recently married Margaret Beshore, a peach of a person, whom I had come to know when we worked together in Washington. And then, nothing was likely to happen in Costa Rica to test a man's mettle—a reassuring thought.

A period of frenetic activity is inevitable when a new Chief of Mission arrives at post. He has to get acquainted with his section chiefs and agency heads on a less formal basis than across the table at staff meetings. That means an informal reception at the residence of the Deputy Chief of Mission which includes section chiefs, agency heads and their wives—perhaps 40 people in all at a post like San José.

Next, the new ambassador and his wife should meet the other members of his staff, as well as the staffs of other US agencies represented in the country. The Deputy Chief of Mission hosts another informal reception for the embassy's staff—possibly 150 in all. There follow informal receptions offered by the heads of other US agencies to introduce their staffs.

While all of this is going on after hours, the new chief is trying to get a firm grip on the helm at the office, while he simultaneously begins to make courtesy calls on Cabinet ministers and his fellow Chiefs of Mission. Of course, that is followed by return courtesy calls, dinners in his honor, return dinners, and so on. It's enough to drive a man to drink—which it sometimes does. Superficially, it seems like a stupid and useless exercise, but it is not. There is a sound reason for each move in this formalized dance that has evolved over the centuries, and you must go through all the steps or live to regret it.

Things at the embassy had returned to normal, and I had found an occasion or two to lean back and put my feet on the desk—if I was reasonably sure the ambassador wasn't likely to walk in and catch me—when the second shoe fell.

The young man from the communications section came into my office and closed the door behind him—most unusual. He had an odd grin on his face, like the cat-that-ate-the canary. Then he brought his hand out from behind his back and put an envelope on my desk. I'd seen many like it before, but not often since my last Washington assignment. Those envelopes were used to hand carry highly sensitive communications. We didn't get many at San José.

The single sheet of paper inside the envelope was a copy of a telegram, addressed for action to the United States embassy at Managua, Nicaragua. It was marked "For Your Information San José Eyes Only for Crockett." The text read:

President desires appoint Kennedy McCampbell Crockett Ambassador to Nicaragua. Request written agrément. Inform Department by telegram when agrément received. Request Nicaraguan officials keep proposed appointment in confidence pending White House announcement nomination. President would like to make announcement ASAP. Leave to your judgment extent to which you can press for speed without prejudice to bilateral relations.

It was dated 7 June 1967 and signed by Secretary of State Dean Rusk.

My surprise and shock couldn't have been more complete. I was utterly dumfounded. It must have showed. The young man from the communications section beamed.

"I really *am* the first to tell you! Congratulations, Sir. You'll make a great ambassador. How does it feel?" I had no idea what to answer. The best I could manage was, "Thank you. I don't feel anything yet." We shook hands, and he went on about his business. I sat looking at the sheet of paper on my desk. I wasn't sure what I should do next—except that Mary had to know as soon as I could tell her. I don't remember if I told my secretary where I was going when I walked out of the office. There were too many things churning about in my mind for me to make sense out of any of them.

If my surprise had been complete, it was as nothing compared to Mary's. We looked at that single sheet of paper and back at each other, time and again. Finally, it dawned on both of us how perfectly unbelievable it was that Ambassador and Mrs. Kennedy McCampbell Crockett sat there acting like a couple of fools. I don't remember who laughed first, but there was soon a duet that went on and on. It seemed the funniest thing that had ever happened to us.

The odds against me being selected as the United States ambassador to Nicaragua, or anywhere else, were astronomical. As a starter, some 15,000 candidates apply to take the Foreign Service officer entrance examination each year. Of these, about 2,500 pass the written examination. The oral examination that follows eliminates another 2,000. Inability to meet physical or security requirements pares the remaining 500 to around 375. Of these, about 150 enter the Foreign Service. Of the roughly 4,000 officers in the Foreign Service at any given time, 200 or so serve in ambassadorial or equivalent assignments. That's a long way from Shipping Clerk, miscellaneous-unclassified.

There was reason enough for Mary and me to laugh, and we continued to for days afterward, every time we looked at each other in private.

Kennedy Crockett. . . of Virginia

June 7, 1967 to July 4, 1967 was the longest four weeks of my life. President Johnson was notorious for the tantrums he could throw when news of an appointment he planned to make got out to the press before he was ready. He had, on more than one occasion, changed his mind simply because his plans leaked prematurely. The longer it took before my nomination was announced, the greater the risk the same thing might happen to me. It was a period of walking on eggshells and keeping fingers crossed.

The embassy at Managua had estimated that the agrément of the Nicaraguan government to my appointment would be forthcoming quickly. It was not a good estimate. Days passed and there was no word, except that the Mayor of Miami, Robert King High, had visited Managua and talked to President Somoza. He returned to Miami on the same plane that took him to Nicaragua. Our embassy reported the local rumor that His Honor wanted President Somoza's support in his campaign for the job of United States ambassador to Nicaragua. The more time passed, the more rumors there were. Finally, on June 19, Nicaraguan Foreign Minister Lorenzo Guerrero sent a formal note to our chargé in Managua informing him agrément for my appointment had been granted. Twelve days had passed without a leak.

On June 22, I was instructed to go to Washington right away. "Your initial appointment will be with Mr. Marvin Watson, special assistant to the president," the telegram read. When people wanted to know what the trip was about I fell back on the lame excuse that I had been called to Washington for routine consultation. They were polite enough not to ask why the hell anyone would want to consult with me.

When I got to Washington, I discovered the cart had somehow gotten before the horse. Mr. Watson wanted to know if I was interested in the job President Johnson had in mind, and if so, was there any reason why I shouldn't be appointed, i.e., "Are there any skeletons in your closet that may come out to embarrass the White House later on?" I answered the question truthfully—I didn't say there were none, I said I didn't think it likely any would get out. He seemed satisfied, but suggested I stick around Washington for a few days.

I had a little trouble explaining to people in the State Department what I was doing in Washington. No one asked who I had come up to consult with, although I'm sure those directly concerned with Costa Rica and the Central American area must have wondered.

To avoid embarrassing questions, I stayed away from the State Department as much as I could. It was summer, the weather was lovely, and outside always appealed to me more than inside. I found ways to pass the time quite pleasantly.

Mr. Watson finally got back to me. "Everything is on track," he said. "You can go on home." I was able to make a reservation for July 4. Sometime during my flight from Washington to Costa Rica the White House announced my nomination. There was an excited crowd of friends waiting to meet me when my plane landed in San José. For the first time since I opened that special envelope on June 7, I was able to believe it was all true and not some weird dream.

Right away, friends wanted to entertain us—be among the first to host going away parties. It was hard to explain that I had been nominated—not confirmed. I would not be going anywhere until the Senate Foreign Relations Committee scheduled hearings to consider my nomination, the full Senate voted to approve the nomination—presuming the Foreign Relations Committee should so recommend—and I had taken the oath of the office. It wasn't easy, but I stuck to my guns.

Again, it was time to sit and wait. Hearings on my nomination were not scheduled immediately. The Department of State wanted me to go before the Foreign Relations Committee with another nominee, preferably someone who would attract all the attention. There was no desire to expose me to a grilling about what had or had not been done during the Dominican Crisis. I certainly agreed with that. Before too long, President Johnson decided to nominate a political appointee, Benjamin N. Oehlert, Jr., to be ambassador to Pakistan. We were scheduled to appear together. Everything seemed to be set.

Once more it was off to Washington. The congressional relations office of the State Department took over for this part of the exercise. My first chore was to pay courtesy calls on the two senators from my home state, Texas—Ralph Yarborough, a Democrat, and John Tower, a Republican. Both received me courteously enough, although I got the impression I had caught them unawares. That seemed strange. The White House was always careful to take whatever political advantage there might be in making appointments such as mine. I didn't give it much thought—not until later, that is.

The next time I was in the Office of Congressional Relations, I was asked to check a draft résumé the White House would send to the Senate. It seemed OK, except that I was identified as a resident of the State of Virginia. I corrected the error and went on about my business. My next call at the Office of Congressional Relations was with Mr. William Macomber, who would accompany me and Mr. Oehlert, to coordinate what I might have to say at my hearing. I informed him I didn't intend to say anything unless asked. He liked that fine. He then handed me a copy of the résumé that the White House had sent to the Senate. The error about my place of residence had not been fixed. I objected. Mr. Macomber thought I was being stuffy but called the White House anyway when I insisted.

When Mr. Macomber was connected with the special assistant in the White House in charge of résumés, a heated discussion ensued. It seemed the special assistant felt there were already too many people from Texas involved in the workings of the United States government, so he had changed my legal residence to Virginia, where I had lived during my last assignment to Washington. Mr. Macomber wasn't concerned about that. He was outraged because no one had consulted him about the change.

The special assistant was not impressed by Mr. Macomber's outrage. When the conversation was concluded, Mr. Macomber turned to me and said, "There's nothing to be done about it. You'll have to live with it." He seemed surprised when I assured him I had no intention of perjuring myself before a committee of the United States Senate. My nomination could be withdrawn as far as I was concerned, if that was what it took. That got his attention. He said he would see what he could work out.

When Mr. Macomber and I met the next morning to ride up to the hill for the hearing, I told him I had given some thought to what I might say if the question of my legal residence should arise. I would point out that my ancestors had lived in Virginia for generations, that the old homestead at Crockett Springs could still be identified, that I would be honored to be a Virginian, but, fate had determined that I should be a Texan, and a Texan I was. Mr. Macomber mumbled that he doubted the matter would come up and hoped I wouldn't bring it up. I assured him I wouldn't.

I took with me to the hearing a 3x5-inch index card containing my notes. They consisted of three words: "Don't get mad." Since most of the trouble I had gotten myself into in my life usually came about because I lost my temper, I was determined not to make that mistake this time. As it developed, I need not have concerned myself. The questions put to me by members of the committee were perfunctory. The Department of State had guessed right, Mr. Oeh-lert drew all the attention. And no one asked me about the place of my legal residence.

It did occur to me that the senators from Virginia might wonder why I hadn't paid the customary courtesy calls.

Miss Pierce, Rubén Darío, and Margarita

The last steps on the long road to becoming Ambassador of the United States of America and Mrs. Crockett were most pleasant. Once the Senate had voted to confirm my nomination, Mary and I were invited to Washington, along with our daughters Linda and Terry, who still lived at home. We were briefed about our new assignment, informed about facilities that would be available to us, asked what special requirements we had, and yes-sired and yes-ma'amed half to death. At some point, I was given a list of candidates for deputy chief of mission. I had no trouble picking Malcolm R. (Dick) Barnaby, whom I had known when we were both office directors. I never had reason to regret the choice.

It was nice to have so many people interested in seeing we were completely satisfied after nine previous assignments when we either found out what we needed to know on our own or didn't find out at all. Being a presidential ap-pointee does have its advantages. When the time came for my oath of office, the State Department sent engraved invitations to those we wished to have attend the ceremony. The chief of protocol was there to administer the oath. Secretary of State Rusk made a polite little speech. It went very smoothly until the chief of protocol said, "Repeat after me: I, Kennedy McCampbell Crockett of Virginia, do solemnly swear. . ." There was no way to get out of it. I repeated after him. What the hell, you can't win 'em all—and besides, there's nothing wrong with being Kennedy M. Crockett of Virginia.

The final act of the induction exercise was a call on President Johnson to receive his instructions and to have my picture taken with him. It was the first time I had ever been alone with the president. If he remembered that he had seen me before, he gave no sign, although he was relaxed and cordial. He told me he had met with President Anastasio Somoza after his election, had been impressed with him and felt we should "Help him help his people." Rural elec-trification was mentioned as a good example of the type of project Johnson favored. The other subject was Vietnam. "You tell him [Somoza] we need as many flags there as we can get."

I guess Mary and I could be forgiven for wanting to swing by Laredo on our way back to Central America. After all, my appointment had been headline news in the town where we were raised. Who wouldn't want to bask a little while the basking was good? In addition, there was no way of knowing when we might see Mary's aging mother again. I broached the prospect in the department and came up with a firm, "Sorry, Managua has been vacant far too long already."

That didn't seem right to me—and I was getting used to being pampered. I had an idea. I called my friend Dave Bintliff in Houston, who had interests in several Central American countries, including Nicaragua. "Dave, would you like for me to come by Houston and address a group of your friends—businessmen, prospective investors and others interested in Nicaragua?" Dave thought it was a great idea. "Do I call Lyndon?" he wanted to know.

The people Dave Bintliff invited for my speech at the Petroleum Club were genuinely interested in Central America and knowledgeable about conditions there. Agriculture, oil, manufacturing, construction, transportation and banking were represented. Questioning continued throughout the luncheon hour, and coffee was served before I had a chance to take a bite. No matter, the exercise served a worthwhile purpose, and when it was all over we were able to slip away for a long weekend at Laredo. If anyone in the State Department knew, or cared, I never heard about it.

When you've been gone from the old hometown for over 20 years as Mary and I had, you find the place and the people changed. Relationships cool over the years. Where once there were so many friends you couldn't find time to see them all, one day there are pitifully few you really want to see—or who want to see you. No matter. The ones that are left become that much more precious. Foremost among these, for both Mary and me, was Miss Alma Pierce.

Miss Pierce had taught Spanish at Laredo High School. She had been teaching Spanish there for as long as anyone could remember. Contemporaries of my father had attended her classes, and she continued to teach many years after Mary and I went on to college. As long as she was there, she also sponsored the Patrick Henry Club, the debating society. Miss Pierce may not have had children of her own, but she always had "her boys," and no mother was more diligent than she in trying to make something of them.

It wasn't until many years after high school that I began to realize how much influence Miss Pierce had over the direction of my life—and, I'm sure, over the lives of many others. Two of "her boys" that came before me, Tom Mann and Covey Oliver, were US ambassadors and went on to hold senior positions in the Department of State. One of my classmates, Abe Kazen, was congressman from our district for many years. There were many others whose accomplishments must have been a source of great satisfaction for her.

We found her in a nursing home, so thin and frail she seemed almost transparent. Mis Pierce was at the end of a long life. Mary and I stood at her bedside, not knowing what to say. She studied each of us carefully. A smile spread across her face and two tears trickled down her cheeks. "Mary and Kennedy," she whispered in a small voice, "how very nice. I have been expecting you for a long time."

Her body may have been frail, and her voice little more than a whisper, but Miss Pierce's mind was strong and eager. Together we reminisced about her visits with us in Mexico City, Washington and Guatemala, the fun we had, the cute things our children had said or done. There was much Mary and I had long since forgotten, but Miss Pierce seemed to remember it all. Only then did Mary and I realize how much those visits had meant to her.

For the third time, a person in white uniform appeared at Miss Pierce's door, cleared her throat and consulted her wristwatch. How quickly time passed. As we said goodbye and rose to go, Miss Pierce looked at me with mock sternness and asked, "Kennedy, do you remember when I wouldn't pass you in Spanish II and you had to make the course up in summer school?"

"Yes, Miss Pierce," I answered.

"Do you remember why I wouldn't pass you?"

"I'm sorry, Miss Pierce, that was a long time ago. . ."

"I wouldn't pass you, Kennedy, because you refused to memorize the poem *Margarita*. Now you will know how important that was. Rubén Darío, the poet laureate of Nicaragua and one of the finest poets of his age, wrote that poem. The United States ambassador to Nicaragua must know about Rubén Darío— and *Margarita*."

Mary and I somehow managed to hold back tears until we touched Miss Pierce's hand one last time and reached the hallway. Sad as we were, I felt a strange sense of elation as we tried to compose ourselves. My parents had both gone the year before. But Miss Pierce, at least, knew that the extra effort she had put into trying to make something out of an unruly and rebellious youth had not been entirely in vain.

Moving On

It's nice to know people think enough of you to go to the trouble of hosting a send-off party. On the other hand, too many despedidas can be exhausting. The problem had serious potential for us in our move from San José to Managua. By air, the two posts are less than an hour apart, leaving no time to rest in between, and we knew breaking in at Managua would be more of a drain on our energies than getting away from San José. The best solution we could work out was to limit the time we would spend in San José before going on to Managua. Every minute of that time was quickly scheduled, including the evening we were due to arrive back in town from Laredo.

As our flight circled San José for a dusk landing, we could clearly see the airport lights, although we could also see the heavy ground fog, not uncommon during the rainy season. When the pilot let down for his approach, we were engulfed in the ground fog well before we reached the end of the runway. Visibility dropped to zero. The pilot pulled the plane up and we gained altitude to circle and make another try.

From above, the lights of the runway were again plainly visible. But as we neared the ground, we were quickly smothered in the dense fog. This time, we came alarmingly close to the control tower before the pilot pulled back on the controls to gain altitude. Once out of danger, the voice of the captain came over the loudspeaker. "I'm sure all of you will agree with me that it would be much nicer to spend the night in a hotel in Panama than in a morgue in Costa Rica. We'll have to overfly San José this evening." Scratch one despedida. I hoped the guests would enjoy our party.

We attended luncheons and cocktail parties and dinners back-to-back for the next several days. It was all very flattering, and exhausting. One of the best despedidas was organized by Bob Gershenson, our administrative officer. He wrote a hilarious skit roasting me good for being more interested in hunting and fishing than my work at the chancery. It was a riot—and not too far from the truth. Margaret Beshore Boonstra hostessed a delightful dinner for us at the ambassador's residence to say goodbye to our best Costa Rican friends.

When the last party was over, I played my ace in the hole. We would drive to Managua, rather than fly, with an overnight at our favorite hotel on the beach at Puntarenas. We desperately needed at least one night of rest in between going away and getting there.

The short drive from San José to Puntarenas wasn't a happy one. We hated to leave Costa Rica for many reasons. Judy would stay on with her Costa Rican husband, Federico Faerron, and our Costa Rican grandson, James Kennedy. Linda and Terry left their friends to go where they didn't know anyone. We all faced the chore of getting acquainted with a new country and a new way of life. Costa Rica had been good to all of us. We had no way to know what Nicaragua might have in store.

Nothing revives the spirit like a nice swim in the ocean, a good dinner, a peaceful night's sleep and a new adventure to look forward to. By the next morning, we'd had them all. We tumbled out of bed for a last swim in the hotel pool, a breakfast of *gallo pinto,* fresh tortillas, eggs and bacon, and the prospect of a pleasant drive to the border on a morning washed clean by an overnight thunderstorm. Things looked a lot better than they had the day before. Don't they always?

Somewhere short of the border we pulled off the highway, snacked out of our cooler and changed into fresh clothes. The pickup carrying our luggage and dogs awaited us near the gate that marked the boundary between Costa Rica and Nicaragua. On the other side, a small crowd stood near the customs station. We were expected. We crossed over into our new life.

Presenting credentials to Nicaraguan President Anastasio Somoza; Managua, 1967.

US Marine guards greet Ambassador and Mrs. Crockett during an official soiree at the embassy residence. Managua, Nicaragua, 1968.

Nicaragua
1967

To Live Like a Millionaire

There aren't many ways a person of modest means can live like a millionaire without resorting to practices frowned upon by the law. One of the few legal avenues available—and possibly the best one—is to be a career US ambassador.

The official residence of the United States Ambassador in Managua, Nicaragua, was built in the late 1930s. The grounds, over 50 acres on the outskirts of Managua, encompassed the top of a prominent hill known as Las Piedrecitas—the small rocks. Some 15 acres of the total area was cleared, planted in lawn, shrubs and trees and maintained by a staff of five gardeners. The remainder, during my time, was heavily overgrown with native grass, bushes, vines and trees. Small animals (including skunks, opossums, rabbits and raccoons) lived there. Several coveys of bobwhite quail were also resident on the grounds. But the sight of deer stepping out of the undergrowth in the evenings to feed on the flowers and shrubs gave us the greatest thrill.

The residence itself, situated to afford a sweeping view of Managua, Lake Xolotlán and the surrounding volcanoes, provided 42,000 square feet of living space on three floors. A smaller, four-bedroom residence reserved for the Deputy Chief of Mission (DCM) was located on the same grounds within hailing distance of the ambassador's bedroom. Then there was a large swimming pool, complete with dressing rooms and showers; a greenhouse, a gatehouse for off-duty guards, a cottage for the maintenance man, a tennis court and other odds and ends in addition to the corral and tack room we built for our horses—at our own expense and mostly with our own hands.

Overall, the place was entirely inappropriate for a small country like Nicaragua and unnecessary to the needs of any US ambassador posted there. It was also one of the least comfortable houses we ever lived in. It took well over 100 steps to get from the master bedroom to the kitchen. Of course, there was a buzzer system (that didn't work) and telephone service between the dozens of rooms—even if there was no current directory.

The entire domestic staff, dressed in starched black and white, awaited us as we wound our way up the drive and stopped beneath the portico at the main entrance. It was an impressive entourage, indeed. Carlos, the majordomo, headed the line, followed by several maids, the cook, the laundress, the house-boy and the chief gardener with his four assistants. There were, in addition, the two chauffeurs who had met us at the border, one or the other of whom was always on duty, 24 hours a day, seven days a week. There may have been others that I do not now recall. What I do remember is my first impression: "My God, with this many servants, there'll be a squabble of some sort going on all the time." I was right.

We were introduced to each of the servants. We toured the entertainment rooms and library on the main floor. There were 24 chairs around the formal dinner table. I shuddered at the thought of endless crowds in black tie and evening gowns sitting along its length making small talk with Mary at one end and me at the other, bored to tears. Then a horrifying thought crossed my mind: "What if we are expected to take our own meals here?" I was relieved when we were shown into the family dining room—lots of windows with mar-velous views, informal wrought-iron furniture, plants in hanging pots, more plants in beds along the walls, and a beautiful plant under the plate glass tab-letop. It was a lovely room—the best in the house.

The tour of our new home came to an end in a spacious, glassed-in veranda with another excellent view. Carlos stood at attention nearby as we found the places where each of us would sit whenever we gathered there over the next three years. I need not have hesitated to ask—the bar was stocked.

When our orders were filled, I raised my glass to Mary and said, "Welcome home." She made a face in response but touched her glass to mine with a smile. For the first time since we had walked through the door, I was beginning to like the place. By the time I reached the bottom of my glass for the second time, I began to feel at home. And when Carlos announced that dinner was served, the four of us rushed for the family dining room as if we had lived in the place for years. It doesn't take long to adjust to new surroundings in the Foreign Ser-vice—you get lots of practice.

Our first day in Nicaragua had been a long one. A rather large group had met us at Peñas Blancas on the border, including the Nicaraguan chief of protocol and an assistant or two, the embassy's administrative officer and an assistant or two, the Nicaraguan colonel in charge of the Rivas military zone, the officers in charge of the Nicaraguan immigration and customs detachments, each with an assistant or two, our two chauffeurs, an embassy officer with whom we had served at Tijuana, and Colonel William P. Francisco, the chief of our military mission, his wife and teenage daughter, both named Nancy.

Photographers recorded our reception and the customs and immigration formalities before the entire group moved on to the residence of Colonel Someone-or-Other of the Nicaraguan Guardia Nacional. There, a three-piece band played the national anthems of both countries and then drinks were served—even if it was still before noon. Nicaragua was like that.

Next the band struck up popular music, and someone whispered in my ear that I would be expected to dance with each of the ladies present. I don't know how many there were, but there were plenty. What there wasn't was air conditioning. By the time I had swung the first lady around the dance floor a couple of times to the beat of "Managua, Nicaragua is a Beautiful Town," I was sweating profusely. Before I finished with the last, a couple of hours later, I was soaked down to my shoe soles. In those conditions, it was absolutely necessary to ward off dehydration. And it was no fault of mine that there was nothing on the trays that passed my way that wasn't alcoholic. We all had a real jolly time of it— Mary included. She had to dance with each of the men.

From Peñas Blancas, the schedule called for driving to San Juan del Sur for lunch at the Francisco's beach house. What the cool waters of the Pacific didn't do for what ailed me, the luncheon spread did. By the time I got up from my nap and took another long swim in the surf, I felt human again. The sun wasn't too far above the western horizon when we decided it was time to go on to Managua. It was then that I really appreciated having a chauffeur. Without one, we simply wouldn't have gone.

None of us felt the least bit uncomfortable about being ready for bed immediately after the first meal in our new home. Besides, we were eager to see our sleeping quarters. We climbed the long, circular staircase behind Carlos like a troop of cub scouts. The thought crossed my mind that with so much opulence, it was strange no one had thought of installing an elevator.

There were two master bedrooms on the second floor of the residence, each with separate dressing room, bath, his and her closets and open balconies. Those off our suite provided a striking panorama of Managua at night—much more beautiful than during daylight hours. There were four other double bedrooms, a furnished, screened-in veranda and a spacious family room.

Our bags sat on stands awaiting our attention. Our beds had been turned down and the lights turned low. It was a struggle to stay awake long enough to find pajamas and get a shower. Just as I was heading for bed a dim red light in one corner caught my eye. No one had mentioned a radio, but this was obviously a portable shortwave. I picked up the handset and asked, "What happens when I speak in here?"

"On this circuit you will reach an officer of the military mission," came back the reply in Colonel Francisco's crisp voice. "On the alternate circuit, you will reach an embassy duty officer or the Marine guard at the chancery. Can I be of assistance, sir?"

"No thanks, Bill," I replied, "Goodnight." I was beginning to like that guy—very much on the ball.

As I crawled into bed, Mary rolled over and said, "Be it ever so humble, there's no place like home. Sweet dreams, Mr. Ambassador."

Getting Started

Custom dictates that a newly arrived chief of mission shall maintain a low profile, except within his own bailiwick, until he has presented his credentials to the chief of state. The interval in my case was from August 13, 1967 when we crossed the border at Peñas Blancas until the afternoon of August 21, 1967 when I handed President Anastasio Somoza the letter President Lyndon Johnson had addressed to him stating that I would be his man in Nicaragua until further notice. It was one of the busiest weeks ever, considering I wasn't supposed to be doing anything.

Monday morning, August 14, began with an embassy staff meeting at 8:00 a.m. At 9:00 a.m. we left for the Nicaraguan foreign office to start arranging for me to present my credentials. After an initial meeting with Humberto Arguello, the Nicaraguan chief of protocol, we met with Lorenzo Guerrero, the Nicaraguan foreign minister. Both looked over copies of the letter I would hand to President Somoza when the time came.

By 10:30 a.m. I was back at the office listening to briefings from the various embassy section chiefs about what was going on in Nicaragua. There was a break for lunch, followed by an early afternoon briefing by the chief of the Agency for International Development and a tour of his offices. Next came the United States Information Agency chief and, of course, a tour of his layout. At 5:30 p.m. I was allotted time to go home to shower and change clothes so I would be socially acceptable for the 6:30 p.m. reception at the DCM's residence to bend an elbow with the men I had been listening to most all day. At least the wives were brought into the picture at this stage. The day's schedule ended sometime after 9:00 p.m.

This wouldn't have been too bad, except that it went on for the rest of the week. Before it was over, we had met some 450 people, including wives. Never have I been happier to see a week come to an end. We had been through the same routine day after day until I had trouble sorting out who worked for whom. There is, however, one worthwhile benefit in an exercise of this type. It's a chance to spot the best and the worst among those Washington has provided, even if it doesn't make it any easier to get rid of the worst or hang onto the best.

It was nice to have the monotony broken when time came for the presentation of credentials ceremony—not as formal in Nicaragua as in many other small countries, but formal enough. At the appointed hour, President Somoza's bulletproof Cadillac pulled up at the residence to take me to the presidential palace. The chief of protocol and President Somoza's senior military aide came along as escorts.

As we arrived at the palace, a group of cadets from the Nicaraguan military academy snapped to attention and stood stock still as we exited the vehicles and climbed the steps. At the top, we turned and bowed in the direction of the honor guard, and a military band started playing the national anthems of both countries. That finished, we bowed again before turning and entering the reception hall where President Somoza awaited at the far end, with the entire Nicaraguan cabinet lined up against one wall and the chiefs of all diplomatic missions accredited to his government lined up against the other. Military officers were dressed in white uniforms and civilians in white linen suits, black bow ties and black shoes. Quite impressive.

There were at least a couple of stops for bows in President Somoza's direction as we marched up the long hall to the dais where he was seated, the foreign minister on his left and an empty chair on his right. Once I had been introduced by the foreign minister and had handed over my credentials, I introduced the senior members of my staff—sort of silly because President Somoza had known most of them much longer than I had and managed to correct me when I bobbled one name. The chief of protocol then took me down the line of cabinet officers, introducing each in turn, after which we went down the line of chiefs of mission as I was introduced to each of them. It occurred to me that since I was the new kid on the block, my place would likely be at the end of that line until some other chief of mission arrived to take last place from me.

When all the introductions had been made, I was marched back up to where President Somoza sat and ushered to the chair at his side. While the rest of those there assembled marked time, he and I drank coffee and had a get acquainted chat, which wasn't as difficult an exercise as it might have been, all things considered. I had a few things to say, and President Somoza was content to listen.

I started with President Johnson's personal greetings and his special thanks for a letter of appreciation President Somoza had written him when we helped fight a recent outbreak of polio. I then delivered a couple of private messages from our own chief of protocol, Ambassador James Symington. I also had a message from the Costa Rican foreign minister thanking President Somoza for leaving Nicaraguan Ambassador Juan Bautista Lacayo in Costa Rica. The Costa Ricans liked him, something that could be said of few Nicaraguans by any Costa Rican.

Next came my own thanks for the cordial reception I had received on my arrival at the Nicaraguan border, followed by greetings from former Undersecretary of State Tom Mann. Having taken care of the niceties, I then told President Somoza that while I would do all within my power to promote cordial and productive relations between our two governments, my mission in Nicaragua would be considerably broader than that. I would also seek to promote better understanding between our two peoples, including those Nicaraguans who made up his non-communist political opposition.

The smile faded from President Somoza's face and I braced for a sharp response. I had counted on that possibility and was ready with a rejoinder. Better get the ground rules established now than run into difficulties later. President Somoza must have read my mind. A bitter little smile crept across his face as he rose to bid me goodbye and said, "I trust you will permit me the luxury of such frankness when my turn comes."

From the moment we arrived in Nicaragua, we had been besieged with requests from the media for interviews. It was easy enough to beg off prior to my presentation of credentials, but once that was behind me, there was no way to get around doing something more positive. My solution was an afternoon press conference at the residence with perhaps 50 representatives of the press, radio and television.

For two hours I fielded questions ranging from Vietnam and the summer's race riots in the United States, to "US support for dictatorships," and our inability to deal with Fidel Castro, ending with harsh criticism of the paucity of our foreign assistance programs. It was a challenging exercise, but I stuck with it until everything they could think to ask had been answered as fully as I knew how. The applause when the end came was worth the effort it took to suffer so much abuse in one sitting.

Throughout the exercise, my eye had kept coming back to an enormous, bearded man sitting toward the back of the audience. I would later learn he was Col. László Pataky, a radio commentator and former French Legionnaire. His visage was as formidable as his size, and he must have weighed over 350 pounds. I couldn't help feeling some apprehension about what he would have to say when it was his turn to have at me. Col. Pataky did not choose to ask for the floor until toward the end of the session. When he stood, it seemed his head would brush the ceiling—he was that intimidating. His voice boomed out like thunder when he spoke.

"Mr. Ambassador," he said, "I wish to thank you for your courtesy in receiving us. It has been a pleasure to hear what you have had to say about so many subjects." And with that, he sat down.

When the press conference was finished, I sent for Mary and the girls to introduce them, after which the waiters served drinks and canapés and we all had a nice visit together that lasted at least as long as the press conference. I forgot about Col. Pataky and my initial impression—that is, until sometime during the night when Mary shook me awake to tell me I was moaning and groaning something awful.

"What's the matter, Kennedy?" she asked. "Can I help?"

"No," I answered, "unless you want to wrestle Col. Pataky. He just challenged me to a match—no holds barred."

Anastasio Somoza Debayle

I'm sure Anastasio Somoza Debayle, the son of President Anastasio Somoza García and the younger brother of President Luis Somoza Debayle, couldn't remember a time when he didn't fully expect to be president of Nicaragua one day. I'm also sure he had no idea that so many who had supported his father and his brother saw him as unsuited for the job. He had been trained to be a soldier, not a politician. He lacked the natural charisma which both his father and his brother had been generously endowed. He couldn't hide an unfortunate streak of arrogance and made no attempt to hide his disdain for those who served him. He was not easy to like.

But he had the brains, determination and singleness of purpose required to overcome all these faults, and he was flushed with his triumph when I came to Nicaragua as the first US ambassador accredited to his government. I didn't expect him to be easy to get along with.

There was good and historic reason for President Somoza to have reservations about any career State Department man. State Department men had held the point when the United States attempted to curb the excesses of his father. While his brother, Luis, had enjoyed a live-and-let-live relationship with the US government during the period of his presidency, the winds from Washington had been distinctly cool since the Kennedy administration took office in 1961. Aaron Brown, an able and disciplined career Foreign Service officer, had been sent to Nicaragua as United States ambassador early that year, and much of his energy during the six years he held the job had been devoted to thwarting Anastasio Somoza's drive for the Nicaraguan presidency—to such an extent that Somoza had gone through US military channels to request Brown's withdrawal. It was against this backdrop that I appeared on the scene. I may have been appointed by President Johnson, who was favorably disposed toward Somoza, but Kennedy men continued to hold much of the power in the State Department—and I was a State Department man.

I was never able to think of Somoza as Hispanic. He had been educated in the United States (West Point), as had his wife, Hope Portocarrero. Both spoke perfect, unaccented English, and I suspect spoke it better than either of them spoke Spanish. I know Somoza thought in English when speaking extemporaneously in Spanish, because his sentence structure betrayed him, as mine often betrayed me. Their children were also educated in English. Their family life together was patterned on the American style, as was their residence, a copy of one of San Antonio, Texas' better homes.

In the beginning, there was no way for me to know how President Somoza intended to do business. Both of us were new at the job and had no experience dealing with one another. It didn't take long for me to find out, however—the hard way. A new president for the Organization of American States was to be elected and the State Department informed me the candidate the United States favored was former Ecuadorian President Galo Plaza. I was instructed to seek a Nicaraguan commitment to support Plaza.

I asked for an appointment with Foreign Minister Lorenzo Guerrero, a former president of Nicaragua himself, and after stating our preference for Plaza and why, was given assurances of Nicaragua's support. I so reported to Washington. Much to my surprise, in a few days I was informed from Washington that Nicaraguan Ambassador Guillermo Sevilla Sacasa, Somoza's brother-in-law, had told the department that Nicaragua was unalterably opposed to Galo Plaza's candidacy and could not support him. Washington suggested I might try to explain what the hell was going on.

I couldn't go back to Foreign Minister Guerrero, a pleasant and compliant old man—it would have been too embarrassing for us both. That left President Somoza. I imagine he expected to hear from me, because I was granted an audience promptly. "Come to lunch."

During lunch, each of us waited for the other to bring up the subject at hand. When dessert had been finished and coffee served, I blinked. "I suppose you can imagine the pickle I'm in, Mr. President. After I assured Washington that Nicaragua would support Galo Plaza's candidacy, Don Guillermo has told the State Department that Nicaragua is unalterably opposed to him."

Somoza broke into a broad grin and replied, "I felt confident you would understand. Galo Plaza has done many things against Nicaragua (read: *The Somozas*)."

"Mr. President," I replied, "there may have been misunderstandings in the past, but in politics there always has to be a way to make amends. Would you be willing to receive Galo Plaza if he asked to see you?"

"I would see him if the United States requested it, but what has been done has been done, and there is no way to change that."

In reporting back to Washington, I suggested that our problem could well be Somoza's ego. After all, the press had reported on frequent trips by Galo

Plaza to major Latin American capitals seeking support for his candidacy. Where Nicaragua was concerned, he hadn't bothered to ask for support but left it to the United States to take care of that detail. I speculated that if Galo Plaza were willing to seek an interview with Somoza on his own, and handled things right, we might be able to save the day.

In due course, Galo Plaza came to Nicaragua, made his obeisance and went home with a commitment for Nicaragua's support. Somoza had made his point. He didn't intend to be taken lightly. I learned my lesson, too. Never again did I go to Foreign Minister Guerrero on a matter of any significance—I went directly to Somoza.

It didn't take Somoza long to find an opportunity to complain bitterly about my predecessor.

"He did everything he could to block my way to the presidency," Somoza protested, "and he never gave me a chance to talk things out with him." Although Somoza skirted around it, I gathered the most damage to his ego was caused by Brown's refusal to be photographed with him. The implied question was clear. "Are you going to be the same?"

I had come to Nicaragua determined to find a way to do business with Somoza while keeping a respectable distance. I knew from the beginning that would be difficult, and I soon realized that what I had planned was impossible. If I expected to get Somoza's cooperation when we needed it, I was going to have to be on good terms with him before I came asking. Now seemed as good a time as any to get started.

"Mr. President," I said, "what would you think of getting together for a US style barbecue one weekend out by the embassy pool? Our families could get acquainted, you and I could talk, and I'll see there's a photographer around to take pictures. How about it?" Somoza didn't have to think twice. "Would this weekend be too soon?" he responded. The deal was cut.

The picnic was a huge success. Somoza's advance guard started arriving shortly after daylight on the appointed morning. Our regular delegation of Nicaraguan soldiers was augmented by perhaps 30 additional riflemen who were posted around the grounds at strategic intervals. Several Guardia Nacional officers supervised them, keeping in touch by walkie-talkie.

At the stroke of eleven, the presidential limousine wound up the driveway, preceded by a jeepload of men dressed in plain clothes, each carrying a briefcase designed to accommodate an Uzi machine gun. The president's car was followed by a large station wagon, which, in turn, was followed by an elongated limo. I would learn this 10-doored monster was known as "The Centipede" in Nicaragua, and in addition to more security people, carried Somoza's manservant, complete with a supply of Upmann cigars and Napoleon brandy.

Somoza's immediate party included his wife Hope and their two youngest daughters, the girls' Spanish governess, and a retired White House Secret Service Agent named Frank Berry, who advised Somoza on personal security measures, escorted Hope when she traveled abroad without Somoza, and generally played the part of a favorite uncle around the presidential household. There were probably others I didn't notice.

For our part, we tried to keep things as informal. Hammocks were slung under shade trees, there were horses for the children to ride, along with a man to fetch and take them as needed. Carlos, the majordomo, doubled as bartender. Besides Mary and me and our two young daughters, Pancho the parrot and Taffy the cocker spaniel helped entertain our guests. When it was time to eat, I broiled steaks and fillets of alligator gar Somoza had brought along with him. Two maids in black uniforms with white trim and white aprons served us. It was quite a picnic!

I remember two items of significance from our first informal day together. Somoza may have been quite tall and husky in appearance when fully clothed, but in a bathing suit it was easy to tell he was not and never had been athletically inclined. More important to me, and to Somoza, was he would never make the grade when it came to personal charm. He was intelligent and interesting . . . but he was not the kind you could ever develop real affection for. In some ways, he reminded me of LBJ. That may have been why they hit it off so well together.

The US Ambassador

Having been a US ambassador, it is reasonable to conclude that one of the easiest questions for me to answer should be, "What is a US ambassador and what does he do?" I've been asked the question enough times that it no longer catches me by surprise. But despite the thought I've given over the years to how best to phrase a reply, I still have nothing better to offer than, "Everything." True as that may be, it is hardly modest and certainly not informative. The problem is, there is no short answer—and probably no complete answer, either. Each ambassador does whatever has to be done at any given time and place. The range of possibilities is limitless.

I have no intention of attempting to give a complete answer to the question here, but I will quote from a publication released by the Department of State which is supposed to provide a good summary.

> "The US Ambassador is the nation's highest diplomatic official. His full title is Ambassador Extraordinary and Plenipotentiary (*extraordinary* in that he represents the person of the President of the United States and *plenipotentiary* because he has full power to negotiate). He is charged with four basic responsibilities that ranking diplomats have carried throughout history . . . protection of his country's interests abroad . . . reporting to his government on conditions in the country of his assignment . . . negotiation of agreements [treaties]…and ceremonial representation.
>
> "The problems confronting the Ambassador in his daily schedule may range in subject matter from atomic energy to educational exchange, from provincial elections to agricultural imports, from technological development programs to immigration policy, currency stabilization, military capabilities, or many other equally complex and varied fields.
>
> "He is concerned with and must be knowledgeable about all aspects of human activity—politics, economics, commerce, industry, agriculture, finance, labor, standards of living, transportation and communication, social welfare, education, science, art, religion . . . in short, all aspects of life in the country of his assignment. He may rely on counselors and attachés and upon specialists for details, but he, himself, has to have a thorough grasp of fundamentals in each pertinent field of human enterprise in order to understand the problems for which he has ultimate responsibility."

The most onerous of an ambassador's duties fall under the heading of ceremonial representation. A great deal of time is wasted standing around, being there to lend dignity and prestige to some other ambassador's show. Ceremonies marking some country's "national day," the equivalent of the Fourth of July, inevitably come when you desperately need the time to take care of an emergency in your own shop. There is no way to avoid these. Failure of the representative of the US president to be in attendance would never go unnoticed by the other country's ambassador and would certainly be reported to its president. Often these events involve a flag raising, speeches and a reception during the day, followed by a black-tie dinner in the evening. Even in a small country like Nicaragua, you can expect several foreign "national day" celebrations each month.

Far more time is spent by the US ambassador attending special ceremonies organized by the host government. Holidays are more numerous abroad than they are in the United States, and each cabinet minister has pet projects of his own to inaugurate. And then there are the endless formalities when a new ambassador from any of the 25 nations maintaining fulltime diplomatic representation in Nicaragua arrives in country—or departs.

One cannot, of course, overlook one's own ceremonies. Besides the Fourth of July, the Marine Corps Birthday Ball, and receptions for visiting dignitaries and delegations, each United States agency active in the country has its own ceremonies. The Agency for International Development can always be counted on for regular ribbon cuttings to inaugurate new roads or low-cost housing; or The Peace Corps wants recognition on the completions of clinics, schools, water wells, and community latrines; and The Department of Agriculture couldn't hope to get the president of Nicaragua interested in its program for biological control of boll weevil infestations of the cotton fields without a ceremony of some sort involving the US ambassador; and The Inter-American Coast and Geodetic Survey wants coverage of the delivery of new mapping equipment to its Nicaraguan counterpart.

Somewhere in between all of this, the ambassador must find time to take care of business back at the office. One way or another it gets done. But believe me, it often is not the least bit easy.

Much of an ambassador's time inside his place of work is devoted to reading what the various Washington agencies have instructed their offices abroad to do—or not do. Failure to keep abreast of the day-to-day guidance sent forth by the wise men of the Potomac can trip you up when you least expect it. But you have to go through reams and reams of chaff if you are to have any hope of spotting that grain of intelligence vital to your operation.

When something worth knowing pops up, likely as not it will turn out to involve a conflict of interest between competing US bureaucracies. For instance: The Agency for International Development wants its police advisor to train the host country's border guards, while the Department of Defense feels this should be the responsibility of the US Military Mission. It is futile to send the problem back to Washington. If it could have been solved there, the conflicting instructions wouldn't have been sent out in the first place. It is in finding solutions to intramural problems of this sort that the ambassador exercises his negotiating skills most frequently—not in working out agreements with the host country. It shouldn't be that way, but it is.

From time to time in the past, the question has been raised as to where ultimate authority rests among and between representatives of the various agencies of the government of the United States when operating abroad. The White House attempted to clear up any doubts by issuing Executive Order 10575 on November 6, 1954 which provides, "The chief of the United States diplomatic mission in each country, as the representative of the president, shall serve as the channel of authority on foreign policy direction to all representatives of United States agencies in such countries."

It seems reasonable to conclude this Executive Order would have settled the question once and for all. Unfortunately, it did not. Human nature being what it is, all too frequently some agency chief decides he is not bound by it. The ambassador may have the authority to send him packing, which sometimes happens, but most ambassadors would consider that a defeat. Any ambassador worth his striped pants should be able to work out some less drastic solution—but the time involved in doing so is often a high price to pay in a job that requires 36-hour days to begin with.

I would be less than candid if I closed out this section leaving the impression that being US ambassador to Nicaragua was such a full-time job for me that I spent all my time trying to do it perfectly. Sometimes I did. And then, sometimes, I did not. The urge to shoot a few quail, catch a few golden snappers, or ride a horse along the trails winding through the coffee plantations sometimes became irresistible. And when that happened, I surrendered and quit being an ambassador long enough for the spell to pass—or until someone got on my shortwave frequency and told me the time had come to get back on the job. Whichever came first.

Nicaraguan Politics

In the United States, we are conditioned to think of politics in Central America (and particularly Nicaragua) as exciting, suspenseful, violent and mysterious—because that's when we hear about it. I've been tempted to write this section against such a background. However, the facts wouldn't bear out that kind of an approach. Although Honduras did go to war with El Salvador over the outcome of a soccer game, and in downtown Managua an opposition faction had to be routed out of the Gran Hotel with tanks, cannons, and machine guns shortly before I arrived, everything is relative. And relatively, Nicaragua was quiet and calm during my tour as ambassador.

Things were quiet and calm because that's the way most Nicaragua's citizens wanted them. The poor and underprivileged (the bulk of the population) found it hard enough to hold body and soul together, but if there was no trouble, most could find a way to feed, clothe and house themselves. Although conditions were primitive and privation the rule, the country people fared better than their urban counterparts. A man willing to work could build his own house out of native materials and grow much of his own food. Hard cash might be scarce, but wage paying jobs were to be had during at least some months of the year.

At the upper levels of society, where the leaders of Nicaragua's traditional political opposition were to be found, there was little complaint about government (Somoza) policies. The Nicaraguan economy was sound and hard currency (dollars) was readily available at an exchange rate that had been stable for many years. There was some grousing over the predominance of the Somoza family in many enterprises, but this was most often heard from those who wished they had the advantage of being in the driver's seat themselves. By and large, conservatives with money had more confidence in Somoza's leadership than they would have had in their own party chiefs.

Except for the Sandinistas, discontent and overt opposition to Somoza was concentrated in the academic community (students and faculty of both universities) and the media, notably the opposition daily *La Prensa*, but also including several radio newsmen. These sectors did not represent any threat to maintenance of law-and-order by the Guardia Nacional.

The fact that the Somoza family had dominated Nicaraguan politics for over 30 years (since 1936) would not become a general rallying cry for some years to come. There had been far too much instability in Nicaragua historically for any movement aimed at overthrowing a relatively prosperous and stable status quo to generate much enthusiasm. Dynasty had gone out of style in Latin America, and it was obvious the Somoza family domination of the body politic must come to an end—one way or another.

I spent a good bit of time getting acquainted with Somoza supporters and opponents. I came to know Alfonso Callejas, the Minister of Public Works and Ambassador Aaron Brown's candidate for president of Nicaragua if a way could be found to get him elected. I also came to know Ramiro Sacasa Guerrero, Minister of Education and Francisco Aguirre's candidate for president of Nicaragua if a way could be found to get him elected.

And then there was Luis Manuel Debayle, Somoza's uncle who headed up the power and light company, mostly his own candidate for president of Nicaragua if a way could be found for him to get there—with or without elections. These men were, of course, all affiliated with the Liberal Party.

On the conservative side, there were two serious contenders—Pedro Joaquín Chamorro, editor and publisher of *La Prensa*, and Dr. Fernando Agüero, titular head of the Conservative party. That these men were free to go about their respective businesses and consort with the US ambassador at will was a testament to Somoza's confidence in his control of the country. Both had been in open, armed rebellion against the government within months of my arrival.

Dr. Agüero may not have been a threat of any significance, but Pedro Joaquín Chamorro hated Somoza so vehemently that he would gladly have given his life if that was what it took to overthrow Somoza. I would like to be able to say that both opposed Somoza for reasons of patriotism and principle, but I cannot. Both were also motivated by a strong desire to sit in the presidential palace in Somoza's stead.

The Sandinistas (Frente Sandinista de Liberación Nacional–FSLN) had been organized since 1961 but had been unable to make any headway in overthrowing Somoza and converting Nicaragua into a "Marxist paradise," the party's goal. To me the most intriguing aspect of the FSLN was its leader, Carlos Fonseca Amador, the illegitimate son of Don Fausto Amador, a Somoza sycophant who served as a major manager of Somoza family enterprises, a circumstance that saved Fonseca's life on more than one occasion when the Guardia Nacional had him cornered and then let him "escape" on Somoza's orders.

The Sandinistas had tried (unsuccessfully) one tactic after another to mount an insurgency during the early 1960s. In December of 1966 they infiltrated the northeastern area of Nicaragua from Honduras and set up a base at Pancasán, a mountainous area in Matagalpa.

From Pancasán the Sandinistas tried to extend operations by recruiting campesinos, without success. The guardia caught up with them in August of 1967, at about the time I arrived in Nicaragua, and killed over half of the band, which never numbered more than 50.

Pedro Joaquín Chamorro was incensed that "these innocent and idealistic young men" had been "ruthlessly murdered" by Somoza's "villainous Guardia Nacional." He harped on variations of the theme day after day on the editorial page of his newspaper. The Somoza-owned newspaper *Novedades* did the best it could to defend the guardia's action at Pancasán but was hardly a match for Pedro Joaquín's *La Prensa*, which, for some reason I never understood, took the position that so long as a young man was a student, it didn't matter how badly he misbehaved. At this point, someone in the Somoza camp decided on a change of tactics.

Somoza also owned an afternoon tabloid called *La Prensa Gráfica*, a yellow sheet in every sense of the word. *La Prensa Gráfica* mounted a violent attack against Pedro Joaquín Chamorro, accusing him of being a communist, a traitor to his country, and anything else the paper's editors could think up. These daily attacks were accompanied by broad suggestions that it would be a service to the country if someone "put a bullet (or several) through Chamorro's black heart." Each day brought a more virulent attack than the day before.

At this point, Chamorro telephoned to ask if he could see me—urgently. No one could remember when, if ever, he had called the embassy before, much less set foot inside it.

"You know what they're doing, Señor Embajador?" Chamorro asked, his pupils widening. "They're encouraging a volunteer to come forward and kill me."

"It does look like they're upset, Pedro Joaquín," I answered. "You've been pretty ruthless in your attacks, too," I reminded him. "You must know most of those 'boys,' as you call them, are at least communist sympathizers. What do you want me to do?" I asked.

Chamorro looked me full in the face for a long moment before answering. "Señor Embajador, they're going to shoot me down in the street like a dog unless there is some way to stop them. I have come to ask your help."

"The problem, Pedro Joaquín, is that you're attempting to make martyrs of a bunch of men who are associated with international communism, who have been trained and indoctrinated behind the iron curtain, and who would stand you up against the wall like anyone else. I don't know of any way I can help until you're ready to change your tactics."

"What do you suggest, Señor Embajador?"

"I think the best way you can make amends is to publish the truth about the background, training and experience of each of those 'boys.' Would you be willing to do that if I can pull the information together for you?"

"If you can assure me the information is true and if it is as damaging as you say, I will do it," Chamorro replied.

I had an idea there was a trade-off in the making. I told Chamorro I would see what I could do and get back to him shortly.

Somoza tried to keep his face expressionless while I told him as much about Chamorro's call on me as I thought he needed to know, but he couldn't hide a grim set to his jaw, or a slight twitch of his lip every time Chamorro's name was mentioned.

"I have nothing to do with the editorial policy of *La Prensa Gráfica*," he protested when I had finished. "The people of Nicaragua have had enough of Chamorro's attacks on the Guardia Nacional and his defense of every communist in the country. He is a mere annoyance to me alive—dead he would be a real problem. I want to see what he publishes before I make any promises. But when you think he has done the right thing I suppose I'll be ready to go along."

Back at the embassy, I got our intelligence people together and we went over biographic data in our files on the Sandinistas involved at Pancasán—both those who were killed and those who managed to escape. There was a lot, and it was damning. Summaries were drawn up, sanitized and submitted to Washington with the embassy's request for authorization to publish in *La Prensa*.

Except for a few minor changes, the several agencies involved went along with our request. True to his word, Chamorro published the biographies without comment, except to attribute the information to reliable sources. The campaign against Pedro Joaquín in *La Prensa Gráfica* came to an abrupt halt, as did the criticism of the guardia in Chamorro's *La Prensa*.

Pedro Joaquín Chamorro lived on another 10 years, fighting Somoza at every turn, with every tool available to him. But in the end, he was shot down in the street. There were many who blamed Somoza, but I doubt he had anything to do with it. He understood much too well what the consequences would be.

Chamorro's assassination in 1978 sparked the final phase of the revolt that sent Somoza into exile and started him on the road to Asunción, Paraguay, where he, too, was shot down in the street in 1980. That was the nature of politics in Nicaragua, where change had always come about through the muzzle of a gun.

The Guardia Nacional

During the 10 years I lived in Nicaragua as the US ambassador with residence in urban Managua, and later as a cattle rancher in rural Rivas, the Guardia Nacional was much more than Nicaragua's Army. The guardia was the police department, the customs service, the immigration service, the coast guard, the air force and the navy. The guardia also ran Nicaragua's telephone and telegraph service. Nicaragua had no FBI, no CIA, no NSC. The guardia was responsible for all the functions these agencies perform in the United States. This is not a complete list, but it is enough to provide a good idea of how diverse the guardia's responsibilities were.

The men of the guardia were as diverse as the organization's responsibilities. Some were bad—very bad—but many, I believe most, were ordinary, average men doing ordinary, average jobs in the Nicaraguan public sector. I did not find the military establishment in Nicaragua essentially different from that of several of the other Latin American countries I had become familiar with over the years.

Often, the bad things done by some of the Guardia Nacional came at the most inopportune time and caused Somoza real embarrassment. Major Oscar Morales beat a university student agitator to death with a length of electrical wire and disposed of his body in the crater of an active volcano while I was ambassador. "Moralitos," as he was popularly known, was therefore relieved of his command and somewhat restricted in his movements. Col. Iván Alegrett was guilty of many abuses but at most was reprimanded orally. Eventually he became a general. From where Somoza sat, there was good reason for his leniency. Both men had served him long and well, and he wanted to demonstrate that loyalty paid off.

In Nicaragua, as in most places, it was not news when a guardia officer went about his business the way he was supposed to. It was the guy who abused the public trust or violated society's accepted norms who got the publicity. Both the good and the bad officers were educated and trained to serve in the guardia, and implicit in that service was loyalty to the Jefe Director—who since the beginning (and for more than 30 years) had always been a Somoza. By the time an officer had enough maturity for independent reasoning, he had accumulated enough seniority to create a real vested interest. The system was cleverly devised and kept well honed.

The Somozas developed several techniques for insuring the continued support of the guardia. Graduates of the military academy who evidenced the greatest enthusiasm for the family were given the choicest first assignments. Young officers who showed exceptional ability in addition to enthusiasm were singled out for rapid promotion. Many positions occupied by more senior officers afforded opportunity for substantial earnings, over and above basic salary. Some agency chiefs could take in hundreds of thousands of dollars each year in "special payments" for services that were otherwise difficult, if not impossible to come by.

The Somozas also resorted to a shrewder strategy to help insure the continued loyalty of the guardia. They cultivated the belief that one of the first things the opposition planned to do if it ever came to power was replace most of the guardia officers with their own men. This had been common practice historically, so it wasn't difficult to make the threat sound plausible. It was believed (and perhaps true) that any guardia officer who might become friendly with a person prominent in the opposition could kiss his chances for advancement goodbye.

The result of these tactics was to maintain a wide gulf between officers of the Guardia Nacional and leaders of the political opposition. They did not know each other, and they were afraid to get acquainted. It was here I thought I might be able to provide an opportunity for some mutual understanding.

It was no simple matter to find a propitious occasion to bring senior guardia officers and leaders of the political opposition together on the neutral ground of the US embassy. There had to be some valid rationale, or I could find my efforts thwarted, and myself persona non-grata. The transfer of Col. William P. Francisco provided the opportunity I had been waiting for. Mary and I would host a despedida for Bill and Nancy. It would be natural to invite all the senior Guardia Nacional officers. Bill and Nancy had mingled in social circles that included leaders of the political opposition, and we could legitimately invite them. It was an opportunity that wouldn't come again during my time. I decided to go for it.

There was a major obstacle to get around if my plan was to bear fruit. Bill and Nancy would want the president and Hope to be invited to their despedida.

They had enjoyed a close personal relationship before Somoza became president. I felt sure President Somoza would expect to be invited and could be counted on to attend. The problem arose because of the insistence of the Nicaraguan chief of protocol that the president of Nicaragua attend only functions given in his honor. Thus, I would have to invite my guests to a function in honor of President and Mrs. Somoza, on the occasion of the departure of Col. and Mrs. Francisco. Normally, that would have been fine, but I knew the leaders of the political opposition would not attend a function in honor of Somoza.

By the time Col. Francisco's transfer was announced, Somoza and I had come to know each other pretty well. We did not, by any means, always agree, but we did understand one another. I asked to call on him and as best I could, without declaring my strategy, I told him he would be welcome to attend our despedida for Col. and Mrs. Francisco and I would be delighted to send him an invitation. However, there were others I intended to invite who would not come if the function was offered in his honor. Therefore, I did not propose to do so. I hoped he would understand.

Somoza had many faults and shortcomings, but a dull wit wasn't one of them. I could virtually see the wheels turning. A small smile on Somoza's lips did not match the furrows on his brow. It is quite possible that he saw through my strategy immediately. But if so, he also knew me well enough to understand I would do what I planned whether he liked it or not. After a long moment of silence, he allowed himself a short laugh and said, "I'm fine with whatever you would like to do, Kennedy. Hope and I will be there to say goodbye to Bill and Nancy. They are our good friends, and we will be sorry to see them go." I was relieved to have gotten past a tricky situation so easily.

At about this point, there was one of those unrelated and entirely unanticipated developments that always seem to turn up at the wrong time. The Nicaraguan coast guard out of El Bluff on the Caribbean coast took into custody a US snapper fisherman from some backwater port in Louisiana on charges of fishing in Nicaraguan territorial waters. There were complications. The cutter that apprehended the snapper fisherman had been given to the Nicaraguan government as part of our military assistance program.

Even worse, the distance offshore of the apprehension, a key factor, was confused because of our embassy's mistranslation of a single word, "*avistado*," in the Nicaraguan report of the incident. Our people assumed there had been a typographical error and translated the word as *"avisado"* (advised). *"Avistado"* actually means "seen from afar," as I had learned during my involvement with the Mexican shrimp wars. Because of our mistranslation, the Nicaraguan report we sent on to Washington appeared to be a self-indictment.

The mistake was brought forcefully to my attention when I received a phone call from Regina Eltz, our desk officer in Washington, warning me the fisheries people in the Department of State were looking for an incident they could use to test a recent amendment of the Foreign Assistance Act, which prescribed stiff penalties for any country interfering with US fishermen on the high seas. They intended to shut down all US assistance in Nicaragua—make an example for all the world to see. The call got my attention, I can tell you.

By the time I got out of the business of setting up a despedida for the Franciscos and into finding a solution to the more urgent fisheries problem, events were moving rapidly in Washington and I was falling farther and farther behind in Nicaragua, mainly because of poor communications between Managua, El Bluff and the coast guard cutter at sea. If I was to find out what had happened out there on the snapper banks in the Caribbean, I would have to get a lot closer than my office in the embassy on the Loma de Tiscapa. I asked the military mission to get our C-47 ready to take me to the north coast.

Before setting out, I called in our protocol officer, a senior first secretary of embassy, and gave him my instructions for carrying on with preparations for the Francisco despedida. I went over the business of the Nicaraguan chief of protocol's insistence that any party President Somoza attended had to be given in his honor. I told our protocol officer we were not going to go that route this time and explained why. I did not tell him I had discussed the matter with the president. The fewer people who knew about discussions of that sort, the better. I reminded him time was running short and he should have the invitations engraved and delivered quickly. It would undoubtedly take me several days to get things straightened out in El Bluff. Was everything clear? Yes, he said, everything was clear.

Once up on the north coast, it took a good bit of doing to find out what had happened between the Nicaraguan coast guard and the Louisiana snapper fisherman. The commander of the coast guard cutter had difficulty grasping the import of my questions. All he had done was bring the US fisherman into port where he was warned to stay out of Nicaraguan territorial waters. There had been no fine or other penalty. What was all the excitement about?

In the end, I had to go out where the events had taken place and have the captain reenact it all, step by step. We finally got it clearly established the fisherman had been warned because he was within 12 miles of the Nicaraguan coast. This was acceptable practice. By then, four days had passed.

As I sat at my desk in the embassy the next morning working my way through the accumulated papers, I came to a copy of the invitations that had been distributed for the Francisco despedida. I had to read the text twice to be sure my eyes weren't playing tricks on me. It read, in part, ". . .to a reception in honor of the President of the Republic of Nicaragua and Mrs. Somoza, on the occasion of the transfer of Col. and Mrs. William P. Francisco." It was inconceivable, but there it was—no way to get around it.

Our protocol officer was a prince of a fellow, married to a charming woman of great personal warmth. Both were well liked by their colleagues in the embassy, popular with their counterparts in the other diplomatic missions, and got on well with the Nicaraguans. But this was not the first lapse. True, the world would not come to an end because the ambassador's instructions had not been carried out. It was possible the whole idea behind my maneuvering had been faulty and no purpose would have been served had my plan been executed without a hitch.

But the problem was much deeper than that. My man had either thought he knew better than I what should be done or had been outmaneuvered by the Nicaraguan chief of protocol. In either case, he had failed miserably to discharge his responsibilities. There is no place at the senior level of an US embassy for an inadequacy of that magnitude. It was one of the most painful responsibilities of my Foreign Service career to have the man transferred to a less demanding assignment at a different post. Why in hell couldn't it have been some jerk I would have been delighted to bust?

Now, almost 20 years later, I look back and wonder—would the guardia have fallen to pieces so quickly when Somoza was forced to cut and run if there had been someone else they could turn to? Had the guardia stood firm, could the Sandinistas have taken over Nicaragua so swiftly and completely? Had a dialogue between Somoza's non-communist political opposition and the guardia leadership been established beforehand, would things have turned out differently? We would never know. Long shot that it was, we missed the only chance I had to find out.

A Place to Talk

Discussing local politics with Nicaraguans presented special problems. It was to be presumed that those associated with Somoza would report back to him any noteworthy comment or question that might come up in a discussion with the US ambassador. On the other hand, those same people were cautious about what they said about Somoza or his policies for fear their comments might get back to him. An additional complication was the fear that what was said at the US ambassador's residence might be picked up by a hidden microphone or overheard by a servant in the pay of Somoza's security people. Our majordomo, Carlos, was suspect in the eyes of many Nicaraguans.

I needed a place at the residence that was secure, where people could speak frankly without fear of being overheard or recorded. Across the circular drive that led to the main entrance, and roughly between the residence and the swimming pool, were two stately Indian laurel trees, each shading an area about 75-feet in diameter. It was a simple matter to pave the area beneath their branches with colonial tile and scatter wrought iron tables and chairs about at random. Here you could lounge quite comfortably and see some distance in every direction. When I entertained there, Carlos was to stay out of sight inside the residence but alert for a signal should his services be needed.

This arrangement worked perfectly except for one detail. Carlos didn't like it. He was conveniently too busy with other duties to see my signals that drinks needed refilling or hear my shouts when it came to that. Alfredo Palacios was with me one afternoon when Carlos was exceptionally balky.

"Señor Embajador," Don Alfredo said, "what you need is a bell. I have collected ships' bells for years and have a perfect one for you. I'll send it around tomorrow."

My new bell arrived promptly as promised. It was made of bronze and had come from a ship named *Alma*. We hung it from a low limb by a sturdy chain, and the clang it made when the lanyard was pulled could be heard clear out into the coffee plantations. Carlos was given to understand that when I rang, he was to come. He didn't have much to say about the arrangement, but he nodded assent.

My first chance to use my new toy came several days later when my visitor and I needed another round. I reached for the lanyard of my new bell and looked toward the house to see how quickly Carlos would appear. As if by magic, I saw him walking toward us at a brisk pace, tray in hand, fresh drinks at the ready.

My bell hung from the laurel branch for upward of two years—but I never got a chance to ring it. Carlos always beat me to the draw. Today, it hangs out on my deck. There's no reason to ring it now—there's no one to come—but I give it a good clang every now and then, for old times' sake.

As Somoza and I got to know each other better, we, too, came to understand the need for a convenient and secure place for us to relax and exchange views candidly, without fear of being overheard. The incident that brought this forcefully home came about one day as we sat over coffee after lunching together in the national palace on the Loma de Tiscapa. We had been discussing the political opposition's carping complaints about the lack of freedom to organize and campaign.

"What do these people want?" Somoza asked rhetorically. "They have freedom to attack me in their newspapers. They have freedom to attack me on their radio stations. They have freedom to campaign. They put up political posters on every tree along every highway in the country. We don't interfere with their conventions or their demonstrations. What more can I do?"

Without thinking, and possibly much louder than necessary, I came back with, "You could drop dead," and then in a lowered voice, "Anything short of that won't be enough."

Somoza blanched, gave a furtive look around and all but brought his index finger to his lips. Without further ceremony or another word, he arose and escorted me toward the door where we said our goodbyes and went our separate ways. Subsequently, Somoza was careful to limit our informal exchanges to a time and a place where he and I were the alone.

There were plenty of places where Somoza and I might have met informally. Nicaragua's first family owned many country estancias within an hour's drive of Managua. However, for us both to drive to any one of these, no matter how separate the routes taken, was to announce to the entire country that we were meeting and thus to invite inconvenient questions from the media and often from our own staffs.

We soon discovered, quite by chance, that the most convenient and private place we could get together was at Somoza's residence, located south of town off the road to the Nejapa Country Club. The embassy residence at Las Piedrecitas was east of town off the highway to Casa Colorada. The two places were separated by a couple of miles of open country, and it was a simple matter for me to ride horseback over the back trails from my house to Somoza's for Sunday brunch, which became our custom once or twice every month.

Daughter Terry and I had discovered this back route between our two places quite by accident, and she often came along with me to check out Somoza's horses while he and I sampled Bloody Marys, huevos rancheros, chorizo and hash browns under the *matapalo* trees in his back yard, accompanied by a friendly red and yellow macaw who walked around on the table, leaving his calling cards wherever the urge happened to strike him. It proved to be a convenient arrangement and provided an ideal setting for me to say some of the less pleasant things Somoza needed to know but would never hear from his own people.

Telling any president what he needs to know but doesn't want to hear is risky business. When the job is undertaken by a foreign ambassador, the risk is compounded. When the ambassador is acting without instructions from his own president, things really get dangerous. My case was worse than that—both presidents I represented during my time in Nicaragua looked favorably on Somoza and appreciated having his support in the Organization of American States and the United Nations. Had I offended Somoza, or in any way alienated him, my tenure would have been a limited one, indeed. I took the risk because if Somoza were to be saved, there were unpleasant facts of life that had to be brought to his attention—and I believed it was in the interest of both Nicaragua and the United States that he be saved. I have not since had reason to change my mind.

Somoza did not do a bad job of governing Nicaragua. He may have been a dictator, but he was a benign one. There were supporters and underlings who were abusive of the offices they held in Somoza's name. There are that sort of people in most all governments of Latin America—and that includes the Latin American governments that we call "democratic."

It's all too easy to scoff at any suggestion that Somoza was democratically elected to the Nicaraguan presidency. After all, his people controlled the polling places, his people controlled the means of getting out the vote, the public at large was apathetic, and so on. This was, of course, all quite true. It was also equally true in Webb County, Texas, where I grew up, and undoubtedly in many other areas of the United States. Relatively speaking, elections during my time in Nicaragua were reasonably democratic, when compared to the rest of Latin America that I am personally aware of.

The non-communist political opposition in Nicaragua held a large number of seats in the National Congress—at least as many seats as the political opposition held in the Mexican Congress at that time. Legislation under consideration in the Nicaraguan Congress was debated at length. True, what was finally enacted was what Somoza wanted. As someone with experience in most countries between the Rio Grande River and the Panama Canal, I don't find that at all unusual.

The problem with Somoza was his name. Had his name been García, or Martínez or González, he would have been considered an enlightened chief of state who operated a tight ship, kept his country solvent and allowed about as much personal liberty as prudent, given the relative lack of sophistication of his electorate.

When conditions were right, which wasn't often, I did my best to get this message across to Somoza—as diplomatically as I could. I went so far on one occasion to use a variation of the "if your name weren't Somoza" theme, which went over like a lead balloon. Somoza did not want to believe his family had been in power too long or that he should be succeeded by someone outside both the Somoza family and his control. There were too many people feeding him an entirely different, self-serving line that his country needed him; that no one else could hold things together; that the communists would take over the minute he was no longer in power.

As things worked out, we were both right.

Night Landing

The US ambassador to Nicaragua couldn't get away from his responsibilities to do a little fishing or hunting nearly as easily or as often as the US consul at Tampico had managed a dozen years earlier—but manage he did every now and then. Nor did Nicaragua offer the variety or the abundance of fish and game to be found in northeastern Mexico, but there was more than enough to make a morning on the water or an afternoon in the field interesting, exciting and productive. And there was no pressure on the available resources. I doubt there were more than a dozen shotgunners in all of Nicaragua, and not a whole lot more sport fishermen.

Less than an hour's drive north of Managua on the southwestern shore of Lake Xolotlán, Don Luis Manuel Debayle had a dairy farm at a place called El Tamagás. There he cultivated several hundred acres of grain and fodder to feed his cows, which produced ideal conditions for what often seemed to be limitless numbers of bobwhite quail. If we could manage to drive out to Don Luis Manuel's finca for a late afternoon shoot, we were certain to come home with heavy game bags. It was nice to have quail for special occasions, which seemed to come along often after President Somoza discovered we shot quail, a delicacy he very much enjoyed.

When conditions weren't right for quail, or we decided we would like to have a little dark meat for a change, we could usually count on a good afternoon flight of mourning doves at a place near Mateare, on the road to Don Eduardo Montealegre's finca, also on the western shore of Lake Xolotlán. I never knew where the doves fed, but they flew in from across the water in the late afternoon to roost in the trees along the road. The pass shooting was fast and furious for an hour or so before dark whenever there were doves in the area. Our luck was often good enough for us to enjoy the luxury of boning our doves, so Mary could make stroganoff out of the meat, a treat much favored by Hope Somoza.

One afternoon not long after we arrived, the shooting was so good Mary and I stayed with it until it was too dark to see any more. We ended up cleaning our birds and eating our picnic supper by the meager glow from the back-up lights on the jeep. When we were ready to head home, something had fused in the distribution system, and the jeep wouldn't start. Mary and I and the girls rolled up in a tarpaulin behind the jeep and went to sleep while our driver, Octavio, walked out to the highway to find help. Our people back in Managua were not too happy by the time we got home in the wee hours of the morning.

A half-hour's flight due north of Managua, around San Francisco del Carnicero (now known as San Francisco Libre), thousands of acres were planted in sorghum each season. When the grain ripened, blue rock pigeons and whitewing doves fell upon the heads of grain in such vast numbers that the harvest was all but ruined. I have seen hundreds of acres where just a few scattered heads of grain remained upright—the rest broken down by the sheer weight of several birds feeding on each stalk at the same time. Here, in a single morning, you could bag more birds than you could carry if you desired, and were a reasonably good wing shot. Few of us hunted this area during my time in Managua, but after I had moved on, charter-planeloads of hunters were flown in from the United States during the season—to the delight of local farmers.

There were other spots within easy reach of Managua where we went bird hunting, but these were the best and the ones we visited most often.

Good fishing was to be found in many areas of Nicaragua, mostly in saltwater, although the lower reaches of the San Juan River boasted excellent tarpon fishing and, at times, equally good fishing for snook. Unfortunately, this area was remote, and access was difficult. I managed one trip down the Río San Juan, but only as far as the rapids at El Castillo.

There was good surf fishing at many locations along the Pacific coast between San Juan del Sur and El Ostional. The bays fronting my friend, Frank Kelly's, ranch at La Flor were favorites of ours, although far enough from Managua to require an overnight or two to make the trip worthwhile. For a day's outing, we were pretty much restricted to the Masachapa-Pochomil beaches, which were easily accessible and at times produced good catches.

Masachapa and Pochomil were close enough for us to drive down for an afternoon swim and a picnic supper whenever we had the time and inclination. If we could get away for a weekend, we sometimes took the hammocks and enough camping gear to spend a night or two. At low tide, we could drive south of Pochomil toward La Boquita to an isolated patch of forest right at the edge of the sand, where there was a small freshwater stream and plenty of trees to make deep shade and convenient hammock hangers. Fishing in the surf wasn't the best, but it was good enough for us to have all the fish we wanted to eat, and some left over for a batch of my Acapulco style ceviche—a dish Hope Somoza thought was the best ever.

I look back on those beach camps south of Pochomil with special pleasure. One of the drivers always stayed with us and we usually took Manuel, the houseboy, to cut wood, wash dishes and keep an eye on the children's horses. Our trips there could hardly be called "roughing it."

There was never enough time for hunting and fishing to suit me during our assignment to Managua (or anywhere else, for that matter) and I was always ready to squeeze in a little outing between official responsibilities if I could. Sometimes this took ingenuity—such as during a brief visit by General Sanborn, the Air Force commander at the United States Southern Command in Panama, to inspect some helicopters we had provided the Nicaraguan Air Force.

The general's program called for an early morning arrival, a briefing by Col. Francisco and his military mission staff, a visit to the Nicaraguan Air Force for honors and to inspect the new equipment, lunch with President Somoza, a briefing by me and my staff in the afternoon and, finally, a reception at the embassy residence in the evening. The general would go on to his next stop early the following morning. He sent me word he hoped we could find time for a little bird shooting, too.

I liked General Sanborn and was always glad to have him visit. My immediate problem was how to fit a little wing shooting into a program as tight as the one scheduled. An additional complication was that at this time of the year, there were no birds to be found at the nearby places we normally hunted. We had to drive north on the road to Leon as far as El Trapiche and then work back toward the coast where mourning doves gathered in the late afternoon to roost in low shrubs.

It was obvious we would have to make at least part of the trip by air. There wouldn't be enough time otherwise. We couldn't use a fixed wing plane because there wasn't any landing strip that I knew of where the birds were—but there was a salt flat where a helicopter could land. Clearly, General Sanborn would have to check out the new equipment somewhat more thoroughly than his program called for if he wanted to get in any shooting.

With the help of Col. Francisco and the Nicaraguan pilot assigned by the Guardia Nacional to fly us, we selected a spot on the lawn in front of the residence for the helicopter pad. The area was free of trees, wires and light poles. We then marked on the pilot's map the place where I planned to shoot, and arranged for him to meet us there no later than 5:00 p.m. If we got started home by 5:30 p.m., there would be plenty of time for the pilot to get us home —and more importantly, on the ground—before nightfall. So far, so good.

In order to get as much time as we could for our drive from Managua to the designated hunting spot, I scheduled my briefing for the trip out. One of our Marine guards substituted for my Nicaraguan driver, and I took along a senior political officer for his support and collaboration in the briefing.

Everything went according to plan, although President Somoza wanted to linger over lunch, something he often did when he had a fellow West Pointer to exchange yarns with. We made it to our destination in good time and had taken our stands by 4:00 p.m., but there was a problem. There were no doves— absolutely *none*!

An hour passed, the sun was swinging low toward the western horizon, and we could hear our chopper approaching in the distance before the first dove skimmed the tops of the low brush in our direction.

"This one's yours, General," I called as I spotted a second bird following close behind. Our shots rang out and we both scored. From there on, we had birds in sight continuously. It was exciting shooting. The birds came in low and tended to weave through the topmost branches of the bushes. They became progressively harder to hit, the lower the sun dipped.

In our concentration, we were oblivious to the deepening dusk until our pilot cranked up his engine to signal we could delay no longer. By the time we loaded our gear in the station wagon, sent our Marine driver and political officer on their way home, and boarded the chopper, it was almost pitch dark.

A half-hour later we approached the embassy residence, where security lights glowed in the moonless night. When the pilot switched on his landing light we could dimly make out the cross marking our makeshift pad. I held my breath nervously, but our pilot settled his craft precisely astride the marker without hesitation. As the general and I disembarked, our pilot climbed out too.

"That was a very skillful landing," the clearly-relieved general remarked as he shook our pilot's hand. "How many night landings have you made, Lieutenant?"

Our pilot swelled with pride, drew himself up to full attention and saluted smartly.

"Counting tonight, Mi General," he replied, "one."

Thirty Minutes at Las Mercedes

The year 1968 was not a good one for President Lyndon B. Johnson. The Civil Rights Movement he had long espoused and worked mightily to promote didn't move quickly enough to suit those who were most directly affected, and peaceful demonstrations degenerated into mob violence, looting, sacking and burning. The war in Vietnam dragged on, casualties mounted and resistance to the sacrifice of more young men to a lost cause grew violent.

Speakers who would defend our nation's policy were denied the podium at the country's institutions of higher learning. The time came when Johnson could not appear in public without risking vilification. *Hey, hey, LBJ, how many boys have you killed today?* became a prevalent chant. Johnson could not even count on winning his party's nomination for reelection, much less the election itself. He withdrew from the race.

Johnson's temperament was not suited for cloister. He needed to be out with the people, preferably looking down on a sea of upturned faces, hearing his name cheered, seeing hands reaching out to touch him, pressing the flesh, feeling the adulation. If this was no longer possible for him at home, then he would have to go somewhere else. His choice was Central America. Here he would be safe—and here it would be possible to guarantee "spontaneous" crowds of "friendly admirers."

He therefore invited himself to a mini-summit with the presidents of the five republics stretching along the isthmus between Mexico and Panama. The meeting would be held in El Salvador. When it was over, Johnson would give each of his colleagues a ride back home aboard Air Force One. Thus, he would be able to look down on "spontaneous crowds" of "friendly admirers" in five different countries during the space of a single day.

Word of the meeting hadn't leaked to the press before advance parties began to come through Central America surveying airports, checking security arrangements, coordinating plans with local officials, picking the brains of US representatives assigned in each country and generally making sure they would each have a voice in whatever was decided. No sooner would one bunch finish and move on than the next would fly in. All too often, several groups overlapped. There was no end to it.

As for Nicaragua, it seemed to me like a hell of a lot of bluster over a visit to Managua's Las Mercedes Airport that wouldn't last more than 30 minutes. But I wasn't surprised. It had fallen my lot to coordinate the Washington end of then-Vice President Johnson's visit to the Dominican Republic when Juan Bosch was inaugurated. I had learned in that exercise how carefully you had to plan anything for a man with an ego the size of LBJ's.

We rebuilt the shower stall in his quarters in Santo Domingo so the water would spray out from precisely the height the vice president demanded. We made sure the supply of Cutty Sark was always adequate. The practical, Jeep-type ambulances Ambassador John B. Martin ordered for presentation at the inauguration had to be replaced by bright red, heavily chromed monstrosities because LBJ thought the 4x4s much too plain for him to present. No one wanted to risk Johnson's ire over any overlooked detail.

One of the contingents that came through Managua was headed by a rather seedy fellow who identified himself as "Retired Air Force," representing some group or another. The man took me aside to tell me it had "been decided" that each US ambassador along the way would give President Johnson a pair of cufflinks made out of antique gold coins from his country of assignment.

"Ya know," he said, "ol' LBJ sure does like to get somethin' for nothin'. I know you boys don't make a whole lotta money, but you can charge these 'momentos' to confidential funds—no questions asked. Jus' be sure you're ready when he gets here."

I didn't like the idea from the beginning. I liked it less when I discovered there had never been any small Nicaraguan gold coins minted. But it was one of those situations where there is no acceptable excuse for failing to come through. Something had to be worked out.

Several days of frantic query turned up the intelligence that one of Managua's leading radio broadcasters had once presented a pair of gold coin cufflinks to President Somoza. When I got in touch with the man, he told me that years past, someone had designed a small denomination gold coin and proposed that it be minted as Nicaraguan legal tender. The proposal didn't prosper, but a local jeweler still had the molds. Somoza's gold coin cufflinks had been made from them. I got the name of the jeweler and took it from there.

When the time came, I made my presentation without blinking an eye. I didn't think it would be helpful to mention there was one other pair of cuff links made from antique Nicaraguan gold coins—or that they were counterfeit. I don't know what the other boys did up and down the line, but I paid for my gift out of my own pocket. I figured that being the case, I was under no obligation to go into the details of where I got what, or how.

One good thing did come from all the scurrying about in preparation for the El Salvador mini-summit—at least from where I sat. When I took over in Nicaragua, my first order of business was to get my staff busy on the projects Johnson had told me he was interested in. Our local technicians from the Agency for International Development had long since worked up a nice rural electrification project, but there had been no implementation because we couldn't get Washington to allocate funds. When Johnson decided he wanted to sign a major development project with each of his Central American colleagues while in El Salvador, we proposed rural electrification. Once Johnson had signed the agreement, funding took care of itself.

I had also persuaded Somoza to offer a Nicaraguan group for service in Vietnam, the other project Johnson favored. We never got any response to that one. Someone up the line in Washington decided it wouldn't be good policy to have Nicaraguan National Guardsmen fighting communists in Vietnam. Not even the president of the United States gets everything he wants.

Finally, the time came for the great Central American mini-summit. At the last minute, someone decided it might be handy to have the US ambassadors from the other Central American Republics on hand and we were all ordered to San Salvador. By then there were no hotel accommodations to be had so we were farmed out to the homes of local embassy officers who were unfortunate enough to have spare bedrooms. We spent our time during the conference standing around on the fringes trying not to look as useless as we actually were.

When the conference was over and the time came for LBJ to fly each president to his respective capital, an occasion did arise for us to play a part. Johnson's people had planned for all the presidents to board Air Force One at San Salvador and fly directly to San José, the southernmost Central American capital, where Costa Rican President José Joaquín Trejos would be dropped off—and Johnson would greet the first crowd of spontaneous, cheering admirers. Air Force One would next fly north to Managua where Somoza would be dropped off—and Johnson would greet the second contingent of spontaneous, cheering admirers, and so on until the president of Guatemala, the last Central American country to the north, had been dropped off and Johnson had greeted—by now you know the rest.

This seemed like a good plan except for one detail—Costa Rican President José Joaquín Trejos would have none of it. Trejos said he would make his own arrangements for getting back home. He refused to give any reason why, and no amount of persuasion would sway him. It was at this point that we stand-by ambassadors were brought into the picture. Clare Boonstra, our ambassador to Costa Rica, and I knew what the problem was as soon as we heard there was one. Trejos had no intention of sharing the same podium with Somoza in Costa Rica. He had been unable to avoid doing so in San Salvador, but in Costa Rica, *never*. It was quickly decided the simplest solution would be to drop Somoza off first. We could hardly ask him to stay inside Air Force One while it was in San José.

There were three questions to be answered before this alternative could be accepted. Could Trejos then be persuaded to change his mind? Could Somoza's ego be massaged when he was informed of the change in plans? Would the weather in Managua in July, the height of the rainy season, permit such an early arrival? Boonstra said he could take care of Trejos if the problem of Somoza could be eliminated. I gave assurances I could handle Somoza, who probably didn't relish showing his face in Costa Rica, where his family had been hated for generations. And as for the weather, I was confident there wasn't anything to worry about and gave assurances it never rained in Managua in the early morning. The deal was struck.

The delegation of US ambassadors departed San Salvador for home base the afternoon before Johnson planned to deliver the chiefs of state to their respective capitals. I wasn't the least bit worried about everything going well at Managua. So many people had toiled so hard for so long that nothing could possibly go wrong. And besides, nothing was expected of Mary or me except to be there—this would be a Johnson-Somoza show.

Everyone involved (and there were many) stood ready on the Las Mercedes tarmac well in advance of the time Air Force One was scheduled to touch down the next morning. I was a little uneasy. The sun shone brightly at the airport, but off in the distance I could see a very large and very black cloud boiling higher and higher. I felt some relief when Air Force One appeared on the horizon a full 15 minutes early. That portion of the ceremonies programmed for outdoors would be over and we would be inside before there could possibly be any rain. And besides, everyone knew it never rained in Managua before 11:00 a.m.

Air Force One circled in the distance, well away from the landing approach. The black cloud became larger and larger as it advanced toward Las Mercedes. By the time Air Force One touched down, my black cloud had moved directly over Las Mercedes, and as the door opened for the president to step out and greet the crowd, so did the heavens. I have rarely seen such a cloudburst.

There was nothing to do but go ahead with the introductions, the speeches and related formalities, cloudburst and all. The day's schedule was much too tight to spare a minute because of the rain. By the time we moved into the VIP reception room, everyone was wet, and some were thoroughly drenched. Mary and I fell in this latter category. And just for the record, LBJ was fully capable of holding me personally responsible for the rain coming at such an inopportune time.

There were more introductions once we were inside the terminal, Johnson was escorted to a small anteroom so I could present his cufflinks and there was a press conference, Somoza interpreting. Then, without warning, Johnson arose and headed back out toward Air Force One, the rest of the entourage crowding along behind. When I could find a place to squeeze in, I followed the others.

The show was over, and I had begun to forget about the whole nonsensical business when the pouch from Washington brought a large envelope prominently marked with the seal of the president of the United States of America. Inside was a photo album with pictures of the president taken during his mini-summit. The cover bore the inscription, "To Ambassador Kennedy M. Crockett, A Recuerdo of a Happy Visit," and was signed "LBJ."

The End of an Era

President Johnson wasn't the only one who had a bad year in 1968. It was even worse for Gordon Mein, LBJ's ambassador to Guatemala, who was killed by terrorists a block from the US chancery. It was the first incident of its kind in Latin America, and the beginning of open season on US ambassadors worldwide. That year marked the end of an era for those of us who served the United States government overseas. In reality, the end of an era for Americans everywhere.

It was some time before that deadly ambush that both United States and Nicaraguan intelligence agencies began to pick up rumors that plans were afoot to kidnap the local US ambassador and use him (read: *me*) to bargain for the release of leftists imprisoned in Nicaragua for a variety of crimes ranging from bank robbery to sabotage of public utilities to murder. I was advised to take precautions and did, after a fashion. I wasn't terribly concerned because I couldn't believe there was any real danger—there never had been before.

Not long afterward, local intelligence services passed on to our people a report they had picked up that preparations were being made to intercept me on the way to San Juan del Sur, where we were planning a family outing for a long weekend. I was concerned that anyone outside our immediate family knew about our plans and decided to get President Somoza's opinion of how seriously the report should be taken.

Somoza reminded me he had been taking special precautions for many years and suggested I do likewise. He offered the loan of a helicopter to fly us down to the beach house we used in San Juan. I thanked him for the offer but explained Mary would stay home before she would get into a helicopter. Somoza laughed and suggested the girls and I could fly while Mary drove. He would send his bulletproof Cadillac around to pick her up, to be on the safe side, although he doubted she would be in any danger. I protested but Somoza insisted.

Early on the morning of our outing, I sent our driver, Octavio Flores, on his way to San Juan in the Wagoneer loaded with our food, fishing gear and beach equipment. Mary left next in Somoza's big black limousine. Then the girls and I took off from our front lawn in the helicopter, enthralled by the beauty of the landscape below as we traversed the country. We briefly landed on a remote, deserted white sand beach near the Costa Rican border before landing on the beach at San Juan well ahead of everyone else. In due course the others arrived without incident, we unloaded, put on our bathing suits and settled in for the weekend.

Once in San Juan del Sur, we considered ourselves safe. There was one paved road that led into town, and it was reasonably well patrolled. In addition, the local military garrison (only a few doors up the street from our quarters in the fully-staffed Customs guest house) had been alerted to exercise special vigilance. We relaxed and enjoyed ourselves—until the afternoon son Jack joined us and we decided to drive to the beach at La Flor on Frank Kelly's ranch.

La Flor was one of our favorite places and we went as often as we could. There we enjoyed complete privacy on a crescent moon beach over a mile long, and conditions for swimming and fishing were excellent. As usually happened when we spent an afternoon at La Flor, the sun had set, and our campfire reduced to embers before we were ready to head back into town.

We had forgotten any concern about security until we came to a gate that had been wired shut, a standard ploy in Nicaragua when mischief was in the making. Was this the real thing or some country bumpkin's idea of a fun trick to play on the gringos? We had no way of knowing. I groped for wire cutters in the Wagoneer's toolbox, but my hand came up empty—there were no wire cutters.

I was driving that day, as Jack rode shotgun, and Terry sat between us. Mary and Linda were in the back seat. At each gate, it was Jack's job to jump out, unhook and drag open the rickety barbed-wire gate, hold it until I drove through, then close it and get back in the jeep. This was an entirely different situation.

There was no point in changing our routine, but I quickly turned off the headlights and reached into the glove compartment for the .45 automatic, which I gripped tightly in both hands as I aimed out the window. I heard Mary draw in a sharp breath as I fired a few warning shots into the air—this was more than any of us had bargained for and there was no question we were damn scared.

Terry held the door slightly ajar as Jack moved cautiously through the dark toward the gate, not at all sure how much trouble we were in. We were, after all, miles from help, and there was no question the gate had been wired shut after we came through on our way in.

It felt like a very long time before the distinct sound of the dragging gate reached my ears. As my foot stomped on the gas pedal, Terry flung the door open for Jack and he jumped back in. We sped over the cattle guard and the Wagoneer bounced and careened as I maneuvered in the dark, finally realizing we were in as much danger of hitting a tree as we were of being ambushed. It was a long while before I noticed Terry staring down in shock at Jack's bleeding hands.

Our elapsed time into town was the best ever, but none of us slept well that night—least of all Jack.

There were other, inconclusive incidents. In retrospect, I wonder if we were being subjected to a series of probes designed to test the extent of our security precautions. What bothered me most at the time was clear evidence that the bad guys often knew in advance where we would be going and when. It had to be someone with access to our personal entourage who was passing this intelligence to the other side. I never did learn who.

Any doubts we may have had about the seriousness of their intentions were dispelled by Ambassador Mein's assassination. The shock of realization was enormous. When we came to Nicaragua hardly more than a year earlier, there were no restrictions on where we went, when we went, or what we did when we got there. The US ambassador, his family and entourage were inviolable.

Shortly after our arrival, President Somoza arrived at a black-tie inauguration at Las Mercedes Airport unable to sit down because of his bulletproof underwear. His people had learned there would be an attempt on his life that evening. Somoza quickly removed himself to an anteroom where he remained surrounded by his best bodyguards the rest of the evening. The chief of protocol escorted Somoza's wife, Hope, to our table and whispered in my ear that the president would appreciate it if she could sit with Mary and me, where she would be safe from harm. Hope and I had opened the dancing without any thought of potential danger.

Now everything had changed. There had always been uniformed guards posted at the residence security gate and stationed at strategic positions around the perimeter of the property. Mostly, we saw these people when we drove in or out. Now, there was always an unmarked Land Rover or Toyota jeep within view, carrying four or five men in civilian dress who carried oversized briefcases suitable for machine guns.

Wherever we went, at least one jeepload of security people went along, and often two. We had no privacy except within the four walls of our personal quarters. We soon gave up going out in the country, our favorite diversion. There was no way we could be alone. Mary and the girls couldn't step behind a convenient bush to answer nature's call without one of our protectors following along.

Being in the Foreign Service had ceased to be fun. I consoled myself with the knowledge that in fewer than eighteen months I would be able to give them back my job—and the trappings that went with it. I had outlived my time.

The Embassy at San Juan del Sur

In the fall of 1968, Richard Nixon was elected to be the next president of the United States. Simultaneously, we in the State Department who had been appointed by Lyndon Johnson became lame ducks—regardless of whether we happened to come from the ranks of the career Foreign Service or were plain old political hacks. To make sure there was no misunderstanding, each of us received polite instructions from Washington on how to submit our resignations.

Some ambassadors from the career ranks are carried over from one administration to the next, even when this involves a change of political parties in the White House. This happens when there are special circumstances to be considered. Generally, however, most presidential appointees from the ranks of the career service can expect at least a change of posts, if not a change of status. My colleagues in Washington seemed satisfied there would be no exceptions in my case and were quick to inquire if I would prefer to be assigned as a senior inspector or a scholar in residence at some university when I was replaced.

I knew the rules of the game and was prepared to play by them, although I didn't look forward to a change of station during my last year in the Foreign Service. I would celebrate my fiftieth birthday at about the same time Nixon completed his first year in office, and I fully expected to retire as soon after that. I had no interest in being either a senior inspector or a scholar in residence. However, I had to give some sort of an answer and decided that if I had to move, it might as well be to a job I was interested in having. I asked to be considered for assignment as consul general at Monterrey. The people in the Department of State wasted no time telling me my request had been approved and formal action to affect my transfer would be taken as soon as my replacement was named.

I don't suppose it's necessary to point out that being a lame duck isn't a pleasant position to be in. But you eventually move on to other pursuits and time dims memories of slights, both real and imagined. I gritted my teeth and went ahead as if nothing had happened, although I earnestly hoped the interval wouldn't last too long.

My team in Nicaragua was mostly considerate and continued to treat me the same as always. But relations with my colleagues in Washington was an entirely different matter. Whether it was true or not, I felt that all too many of them missed no opportunity to ignore my needs—or worse, to ignore me. Most of them were candidates for ambassadorial appointments and didn't intend to be the least bit helpful to an incumbent they might get an opportunity to replace. I didn't like it, but I did my best to understand.

The first few weeks after I was told I'd have to move over for someone else passed reasonably quickly. However, the first few weeks stretched into the first few months, and I still heard nothing definite about when I would be relieved. The rumor that got down as far as Managua was that the man the White House had selected to replace me didn't want the job. I can't deny that the longer I waited, the more fidgety I got and the less charitable I felt about the whole damned business. The day was nearing when I would inevitably say to myself, "To hell with it. I've sat around long enough. It's time to do something."

In the traditional sense, the place where the ambassador lives is "The embassy." Technically speaking, our offices in Managua occupied "The Chancery" although the building they were located in was popularly known as "The embassy." That being the case, I saw no reason why I couldn't take up residence in a beach house at San Juan del Sur and declare that to be the US embassy in Nicaragua. The more I thought about it, the more I liked the idea. What did I have to lose? We took down the great seal over our front door, the flag that flew out front, and selected a modest staff of four to accompany us. We were ready to move.

The place we selected for the embassy at San Juan del Sur was a spacious beach house called La Pepesca, which belonged to a prominent family from Granada, associated with the conservative party, Somoza's political opposition. La Pepesca offered numerous advantages. It was located across the estuary from San Juan del Sur proper and near the end of the single lane road that stopped at a steep mountain at the northern extremity of San Juan del Sur Bay. It was a simple matter for the local authorities to keep unwanted visitors out. The house was large and boasted a phone. There were lots of open porches and the yard was well shaded by native trees. Only sand separated the front yard from the water's edge. Best of all, the owners were willing to lease the place for a sum I could easily afford. I don't think we could have done better in all of Nicaragua.

The telephone at La Pepesca (an old model that had to be hand cranked) was an important consideration. I needed some way to keep in touch other than courier given that we were well over an hour's drive from Managua. I had taken for granted the phone was in working order when I leased the place. That proved to be overly optimistic. We had hardly moved in before one of the girls discovered the instrument was dead.

Nicaragua's communication facilities (mail, telephone and telegraph) were all controlled by the Guardia Nacional. I sent Octavio down to the military garrison to report our problem. He returned shortly and told me he had made the report but didn't think we should expect much to be done about it. The sergeant in charge of telephone service had a good laugh before responding that most telephones in San Juan del Sur were out of order most of the time. As for our problem, the strand of fencing wire connecting our instrument to the San Juan del Sur switchboard was stretched from one tree to another most of the way, and there had been no recent effort to trim branches rubbing against it. As far as the sergeant was concerned, that was a problem for the subscriber.

I decided to let things ride. I needed to mount the great seal over our front door and see about cutting a tree out in the jungle to fly our flag. Sooner or later President Somoza would call, and when he was unable to get through, we could expect our problem to be solved immediately. I did send a warning back to the sergeant, but he wasn't impressed. He was much too important a man in San Juan del Sur to take any guff from anybody.

Early the next morning I took José Sandoval, our #2 driver, and headed south on the dirt road leading to the Costa Rican border to look for a flagpole. We quickly found what we wanted in a thick stand of jungle where each tree tried to reach higher than the next. When our selection had been cut and lashed to the rack on top of the Wagoneer, it protruded several feet beyond the car, fore and aft—a truly magnificent pole for the flag at the embassy at San Juan del Sur.

We were back in town by the time the sun crested the low range of mountains that passed for the continental divide to the east. Long before we came in sight of La Pepesca, I knew President Somoza had tried to call. There were soldiers in every tree along the road trimming every branch that might rub against our telephone line. For the rest of our stay in San Juan del Sur, we never drove in or out of town without seeing at least one soldier along the way armed with a machete looking for branches to trim. And at least twice each day, we had a call from the sergeant in charge of telephones to inquire whether there were any problems he needed to be aware of. He may have learned the hard way, but he learned.

During our stay at La Pepesca, we managed to get all the children and grandchildren from near and far to visit and share the pleasures of life at the beachfront embassy. There were horses to ride along the beach and a fishing boat for expeditions offshore. For the less energetic there were hammocks under the shade trees in the yard. There was plenty of good food and even more good cheer. It was a good life.

Looking Out for Número Uno

The initial months of the Nixon administration passed without any change in my personal status. The Rockefeller group came through Central America preparing a study commissioned by the president, and one of the governor's senior aides told me in confidence that Rockefeller would recommend that Nixon confirm me as ambassador to Nicaragua. I thanked the man but didn't hold my breath. It was a good thing, too—if anything ever came of it, no one bothered to tell me. I eventually decided it was time to take an initiative on my own.

Any Foreign Service officer who has worked in Washington for two tours should have friends on both sides of the political aisle. I took an inventory of my own assets and was pleased to find there were people in the Republican hierarchy that I could turn to. What I wanted did not seem unreasonable or out of line, so I did something I had never done before—I turned to outsiders to ask for help in staying on at Managua until my fiftieth birthday. I got what I wanted.

I may have known I would be staying on for the time being, but few others did. I felt obliged to inform President Somoza, as we still needed his cooperation and he and I had a good working relationship. One of the things I wanted to wrap up before leaving was negotiating the repeal of an old treaty we had imposed on the Nicaraguans during the days of gunboat diplomacy, which granted the United States exclusive rights in perpetuity to construct a canal across Nicaragua. For years the Nicaraguans, including Somoza, had beat us over the head about this prime example of "Yankee imperialism," when it suited their purposes.

I had undertaken the negotiation after our Canal Study Commission decided it would not be feasible to build a canal across Nicaragua under any circumstances. Our Nicaraguan desk officer in the State Department, Regina Eltz, had things lined up in Washington and we were ready to move forward. I anticipated Somoza would try to take any advantage he could, but I underestimated him. He took the position that the United States owed Nicaragua compensation for having failed to make use of this exclusive right for so many years—and suggested we should ante up before he agreed to the repeal!

Somoza caught me by surprise, and I wasn't in too good a mood anyhow. I snapped back that he could forget the whole deal as long as I was around. I would never agree to one penny of what he chose to call compensation. Somoza smiled and said I should understand he was trying to protect the interests of his people. I smiled right back and told him that was fine and dandy from where he sat, but from where I sat, I wanted no part of it. There things stood when I eventually left Nicaragua—yet another consequence of my lame duck status.

The final straw was yet to come. Before my arrival in Nicaragua, much effort had been devoted to raising funds for the construction of a national theater for the performing arts. The diplomatic corps had organized many fund raisers, as had every civic organization in the country. Mary and I had done our part, with the support of embassy staff. Hope Somoza was the main organizer for the undertaking, but it was in no way a partisan affair. She got help from many Nicaraguans who were opposed to Somoza politically but as eager as the rest of us to see the project to a successful conclusion. If there was such a thing as a bi-partisan project in Nicaragua, it was the Rubén Darío Theater.

Construction was completed in the second half of 1969. For Nicaragua, it was a substantial undertaking. The Rubén Darío Theater cost each Nicaraguan more than it cost each US taxpayer to build the Kennedy Center for the Performing Arts in Washington. It was understandable that those involved were proud of what had been accomplished and eager for the inaugural performances in their new theater to be the best available. Mexico was invited to put on the first show. The United States was asked to put on the second, to follow a week later.

Mexico offered the Ballet Folklórico Nacional—one of the greatest stage performances in the world. But now the US needed to identify something suitable to follow an act like the Ballet Folklórico.

It took considerable prodding to get a response to our request for help. When it came, I couldn't believe the suggestion was serious. Our Cultural Affairs people in the State Department proposed sending someone to recite selections of Rubén Darío's poetry—after an act like the Ballet Folklórico—in a country where every man in his heart of hearts believes himself to be the absolute best there is when it comes to reciting Rubén Darío.

I suppose I wasn't as delicate as I might have been in rejecting the suggestion, but I don't think I did anything to deserve the deafening silence that greeted our later pleas for Cultural Affairs to hurry up and find something appropriate. When time grew alarmingly short and we still had nothing to offer, I resorted to urgent, personal appeals. That didn't work, either.

When I was a boy, I learned a hard lesson. Pleading, alone, doesn't get the job done. You must be willing to fight. I had hoped to avoid fighting, but I didn't intend to let a situation continue where the personal representative of the president of the United States could be ignored with impunity. At least not when the man was asking on behalf of the president in Nicaragua. I got a plane reservation for Washington to take up my problem in person. I intended to get something acceptable nailed down for the Rubén Darío Theater—and I intended to make clear I would not tolerate being ignored.

The first of my problems was solved before I could get away. The embassy's military people discovered the United States Army Field Band and Chorus were available to fill our commitment at the Rubén Darío Theater if I was interested. I had attended several of their performances and jumped at the opportunity. I don't know which was greater, my satisfaction at having chanced upon such an ideal solution to our problem or my satisfaction at having done so without any help from Cultural Affairs.

Now I had another dilemma—I could hardly go to Washington to fight over a problem that was already solved. But I couldn't afford to let anyone believe I could be ignored. It didn't take long to figure out what to do. I drafted and sent the following telegram, unclassified, to be sure it got wide circulation:

> Action: Department of State
> Attention: Mr. Smith, Cultural Affairs
> Subject: Cultural Presentation for Opening of Rubén Darío National Theater
> I want to give you the satisfaction of knowing that your discourtesy in failing to acknowledge or respond to the personal and urgent appeals which I addressed to you on November 7 and November 11 has not gone unnoticed, and to tell you that your inaction is in keeping with the tradition of unresponsiveness and ineffectuality which your organization has established over the years in reacting to the needs of those of us who serve in this area of the world. At least we can be thankful that the responsibilities with which your Bureau is charged in servicing us are significantly less than vital to the attainment of our more important foreign policy objectives. Otherwise we would be in a hell of a fix.
>
> [signed] CROCKETT

It is decidedly poor form in the State Department to rock the boat, make waves, or put criticism down in writing. My telegram violated all three of these maxims—and probably several others as well, but it did serve my purpose. None of my requests from there on in were ignored.

A Time for Reflection

It had been a simple matter, 15 years before my fiftieth birthday, to decide when I would retire from the Foreign Service. It was an entirely different matter when the time came to implement the decision. I couldn't afford to be wrong on this one. There was too much at stake. I needed peace and quiet and time alone to think things through. I saddled Max and slipped out the back gate of the embassy grounds for a long ride through the coffee plantations.

A major consideration had to be what I might do next if I decided not to retire. While there was no assurance I could get another ambassadorial post, nowhere was it written that I couldn't if I was prepared to go to the right peo-ple. Being ambassador to Nicaragua had been at least an interesting experience, and there had been some challenge to getting acquainted with Somoza. He taught me a lesson early on when I failed to check with him before telling the State Department that Nicaragua would support the candidacy of Galo Plaza for Secretary General of the OAS. I got my turn when he criticized the United States while I sat on the platform behind his podium. As I walked off, his aide followed to tell me the president wouldn't like it. I told him to tell the president I didn't like what he had to say about the United States, and I stayed where I was until the ceremony was over. Somoza got the message—it didn't happen again.

There had also been occasions for good laughs. One Sunday morning So-moza called to say he needed to talk with me urgently. He was leaving for his place on the beach at Montelimar and was in a hurry. Could I meet him at an open-air restaurant on the highway by the embassy? That was fine with me—Max and I just happened to be getting ready for a ride.

People had started to stir at the drive-in. Chairs were turned upside down on tables and someone was mopping the floor. I tied Max's reins to a tree over-hanging the parking lot and ducked under the thatched roof. I was quickly greeted with, "No hay servicio todavía—regrese en un par de horas." ("We're not open yet—come back in a couple of hours.")

I didn't see any point in identifying myself and risking the embarrassment of being told the same thing again. Instead, I explained that the President of the Republic would be stopping by shortly, and it might be a good idea to get a table and a cup of coffee ready for him. The waiters exchanged bleary-eyed glances and continued with their chores. I decided to go wait with Max to see what happened next.

Within a few minutes a jeepload of Somoza's plainclothes guards pulled into the parking lot, piled out and took stations. I could see the beginning of a stir inside the drive-in. A Mercedes-Benz with more beef pulled in on the heels of the Jeep. There was a marked increase in the pace of activity inside. I could hear tables being dragged across the floor and the sounds of related scurrying. Somoza's Cadillac came next. His military aide ducked under the thatched roof as Somoza stepped out and waited for me to join him. Together we walked in-side.

Two waiters in fresh jackets stood beside a table covered with a spotless cloth. Chairs were pulled back and coffee cups set at each place. I recognized the fellow who had a few minutes before told me to come back in a couple of hours. He did his best to smile and look nonchalant. I winked at him and took my seat. "Excelencia," the man said as he bowed in Somoza's direction, "we have been expecting you. May I serve Your Excellency a cup of coffee?" Wonderful what a man can do when he's motivated.

Then there was the family outing we had planned for months but hadn't been able to bring off before we found ourselves saddled with our own guards. When we got the chance, we decided to go ahead with our plans, guards and all. Our destination was an isolated beach we had spotted from the air. It was beautiful, shaped like a cloverleaf, with a narrow opening to the sea and three crescent-shaped beaches with lots of white sand against a backdrop of dense jungle.

When we reached the spot where we hoped to find a way in, on a narrow dirt road between San Juan del Sur and the Costa Rican border, we told our guards they could relax until we came back out but not to expect us for several hours. They would hear nothing of it. Their duty was to go wherever we went. Clad in their business suits and carrying their oversized briefcases, they piled out to follow along. There was nothing to do but shrug and go ahead.

A half-hour of steep climbing over a narrow jungle trail brought us to a ridge high above our cloverleaf bay. Here and there on the trail behind us we could spot one or another of our security contingent, sweating up the grade. We had all reached the beach and found bushes where we could change into our bathing suits before the last guard made it down. It was then that the excitement began.

Our guards suddenly realized we had all vanished into the jungle. There was an anxious order to "Fan out and find them," along with the admonition, "Be ready for any eventuality." Briefcases snapped open and machine guns were armed as the men prepared to search. I hate to think what might have happened if I hadn't managed to get my pants zipped up and stop the show before one of the girls was flushed out of hiding. Everybody joined in a nervous laugh.

Our security people found a shady spot where they could rest for the return trip while we went down to the water. When we had finished our swim, and were about to hike back out, someone pointed to a message in Spanish scratched on a large rock.

It read: "Sandino estuvo aquí." (Sandino was here.) Maybe it was meant to be funny. . . maybe it really *was* funny and there was something wrong with me. None of us knew then that the Sandinistas would be all over Nicaragua 10 years down the road—and there was nothing funny about that.

My train of thought was broken when Max and I came to the big guanacaste tree high up the mountainside where we always stopped to rest the horses. As I swung down I held onto the saddle horn to be ready in case my knees buckled. That was something else that bothered me about the life I led—not enough exercise to keep in shape. I loosened the saddle girth and slipped Max's bridle. There was always green grass here, even during the driest months of the year. Max chomped enthusiastically while I settled into my favorite spot among the gnarled guanacaste roots. The sun was warm, the air was calm, there was peace. I closed my eyes for a minute.

Max's whinny startled me to attention. I immediately recognized the rider approaching down the road. There was but one Col. Iván Alegrett in Nicaragua—gracias a Dios, as the campesinos would say. Alegrett was smart, bold and ruthless. He was also powerful. As a younger man, he had been an aide (some said procurer) on Somoza's staff. When Pedro Joaquín Chamorro and Dr. Fernando Agüero had tried to overthrow Somoza in 1967 and the generals held back to see which way things would go, it was Alegrett who got out the tanks and put down the rebellion. Somoza was understandably grateful and rewarded him with the job of director of immigration, an assignment that offered many opportunities for large-scale graft.

Alegrett and I were civil to one another, but there was no love lost between us. I once had his Cuban business partner captured and flown to Miami to face drug running charges. Alegrett had barely escaped the same fate.

Col. Alegrett had weaknesses for many things. He had a yacht and an airplane and beach buggies and whatever else struck his fancy. But his first love was horses. This morning he was mounted on a pure white Andaluz stallion—a gorgeous animal—one of a kind in Nicaragua. After greetings had been exchanged, I complimented the colonel on his taste in horses, and for lack of anything better to say, mused that, "A horse with so many fine qualities must be expensive, Colonel."

Alegrett patted his stallion on the neck with genuine appreciation before giving me a wide grin and responding, "Not really, Señor Embajador, only a Chinaman and a half."

It took me a couple of seconds to get in step. Alegrett was saying the horse had cost one and a half times the bribe he would collect from a native of China for letting him into Nicaragua. Well, everyone knew Alegrett had no shame. I was glad when he and his horse moved on.

Eventually, it came time for Max and me to head back home—I reluctantly, Max enthusiastically. We would both eat when we got there, Max in the privacy of his stall, I in the discomfort of black tie.

There was no denying it had been interesting and rewarding to be an ambassador, but once was enough. I liked the substantive part of the job fine. It was the ceremonial end I couldn't take. It was a drag, and it took far too much time that could have been invested in more enjoyable pursuits. I resented every wasted minute. And now, security considerations ruled out many of the things we enjoyed most in life. No, I didn't want another ambassadorial assignment, assuming I could swing one.

What about another Washington assignment? It would be easy enough to get back to the Department of State—not a choice assignment, but that wasn't too important. I knew from experience there were never enough people available to fill the demanding jobs. My turn would come again, as it always had before. But why go back to Washington? Why seek out another tough job? Where would that take me? The answer to that question was an easy one: Nowhere! If I never got back to Washington that would be entirely soon enough.

And there was something else. During the early years of my career, I had taken great pride in being an officer of the United States Foreign Service. My profession was an honorable one, people treated me with respect, and I walked with my head held high wherever I went. Along the way, this had changed—almost imperceptibly.

Being an employee of the United States government, even one with the rank of ambassador, was no longer the honorable profession it had once been. Too many government employees had done too many unethical, dishonest things. Integrity was no longer taken for granted. I could still hold my head high, but there were far too many who could not—people who in failing themselves had also failed me.

I would have gone back to being a consul general rather than take an assignment as an inspector or a scholar in residence if it had come to that, but it hadn't. That would have been a hard choice to make—going back instead of forward. Being a consul general is no place for a man who has already made FSO-1 and been an ambassador. In life you must not look back.

If there were other alternatives, something else I might do, I couldn't think what it might be. The conclusion was inescapable—I had done what I was interested in doing as far as the Foreign Service was concerned. The time had come for me to move on to something else.

Max raised his head and quickened his pace. Home was around the bend. This was the best part of the ride for him—he always surged at the prospect of being unsaddled and let loose to graze. I slackened the reins gently and Max stretched out. As he raced up the winding drive to the front door I felt elation and relief. This chapter of my life was winding down, and I found myself looking forward to new adventures ahead.

I threw a leg over the horn and slid down. Not bad for a man who would turn 50 tomorrow.

**Kennedy and Mary Crockett during post-retirement RV trip
in the Southwestern United States, 1970.**

Afterword

By Judith Crockett Faerron

El Alamo, San Antonio

Following Kennedy's retirement, the Crocketts spent a summer traveling throughout the Southwestern US looking for the perfect place to settle down—only to find their love for Nicaragua calling them home.

They returned to Managua and rented a house in Colonia Wheelock on the southbound Pan American highway, a few miles from the embassy residence at Las Piedrecitas.

Kennedy decided to follow his lifelong dream of cattle ranching and purchased 488 overgrown hectares (1,200 acres) near Rivas in southern Nicaragua. Located in an area known as San Antonio, the ranch was called El Alamo—the same as the fort where Kennedy's distant ancestor Davy Crockett had died fighting for Texas's independence from Mexico in 1836.

In the early days of his ranching venture, Kennedy lived in a tent, attracting the attention of one of Managua's newspapers which published a lengthy article on the former ambassador's new accommodations.

In a November 1971 letter to family abroad, he wrote:

> The ranch has come to take up most of my time. We are now in the second week of clearing vegetation. When I arrived out there last Tuesday morning at daylight several workmen were walking off the job, for lack of "comforts and resources," they said. It's the contactor's responsibility to take care of his people, but I agreed to hear their grievances, which turned out to be reasonable.
>
> The men complained about sleeping on the bare ground and I agreed to get flooring for them. They complained that the contractor did not have enough machetes, so I agreed to stock ten extra. They complained about having only two sharpening stones, so I agreed to buy another.

I took the contractor and my foreman to the town of Rivas, about an hour's drive by jeep, to recruit more workmen. Then I left them to go see about "comforts and resources."

It's fairly simple to get flooring here. All you have to do is find logs that suit you, take them to the sawmill and have then sawn down in the sizes you want. I found two suitable logs at the sawmill and arranged for delivery later in the week.

The machetes were easy enough, as was the sharpening stone. I settled on 40 jute bags for hammock material, or at least something to sleep on, and delivered the items to the ranch gate before returning to Managua.

Early Thursday I went back to Rivas with seven plywood panels in the trailer and arranged for the newly sawn lumber to be hauled out to the ranch entrance. The terrain is too rough to drive anything all the way in. I managed to get the lumber unloaded and hired an oxcart to haul it the rest of the way.

Friday morning, I rode into the property on horseback and spent several hours looking over work accomplished and planning future operations. Also started negotiating with the contractor for preliminary fence clearing on the eastern division which remains overgrown.

Early Saturday, I was back at the ranch on horseback, inspecting the work and estimating how much I could advance the contractor against his final payment. He always wants to stay quite a bit ahead of me and I want to stay at least a little ahead of him. So far, he has come out on top!

It took an hour and a half before we could come to terms and I had finished counting out C$1,000 Córdobas, [about US$143 at the going rate of US$1=C$7] in small bills which he needed to pay his men. I managed to get started back to Managua by 11 a.m. after looking in on a worker who is in the hospital recovering from injuries caused by a tree falling on him. He has several broken ribs and a broken ankle, but is not as badly hurt as feared.

In December 1971 he wrote:

Had things to do in Managua last Monday which kept me busy but managed to get off for Rivas fairly early Tuesday morning. That afternoon I met with my new foreman, Domingo Antonio Siezer where he has been living, which is about 20 miles from where I stay when I'm there.

I loaded him, his wife, a 40-day-old daughter, his mother-in-law, a seven-year-old brother-in-law, two dogs, and what little they had in the way of personal and household possessions into the jeep and trailer with room to spare. Their prized possessions appear to be several game cocks and a half dozen or so game hens.

Took the whole works to Finca Santa Clara, adjoining our ranch, where the foreman and Domingo are old friends. They stayed there until the family living in the small house at El Alamo moved out. I have learned little by little that there is bad blood between the men—they don't even speak when they pass on horseback.

The dogs threw up in the back of the jeep during the trip and one game cock had to be brought into the jeep from the trailer as he was trying to peck out the eyes of another—tied down and all!

On Wednesday, I picked up my new ranch family shortly after daylight and drove them to their new home. It isn't much—but a heck of a lot better than where I brought them from.

As soon as we got the women, children, dogs and chickens unloaded, I took Domingo Antonio into Rivas, and we spent the rest of the morning buying essentials so they will be able to get by out on El Alamo. We also went to see about two horses some of his friends were selling for a total of C$750. That is a rather long story.

The first horse was OK—I would have paid C$350 for him. The second was a young stallion in excellent shape and a very promising animal. I told the men I would take both, only to be told the price was now C$1,050.

After several offers and counteroffers, the owner of the horse I liked accepted C$400 for him.

I couldn't do any business with the owner of the first horse, who wanted C$650. We arranged for someone to ride the stallion halfway to El Alamo the next morning where Domingo Antonio would meet him and ride it the rest of the way.

I picked up Domingo Antonio at Finca Santa Clara about sunup on Thursday and drove him to the meeting place with his new *albarda*, the local version of a saddle. I drove back to Santa Clara, where I borrow horses, mounted up and rode into El Alamo to see how work was going on the clearing contract. After riding around the 400-acre pasture where the men were working, I still hadn't been able to find them, and I gave up when my horse fell trying to cross a river. It was the same horse that tried to throw me the week before and I won't ride him again.

When I got back to Santa Clara about 10 a.m., Domingo Antonio had not yet shown up, so I unsaddled and took the jeep to look for him. He was still where I had left him at 6:30 that morning. We drove back to the little town where the stallion was bought, but the stallion and the owner were nowhere to be found. We finally located the boy who was supposed to have ridden the horse out and he informed us that the owner had changed his mind and would not sell for less than C$450. The boy had my C$400 and after recovering that I gave him a message for the owner of the stallion in language he would well be able to understand.

Friday morning, I rode in to the finca early enough to find Domingo Antonio at home with his horse unsaddled. Together we located the clearing contractor and got semi-straightened out with him, so I could go to the bank before noon and withdraw the Saturday payroll—C$2,000 this week. He is way behind schedule and I'm pretty sure he will not be able to fulfill his contract.

Maybe I beat him down too much in price. The next clearing contract will be arranged on different terms which will leave me free to lay out the work plan—sort of a cost-plus arrangement with a minimum performance clause. I think I'm learning, but have a long way to go.

That afternoon I arranged with a neighbor to put 100 of his steers on part of the property to help with the clearing. Also arranged to transport the horses we still have in Managua—Jerry and Daisy along with a gelding I bought last week for C$500, and which I have named Alamo.

Early Saturday I drove into the ranch with my friend Manuel Joaquín Barrios whose father once owned the land. At that time Manuel was a young man and he put up much of the fencing that still exists. He was impressed with how the place looks now. Manuel is one of two friends who will do my cattle buying, at least until I learn a little more about it. Purchasing is a key part of the operation and can make the difference between a profit or loss at the end of the year.

I contracted a man to cut *jaragua* (a local variety of sorghum) seed for me as I have a great deal and will likely need to plant more next year on land that is now being cleared. We plan to cut 20 gunnysacks, which will plant 200 acres, and if I don't need it all, there is a good market to sell. I bought some earlier this year to plant in the horse pasture at the house in Managua and not a single seed germinated. If I can sell mine for half of what I paid for the sacks I bought, I'll make 100% on the deal.

Early this morning Mary drove me down to pick up the gelding I bought last week. There was a stray German shepherd at the pen, and when I started to bring the horse out, the dog started to bite it fore and aft. The horse, the dog and I went around and around, with me trying to swat the dog with a rope, the horse thinking I was after him as well, and trying to get away from me and the dog.

Finally, the horse cut out in a run—with me trying to hold on to him until I burned both hands with the rope and let go. I should have let go in the first place, since once the horse was sure he was free, he gave the dog a swift kick in the ribs. That ended the problem for everyone, except the dog, but after all, he started it.

The horse was a pleasure to ride, with a road pace as smooth as my favorite, Max. Terry has since taken him out and while she says he gallops pretty rough, that won't bother me as I rarely get beyond a good fast road pace and never let a horse clear out like she does. I am pleased with the purchase. He is quite gentle, which is what this old man of 51 needs.

Disaster

And so went Kennedy's first year. He stocked 200-plus steers that year and learned the ropes around the ranch. Whenever possible, he visited Jack and family in nearby San Juan del Sur and went home to Managua on weekends.

That's where he was in the wee hours of December 23, 1972, when a 6.2-magnitude earthquake and considerable aftershock destroyed most of Managua, killing 10,000 people and leaving 250,000 homeless.

His letter describing the event and aftermath reads:

We have been through many earthquakes over the years in Central America and Mexico. At least one that occurred during our stay in Mexico City was stronger than the Managua quake of December 23. But I know of no way to describe the difference between the Managua quake and those we experienced before. It is an experience you must live through to fully comprehend.

The quake centered in downtown Managua and the area of major damage fell off sharply some four kilometers short of our house, located 13.5 kilometers by road from the center of town. We can be thankful for that.

People report that light quakes occurred on several occasions during the evening of December 22. I had come in from the ranch late that afternoon, dead tired, and slept through the preliminary quivers. Mary can't remember feeling any quakes either, until the first major quake hit a little before 12:30 a.m., December 23.

The preliminary to every severe earthquake we have experienced is a deep rumbling, grinding noise like nothing else you have ever heard. I woke up with a start, too groggy to anticipate what was coming, but alert enough to reach for Mary as the tremor (a most inadequate word!) hit. There was nothing to do but cling to each other and try not to be thrown out of the bed until it subsided.

The noises were more terrifying than the quake itself, but it got worse. In addition to the grinding and rumbling from the earth itself, the house creaked, groaned and rocked. Loose objects fell to the floor, including every lamp in the house, although the glass and china cabinet suffered surprisingly little damage. The lights went out immediately—and were not to come back again until ten days later.

Terry slept through the worst but the rest of us got up, found flashlights and surveyed the damage, which was surprisingly light. We were still at the task some 20-30 minutes later when the second quake started—the approaching roar twice as loud, and the quake itself twice as severe. Mary and I were at the doorway between the kitchen and the dining area and by clinging to each other and the door frame, managed to keep from being thrown to the floor. The maid went down, along with a good many other things, including my surplus liquor stored in the cabinet over our bedroom closet.

The odor of tequila permeated the house and it was still dribbling onto our clothes an hour later. There was more glass breakage but overall, surprisingly little. All the lamps still in one piece after the first quake went down again and every piece of furniture in the house shifted location from a few inches to a couple of feet. Terry slept through that one too!

There had been no communication between the neighbors following the first quake. It seemed hardly stronger than those often experienced in Managua during December and January, "the season." However, everybody headed outdoors after the second one. Those with transistor radios tried to pick up something, but there was not a single station on the air, a situation that continued for 36 hours.

One neighbor tried to drive down to his place of business but found the highway cut by crevasses and landslides some three kilometers toward town from our colonia. He did say he got far enough down to see large fires throughout the city.

I surveyed the house as best I could and found little evidence of serious damage. Plaster had fallen and there were small cracks here and there. Roof tiles had shuffled down in places. Other neighbors reported similar conditions and after a couple of hours, most of us went back inside to get a little rest for what was to come—and it was damned little rest, as small shakes and quivers continued, each with its own rumble and roar, giving us chills of fear for worse to follow.

By about 6 a.m. on the 23rd I was able to pick up broadcasts from Costa Rica, Tegucigalpa, San Salvador, and Guatemala on the Torino [Mary's car] radio, which is very large for an automobile. For once it turned out that preliminary reports from the wire services were not exaggerated.

Managua was in shambles and relief missions from all over the world were being readied. By about 7:30 a.m., I managed by chance to tune in on the emergency frequency being used by the Red Cross. Calls went out for doctors, nurses, and above all, blood plasma for the thousands of injured spread out on the hospital lawn. The hospital had suffered severe damage and it was feared some 60 patients trapped inside were dead. That turned out to be an underestimate.

I've never had trouble making decisions, and I have confidence in my ability to reason things out and come to the right decision. Not so this time! Although I was not to realize it until several days later, I was in a state of shock like everyone else, and the dimensions of the situation we faced, although still unknown, were monumental for us all. It was strange sitting out on our quiet lawn, in our quiet neighborhood and realizing there were tens of thousands of people injured or dead a few miles away with an entire city of some 400,000 in ruins. I didn't try to go down to see where I might help out—I was unwilling to leave the girls alone.

I felt guilty, but I knew what was bound to come next, although I had no way of knowing how soon it would start. I worried about local gasoline supplies running out, but luckily, both vehicles had well over half a tank of gas.

Jack came in from Rivas about 8:30 a.m. with a refrigerated truck and several of his workers, hoping to save 15,000 pounds of shrimp he had been holding in storage in downtown Managua, awaiting shipment to the US. He stopped briefly before heading into town.

When he came back several hours later he reported that after great effort he had found a way to the storage plant, only to find it had burned to the ground.

Jack urged us to leave Managua and spend a few days with his family in San Juan del Sur until we could decide what our eventual course would be. I told him we would sit tight for the moment, so he reassured us that he, Mayra, and baby Nicole would be back the following day to spend Christmas with us as planned.

As the day wore on, we gathered bits and pieces of information, including verification that both the embassy chancery and American Nicaraguan High School were nothing more than stacks of rubble. A teacher from the school said it was doubtful they would be able to resume classes until the fall term.

By afternoon, the looting I had anticipated was already widespread downtown and moving out our way. The mobs were large, some in the hundreds, and were not of a mind to be stopped, particularly where they might find food and water. Our favorite store, some 6 km. toward town, had already been sacked including shelving, scales, countertops and all the shopping carts, which were handy for people to carry off their loot. Several soldiers there were unwilling to do more than fire warning shots, which the mob ignored.

Some private residences were being similarly invaded and emptied, a practice that was to increase over the next week or so. By way of saying thank you, some looters were setting fire to any structure that would burn. I was afraid to stay on and afraid to leave the home unoccupied, despite the "guards" sent in by the people who own the houses in our small colonia—most armed with machetes and muzzle loaders.

The night of Dec. 23 was an uneasy one—no lights, no moon and a steady stream of vehicles leaving town. There were also a number of minor tremors to remind us of what had happened the night before, each one sending a chill down our spines. Most people slept outdoors, although we fatalistically slept in our beds—if you could call it sleep.

By 3:30 a.m. I had managed to reason things out to my satisfaction. We were, after all, lucky to be alive. If we stayed on and a mob of looters came through, there was nothing I could do except try to defend the girls. The situation we faced would not change for at least several months, and I could not let more than a few days pass without looking into our interests at the ranch, where we were in the midst of the marketing season, and where ten families depend on me for much more than a livelihood.

I could not go to the ranch as there was not enough gasoline to come back, to say nothing of my unwillingness to let any of the girls out of my sight for more than a few minutes. The conclusion was obvious—we would pack what we could take in the Torino, the jeep and my one-ton trailer and move to San Juan del Sur until the future was clearer. The house and furnishings would have to take their own chances.

I routed everyone out of bed, and we started packing, each giving priority to their most cherished possessions in the understanding that the next time we saw the house, it would probably be empty, if not burned to the ground. It was not a pleasant morning for any of us.

Jack showed up with Mayra and Nickie sometime during the morning of December 24. However, they came in a 2½ ton truck, prepared to urge us to make the decision we had already reached. He also brought 40 gallons of gasoline and 400 pounds of ice in case we decided to stay on. By then, Mary and I were exhausted, and the truck got loaded between Jack and Linda, without whom we would never have been able to make it through the past couple of months. They have both been pillars of strength when we have faltered, which has been often.

We left the icebox and ice with the neighbors and managed to get away from the house about 5 p.m. We loaded our four best beds onto the truck, for which I will be eternally grateful—at least we would sleep comfortably during the following months while most of our household effects were stored in nooks and crevices wherever we could find room.

On the trip to San Juan that evening, we had many exciting experiences trying to keep together in traffic where most drivers had gone mad. Our jeep started to sputter by the time we hit Rivas, but I managed to pull into my regular station. The military had already emptied the gasoline storage tanks for emergency evacuation of 150,000 people who had survived in downtown Managua. We siphoned from Jack's foresighted oil drum and made it to his house in San Juan del Sur by 9 p.m. on Christmas Eve.

Christmas morning was devoted to figuring out what we should do about emergency supplies—or hoarding, if you want to call it what it really was. Mary had already bought 10 pounds of rice and we were able to pick up 100 pounds of beans, partly for our own use, but also to take care of people on the ranch. Jack anticipated the military would requisition the diesel and gasoline from his shrimp processing plant tanks and had loaded five drums with 200 gallons into my ranch trailer sometime during the night of December 24-25. It was obvious what the trailer contained, despite the canvas he tied over it, so we decided to take the load out to the ranch, where it would be less likely to be lost.

We got off about 10 a.m. and drove up to the foreman's house about 11:30 a.m. Christmas morning. There were a good many horses and people around the house and we surmised they were there for a Christmas celebration. It was something more than a shock to learn that the foreman's 10-day old son had died the afternoon before, and the group was preparing to haul the tiny homemade coffin some 13 km. by horseback to the nearest cemetery so burial would be on consecrated ground. There was nothing to do but help out as best we could.

We unloaded the gasoline from the trailer and the supplies from the jeep; padded the trailer with sleeping bags and managed to get the 20-some-odd mourners and the tiny coffin all inside—or on board, as it were. I was unwilling to go to Rivas and pick up the foreman's mother-in-law, as there had already been attempts to commandeer Jack's jeep and we would have all been in a hell of a fix left on foot some 50 miles from home with a small corpse and small chances of finding anyone willing to haul us back.

We managed to get the sad task completed by mid-afternoon and arrived back "home" by 5 p.m., in time to "celebrate" Christmas. We all tried hard, but it wasn't a very happy one, I'm afraid. Considering the plight of thousands of others in the country at that moment, we had a great deal to be merry and thankful for. Somehow it was a little difficult to reconcile our various emotions and come out that way. I felt guilty eating the turkey Mary had struggled so mightily to salvage.

Although we had not decided to permanently leave Managua, Jack took men and a large freezer truck from his plant on December 26 to bring back a load of household effects. He anticipated the truck would be requisitioned by the military and wanted to salvage what he could beforehand.

Jack's instinct turned out to be right and some 24 hours later he had been able to pack, load and haul to San Juan del Sur all our silver, china, crystal and much of our furniture. Between Jack's efforts and ours a few days later, we managed to salvage all our effects—at least those that survived the trip by freezer and cattle truck. I was able to find a truck with a driver tough enough to go into Managua, but it was Linda and Mary who carried the ball getting things packed.

We vacated the house in Managua before the end of December and a relative of the owner moved in as quickly as we moved out. Jack and Mayra were wonderful to us while we were with them, although I know it was a strain on them. We made two separate four- or five-day visits to the ranch where I had prepared three thatched-roof *ranchos* for our summer use. Judy, Federico and the boys drove up to Jack's house just as we were leaving for a week at the ranch and followed us out there. We did relax and have a good time with them between Christmas and New Year.

Rivas and Ranching

Although the family preferred to settle in San Juan del Sur, there was nothing available for lease. Near the end of January Jack learned that a place near Rivas was coming on the market for $100 a month—a sum considered outrageous in that part of Nicaragua, but a fraction of the rents prevailing in what was left of Managua after the earthquake.

The three-bedroom house was on five acres of land, which included a mango and citrus grove. It was directly on the Pan American Highway, two km.

south of Rivas and 21 km. (30 minutes in the dry season) from the ranch headquarters. It was almost exactly the same distance from Jack and Mayra's place
in San Juan del Sur. The location was ideal.

In a March 1973 letter to family abroad, Kennedy wrote:

> The ranch stocked 526 steers and bulls last year between mid-June and
> the early August, when my credit at the local bank dried up. I can't blame
> them. They took a hell of a risk on an old retired ambassador as it was.
> But it wasn't enough stock to make a profit, given our overhead, especially
> when much of the work is still investment, rather than maintenance and
> operational costs.
>
> But we didn't lose anything either and would have done fairly well were
> it not for the 10% earthquake surtax we were hit with around the time the
> local market started its annual dry season upswing. So far, we have mar-
> keted 444 animals and have 45 more scheduled for the 27th of this month.
> If current prices hold steady until then we will do well on these last 45
> steers and come through the year with a small profit, based on my ac-
> counting.
>
> The banks are impressed and have already told me I can set my own
> credit limit this year.
>
> There is a saying in Spanish: *No hay mal que por bien no venga* ("there
> is nothing so bad that some good doesn't come from it.") This has been
> the case with the ranching operation. For lack of credit, I was understocked
> and consequently had several large, semi-cleared pastures to go to seed
> (jaragua) for my own use.
>
> Despite the drought, my seedbeds prospered while other areas did not,
> and the price for jaragua seed has gone sky high. I decided to gamble and
> instead of harvesting 10,000 pounds of seed as planned, I have thus far
> harvested 128,900 pounds, and will probably keep going for another
> 50,000 pounds. I have sold 51,500 pounds, generously priced at twice my
> cost and the buying season hasn't gotten started yet. This will help a great
> deal.
>
> This leads me to one of my other current operations. We are busily
> building the second half of the barn which we had to leave unfinished last
> year when the rainy season caught up with us. This starts with chopping
> down the trees, then hauling the logs out with oxen, then to the sawmill
> by truck and back to the ranch ready for use. It keeps a person busy as
> hell, as something is sure to go wrong and the whole thing will come to a
> standstill unless the project is closely supervised.
>
> We are also digging a well, located it at the junction of three pastures,
> two of which have water, but of poor quality, this season of the year. So
> far, we are down 28 feet, the last 12 solid rock, and have an accumulation
> of about three feet of water every morning. I hope to get at least three

feet deeper, but the going is tough, and it takes half the morning to bail out, so the men can start digging. All of this is done by hand, incidentally.

We are also building something less than a kilometer of new fence and have to take down about 500 meters of fence we built last year. There is no substitute for experience on a ranch and after working it for a year, we find we made some mistakes. They are not many, nor serious, but we seem to always have a little more to take care of than we can manage with all the men and facilities available to us. And there are damned few facilities—or men that I can trust to do the job right if left alone for more than ten minutes at a time. Thank goodness I have a reliable and intelligent foreman. I could not make it without Domingo Antonio.

Although the family was thrilled to have a permanent home near Rivas, they never passed up an opportunity to spend a few days at the ranch. While Kennedy—often with Jack or one of the girls—was out inspecting the ranch, Mary could usually be found fixing a meal in her thatched-roof kitchen or relaxing in the shade by the stream with a good book. Visits from the children and grandchildren in the US and Costa Rica were frequent. The grandchildren learned to ride horses and enjoyed camping in thatched-roof ranchos. They loved having their own campfire to tend, playing in the shallows of the creek, and fishing in the deeper pools. It was gloriously idyllic.

Then came what Kennedy later referred to as "the beginning of the end." In 1974 Mary was diagnosed with cancer. She traveled to Costa Rica for surgery, then Texas for treatments, and endured crude and painful experimental chemotherapy at home in Rivas. Kennedy bought a VW bus outfitted with a bed and sink so Mary could continue to visit the finca whenever she felt up to it, and family life revolved around her and the finca for the next couple of years. Mary lost her battle with cancer in May of 1976 and was buried on a hilltop in the Rivas cemetery.

Kennedy continued to put in long hours at the finca, but became increasingly wary as Sandinista rebels escalated their efforts against President Somoza, and telltale signs suggesting intruders cropped up at the ranch and home properties.

Kennedy was abruptly forced to leave Nicaragua in 1978 when US officials informed him they could no longer guarantee his safety. The Sandinistas had expanded their range throughout the southern part of the country, and evidence confirmed they had infiltrated his ranch, surveilled his home, and plotted to abduct him. Linda opted to move to Costa Rica and was picked up at the border by Judy and family. Terry had moved to Panama the year prior.

Towns along the southern stretch of the Pan American Highway were blitzed by Sandinistas as Kennedy, then 58, was evacuated by American security agents who drove off-road through banana and coffee plantations to avoid war zones, and get him on one of the last airplanes out of Managua.

Safely back in the US, Kennedy purchased an RV and indulged his love for discovering new places while working intermittently on this memoir. He eventually settled in the Hill Country of Texas, where he enjoyed a life of travel, hunting, fishing, exploring the great outdoors, and visits from friends and family. In 1982 he was inducted in the Cadet Corps Hall of Honor at the University of Texas/Arlington.

In May 2001, at the age of 81, Kennedy died peacefully, surrounded by loved ones. Later that week as the five Crockett siblings scattered their father's ashes at his hunting lease, they saw a hawk—a hunter, like their dad—fly languid circles above them before it glided down and dipped its wings, as if to say goodbye.

Epilogue

By Teresa Crockett Esquivel

Twenty-five years had passed since I left Nicaragua before I was finally able to return. One by one, all my reasons for delaying a trip back had disappeared, and a small group of my American Nicaraguan School friends from the 1970s were planning a high school reunion at the Montelimar beach resort on Nicaragua's Pacific Coast.

This was an opportunity to revisit the places where our family had lived and enjoyed our ten years in Nicaragua. My husband Gene was at last going to be able to see the beautiful land I had told him so much about. I was going back to the country where I had grown up.

Our brother Jack was living in Honduras at the time, and he agreed to drive to Managua to join us. I couldn't have been more thrilled that we would share this trip of a lifetime together. Gene and I were to meet him at the international airport—the same Las Mercedes Airport where President Lyndon B. Johnson had arrived on Air Force One back in 1968.

It was wonderful to exchange hugs with Jack in the main terminal. Our flight had landed early enough that we expected to arrive in Montelimar by evening, but there was no time to waste—we had a stop to make along the way.

Jack expertly navigated the crazy Managua traffic and got us on the southbound Pan American Highway. Passing through the outskirts of Managua, I noticed high walls surrounding many homes—a change since the late '60s and '70s when houses were clearly visible and unprotected by the barriers so common now in many parts of Latin America. Nonetheless, we easily found the entrance to the old Colonia Wheelock at kilometer thirteen and a half. We drove to the last house in the colonia and stopped for a moment to take it all in. This was where we had lived after our father retired from the US Foreign Service. This was where we were during the earthquakes that destroyed Managua on December 23, 1972—the catastrophic event that resulted in our immediate evacuation and relocation to the town of Rivas in southern Nicaragua, much closer to our father's cattle ranch. So many memories, but no time to linger.

Back on the Pan American Highway, we headed south towards Casa Colorada in El Crucero. As we gained altitude, we were surrounded by lush vegetation on both sides of the two-lane highway. This was the Nicaragua I remembered. Coffee and banana plantations abounding on the fertile mountainside where we loved to ride our horses along the back country roads. El Crucero is also known as Las Nubes thanks to thick fog that enshrouds it much of the time—even though its highest point is barely over 3,000 feet above sea level. It was here that we turned off the Pan American Highway and headed west toward Montelimar. We descended rapidly, in silence, enraptured by the multiple shades of green around us and the sprawling view below.

Montelimar held many fond memories for me. During the time our father was US ambassador to Nicaragua, the seaside mansion belonged to President Anastasio Somoza. We were often invited for weekend visits where we had the place entirely to ourselves. I wondered how much had changed over the years since its purchase by a large Spanish hotel chain. I was thrilled to find that the swimming pool where our mother loved to float in an inner tube under the palm trees was well maintained. The huge round thatched cabana where we sat in the shade next to the pool was exactly as it had been. The coconut grove continued to thrive as it had decades ago.

As much as I wanted to bask on the beach in this beautiful place, we had little time to enjoy the reunion and take advantage of our proximity to Managua. Weeks before, I had arranged with the US embassy in Managua to visit the former embassy residence at Las Piedrecitas where we had lived from 1968 to 1970.

We excused ourselves from reunion events the day of our appointment and headed back towards Managua. When we approached the embassy residence's main gate, we were stopped by uniformed guards bearing guns. Our identification was checked, and Jack's truck was carefully inspected. We were instructed not to take any photographs during our visit and given the green light to proceed. As we made our way up the long, winding drive towards the residence, I vividly recalled the exhilaration I used to feel riding Max bareback, galloping up this hill at full speed. Near the top of the hill the nearly 70-year-old, 42,000 square foot mansion came into full view. The embassy intern assigned to meet was waiting when we entered the circular driveway.

From the outside everything looked exactly as it had when we lived there. The grounds were immaculately manicured. The enormous Indian laurel trees across the circular drive that led to the main entrance continued to thrive and provide massive amounts of shade. I remembered the many parties that were held here. The residence's façade was still painted the same cream color which contrasted sharply with the terracotta Spanish roof tiles.

The moment we entered the residence through its imposing black wrought iron doors, my heart fell. The interior was a shadow of its former elegance. The polished black and white tiles in the large, round foyer, and the circular marble staircase remained the same, but the entire area was devoid of furnishings. The same was true for the expansive living room and veranda.

Where once there had been beautiful large rugs, lounge chairs, antique furniture tastefully arranged in seating areas, colorful oil paintings, and a baby grand piano—now there was nothing but empty space. In the main dining room, the scenario was repeated. The area formerly furnished with dark cherry wood buffets, a long table, and chairs that comfortably sat 24 was now starkly empty. The vast spaces once filled with bustling life, chatter and music during innumerable diplomatic social events, were now eerily silent.

As we ascended the curved marble staircase, our guide recounted what had happened. After the property was justifiably deemed too ostentatious to serve as a residence for the US ambassador, it became a guest house for temporary personnel assigned to the embassy. It was left unoccupied for a while and later used to headquarter the embassy's Hurricane Mitch relief efforts. Now it stood empty.

Walking down the wide second floor hallway we found many doorways leading to bedrooms boarded shut. I longed to enter the corner suite with its panoramic view that had been our parent's bedroom, but it too was boarded up.

As we took our leave, we shook the intern's hand, smiled and thanked her for such a special experience, but driving away, our hearts were filled with mixed emotion. We were in awe of our good fortune to come back and see the grounds after so many years, and yet we were sad that such a beautiful residence was left to deteriorate, empty and unused. We had lived here during a bygone era.

Heading back for our last night at Montelimar, we made plans for the next day. We would leave first thing in the morning and get back on the southbound Pan American Highway. We expected to arrive at Rivas by noon and would spend the afternoon there before driving to San Juan del Sur and its better hotel options near the beautiful crescent moon beach where we had once spent so much time.

Early the next day we said goodbye to our friends from the American Nicaraguan School and began our drive to Rivas. The road I had traveled so many times before seemed much narrower than I remembered. In fact, it was largely unrecognizable to me. It wasn't until we pulled into the town of Rivas that things started to look familiar. Rivas had grown up but was basically the same. I recognized the streets and was thrilled to find the central plaza exactly as I remembered it. Brightly colored horse carriages were parked along one side of the plaza waiting to take passengers on errands through town, just as when we lived here in the '70s. The Chop Suey restaurant on the plaza corner was still there, its façade painted the exact shade of teal that I remembered. On the days my father was out at the cattle ranch, my mom and I often ordered takeout from this restaurant. It had reminded us of the evenings we would stop for Chinese food after taking my father a clean shirt and a sandwich during the times he worked around the clock at the State Department in Washington, DC. Jack, Gene and I decided to stop at the Chop Suey for lunch.

I realized I had never eaten inside this restaurant—in fact, never been beyond the front counter where takeout orders were placed. We opted to sit in the garden patio, and when our order of chop suey arrived, it looked and tasted exactly as I remembered. The primary condiments were still mustard and ketchup, which used to make my mother and me chuckle, even though we immensely enjoyed our meal—it was the only Chinese food available in the area.

With lunch taken care of, the main reason for our visit to Rivas became front and center. Our mother had lost her battle with cancer in 1976 and was buried at the Rivas cemetery. We struggled to get our bearings once we entered the cemetery. We remembered she had been buried on a hill, under a lone tree, but where exactly? There were many hills and more headstones now than back then—which way should we go?

Jack had no trouble recruiting the help of several enthusiastic local men with machetes. As it turned out, they readily remembered that "una Americana" had been buried here many years before. They did not recall exactly where, but they swung their machetes in unison through various overgrown areas, determined to find her headstone. Time passed with no luck. In the meantime, I had lost my sense of direction.

After nearly two hours of searching and clearing overgrown vegetation in various locations, we heard encouraging cries. We rushed to the spot where the men excitedly continued to clear the shrubbery and as it fell away, we glimpsed the remains of our mother's worn and mossy headstone.

I stood speechless, overtaken by emotion. On our own we may have never found our beautiful mother's resting place.

The sun was starting its descent towards the horizon. We paid the men for their services and decided to head towards San Juan del Sur in search of a hotel. We planned to spend several days in the area, and be back at the cemetery early the following morning since much work remained to be done. We drove the 30 kilometers to San Juan del Sur in silence.

The first hotel Jack checked out had availability. The property was once the private residence of an acquaintance when Jack lived down the same beachfront street during the '70s. We checked in and Jack and Gene went across the street to a beachfront restaurant for dinner. I was to meet them there shortly.

Sitting on the bed alone in our room, my head was swimming, still trying to make sense of it all. I was not prepared to find our mother's grave completely lost in the overgrowth. As nausea overtook me, I ran to the bathroom.

Revived by a good night's sleep, we returned to the cemetery early the next day. Our To Do list included cleaning up the headstone, laying new ceramic tiles, giving the little metal fence around the grave a fresh coat of paint, and planting tropical ornamentals in the surrounding area. As the workers arrived eager to get started, Jack pointed to a bullet hole in the metal fence, and the workmen told us about gun fights in the cemetery during the Sandinista revolution. The images that came to mind were almost incomprehensible. We headed for town to gather supplies, and the work began.

That evening, while we enjoyed freshly caught fish on the beach in San Juan del Sur, we decided that I would contact the man who had agreed to purchase our father's cattle ranch back in 1978. When I dialed the phone number the following morning and identified myself, the gentleman on the other end of the line knew exactly who I was. Would we be interested in seeing the ranch? He gave directions where to meet him the following day and assured us he would be there waiting for us.

True to his word, he and several others were already waiting for us when we pulled up to the appointed meeting place, not far from the ranch. One of their two vehicles led our small caravan, and the other pulled up the rear. This entrance to the ranch was unfamiliar to me. I imagined that we had driven through the adjoining ranch, Finca Santa Clara, that had belonged to Candelario and Socorro Castillo, wonderful friends of ours who were brutally murdered during the Sandinista revolution.

Entering the ranch gate and driving onto the property, I was struck with the sense that it had become exactly what our father had envisioned when he bought the place from Violeta Chamorro in 1971. Back then, the land was largely covered with jungle and required extensive clearing. Now golden jaragua grass blew in the breeze on the rolling hills. The property was well maintained. The main corral, tack room and bunkhouse were still where Dad's men had built them. The roads were now compacted and looked to me like they could be driven during the rainy season, something that had always presented a challenge when deep mud left them unnavigable.

Reflecting on the beauty of the land, and all that had come to pass since we left Nicaragua, I wondered if Violeta or our father could have ever imagined the events that lay ahead when they signed the sales contract in 1971.

A catalyst to the overthrow of the Somoza regime, Violeta's husband, journalist and publisher Pedro Joaquin Chamorro, was ambushed and shot to death as he crossed a Managua street in 1978. As fate would have it, Violeta became president of Nicaragua from 1990 to 1997. Did she have time to enjoy her own beautiful cattle ranch in southern Nicaragua? I imagine it was a place of refuge during difficult times.

Our visit to Nicaragua had come to an end, and we had accomplished everything we wanted to during our trip. We visited the places where we had lived over the years, and our mother's gravesite was now well-maintained. It was difficult to know if I would ever be back, but I found solace in knowing we had done all we could during our short time here.

At the time of this writing, it has been over 40 years since we left Nicaragua. Our parents are long gone; our eldest sister, Laura Buckner, is recently deceased; and the four remaining Crockett children are faced with our own mortality.

As we inventory our life's experiences, there is one thing we know for sure: our parents lived a life of adventure, confidently forging ahead to meet each opportunity that awaited them. In the process they gave us a profound sense of appreciation for who they were, the awareness that we lived a unique life during a special time, and we were forever imprinted with extraordinary childhood memories.

September 2020

Thank you for reading **THE DIPLOMAT.**

If you enjoyed this book, we hope you will tell your friends and family on social media, and leave a review on Amazon.

We sincerely appreciate your support!

Made in the USA
Middletown, DE
19 September 2020